In 1883 the radical journalist W. E. Adams described community self-government as 'the essence of all the political liberalism that is worthy of the name'. This collaborative volume of essays enlarges upon Adams' thesis, applying it to the study of various 'currents of radicalism' in Britain and Ireland, ranging from Victorian 'advanced' Liberals to Irish and Welsh socialists in the 1920s.

Citizenship and community explores the links between liberalism, social democracy and nationalism within the framework of classical republican ideals of 'civic virtue' and active citizenship. Its strong comparative emphasis breaks down conventional views of the state, and focuses attention on the regions of Britain, revealing how different forms of collective identity interacted in popular attitudes to political and social debates at a national level.

Citizenship and community

Citizenship and community

Liberals, radicals and collective identities in the British Isles, 1865–1931

Edited by

Eugenio F. Biagini

Princeton University

CAMBRIDGE
UNIVERSITY PRESS

Published by the Press Syndicate of the University of Cambridge
The Pitt Building, Trumpington Street, Cambridge CB2 1RP
40 West 20th Street, New York, NY 10011-4211, USA
10 Stamford Road, Oakleigh, Melbourne 3166, Australia

First published 1996

Printed in Great Britain at Redwood Books, Trowbridge, Wiltshire

A catalogue record for this book is available from the British Library

Library of Congress cataloguing in publication data

Citizenship and community: liberals, radicals, and collective
    identities in the British Isles, 1865–1931 / edited by Eugenio F.
    Biagini.
        p.   cm.
      ISBN 0 521 48035 3 (hc)
        1. Liberalism – Great Britain – History.   2. Radicalism – Great
    Britain – History.   3. Great Britain – Politics and
    government – 1837–1901.   4. Great Britain – Politics and
    government – 1901–1936.   I. Biagini, Eugenio F.
    JC574.2.G7C57   1996
    320.5′1′094109034 – dc20   95-35033   CIP

ISBN 0 521 48035 3 hardback

KS

Contents

Contributors

EUGENIO F. BIAGINI is assistant professor of modern British history at Princeton University. His publications include *Liberty, Retrenchment and Reform. Popular Liberalism in the Age of Gladstone 1860–1880* (1992) and *Currents of Radicalism*, which he edited with Alastair J. Reid (1991).

JOHN COFFEY is a research fellow at Churchill College, Cambridge. He is the author of a forthcoming book on Samuel Rutherford and seventeenth-century Scottish political thought.

CLAIRE FITZPATRICK has completed her Cambridge Ph.D. thesis on Irish labour politics during the period 1900–1923.

GRAHAM GREENLEE is a research student at the University of Ulster at Jordanstown. He is completing a D.Phil. thesis on 'Ulster Liberalism, Constructive Unionism and the Issue of Home Rule, 1885–1914'.

JOSE HARRIS is reader and tutor in history at St Catherine's College, Oxford. Her works include *Private Lives, Public Spirit. A Social History of Britain 1870–1914* (1993) and *Unemployment and Politics: A Study in English Social Politics, 1886–1914* (1984).

ANTHONY HOWE is senior lecturer of international history at the London School of Economics. His publications include *The Cotton Masters 1830–1860* (1984) and a forthcoming study of 'Free Trade and Liberal England'.

RICHARD LEWIS is senior lecturer in British history at the University of Teeside. His works include *Leaders and Teachers: Adult Education and the Challenge of Labour in South Wales, 1906–1940* (1993).

IAN MACHIN is professor of modern history and head of the Department of Modern History at the University of Dundee. His publications include *Disraeli* (1995) and *Politics and the Churches in Great Britain* (2 vols., 1977 and 1987).

MARTIN PUGH is professor of modern British history at the University of Newcastle upon Tyne. His works include *State and Society. British Political and Social History 1870–1992* (1994), *The Making of Modern British Politics 1867–1939* (2nd edn, 1993) and *Women and the Women's Movement in Britain 1914–1959* (1992).

NIGEL SCOTLAND is senior lecturer of British history at the Cheltenham and Gloucester College of Higher Education. His publications include *Agricultural Trade Unionism in Gloucestershire 1872–1950* (1991) and *Methodism and the Revolt of the Field* (1981).

JOHN SHAW is a research student at King's College, Cambridge. He is completing a Ph.D. thesis on the freemasons in nineteenth-century Britain.

JONATHAN SPAIN has worked as a curatorial officer for the Royal Commission on Historical Manuscripts and is a freelance researcher and writer.

PAT THANE is professor of women's studies and social history at the University of Sussex. Her works include *The Foundations of the Welfare State* (1982) and *Maternity and Gender Politics, 1880–1950* (1991), which she edited with Gisela Bock.

FRANK TRENTMANN is a tutor in history at Harvard University. He has published articles on cultural history, political economy and political culture. He is completing a Ph.D. thesis on 'The Survival and Decline of Free Trade: The Transformation of Liberal Political Economy and Political Culture, Britain *c.* 1897–1932'.

Acknowledgements

Many of the chapters of the present book were first presented and discussed at the conference, 'Liberty and Public Control in the Radical Tradition. Great Britain and Ireland, 1866–1923', held at Henderson Hall, the University of Newcastle upon Tyne, on 29–30 March 1993. The editor and the authors would like to thank all the participants in that conference for their helpful comments and criticism, as well as the Department of History of the University of Newcastle upon Tyne for its generous support for the organisation of the conference. Special thanks are due to the following scholars, who acted as chairs and discussants: David Bebbington, John Derry, John Dunbabin, Gareth Stedman Jones, Norman McCord, Bernard Porter, Alastair Reid, Raphael Samuel and Pat Thane.

Introduction: Citizenship, liberty and community

Eugenio F. Biagini

I

In 1883 the radical journalist W. E. Adams described community self-government and community representation as 'the essence of all political liberalism that is worthy of the name'.[1] His comment may serve as an opening statement for the present book. In contrast with the old Thatcherite or 'Newt Gingrichite' stereotypical image of 'Victorian values' – meaning individualism, self-help and *laissez-faire* – and the endorsement of similar myths by some socialist historians,[2] we elaborate on the thesis that politics in the nineteenth and early twentieth centuries ' was not primarily about the individual's rights, but the representation of his community'.[3] The following chapters focus on the tension between concern for individual liberty and commitment to 'community': the latter included the citizen's 'organic' connections and the collective identities underpinning them.[4] In particular, we suggest that 'community' was a crucial concept for both 'advanced Liberals' and supporters of other 'currents of radicalism' with which liberalism was allied, for example, free traders, revivalist dissenters, Celtic nationalists and activists in the women's movement.

This area has long called for a comprehensive reassessment for, though the relationship between liberalism, democracy and community ideolo-

I would like to thank the contributors to the present volume as well as Jeremy Adelman, Stefan Collini, Margot Finn, Molly Green, Peter Lake, William Lubenow and Alastair Reid for their helpful comments on earlier drafts of this introduction. While the preparation of this work has involved a considerable degree of discussion and cooperation among the authors, this introduction reflects only the editor's opinions and is not intended as a collective statement.

[1] 'Franchise at Last', *Newcastle Daily Chronicle*, 12 February 1883, p. 2.
[2] Cf. T. C. Smout (ed.), *Victorian Values*, Oxford, 1992; and J. Walvin, *Victorian Values*, London, 1988.
[3] M. Pugh, *The Making of Modern British Politics, 1867–1939*, Oxford, 1993, p. 5; E. F. Biagini, *Liberty, Retrenchment and Reform. Popular Liberalism in the Age of Gladstone, 1860–1880*, Cambridge, 1992, pp. 313–68.
[4] Cf. J. Harris, chapter 14 below, p. 343–60.

gies has generated a great deal of theoretical discussion,[5] it has not yet received sufficient attention from historians.[6] Thus, very few studies explore the links between community-centred liberalism and free-trade economics in the Victorian and Edwardian United Kingdom. Even fewer works approach that most important and controversial form of communitarian ideology – Celtic nationalism – within the broader context of the radical–democratic tradition of the British Isles. Rather, the prevailing tendency has been to look on the separatist movements in Ireland, Scotland and Wales as fairly distinct forces,[7] ignoring the strong affinities existing both among them individually, and between them as a whole and the main 'currents' and traditions of British radicalism. Yet, this 'common ground' is of crucial importance for understanding the successful working of multinational 'coalition' parties, such as Gladstone's and Asquith's Home Rule alliance or the early Labour Party.

The proposed approach also involves a reflection on basic methodological assumptions for, while there is a strong trend towards comparative history in the field of European studies, the component parts of the United Kingdom are still studied from either a strictly 'national' perspective or one which is dominated by the *English* case. In contrast, we argue that – especially in the case of radical politics – a more sophisticated approach is necessary to account for the plurality of identities and experiences in a multinational context unified by a shared institutional framework. The present volume tries to move in that direction with a combination of general chapters on topics of particular relevance and in-depth case studies. Starting with J. S. Mill's emphasis on 'community' as the historical and moral environment in which civil liberties flourish,[8] we explore the relationship between classical ideals and actual politics, democracy and religion, free-trade economics and collective control, ethnic identity, nationalism and their 'invention' by intellectuals – who often were outsiders. Drawing on the 'currents of radicalism' thesis,[9] we focus on both religion and 'civic virtue' as the main factors of collective identity, as well as the means whereby the opposing claims of individual liberty and duty to one's community could be harmonised.

[5] Cf. A. MacIntyre, *After Virtue*, London, 1981; J. Gray, *Liberalism. Essays in Political Philosophy*, London, 1989; W. Kymlicka, *Liberalism, Community and Culture*, Oxford, 1989; S. Macedo, *Liberal Virtues. Citizenship, Virtue and Community in Liberal Constitutionalism*, Oxford, 1990; C. Lasch, *The True and Only Heaven. Progress and its Critics*, New York and London, 1991.

[6] With few exceptions: *e.g.* E. and S. Yeo, 'On the Uses of "Community": from Owenism to the Present', in S. Yeo (ed.), *New Views on Co-operation*, London, 1988, pp. 229–58.

[7] See, however, C. H. Williams (ed.), *National Separatism*, Cardiff, 1982; and I. S. Wood (ed.), *Scotland and Ulster*, Edinburgh, 1994.

[8] See below, chapter 1, pp. 21–44.

[9] E. F. Biagini and A. J. Reid (eds.), *Currents of Radicalism. Popular Radicalism, Organised Labour, and Party Politics in Britain, 1850–1914*, Cambridge, 1991.

II

The task of reconciling liberty and community, individual rights and social control turned out to be simpler in Britain than anywhere else in Europe, with the exception of Switzerland and the Scandinavian countries, with their original experiments in, respectively, cantonal federalism and Lutheran social democracy. But in most other cases including Ireland – especially with the rise of ethnic nationalism – liberal and labour reformers struggled with problems and contrasting demands and values for which there were probably neither solutions nor possibilities of reconciliation.[10]

Part I outlines what can be seen as the 'classical' radical liberal positions in both politics and religion, including Mill's 'civic virtue', the campaigns for women's emancipation and the crusades for spiritual freedom and church disestablishment. The first chapter traces the intellectual origins of Gladstonian 'rational-charismatic' politics in Mill's understanding of ancient democracy.[11] In the fourth John Coffey explores the parallels between charismatic, American-style religious revivalism in 1873–5 and the mobilisation of popular enthusiasm for political purposes during the 1876 Bulgarian Agitation. It is difficult to imagine two men more different than Mill, the sophisticated intellectual, and Moody, the down-to-earth populist preacher. Arguably, the latter's anti-intellectualism could hardly appeal to sophisticated Millite philosophers. Yet, in the specific historical context of Britain in the early 1870s, these differences did not rule out an 'elective affinity' in practical politics, or a common ground between their respective positions.[12] The chapters by Pugh and Thane on the women's movement, and by Machin on the disestablishment question further examine the Liberal understanding of citizenship.[13] Pugh and Thane assess the substantial ideological affinities between early feminism and classical liberalism, in a context which included suffragism's nonconformist revivalist style and mentality[14] and systematic attacks on 'the centralized power of the state'.[15] In discussing

---

[10] See below, chapters 10 and 11.

[11] See chapter 1, below.

[12] It is worth remembering that the equally large differences between Mill and Lincoln had not prevented the former from admiring and supporting the latter in 1861–5. (Interestingly enough, both Moody and Lincoln had been shaped by Illinois democratic society: see below, p. 102 and n. 66.)

[13] Cf. pp. 45–92 and 120–47 below.

[14] Cf. Thane, pp. 66–92 below. George Lansbury described suffragist meetings in 1913 as 'more like a religious revival than anything else': cited in Sandra Stanley Holton, *Feminism and Democracy. Women's Suffrage and Reform Politics in Britain 1900–1918*, Cambridge, 1986, p. 128.

[15] Susan Kingsley Kent, *Sex and Suffrage in Britain, 1860–1914*, Princeton, 1987, p. 227.

the search for new forms of democracy – inspired by a sort of 'free-market equality' in religious and gender issues – these chapters explore some of the limits of late-Victorian liberalism: such was, for example, the ultimate incompatibility between regarding citizens as 'political consumers', and the emphasis on civic virtue and participatory citizenship.[16] By confirming the continuing importance of religion and the crucial role played by intellectuals in deciphering and articulating popular protest, they link up with both Part II (the role of religion and intellectuals in the development of Liberal and Labour free trade), and Part III (the impact of idealist philosophy and organicist views of society on liberalism and early Labour).

Part II extends this analysis to the social and economic sphere. Again, we deal first of all with a 'classical' position – based on the idea of informed consumer control. Nigel Scotland,[17] examining the agricultural workers' commitment to land reform, links revivalist dissent with popular 'communitarian' traditions, including Owenism, and stresses the importance of free-trade principles in popularising the transition from classical liberalism to forms of collectivism. Jonathan Spain,[18] focusing on borough opinion, shows that from the late 1870s urban support for Cobdenite principles increased in response to the new economic pressures at the onset of the 'Great Depression'. Anthony Howe[19] and Frank Trentmann[20] analyse the reshaping of the free-trade ideology under the impact of class issues and consumerist concerns after 1885: they underline the economic and political novelty of the creed which Liberals, Radicals and Labour conveniently cloaked in the Cobdenite rhetoric of the 'hungry forties', though the expression 'free trade' had begun to mean different things to different people.

During the period 1878–1932 the debate about free trade increasingly provided an opportunity to agitate or oppose forms of political and economic nationalism. As Spain demonstrates, the 1878 Cattle Diseases Bill – denounced by the free-trade lobby as a device to protect the 'agricultural interest' at the consumers' expense – also had wide-ranging implications on British trade policies and international treaties. Defeated in 1878, from 1880 the 'fair traders' and, later, the 'tariff reformers' launched a series of new campaigns which reached a climax in the aftermath of the Boer War, achieved substantial success during the First World War, and finally triumphed in 1931–2, in the wake of the Great

---

[16] D. Marquand, *The Unprincipled Society*, London, 1988, pp. 29–30.
[17] Cf. chapter 6, pp. 151–67 below.
[18] Cf. chapter 7, pp. 168–92 below.
[19] Cf. chapter 8, pp. 193–218 below.
[20] Cf. chapter 9, pp. 219–50 below.

Slump. The latter, as Trentmann writes, 'dug the grave of free trade [but] did not kill it. Free trade, as a secular religion, had died a slow death in previous decades.'[21] Significantly, throughout this period, protectionist revivals coincided with outbursts of xenophobia or imperialism. Both Howe and Trentmann deal extensively with the incompatibility between free-trade liberalism (in its Cobdenite, Gladstonian and Hobsonian manifestations) and the new and more aggressive imperialism which began to spread from the late 1870s – a clash whose full implications became evident in 1916–31.

The nuanced support for 'free trade' that most 'currents of radicalism' expressed throughout the period reflected a parallel kind of community identity. It was based on perceived material interests (most vocally expressed by the consumers' cooperatives) and a Cobdenite and Hobsonian 'internationalist' vision of progress; the latter was equally opposed to both economic autarky and 'monopolistic' capitalism. These values and ideas provided the campaigns against resurgent protectionism with a moral and quasi-religious emphasis which helped to preserve 'free trade' as a component of the tradition of civic-virtue liberalism until the 1920s. It is significant that many of the persons and groups discussed in Part I, including the women's movement[22] and the nonconformists,[23] also figured prominently in these 'free-trade' crusades. Moreover, we find a close interaction between intellectuals and mass politics, as the former played a crucial role in articulating and directing popular protest. From the 1910s their radical vision came under pressure, with growing tensions between 'liberty' and public control: hostility to foreign cartels gradually became a form of economic nationalism, replacing the old uncompromising internationalism of the Cobdenite school. This culminated in a reformulation of the basic assumptions behind the old free-trade 'moral economy'.[24]

Economic and social challenges did not prove as formidable as those posed by Celtic separatist nationalism, with whose various manifestations Liberals and Radicals struggled to come to terms from the early 1880s. The 'currents of radicalism' discussed in the first two parts of the book shared an *internationalist* ideology and *Weltanschauung*: substantially inspired by Christian and Enlightenment humanism, this frame of mind was hardly compatible with ethnic nationalism or economic autarky. Part III assesses the difficulties experienced by radical agitators (both Liberal

[21] *Ibid.*, p. 248.
[22] See chapters 2 and 3 below, pp. 45–65 and 66–92 respectively.
[23] S. E. Koss, '1906: Revival and Revivalism', in A. J. Morris, (ed.), *Edwardian Radicalism 1900–1914*, London, 1974, pp. 76, 86, 91.
[24] For the 'moral economy' of free trade see Biagini, *Liberty, Retrenchment and Reform*, pp. 93–102.

and Labour, British and Irish) in contexts increasingly dominated by sectarian strife or endemically anti-liberal, anti-socialist Irish Catholicism. Nevertheless, in Britain radical democracy was reconciled with the new demands for ethnic revival: in an interesting contrast with the Irish cases discussed by Greenlee and Fitzpatrick,[25] Richard Lewis and John Shaw[26] examine the success of a Liberal-oriented, town-manu-factured 'Celtic' movement in exploiting the myths of a bucolic 'golden age' in predominantly Protestant Wales and the Presbyterian Scottish Highlands.

Both the Highland Gaelic mythology and the Welsh 'democratic community' were largely inspired by various forms of philosophical idealism and historical criticism which were then becoming increasingly influential in the main university institutions of both Scotland and Wales. In a sense, idealism and Celtic nationalism were on the same conceptual wavelength: both shared an organicist view of society, which set them apart from the various kinds of utilitarian individualism of the Millite political economists,[27] but which was being increasingly adopted by both New Liberals and Labour leaders.[28]

The book opens with the commitment to active citizenship of J. S. Mill and the nonconformists, and their awareness of their responsibility to the nation: they insisted on the importance of being rooted in a moral community, championing public issues and giving people a sense of civic responsibility and vocation. The last two chapters of Part III further develop aspects of Part I by examining a later generation of intellectuals who – influenced by German scholarship – elaborated the community theme in regional contexts dominated by ethnic/religious forms of iden-tity. The book closes with Jose Harris's discussion of British sociological organicism at the beginning of the twentieth century. This chapter is, in a sense, a sequel to E. P. Thompson's 'peculiarities of the English' in its critique of historical interpretations based on continental models. As Thompson rejected the reductionism of the Anderson and Nairn model, so Harris criticises the assumption that British progressivism was under-mined by underdeveloped sociological thinking, i.e. in contrast with the 'sophistication' of the French, German and Italian social sciences. It was

[25] Cf. chapters 10 and 11 below.
[26] Cf., respectively, chapters 12 and 13 below.
[27] Cf. J. Lipkes, 'Politics, Religion and the Fate of Classical Political Economy: John Stuart Mill and His Followers, 1860–1875', Princeton University Ph.D. dissertation, 1995. Mill's own position was, however, more complicated, and the younger generation of economists showed marked tendencies towards forms of organicism from the early 1870s: cf. *Alfred Marshall's Lectures to Women*, edited and introduced by G. Becattini, Eugenio Biagini, Rita McWilliams Tullberg and Tiziano Raffaelli, London, 1995.
[28] D. Tanner, *Political Change and the Labour Party 1900–1918*, Cambridge, 1990, p. 26.

not a question of sophistication: indeed, 'a great deal of innovative theorising about modern societies was in fact occurring in many different contexts', though 'not necessarily under the label of academic sociology'.[29] From this point of view the distance between Britain and the continent was not considerable.

Even at the level of policy recommendations liberal and democratic intellectuals across Europe showed substantial affinities in their adoption of the 'progressive' or 'revisionist' turn, as well as in their support for various versions of free trade. However, these ideas found different applications in different countries because of the diversities in the political and institutional systems and in the pace and timing of the process of industrialisation. Likewise, divergences in the relations between liberalism and labour were due more to the specificity of national history and context than to substantial differences in liberal ideology.[30]

The institutional and cultural constraints peculiar to each country contributed to defining not only policy-making and traditions in the social sciences, but also the role and functions of the intellectuals. Indeed, the very concept of an 'intellectual' was different. It is difficult to generalise: between continental countries there were differences as important as those between 'the continent' and Britain. Yet, arguably, in some cases the seemingly greater radicalism and higher profile of continental intellectuals, and their emphasis on the elaboration of highly abstract ideas, were due to their greater isolation from the centres of political power; their status as a special category, as 'intellectuals', was a function of their impotence.[31] But ideas and debates were broadly similar: in Italy, for instance, the environment in which modern social theory developed owed much to the long battle between organicist 'Hegelian liberals' and empiricist Cobdenite economists, in a context in which most intellectuals, including Mosca and Pareto, were basically excluded from the political elites they so effectively criticised.[32] On the other hand, in the case of Germany and France,[33] as well as in that of Italy, *sociological* thinking had institutional links with newly established regimes eager to strengthen their legitimation.

---

[29] See below, ch. 14, p. 344. Cf. R. A. Fletcher, 'Cobden as Educator: the Free Trade Internationalism of Eduard Bernstein, 1899–1914', *American Historical Review*, 88, 3 (June, 1983), pp. 561–78; D. Tanner, 'Ideological Debate in Edwardian Labour Politics: Radicalism, Revisionism and Socialism', in Biagini and Reid (eds.), *Currents of Radicalism*, pp. 271–83; P. Spriano, 'Introduzione', to E. Einaudi, *Le lotte del lavoro*, Turin, 1972.

[30] J. Breuilly, *Labour and Liberalism in Nineteenth Century Europe*, Manchester, 1992.

[31] P. Mandler and S. Pedersen, 'The British Intelligentsia after the Victorians', in P. Mandler and S. Pedersen (eds.), *After the Victorians*, London and New York, 1994, p. 2. Cf. E. P. Thompson, 'The Peculiarities of the English', in *The Poverty of Theory*, London, 1978, pp. 271–3.

[32] Cf. R. Bellamy, *Modern Italian Social Theory*, Oxford, 1987.

[33] See below chapter 14, p. 349.

Moreover it had been shaped by the exceptional social and political experiments involved in the struggle for nation-building (or rebuilding, in the case of the French Third Republic), and influenced by an accelerated process of industrialisation.

From these points of view things were different in Britain. Of course, the 'industrial revolution' there had been a slower, but gradual and precocious phenomenon. Institutional legitimation was not a problem. On the other hand, British intellectuals, especially Oxford and Cambridge dons, had an organic relationship with the ruling elites, who in turn exhibited a greater homogeneity and lack of polarisation.[34] Moreover, the contrast between free-trade utilitarian individualism and idealism was somehow softened by the continuity of an overarching Puritan tradition: this – fully embodied in the philosophies of T. H. Green and Arnold Toynbee, and the economics of Alfred Marshall[35] – added a strongly 'idealistic', community-oriented component to Victorian liberalism. Finally, as Jose Harris shows, continuity was also ensured by the tradition of the study of classics and ancient history, as 'the spell of Plato' and the ideal of the Athenian *polis* continued to influence progressive social thought well into the twentieth century.

III

Of all the questions raised by Jose Harris, that of the closeness of the relationship of British liberalism and progressivism to their continental counterparts is perhaps the most basic. This question seems to admit of – indeed, requires – different answers, according to the particular periods, areas and issues concerned. For instance, during the classical 'liberal age' Gladstone, Cavour and the Belgian Frère-Orban shared a common attitude to the 'concert of Europe', international relations, free trade and nationalism in western Europe. Guizot's and Macaulay's interpretations of history, J. S. Mill's economics and Tocqueville's analysis of contemporary trends in society and politics were widely accepted by liberals throughout Europe and the 'European worlds' overseas – in the Americas and Australasia. Most liberals across Europe had a difficult relationship with Roman Catholicism, despite the efforts of eminent Catholic liberals such as Alphonse de Lamartine, Lord Acton, Alessandro Manzoni and Bettino Ricasoli.

[34] S. Collini, 'Intellectuals in Twentieth-Century Britain: An Unknown Species?', British Studies Seminar, Princeton, 2 December 1994.

[35] Cf. E. F. Biagini, 'The Anglican Ethic and the Spirit of Citizenship: the Economic and Social Context', in G. Becattini, E. F. Biagini, T. Raffaelli and R. McWilliams Tullberg (eds.), *Alfred Marshall's Lectures to Women*, pp. 26–46. See also Collini, *Public Moralists. Political Thought and Intellectual Life in Britain, 1850–1890*, Oxford, 1991, Part I.

Finally, liberals generally shared a concern for the preservation of a limited electoral franchise, the containment of the radical pressure for universal suffrage, and the perpetuation of certain social privileges and inequalities as necessary for the survival of 'liberty'. More particularly, while endorsing the principles of the French Revolution of 1789, continental liberals looked with suspicion or hostility at the heritage of '1793', revived by the 1871 Paris Commune.[36] This suspicion was shared by British liberals as well: indeed Jonathan Parry seems to consider whiggish 'moderation' as the hallmark of true liberalism.[37] However, one reason why Gladstone's and Asquith's Liberal Party survived for so long as the main force of reform and was so effective in steering the Labour Party firmly on to the path of parliamentary democracy was precisely their ability to adopt labour and democratic reforms, even at the cost of painful party splits.[38] On the continent, despite the radicalism of liberal intellectuals, most liberal parties stuck to 'moderation' and were undermined by movements which were fully embedded in a culture of mass politics (though not necessarily of democracy).

The most formidable challenges to liberal democracy – both in continental Europe and the United Kingdom – were offered by both pannationalism and national separatism, with their mutually incompatible claims. Even the Wilsonian–Leninist idea of self-determination proved unable to provide an answer to some of these challenges: in fact, as we now know all too well, in many cases it merely compounded the problem.[39] The Victorian equivalent of the 'fourteen points' – expounded by Gladstone in Midlothian – also proved fairly difficult to operate. Indeed, Home Rule for Ireland – which could be seen as the most consistent development of 'Midlothian liberalism' – was partly undermined by its own logic, when the Protestants in Ulster claimed their right to determine the political allegiance of their own community: a claim which was not without a certain 'nationalist' flavour.[40]

[36] F. Chabod, *Storia della politica estera italiana dal 1870 al 1896*, Bari, 1976, pp. 424–47; cf. J. Parry, *The Rise and Fall of Liberal Government in Victorian Britain*, New Haven and London, 1993, p. 304. To the Hegelian liberal and anti-fascist Guido De Ruggiero hostility to monarchical absolutism and rejection both of Rousseau's 'general will', and later of various forms of collectivism and socialism, were the two sides of the same liberal coin: *Storia del liberalismo europeo*, Bari, 1925, pp. 174–83. Far from sharing the panic of many of his contemporaries, Mill was appalled by the brutality of the suppression of the *Commune* by Thiers (I. Wessel Mueller, *John Stuart Mill and French Thought*, Urbana (Ill.), 1956, p. 225).

[37] Parry, *The Rise and Fall of Liberal Government*.

[38] P. F. Clarke, *Lancashire and the New Liberalism*, Cambridge, 1971, and *Liberals and Social Democrats*, Cambridge, 1978; Biagini, *Liberty, Retrenchment and Reform*.

[39] E. J. Hobsbawm, *Nations and Nationalism since 1870*, Cambridge, 1992, pp. 132–4; H. Grunwald, 'Memorandum to Woodrow Wilson', *Time*, 14 November 1994, p. 104.

[40] Cf. T. Nairn, *The Break-Up of Britain*, London, 1978, pp. 237–45.

Was there any alternative course that the Liberal Party could have followed? One way to try to answer this question is to look at it in a comparative perspective.

IV

'Make it known that I am shooting all peasants caught carrying arms. Quarter will be given only to regular soldiers. Executions have already begun today.'[41] This was the chilling text of a telegram sent by General Cialdini – an Italian liberal and member of Cavour's majority in parliament – to the governor of Campobasso, a town north-east of Naples, in the then inaccessible hills of Molise. It was 20 October 1860. Italy had become a united kingdom only a few months before. The Piedmontese, fresh from the Austrian battlefields, and incorporating the armies of Tuscany, Emilia and Lombardy, had first proceeded to crush the army of the Pope. The next step had been the annexation of the south. Garibaldi had already defeated the bulk of the Neapolitan army, though the last Bourbon king still hung on with his elite forces. The latter were quickly dispatched by Cialdini. But then the real difficulties began.

Thousands of ex-soldiers from the disintegrated southern army took to the hills to join the 'brigands', the social bandits celebrated by Hobsbawm as 'primitive rebels'.[42] At that time banditry was widespread throughout the Mediterranean basin,[43] and in some cases – as for the Greek *klephts* of the 1820s – had a proto-nationalist flavour, eventually generating real nationalism in a few instances.[44] In the territories of the former Kingdom of the Two Sicilies these 'brigands' had always been a power. Though historians have traditionally interpreted banditry in terms of mere social conflict and protest,[45] during the Napoleonic occupation it had played an anti-French – almost proto-national – role, similar to that of the *klephts* in the Ottoman Empire or the guerrillas in contemporary Spain. The perception that the south was 'different' from the north in more than mere socio-economic terms was suppressed by Risorgimento enthusiasts, only to be reaffirmed in the 1860s. Then Italian army officers and northern observers displayed all the vocabulary

---

[41] Cited in D. Mack Smith (ed.), *The Making of Italy, 1796–1870*, London, 1968, p. 327.

[42] E. J. Hobsbawm, *Primitive Rebels*, Manchester, 1959; and *Bandits*, London, 1969.

[43] Cf. G. Koliopoulos, *Brigands with a Cause: Brigandage and Irredentism in Modern Greece, 1812–1912*, Oxford, 1987.

[44] E.g. E. M. Edmonds (trans.), *Kolokotrones: the Klepht and the Warrior: An Autobiography*, London, 1892, pp. 83 ff.

[45] Cf. M. Petrusewicz, 'Society against the State: Peasant Brigandage in Southern Italy', *Criminal Justice History*, 8 (1987), pp. 1–20; J. A. Davis, *Conflict and Control: Law and Order in Nineteenth-century Europe*, Basingstoke, 1988, pp. 168–73.

of Victorian racism in their description of the southern 'brigands',[46] while the latter referred to the new authorities as 'the Piedmontese', irrespective of actual regional background: according to them the south was being 'invaded', not 'liberated'.

Whatever weight we may want to ascribe to these pseudo-ethnic prejudices and this proto-nationalist language, the 'brigands' became a force to be reckoned with from 1860, when their military capabilities were reinforced by professionally trained soldiers. As the new nation-state proceeded to enforce its authority, the ranks of the 'brigands' were further swelled by thousands of peasants fleeing from heavy taxation and military conscription. Cialdini's telegram reflected the fact that what had begun as a police operation had escalated into a veritable civil war, which eventually required the mobilisation of up to 100,000 soldiers for four or five years.[47] From Rome, the exiled Bourbons and the Pope lent spiritual, but little material, support to the rebels, and the uprising acquired the character of what nowadays would probably be described as a separatist movement. By 1861 the situation was so dire that Cavour feared that the south would be lost again. It was not, though, and for two main reasons. On the one hand the Italian government was determined to fight to the bitter end, whatever the cost to the state and the civilian population. On the other, the 'primitive rebellion' and its aristocratic patrons in Rome did not manage to produce a viable ideology, and were unable to appeal to either the nobility or the middle classes in the south, who were rallying around the new Italian state. Yet, even after the military power of the brigands was crushed, guerrilla warfare went on for years. More Italian soldiers died in this war than in the three wars of independence put together. Even without international support or legitimation for the 'brigands', the possibility that the Italian government in the south might end up like the Neapolitan Republic of 1799, which had been swept away by an anti-Jacobin 'church and king' *jacquerie*,[48] did not seem unrealistic at the time.[49] After all, Sicily and the Kingdom of Naples had a long unbroken history as independent centralised states, stretching back to the Norman invasion in the eleventh century: none of the 'nation-states' that achieved or claimed independence in nineteenth-century Europe – including Belgium, Greece and Ireland – could boast any comparable record.

Looking at Europe can help us to put the British and Irish problem in context, for what I have briefly illustrated was the Italian equivalent of

---

[46] J. Dickie, 'Una parola di guerra: l'esercito italiano e il brigantaggio', *Passato e presente*, 26 (1991), p. 59.

[47] Cf. R. Romanelli, *L'Italia liberale*, Bologna, 1979, pp. 29–36.

[48] G. Candeloro, *Storia dell'Italia moderna*, vol. I, *1700–1815*, Milan, 1977, pp. 273–75.

[49] Davis, *Conflict and Control*, p. 175.

'the Irish Question'. In a recent article W. C. Lubenow has observed that 'British Liberals could admire ... nationalism without appreciating the ways in which its central features ran contrary to their own state interests'.[50] In a sense, a similar comment could be applied to Italian liberals, and indeed to liberals elsewhere as well. For instance, there were French versions of the same problem: Thiers, a liberal nationalist, had to struggle tooth and nail with the 1871 Parisian federalists; later the Third Republic had to 'nationalise' the staunchly reactionary peasants,[51] who had forms of collective allegiance different from those of 'the nation', and many of whom did not speak French any more than Calabrian peasants spoke Italian.[52] In the United States, despite greater cultural homogeneity, the Civil War involved contrasting forms of national identity, and nowadays some historians would endorse Gladstone's 1862 statement that Jefferson Davis had 'made a nation'.[53]

The point is that there were – and still are – at least two basic kinds of 'nationalism', whose aims are incompatible. The one seeks the unification of states and regions with similar cultural and historical heritages into a larger 'national-state'; the other seeks the separation of a region or ethnic group from a broader political unit within which the region or group is considered to be 'imprisoned'. From the second half of the nineteenth century both forms of nationalism were *simultaneously* at work, sometimes in the same parts of Europe. Moreover, criteria of legitimacy were changing, as the old right of conquest – for centuries accepted as a valid source of government authority – was being replaced by new ideas of popular sovereignty. These different claims and contrasting sources of legitimacy generated considerable strife and, often, war. The establishment of a viable 'nation-state' was almost invariably accompanied by one side's decisive victory in such civil wars, and by successful propaganda operations which turned the victors' solution into 'the general will'.[54] In other words, it is questionable whether there has ever been a homogeneous 'nation-state', except as the outcome of repression and suppression of pre-existing forms of collective identity: paraphrasing both

---

[50] W. C. Lubenow, 'The Liberals and the National Question: Irish Home Rule, Nationalism, and their Relationship to Nineteenth-century Liberalism', *Parliamentary History*, 13, Part 1 (1994), p. 129.

[51] E. Weber, *Peasants into Frenchmen. The Modernization of Rural France*, Stanford (Ca.), 1992.

[52] As late as 1789 50 per cent of the inhabitants of the kingdom of France did not speak French at all, while only 12–13 per cent spoke standard French: E. J. Hobsbawm, *Nations and Nationalism since 1780*, Cambridge, 1991, p. 60; see also Weber, *Peasants into Frenchmen*, pp. 66–94.

[53] D. A. Faust, *The Creation of Confederate Nationalism: Ideology and Identity in the Civil War*, Baton Rouge (La.), 1988.

[54] Y. Tamir, *Liberal Nationalism*, Princeton, 1993, p. 3.

Bismarck and Cavour, it would seem that national-states were built with 'blood and steel' as much as with 'parliamentary majorities'.

The original example had been set by the French Jacobins in the 1790s, when Catholic Vendée and Celtic Brittany had been 'nationalised' by republican artillery more than by republican ideas. Centuries-old linguistic and political differences were swept away and denied any legitimacy. There was also a religious dimension in this French revolution: as the republic found its most loyal supporters in Huguenot *sans culottes*, the Catholic north-west was made to pay dearly for a century of oppression of the Protestant Languedoc.[55] The world was – indeed – turned upside down.

For better or for worse, the French exported their model throughout the rest of Europe, with one exception – Britain. The United Kingdom was neither a 'nation-state', nor interested in becoming one. It was a rather archaic multinational state, held together by parliament, the monarchy and the Protestant religion.[56] Yet, and significantly, after Napoleon's defeat in 1815, the United Kingdom – with its peculiar political stability, civil liberties, and economic growth – became a model for continental liberals, including the young Cavour. As Lubenow has rightly described them,[57] such liberals were *aristocratic* nationalists, a characteristic with important implications for their outlook. In particular, they tended to dismiss separatism as 'rebellion'. For example, far from perceiving the Irish question as parallel to the Italian struggle for independence, Cavour – and even Mazzini – rejected Irish claims as being motivated purely by religion and rural unrest.[58] The former did not deserve the sympathy of anti-clerical liberals; the latter – well, General Cialdini knew how to 'deal' with agrarian crime.

In its development the movement for Italian unification clashed with other and less sophisticated forms of collective identity. At a later stage and in other parts of Europe, including Ireland, similar feelings would generate separatist agitations, and 'anti-nationalist' nationalisms. On the continent the encounter between these contrasting forms of collective identity culminated in the suppression of the weaker ones, usually the separatists. In Britain and Ireland neither the Liberals nor the Tories could even contemplate the adoption of large-scale military repression before 1916–21, and when they did were unable to carry it out successfully.

[55] Cf. W. Doyle, *The Oxford History of the French Revolution*, Oxford, 1990, pp. 7, 9, 36, 138, 142, 144–7, 300, 410–1.

[56] L. Colley, *Britons. Forging the Nation 1707–1837*, New Haven and London, 1992; cf. M. Finn, *After Chartism*, Cambridge, 1993, pp. 13–59.

[57] Lubenow, 'The Liberals and the National Question', p. 130.

[58] N. Mansergh, *The Irish Question 1840–1921*, London, 1940, pp. 56–82.

Yet, whether they liked it or not, by the 1880s both Liberals and Conservatives had to come to terms with the new realities created by nationalism in the two main forms which it was taking in the United Kingdom – that is, Celtic separatism and militant imperialism. Thanks to Salisbury's ability to manipulate the latter without taking it too seriously, the Conservatives went from strength to strength. For their part, the Liberals were good at managing and absorbing Celtic separatism, turning a potentially destructive force into an important asset for both the stability of the United Kingdom and the electoral success of their own party. It is significant that the one case in which this strategy did not work was Ireland. This raises the question not so much of the compatibility of liberalism and Catholicism (for Greenlee shows that Presbyterian voting patterns in pre-Home Rule Ulster were more complex than is generally believed),[59] but rather that of the general relationship between culture and religion, and between the latter and politics.

Separation between church and state was the answer sought by many liberals. In the case of Scotland and Wales the disestablishment campaigns were a component of their respective nationalist movements.[60] Yet, separation could also be justified on purely theological or 'libertarian' principles. In particular, many Liberal MPs had a congregationalist background: they belonged to denominations whose ecclesiastical polity emphasised the full autonomy of the local congregation and its complete independence of state patronage or control. They saw religion as a matter of personal choice rather than of group or national allegiance. This flexible congregationalist *Weltanschauung*, in the context of Britain's apparent immunity from European wars and revolutions, enabled many, both within and without the Gladstonian coalition, to endorse a revolt against the *English* state from a non-separatist standpoint. From 1871, while unsettled, insecure European nationalists called for 'purity of blood', 'le cult de la terre et des morts', and eventually 'ein Volk, ein Reich, ein Führer', the British 'invented' Scottish traditions, revived the study and teaching of the Gaelic and Welsh languages, and revelled in their multiracial empire. The invention of the 'Scottishness' of the social and political establishment of the United Kingdom was one of the earliest manifestations of the move towards historicist 'inductive thinking', later to be adopted by the Liberals and Labour.[61] Any attempt to impose 'Englishness' on the other component parts of the United

---

[59] See below, p. 254.
[60] Machin, p. 130 below; cf. D. W. Bebbington, 'Religion and National Feeling in Nineteenth Century Wales and Scotland', in S. Mews (ed.), *Religion and National Identity*, Oxford, 1982.
[61] See below, chapters 12 by Shaw, and 13 by Lewis.

Kingdom seemed to betray basic constitutional principles. This was the rationale behind Gladstone's and Stuart Rendel's eulogy of the Welsh nation, as well as their campaigns for Irish Home Rule and Scottish land and church reform.

From the late 1870s 'inductive thinking' and historicism transformed the Liberal approach to land reform and nationalism. As Jose Harris shows, these could be inspired as much by traditional British philosophical schools, such as Platonism, as by positivism or German idealism. Their adoption by the Gladstone governments in 1881–6 showed both their responsiveness to contemporary intellectual innovation, and their ability to renew the British state's hold on the various proto-nationalist movements in Scotland, Wales and Ireland.

In Scotland this strategy worked out very well, and the Scottish Land and Labour League – which had successfully run independent crofter candidates at the 1885 election – was co-opted and transformed into a Liberal pressure group. It was, however, a question of incorporation, rather than manipulation: this is best exemplified by the Liberal Association's sending of delegates to the meetings of the Scottish Land and Labour League 'to determine what course the Liberals should pursue in the Highlands'.[62] It resulted in the painless absorption of the crofters' party before it could generate a nationalist party, and the Liberals in Scotland became 'omnipotent'[63] for another generation. This strategy was also effective in Wales, where the desire for ecclesiastical reform and temperance legislation turned *Cymru Fydd* and its leaders – including the young Lloyd George – into champions of Gladstonianism. When considered against the background of the repression and suppression carried out in continental Europe, these achievements stand out as impressive memorials to Victorian liberalism.

In Ireland too, Gladstone, followed by Asquith and Birrell, very nearly succeeded. Their strategy had been laid out between 1881 and 1886: by co-opting the National Party led by the aristocratic Parnell, Gladstone tried to turn a dangerous challenger into a pillar of empire. A similar operation had been successfully carried out in Canada in 1840–67, in a society resembling Ireland in its divisions along historical, religious, ethnic and linguistic lines.[64]

---

[62] I. G. C. Hutchison, *A Political History of Scotland 1832–1924*, Edinburgh, 1986, p. 170.

[63] J. Buchan, MP, cited in A. Marr, *The Battle for Scotland*, London, 1992, p. 111.

[64] K. McNaught, *The Penguin History of Canada*, London, 1988, pp. 90–137; A. Grier and I. Radforth (eds.), *Colonial Leviathan. State Formation in Mid-Nineteenth Century Canada*, Toronto, 1992. A similar policy – in a similar context of ethno-linguistic and historical strife – was successfully carried out in South Africa by the Asquith government in cooperation with Jan Smuts, from 1908: T. R. H. Davenport, *South Africa. A Modern History*, London, 1991, pp. 216–25. For Gladstone's long-term commitment to devolution see H. C. G. Matthew, 'Introduction' to *The Gladstone Diaries*, vols. XII and XIII, Oxford, 1994, pp. xxxiii–xxxvii; Parry, *Rise and Fall*, p. 255.

Moreover, Gladstone could hope that, after the implementation of Home Rule, Parnell's national alliance would disintegrate and generate a left-wing party, either radical–secularist in the continental fashion, or Catholic and populist in the O'Connell tradition. Whatever the complexion of such a party, it would be likely to focus on social and land issues rather than on nationalism. This had happened in Hungary after the establishment of the 'Dual Monarchy' in 1867 – a contemporary case of successful 'home rule'. During his visit to Budapest in 1892 Sidgwick had observed that 'in the Hungarian Parliament the extreme left seems to be *more* anti-nationalitarian than the government party'.[65] This was hardly surprising given the internationalist zeal of the European left, both socialist and Cobdenite, and their interest in social reform and economic progress. As Fitzpatrick has shown, internationalism remained a powerful current in the early Irish labour movement,[66] and, probably, the only one which could have generated an all-Ireland Labour Party. However, the Easter Rising and the adoption of a nationalist stance imposed a different course on the subsequent development of socialist politics in the Free State. Suddenly, the slow 'forward march of labour' was replaced by a new emphasis on 'blood, sacrifice and purification', seen as the only way to prevent the final success of Redmondite Catholic liberalism[67] – a rhetoric fearfully reminiscent of 'la Terre et les Morts' and other continental proto-fascist movements.[68] Yet, the internationalist/ pacifist identity survived alongside the nationalist one, ensuring that Irish socialists would remain awkwardly divided and in a state of electoral impotence for yet another generation.[69]

The persistent frustration of the Irish Labour Party and socialist republicans and their unsuccessful struggle to square the circle of framing a

---

[65] Henry Sidwick to Oscar Browning, 12 April 1892, cited in Lubenow, 'The Liberals and the National Question', p. 29.

[66] See chapter 11 below, p. 280.

[67] D. G. Boyce, *Nationalism in Ireland*, London, 1982, p. 308; R. English, *Radicals and the Republic. Socialist Republicanism in the Irish Free State 1925–1937*, Oxford, 1994, pp. 50–1. The revolutionaries felt that this was probably the only way to avoid a fate similar to that of Australian nationalists, whose hopes in 'a great nationalist awakening when the people would throw over British rule and British notions and found a republican democracy' were dashed by liberal reforms: the Australians concluded that '[r]epublicanism was not needed in order to achieve control over local affairs and democracy too was established without a disowning of Britain' (J. B. Hirst, *The Strange Birth of Colonial Democracy. New South Wales 1840–1884*, Sydney and London, 1988, p. 272).

[68] Cf. H. Stuart Hughes, *Consciousness and Society*, New York, 1977, pp. 338–40, 353; G. L. Mosse, *The Crisis of the German Ideology: Intellectual Origins of the Third Reich*, New York, 1981, pp. 54–7; Z. Sternhell, M. Sznajder and M. Asheri, *The Birth of Fascist Ideology. From Cultural Rebellion to Political Revolution*, Princeton, 1994, pp. 9, 28–9, 32, 50, 166, 176–7, 187.

[69] M. Gallagher, *The Irish Labour Party in Transition 1957–82*, Manchester, 1982, pp. 121–53.

nationalist socialism[70] provides an interesting parallel to the earlier failure of Ulster Liberals as epitomised by Greenlee. Liberal land reform proposals won both Presbyterian and Catholic seats in 1880, its rhetoric being based on a form of 'class struggle' (tenants *versus* landlords), encouraging people to exchange the reality of a three-century-old sectarian hatred for the hope of a farmer's paradise. Liberal class struggle worked no better than its socialist counterpart would have done forty years later, and indeed to the present day socialist and 'liberal' parties are marginalised by sectarian–nationalist ones in both Northern Ireland and Eire.

Nowadays, in the light of the events of 1989–94 in Europe, Parnellite concepts such as dual allegiance, cultural diversity and divisible sovereignty look much more attractive.[71] Yet, and despite recent hopeful developments, it would still seem that Gladstone stood more chance of implementing a liberal solution to community strife in Ireland than any of his successors in the twentieth century, with the possible exception of Asquith and Redmond.[72] On a different level, in terms of Ireland's internal policy, the failure of Redmondite Catholic liberalism and the later frustration of Tom Johnson's socialism had profoundly negative consequences on the development of democracy in the island. Whether liberals or socialists will ever be successful in dealing with militant nationalism, separatism and religious intolerance remains an open question – both in Ireland and elsewhere in the world.

[70] See C. Fitzpatrick, chapter 11 in this book. For similar conclusions about the socialist republicans of a later period see English, *Radicals and the Republic*, pp. 44–51, 130–8, 275–6.

[71] R. F. Foster, *Paddy and Mr Punch. Connections in Irish and English History*, London, 1993, p. 36; D. Marquand, *The Unprincipled Society. New Demands and Old Politics*, London, 1988, pp. 9–10; D. McCrone, *Understanding Scotland. The Sociology of a Stateless Nation*, London, 1992, pp. 2, 216–18.

[72] P. Bew, *Ideology and the Irish Question. Ulster Unionism and Irish Nationalism 1912–1916*, Oxford, 1994, pp. 152–60.

Part I

Citizenship, populism and liberalism

1 Liberalism and direct democracy: John Stuart Mill and the model of ancient Athens

Eugenio F. Biagini

I

Liberalism is often described as a body of strictly individualistic doctrines based on, and aimed at, the defence of personal rights and liberties, intended as 'absence of restraint'.[1] Furthermore, it is usually assumed that there was a 'crucial moral opposition' between such individualism and the 'classical republican' (Aristotelian) concept of active citizenship typical of democratic and socialist movements.[2] And yet over the past few years this assumption has come under increasing attack from different quarters. Quentin Skinner has demonstrated that the republican tradition included a considerable emphasis on liberal individualism,[3] while more recently I have argued for both a community dimension and a passionate attachment to 'positive' liberty as characterising Gladstonian popular liberalism.[4] A question now to be addressed is whether the latter sat midway between the 'liberal' and 'republican' traditions, or whether the dichotomy between these traditions is just not applicable to British liberalism.

The case of J. S. Mill is almost an ideal one for exploring this question. Not only was he the leading 'libertarian' of his day, but he also paved the

I would like to thank Daniel T. Rodgers, Stefan Collini and Quentin Skinner for their helpful comments and criticism on a previous draft of the present chapter.

[1] J. A. Colaiaco, *James Fitzjames Stephen and the Crisis of Victorian Thought*, London, 1983, pp. 127, 138.

[2] A. MacIntyre, *After Virtue*, London, 1981, p. 241; C. Lasch, *The True and Only Heaven. Progress and Its Critics*, New York and London, 1991, pp. 14–15, 59. Cf. S. Macedo, *Liberal Virtues. Citizenship, Virtue, and Community in Liberal Constitutionalism*, Oxford, 1990, p. 97: 'the contrast between classical citizenship, as conceived by Aristotle and that in liberal theory is striking'. See also C. Taylor, 'What's Wrong with Negative Liberty', in A. J. Ryan (ed.), *The Idea of Freedom*, Oxford and New York, 1979, pp. 175–94.

[3] Q. Skinner, 'The Republican Idea of Political Liberty', in G. Bock, Q. Skinner and M. Viroli (eds), *Machiavelli and Republicanism*, Cambridge, 1990, pp. 293, 302. For a systematic discussion of the relation between 'republicanism' and 'liberalism' see D. T. Rodgers, 'Republicanism: the Career of a Concept', *The Journal of American History*, 79, 1 (June 1992), pp. 11–38.

[4] *Liberty, Retrenchment and Reform. Popular Liberalism in the Age of Gladstone, 1860–1880*, Cambridge, 1992.

way towards experiments in collectivism, and by the end of his career was supposed to have become a kind of socialist. Not surprisingly, scholars have long questioned Mill's consistency, as well as the dynamic of what can be seen as his systematic eclecticism. Curiously, the common thread linking the traditions on which Mill drew has been overlooked:[5] it was a version of the 'classical republican' model which held the key position in Mill's liberalism, and had wide-ranging implications for his attitudes to the issue of liberty and public control in a free society. This chapter sets out to explore this territory.

II

We know that British working-class radicals were not affected by continental polemics about direct *versus* representative democracy: like the Jeffersonian Democrats,[6] they did not see any real dichotomy between the two systems. With their forerunners, the Chartists, they shared much of the 'republican' tradition, the 'Machiavellian moment' which placed great emphasis on civic duty and public-spiritedness as the essential guarantors of liberty, and deplored as 'corruption' the despising of these virtues in the furtherance of private interests.[7] Their ideal was the 'small state'[8] with its popular magistracies and participatory emphasis: like the French Jacobins of the 1790s, they admired the virtuous Rome of early republican times,[9] and their supreme model was ancient Athens.[10]

That this heritage remained alive in the working-class left may not be surprising. What is more so, however, is that it was accepted by leading Liberal thinkers as well. There is little doubt that Gladstonian ideology could not be reduced to Lasch's 'state-nightwatchman':[11] on the contrary, it included the identification of liberty with self-government,

---

[5] Even Turner has failed to mention the case of J. S. Mill, though he devotes a long section to the political and constitutional debate (F. M. Turner, *The Greek Heritage in Victorian Britain*, New Haven and London, 1981, pp. 187–233).

[6] Cf. H. F. Pitkin, *Concept of Representation*, Berkeley and Los Angeles, 1967, pp. 60–1, 63, 191. For the survival of classical models and rhetoric in late nineteenth-century Democratic language see M. Ostrogorski, *Democracy and Political Parties*, vol. II, New York, 1964 (First edn 1902), p. 264.

[7] Q. Skinner, 'Republican Liberty', pp. 303, 304. Cf. J. G. A. Pocock, *The Machiavellian Moment*, Princeton, N.J., 1973.

[8] [Report], 'Political Address by Mr Cowen, MP', *Newcastle Daily Chronicle*, 16 February 1885, p. 2.

[9] Cf. [report], *Bee-Hive*, 18 January 1868, p. 1. For a discussion of the Roman republican tradition in British politics see F. M. Turner, 'British Politics and the Demise of the Roman Republic, 1700–1939', in Turner, *Contesting Cultural Authority. Essays in Victorian Intellectual Life*, Cambridge, 1993, pp. 231–61.

[10] Cf. [leading article], 'Democracy in Olden Times', *Newcastle Daily Chronicle*, 30 October 1885, p. 4; and [leading article], 'The People's Parliament', *Lloyd's Weekly*, 21 December 1884, p. 6.

[11] Lasch, *The True and Only Heaven*, p. 59.

high esteem for a life of public service and the related civic virtues, the idealisation of 'independence',[12] and an emphasis of self-help and education as moral imperatives. As is well known, all these aspects were also typical of the 'republican ideal'.[13]

Even more interesting was the claim that the representative system was 'not primarily about the individual's rights, but the representation of his community'.[14] This had potentially radical implications, as well as conservative applications. Clearly, the liberal position contained elements of ambiguity. Both Tocqueville[15] and J. S. Mill feared a democracy of 'monads', which would lead to a government's undisturbed rule over a mass of isolated individuals.[16] There was the conviction abroad that something more than 'mere numbers' should find representation in parliament, and that between the elector and the representative chamber there should be intermediate forms of collective identity.[17] While this could be construed to justify limited franchises and the rule of the *notables*, to 'advanced Liberals' it meant that there were occasions when the interests of the individual ought to be subordinated to the welfare of his community.

As on many other questions, so on this one Mill's views were close to the aspirations of popular democracy. For instance, he repeatedly expressed his preference for a small-scale society based on face-to-face relationships and virtually co-extensive with a local community. In it, participation and debate would spontaneously arise from the awareness of common interests, and from the feeling of belonging to a socio-cultural entity to which one felt a positive emotional commitment. Moreover, in Mill – 'the Saint of Rationalism' – we find an almost Mazzinian zeal for the cultivation of civic virtue,[18] a vocal condemnation of 'a life devoted to the pursuit of wealth and private comforts ... because it provided insufficient scope for the ambition to excel',[19] and an emphasis on personal development reminiscent of the classical ideal of the *eudaimonia* or 'human flourishing'. This is well illustrated by his attitude to ancient Greek democracy.

[12] For the importance of 'independence' and yeoman property in the republican tradition see J. G. A. Pocock, *Virtue, Commerce, and History*, Cambridge, 1985, pp. 67–8.

[13] Skinner, 'Republican Liberty' pp. 294–6.

[14] M. Pugh, *The Making of Modern British Politics*, Oxford, 1993, p. 4; M. Cowling, *Disraeli, Gladstone and Revolution*, Cambridge, 1967, p. 68.

[15] A. De Tocqueville, *Democracy in America*, vol. II, Part I, Chapt. 5, London, 1968, p. 569.

[16] J. S. Mill, *Autobiography*, in *Collected Works*, vol. I, *Autobiography and Literary Essays*, London and Toronto, 1981, p. 201.

[17] H. J. Hanham, 'Tra l'individuo e lo stato', in P. Pombeni (ed.), *La trasformazione politica nell'Europa liberale 1870–1890*, Bologna, 1986, p. 96.

[18] C. S. Maier, 'Democracy since the French Revolution', in J. Dunn (ed.), *Democracy: the Unfinished Journey 508 BC to AD 1993*, Oxford, 1992, p. 130.

[19] Lasch, *The True and Only Heaven*, p. 174.

Ancient democracy was a 'hot' issue during the decades between the 1790s and the 1870s. Many continental liberals regarded it with suspicion because of the ideological use to which it had been put during the French Revolution. Benjamin Constant seemed to represent the voice of European liberalism when – in his 1819 lecture at the Athenée Royal – he contrasted the 'liberty of the ancients' with the 'liberty of the moderns':[20] the former was the 'positive liberty' of collective self-determination, with its emphasis on participation and civic militancy; the latter involved the law's protection of the individual in the pursuit of his own intellectual and economic goals. Constant criticised the 'liberty of the ancients' because of his own experience of Jacobin democracy[21] and his fear of a repetition of something like Robespierre's attempt to impose the model of 'ancient republican virtue' by heavy-handed interference in private life.[22] To him, Rousseau and Robespierre were the true heirs of the 'ancients', whom they had greatly admired.[23] But the liberals, the 'moderns', were supposed to follow a totally different school of thought:[24] one based on the cooperation of enlightened self-interest in a 'commercial society', rather than on 'Spartan virtue' and disinterested Aristotelian devotion to the commonwealth.[25] Not surprisingly, Constant 'did not indulge in any sentimentalism about the myth of direct political participation';[26] rather, he was the forerunner of those liberals, recently celebrated by Stephen Macedo, who, 'fearing the impassioned instability of direct democracy ... opt for representative government'.[27] For constant 'the mirage of ancient liberty – participatory democracy as the ceaseless exemplification of community in collective public action – was a malign survival in the politics of the modern commercial west, an ideological residue of a very distant world and one which could now do nothing but harm'.[28] French and European liberals seemed to agree; and,

---

[20] B. Constant, 'The Liberty of the Ancients compared with that of the Moderns', in *Political Writings*, translated and edited by B. Fontana, Cambridge, 1988, pp. 308–28.

[21] B. Croce, 'Constant e Jellinek: intorno alla differenza tra la libertà degli antichi e quella dei moderni', in *Etica e politica*, Bari, Laterza, 1931, pp. 294–301; B. Fontana, 'Introduction' to B. Constant, *Political Writings*, p. 18. For the emphasis on the ideal of direct democracy in the French Revolution see B. Fontana, 'Democracy and the French Revolution', in J. Dunn (ed.), *Democracy. The Unfinished Journey*, pp. 112–13; cf. also L. Guerci, *Libertà degli antichi e libertà dei moderni. Sparta, Atene e i philosophes nella Francia del Settecento*, Naples, 1979.

[22] Fontana, 'Introduction' to Constant, *Political Writings*, pp. 26, 34.

[23] J. J. Rousseau, *The Social Contract*, Oxford, 1962, Book 3, ch. xv; Lasch, *The True and Only Heaven*, p. 128.

[24] G. Acocella, 'Costituzione liberale e democrazia totalitaria nella critica di Benjamin Constant al "Contratto sociale"', *Filosofia*, n.s., 27, 1 (January 1976), pp. 67–100.

[25] S. Macedo, *Liberal Virtues*, pp. 97–9, 120; Fontana, 'Introduction' to Constant, *Political Writings*, pp. 15–18.

[26] B. Fontana, *Benjamin Constant and the Post-Revolutionary Mind*, New Haven, 1991, p. 54.

[27] Macedo, *Liberal Virtues*, p. 98.

[28] J. Dunn, 'Conclusion', in Dunn (ed.), *Democracy*, p. 243.

indeed, by the experience of 1848 they were confirmed in the belief that 'direct democracy meant the illiberal restraint of opinion, the curbing of individuality and culture, the mobilisation of mass sentiment to dominate policies and personnel ... continually vulnerable to despotism, whether exerted by the mob or a tyrant'.[29]

J. S. Mill, with his emphasis on the rights of elites, the prevention of the oppression of dissenting minorities by conformist majorities, and the benefits of originality and genius, would seem to fit comfortably into this context.[30] Indeed, charges of elitism have often been levelled against him, and he is believed to have been 'constantly haunted by the fear of working-class despotism'.[31] For many scholars it goes without saying that the 'liberty' defended by Mill was substantially the same as that proclaimed by Constant, and with the same qualifications. However, this view hardly seems compatible with Mill's enthusiastic appraisal of direct democracy and militant citizenship in ancient Athens.

Like most of his contemporaries,[32] the classically educated Mill felt the fascination of the political systems of ancient Greece. He devoted several essays to Greek politics and philosophy, including two long reviews, published in 1846 and 1853 respectively, of George Grote's *History of Greece*. These were, more than reviews, real 'manifestos for democracy'[33] in which Mill elaborated on Grote's ideas and applied the teaching of 'the ancients' to the context of the Victorian debate on democracy – an operation which he was to continue in later works, including the *Considerations on Representative Government*.

Mill's interest in democratic Athens went back to his precocious boyhood, when – sharing his father's admiration for the principles of the French Revolution – he had criticised the anti-democratic and anti-Jacobin interpretation of Greek history contained in Mitford's classical text.[34] In those years, and especially from the 1820s, Mitford became one

---

[29] Maier, 'Democracy since the French Revolution', in Dunn (ed.), *Democracy*, p. 128.

[30] G. Himmelfarb, *Poverty and Compassion. The Moral Imagination of the Late Victorians*, New York, 1991, p. 250; see also pp. 251–3.

[31] R. J. Halliday, *John Stuart Mill*, London, 1976, p. 138.

[32] Cf. R. Jenkins, *The Victorians and Ancient Greece*, Oxford, 1980, esp. pp. 14–15; F. M. Turner, *The Greek Heritage in Victorian Britain*, esp. pp. 187–233; F. E. Sparshott, 'Introduction' to J. S. Mill, *Essays on Philosophy and the Classics*, in *Collected Works*, vol. XI, London, 1978; I. Bradley, *The Optimists*, London, 1980, pp. 78–9. This heritage was one of the main motivations behind British support for the Greek war of independence: cf. D. Dakin (ed.), *British and American Philhellenes during the War of Greek Independence*, Thessaloniki, 1955; A. Fimaras, 'The Other British Philhellenes', in R. Clogg (ed.), *The Struggle for Greek Independence*, London, 1973, pp. 200–23.

[33] S. Collini, *Public Moralists. Political Thought and Intellectual Life in Britain, 1850–1930*, Oxford, 1991, p. 136.

[34] J. S. Mill, *Autobiography* (1873), in *Collected Works*, vol. I, p. 15. For James Mill's admiration for the principles of the French Revolution see B. Mazlish, *James and John Stuart Mill. Father and Son in the Nineteenth Century*, New York, 1975, pp. 236–7.

of the polemical targets of the second generation of radical utilitarians. In 1822 George Grote, a close friend of Mill, decided to write a new history of Greece in order to provide a more balanced and 'correct' – or philo-democratic – interpretation. By the end of that decade other radicals – including Charles Austin, G. C. Lewis and G. Warde Norman – had also intervened on the question.[35]

The first real radical 'manifesto' on Greek democracy appeared in 1826, when Grote published a long and well-argued indictment against the Tory interpretation.[36] Charging Mitford with having manipulated facts and evidence out of blind hatred for the French Revolution,[37] Grote proceeded to dissect two of the anti-democratic prejudices which in those years both affected attitudes to ancient democracy and stimulated apprehensions as to the likely consequences of electoral reform. First, Grote demonstrated that in Athens *arbitrary* judgements and sentences dictated by the populace were rare and purely accidental, and took place *despite* the democratic involvement of the people, rather than because of it.[38] Second, he exploded the notion that in democratic Athens the wealthy – either as a group or as individuals – were subjected to any form of persecution or spoliation.[39]

But the most important part of Grote's essay was the formulation of the outline of a liberal interpretation of Greek history, on which he would eventually construct his monumental work. To the young Grote, classical democracy was a system which promoted not the interests of the poor as against those of the wealthy, but those of society as a whole. He presented it not only as the best political system which had existed in antiquity, but indeed as a better one than that of contemporary England: Athens was seen as an 'open society' based on a maximum of tolerance – including religious tolerance – in which publicity and constant discussion of all questions concerning the public interest had been the key to great intellectual achievement. These advantages were linked to the form of the city-state, within which it was possible to achieve the 'concentration of public' essential to ensuring the proper working of a system based on free

---

[35] *The Quarterly Review*, 32 (1826), pp. 332–56; and C. Austin's answer in *Westminster Review*, 7 (1827), pp. 227–68. Cf. A. Momigliano, 'George Grote and the Study of Greek History', in *Contributo alla storia degli studi classici*, Rome, 1955, pp. 217–19.

[36] G. Grote, 'Institutions of Ancient Greece', *Westminster Review*, 5 (1826), pp. 269–331.

[37] William Mitford's *History of Greece* had been published between 1784 and 1810. Like J. Gilliet's *Greek History* (1786) it was affected by the American Revolution first and the French Revolution afterwards, to both of which both authors were strongly opposed: see Momigliano, 'George Grote', pp. 214ff.

[38] G. Grote, 'Institutions', pp. 294ff; J. S. Mill, 'Two Publications on Plato', *London and Westminster Review*, 34 (Sept. 1840), in *Essays on Philosophy and the Classics, Collected Works*, vol. XII, p. 242. Socrates' conviction and execution were traditionally taken as an example of democratic despotism in Athens, but Mill disagreed (see below pp. 35–6).

[39] Grote, 'Institutions', pp. 192–7.

discussion. Though modern nations, because of their size, were unable to evolve along similar lines, Grote expressed the view that technological progress would eventually compensate for the impossibility of a physical concentration of an educated citizenship in the *agora* – a view that Mill endorsed.[40]

III

The publication of Grote's essay coincided with the onset of Mill's 'mental crisis': an occurrence which may help to explain why there were no reactions or remarks by Mill, though such a literary event was one that could hardly have passed without comment in different circumstances. During the following years Mill was concerned more with poetry than with political theory. He visited France for the second time in 1830, and started his life-long relationship with Harriet Taylor. Under the influence of Romanticism, he began to switch the focus of his attention from the utilitarian 'arithmetic' of pleasures and pains, to the development of the individual. In politics this meant a growing concern for the levelling tendencies of industrial society and the threats this posed to original and eminent personalities.

This theme was closely intertwined with that of the role of intellectuals in society. Following the controversial essay 'The Spirit of the Age',[41] Mill published 'On Genius' in 1832.[42] This work – a powerful vindication of the importance of originality and the individual's right to dissent – contrasted contemporary England with ancient Athens. Mill argued for the superiority of the latter on the ground of her allegedly greater respect for individual genius: among the Athenians wisdom and culture were not 'private ornaments', but essential attributes of full humanity and active citizenship. Socrates left behind no dogma, but rather a method of reasoning an enquiry. Mill lamented that in modern England the general trend was the opposite one: culture was seen as a disposable luxury, and an anti-intellectual, uneducated public opinion asked only for readily consumable dogmas which would save them the trouble of thinking for

---

[40] *Ibid.*, pp. 277–9. Cf. J. S. Mill, 'M. de Tocqueville on Democracy in America', *Edinburgh Review* (October 1840), now in *Collected Works*, vol. XVIII, Tome I, *Essays on Politics and Society*, Toronto and London, 1977, p. 165: 'The newspapers and the railroads are solving the problem of bringing the democracy of England to vote, like that of Athens, simultaneously in one *agora*.' A similar opinion was expressed by Mill's one-time friend, Thomas Carlyle: *On Heroes, Hero-Worship, and the Heroic in History*, The Norman and Charlotte Strouse edition of the works of Thomas Carlyle; introduction and notes by M. K. Goldberg, J. B. Brattin and M. Engel; Berkeley, Los Angeles and Oxford, 1993, p. 142.

[41] *Examiner*, 1831, now in *Collected Works*, vol. XXII, Toronto and London, 1986 pp. 227–316.

[42] *Monthly Repository*, n.s., (Oct. 1831), now in *Collected Works*, vol. I, pp. 329–39.

themselves.[43] In the comparison between the 'ancients' and the 'moderns', the cause of the latter looked so hopeless that Mill signed himself under the pseudonym of 'Antiquus'.

Between 1829 and 1831, with a zeal renewed by mature reflection, Mill devoted himself to the study of the Greek classics, and particularly of Plato's dialogues. He was more impressed than ever by Socrates: indeed, the Socrates 'midwife of truth' of the *Phaedrus* became the model on which he self-consciously began to shape his own intellectual personality.[44]

Though he continued to publish on various topics,[45] Mill did not discuss political theory or history till 1835, when he read the first volume of *La democratie en Amerique*. Tocqueville's work made a deep impression on him.[46] Under the influence of Romanticism, Mill had already lost the typically Benthamite trust in the magical effects of democratic arithmetic:[47] now Tocqueville offered a rigorously formulated and empirically based version of the Romantic fear that the conformism of public opinion in a mass society would endanger individual freedom. Mill's 1835 review of the first volume of *La democratie* constituted a presentation from a democratic standpoint of a book which in England had been welcomed first and foremost by anti-democratic writers.

Though parallel, and on many issues closely akin to each other, the analyses of Mill and Tocqueville differed on fundamental details.[48] To Mill the threats which Tocqueville ascribed to democratic equality were in fact to be laid at the door of commercial, industrial society, with its mass dimension and breakdown of face-to-face relationships and community feeling. The kind of civilisation which thus came into existence was much more impersonal:

The individual becomes so lost in the crowd, that though he depends more and more upon opinion, he is apt to depend less and less upon well-grounded opinion; upon the opinion of those who know him. An established character becomes at once more difficult to gain, and more easily to be disposed with.[49]

---

[43] M. St John Packe, *The Life of John Stuart Mill*, London 1954, p. 133.

[44] R. J. Halliday, *John Stuart Mill*, pp. 30–1.

[45] Of particular importance were his *Essays on Some Unsettled Questions of Political Economy* (now in *Collected Works*, vol. IV, Tome I, Toronto and London, 1967, pp. 229–339), written in 1831–2 though published only in 1844–5. More indicative of his state of mind in this period are his literary writings, which expressed his interest in Tennyson's and Wordsworth's poetry (these writings are now in *Collected Works*, vol. I).

[46] Though not a decisive one: H. O. Pappè, 'Mill and Tocqueville', *Journal of History of Ideas*, 25, 2 (1964), esp. pp. 228–30.

[47] Indeed, Halliday – in *Mill*, pp. 20–43 – goes as far as speaking, for this period, of a 'high Tory' Mill.

[48] Pappè, 'Mill and Tocqueville', p. 230.

[49] 'On Civilization', *London and Westminster Review*, 30 (April 1836), now in *Essays on Politics*, *Collected Works*, vol. XVIII, p. 132.

In this way also the guiding role of public opinion was lost. Whereas the old community was small enough for its citizens to know one another and exercise what amounted to a reciprocal censorship, the modern industrial city was so immense and diffuse that the prevalent attitudes were either indifference or groundless prejudice aroused by demagogy and propaganda. Mill effectively illustrated his case by comparing the shopkeeper in a market town with the general store in the metropolis:

It is in a small society, where everybody knows everybody, that public opinion, so far as well directed, exercises its most salutary influence. Take the case of a tradesman in a small country town: to every one of his customers he is long and accurately known; their opinion of him has been formed after repeated trials; if he could deceive them once, he cannot hope to go on deceiving them in the quality of his goods; he has no other customers to look for if he loses these, while, if his goods are really what they profess to be, he may hope, among so few competitors, that this also will be known and recognised, and that he will acquire the character, individually and professionally, which his conduct entitles him to. Far different is the case of a man setting up his business in the crowded streets of a great city. If he trusts solely on the quality of his goods, to the honesty and faithfulness with which he performs what he undertakes, he may remain ten years without a customer: be he ever so honest, he is driven to cry out on the housetops that his wares are the best of wares, past, present, and to come; while, if he proclaims this, however false, with sufficient loudness to excite the curiosity of passers by, and can give his commodities a gloss, saleable look, not easily to be seen through at a superficial glance, he may drive a thriving trade though no customer ever enters his shop twice.[50]

Thus, the breakdown of community links meant that public opinion degenerated from rational check to an irrational phenomenon easy to manipulate. This was accompanied by the loss of influence of the most cultivated people in the midst of a multitude seemingly deaf to their teaching. Rhetoric was degraded from 'instrument of logic' for the triumph of the truth, to instrument of demagogues anxious only for their own success. It was not a class revolution that Mill feared: rather, it was the crisis of the magistracy of the public moralists in a commercial society.[51]

Democracy, the despotism of an ill-formed public opinion, and the role of the intellectuals remained at the centre also of his later works. In 'On Bentham' (1838)[52] Mill anticipated the argument eventually developed in On Liberty as to the distinction between the rule of the majority on each member of the community, and the rule of each member on

[50] Ibid., pp. 132–3.
[51] Cf. ibid., pp. 133–4.
[52] 'On Bentham', London and Westminster Review, 29 (August 1838), now in Essay on Ethics, Religion and Society, Collected Works, vol. X, Toronto and London, 1969, pp. 75–116.

himself, and emphasised the critical and progressive role of oppositions, anti-conformism and even heresy.[53] And in 'Coleridge' (1840)[54] Mill provided further evidence for those who suspected him of 'elitism', by proposing that the intellectuals – the 'clerisy' – should be publicly endowed to make them fully independent of the pressure of opinion.[55]

About seven months after 'Coleridge', Mill published his second review of *La democratie en Amerique*. As Royer-Collard pointed out,[56] it was not so much a review as an original contribution to the debate on democracy and liberty. In his *Autobiography* Mill remarked that reading Tocqueville was particularly stimulating with regard to two issues: the first was the necessity of developing a qualified form of democracy having institutional safeguards for the rights of minorities. The second was the problem of centralisation. Like Tocqueville, Mill now attached

the utmost importance to the performance of as much of the collective business of society, as can safely be so performed, by the people themselves, without any intervention of the executive government ... He viewed this practical political activity of the individual citizen, not only as one of the most effectual means of training the social feelings and practical intelligence of the people ... but also as the specific counteractive to some of the characteristic infirmities of Democracy, and a necessary protection against degenerating into the only despotism of which in the modern world there is real danger – the absolute rule of the head of the executive over a congregation of isolated individuals, all equals but all slaves.[57]

To Mill the fundamental character that a democracy must possess in order to safeguard liberty was a high degree of popular involvement in public life. Though he agreed with Tocqueville on the existence of a strong trend towards equality – leading to 'the growing insignificance of the individual in comparison with the mass'[58] – he differed from the French aristocrat as to the reasons why such a trend could be detrimental to liberty.

Tocqueville insisted that growing social equality was levelling down those positions of privilege which in the past had provided centres of resistance to despotism as well as to prejudice and fanaticism. To him the new middle classes were, at one and the same time, too weak to feel that they – as individuals – could have an impact on current issues, and too wealthy to feel that they needed to seek collective help and cooperation: believing that they 'owe[d] nothing to any man, they expect[ed] nothing

[53] *Ibid.*, pp. 107–8.
[54] 'On Coleridge', *London and Westminster Review*, 34 (March 1840), now in *Collected Works*, vol. x, *Essays on Ethics*, pp. 117–65.
[55] *Ibid.*, pp. 147–51.
[56] Cited in Pappè, 'Mill and Tocqueville', p. 227.
[57] J. S. Mill, *Autobiography*, *Collected Works*, vol. I, p. 201.
[58] Mill, 'M. de Tocqueville on Democracy in America', p. 194.

from any man'.[59] The individual retreated into the sphere of his own private life, in the pursuance of personal interests, and distanced himself from the business of the community: the *nouveaux riches* lacked any civic spirit.

Mill answered that, if such was the case, the question was not one of equality, but of participation and the fostering of civic virtue. Democracy, he pointed out, is a term which merely indicates the mass involvement of the citizens in national life: in this sense both France and the United States were democracies, though the trends observable in each case were different. The main difference was that in France 'everything was done *for* the people, and nothing *by* the people'.[60] By contrast, in the United States the citizens' interest in the commonwealth had an intensity comparable to that in their own private affairs. What provided the people with political education was their inevitable, almost compulsory, involvement in the activities of the government. They were continually being called upon to sit on various representative bodies, to be invested with one or other of the many popular magistracies, and to man the voluntary committees which were forever springing up to deal with various aspects of ordinary community life. These committees and magistracies, which carried out functions that in France would have been entrusted to bureaucrats, were the means whereby the Americans 'maximize[d] [their] own individual liberty' by taking 'charge of the public arena [themselves]'.[61] In this way the American constitution counterbalanced the centrifugal, individualistic, tendencies of the modern commercial society:[62] every day it exorcised the 'commercial spirit' by forcefully awakening the 'civic spirit'.

IV

This was the background to the publication of Mill's reviews of Grote's *History of Greece*.[63] The latter was widely acclaimed and met with an enormous success throughout the nineteenth century, though nowadays it is perhaps more interesting for what it says about Victorian Britain than for its analysis of ancient Greece. Indeed, Mill's reviews,[64] and particularly

[59] A. de Tocqueville, *Democracy in America*, vol. II, p. 99.
[60] Mill, 'M. de Tocqueville on Democracy in America', p. 169.
[61] Skinner, 'The Republican Idea of Liberty', p. 308.
[62] Mill, 'M. de Tocqueville on Democracy in America', pp. 169, 191–2; cf. Pappè, 'Mill and Tocqueville', pp. 228, 230.
[63] G. Grote, *A History of Greece*, 11 vols., London 1846–53.
[64] Besides the two main review essays in the *Edinburgh Review*, Mill published five short reviews in the *Spectator* between April 1846 and March 1850 (*Newspapers Writings, Collected Works*, vol. XXIV, Tome 3, Toronto and London, 1986, pp. 867–8, 1084–8; and vol. XXV, Tome 4, pp. 1121–8, 1128–34, 1157–64).

the one of 1853, are important just because he examined the *History* with an eye to contemporary Britain, and from a political, rather than a historical, point of view.

Mill's assessment of ancient Greece was dominated by Sparta and Athens, each of which assumed a symbolic 'philosophical' significance. Sparta was dealt with in the first review.[65] After inspiring the Jacobins, she had often stirred up sympathy and interest among British conservatives both because of the moral virtues ascribed to her citizens, and because of the stable character of her institutions. Lycurgus' constitution had been devised in such a way as to inculcate into the citizens the idea of equality under a shared military or para-military discipline.[66] The result had been the 'building' of men for certain social functions predetermined by the constitution. Mill regarded them as 'partial' men whose asceticism concealed a moral fragility which was a by-product of their 'unilateral', 'one-sided' education.[67] The latter was what Mill really abhorred. Raised in privilege and educated to preserve privilege, obtusely and obstinately attached to the values of the ancient days and to traditions *qua* traditions, '[s]uch were the Spartans, those hereditary Tories and Conservatives of Greece'.[68]

At the opposite extreme Mill placed Athens, to which he devoted almost the whole of the review of 1853, totally overlooking the other aspects of the volumes of the *History of Greece* with which he was supposed to deal. The main characteristics of the Athenians was the 'multilaterality' of the development of their culture.[69] This had led to such a luxuriant flowering of humanity that Athens held a position of extraordinary importance in world history.[70] Her pre-eminence 'was wholly the fruit of Athenian institutions. It was the consequence, first of democracy, and secondly, of the wise and well-considered organisation, by which the Athenian democracy was distinguished among the democratic constitutions of antiquity.'[71]

However, it was in the interplay between public opinion and the 'public moralists' that Mill saw the true superiority of Athens. Mill believed that the traditional anti-democratic indictment of the Athenian republic – namely, that it allowed frequent violation of civil liberties – was

[65] J. S. Mill, 'Early Grecian History and Legend', *Edinburgh Review*, (October 1846), now in *Essays on Philosophy and the Classics, Collected Works*, vol. XI, Toronto and London, 1978, p. 273–305.

[66] J. S. Mill, 'Early Grecian History', pp. 301–2.

[67] *Ibid.*, p. 302.

[68] *Ibid.*

[69] J. S. Mill, 'Grote's *History of Greece*', *Edinburgh Review*, (October 1853), now in *Essays on Philosophy*, pp. 307–38.

[70] *Ibid.*, pp. 315–16, 318.

[71] *Ibid.*, p. 324.

devoid of any foundation. On the contrary, he maintained that the rule of law and the greatest respect for the constitutional procedure were the hallmarks of Athens.[72] Far from being an illibertarian republic, Grote's and Mill's Athens was the home of civil liberties.

It is to this point that the 1853 review wanted to call the reader's attention, as if to emphasise that individual liberty could find its most perfect expression only when and where civic spirit was also exalted. Mill ascribed to Athens the same kind of liberty which he would subsequently defend in *On Liberty* (whose first draft was completed in 1855, two years after the publication of the second review of Grote's *History*). Though Mill did not seem to believe that nineteenth-century western civilisation could claim any real superiority over ancient Athens,[73] he was ready to acknowledge that the 'moderns' had improved on it in three respects: (1) the invention of the representative system, making democracy possible even in large countries; (2) the achievement of economic prosperity without slaves; and (3) the emancipation of women. But, as far as civil liberties were concerned, Mill accepted the description presented by Pericles in his 'funeral oration',[74] and, in order to make his point even clearer, he added a long quotation from Grote, which looked like an introduction to *On Liberty*:[75]

The stress which he [Pericles] lays upon the liberty of thought and action at Athens ... deserves serious notice, and brings out one of those points in the national character upon which the intellectual development of the time mainly depended. The national temper was indulgent in a high degree to all the varieties of positive impulses: the peculiar promptings in every individual bosom were allowed to manifest themselves and bear fruit, without being suppressed by external opinion, or trained into forced conformity with some assumed standard; antipathy against any of them formed no part of the habitual morality of the citizen. While much of the generating causes of human hatred was thus rendered inoperative, and while society was rendered more comfortable, more instructive and more stimulating, all its germs of productive fruitful genius, so rare everywhere, found in such an atmosphere the maximum of encouragement. Within the limits of the law ... individual impulse, taste, and even eccentricity, were accepted with indulgence, instead of being a mark, as elsewhere, for the intolerance of neighbours or the public ... That liberty of individual action, not merely from the

[72] In fact, as he pointed out, only one case of irregular judicial procedure has been passed down by history – that concerning the generals condemned after the naval battle of Arginusae: this took place in a situation of national emergency, and, in any case, the citizens convicted were actually guilty: Mill, 'Grote's *History of Greece*', pp. 326–7.

[73] *Ibid.*, p. 314.

[74] *Ibid.*, pp. 317–18. (*History of Greece*, vol. VI, pp. 200–2). Mill was so keen on this oration that he did not content himself with quoting Grote's rendition, but retranslated it almost completely (F. E. Sparshott, 'Introduction' to Mill, *Essays on Philosophy*, p. xxiii).

[75] See A. P. Robson, 'Introduction' to *Collected Works*, vol. XXII, *Newspapers Writings*, Tome I, p. lxxxv.

over-restraint of law, but from the tyranny of jealous opinion, such as Pericles depicts in Athens, belongs more naturally to a democracy, where there is no selection One or Few to receive worship and set the fashion, than to any other form of government. ... To impose upon men such restraints, either of law or of opinion, as are requisite for the security and comfort of society, but to encourage rather than repress the free play of individual impulse subject to those limits, is an ideal which, if it was ever approached at Athens, has certainly never been attained, and has indeed comparatively been little studied or cared for, in any modern society.[76]

At this stage it is superfluous to say that Mill did not accept Constant's distinction between the 'liberty of the ancients' and that 'of the moderns'. Although in his work he nowhere makes explicit reference to the thought of Constant, it is likely that Mill knew it well.[77] He must have read, if not his 1819 lecture, at least his *Principes de Politique*, which contained the same criticism of direct democracy. Moreover, opinions similar to those of Constant had been voiced by Mill's beloved Romantic libertarian, Wilhelm von Humboldt, in his *Spheres and Duties of Government* (1851). Such being the case, it is likely that words like the following were intended to be a direct refutation of the view which appealed so much to continental liberals:

This picture [Pericles' 'funeral oration'] ... wholly conflicts, so far as Athens is concerned, with what we are so often told about the entire sacrifice, in the ancient republics, of the liberty of the individual to an imaginary good of the state. In the greatest Greek commonwealth, as described by its most distinguished citizen, the public interest was held of paramount obligation in all things which concerned it: but, with that part of the conduct of individuals which concerned only themselves, public opinion did not interfere: while in the ethical practice of the moderns, this is exactly reversed, and no one is required by opinion to pay any regard to the public, except by conducting his private concerns in conformity with its expectations.[78]

What is remarkable is that this 'liberal' paradise was not only compatible with the full implementation of the 'republican' ideal of a perpetually deliberating *demos*, but, in fact, it *required* it. In Athens each citizen was continually invested with some public magistracy, almost to the obliteration of private life: the *polis* had not only universal suffrage, but also 'the liberty of the bema, of the dicastery, the portico, the palestra, and the stage'.[79]

Every office and honour was open to every citizen, not, as in the aristocratic

---

[76] Mill, 'Grote's *History of Greece*', pp. 319–20.
[77] Cf. *Newspaper Articles*, in *Collected Works*, vol. XXII, pp. 156, 203, 214, 227; vol. XXIV, pp. 486–7, 792; vol. XXV, p. 1072. Mill had personally met Constant in France in 1830 (*Earlier Letters*, in *Collected Works*, vol. XII, London and Toronto, 1963, p. 58).
[78] Mill, 'Grote's *History of Greece*', p. 319.
[79] *Ibid.*, p. 324.

Roman republic (or even the British monarchy), almost nominally, but really; while the daily working of Athenian institutions (by means of which every citizen was accustomed to hear every sort of question, public and private, discussed by the ablest men of the time, with the earnestness of purpose and fulness of preparation belonging to actual business, deliberative or judicial) formed a course of political education, the equivalent of which the modern nations have not known how to give even to those whom they educate for statesmen. To the multitudinous judicial tribunals the Athenians were also indebted for that habitual love of fair play, and of hearing both sides of a case.[80]

The obvious question is: how could Mill reconcile this interpretation of Athenian direct democracy with episodes of 'popular despotism', the most infamous of which – the conviction and execution of Socrates – was in fact mentioned in On Liberty as a negative example?[81] The answer is to be found in Mill's historical relativism, as revealed in an 1845 review of some writings by Guizot.[82] In that article Mill, following the French historian, distinguished between three kinds of liberty typical of European civilisation: freedom of thought and of scientific research, freedom of religion and conscience, and personal independence. Only the first had been known in the classical world, while the second and the third had been affirmed amidst much strife, as a consequence, respectively, of Christianity and feudalism.[83] Socrates' execution had been due to the fact that the Athenians did not conceive of the religious sphere as one of free choice. As Guizot had pointed out, freedom of religion and conscience derived from the separation of religious and secular authority, which began to take shape in the Middle Ages. Mill concluded:

Toleration cannot exist, or exist only as a consequence of contempt, where, Church and State being virtually the same body, disaffection to the national worship is treason to the State; as is sufficiently evidenced by Grecian and Roman history, notwithstanding the fallacious appearance of liberality inherent to Polytheism, which did not prevent, as long as the national religion continued in vigour, almost every really free thinker of any ability in the freest city of Greece, from being either banished or put to death for blasphemy.[84]

[80] Ibid.
[81] Mill, On Liberty, in Collected Works, vol. XVIII, p. 235; in Mill's day the execution of Socrates was often quoted as evidence that in Greece 'there was no personal liberty' (Lasch, The True and Only Heaven, pp. 189–90).
[82] J. S. Mill, 'Guizot's Essays and Lectures on History', Edinburgh Review (October 1845), now in Collected Works, vol. XX, Essays on French History and Historians, Toronto and London, 1985, pp. 257–93.
[83] It is not totally clear how Mill interpreted Guizot's 'personal' freedom. Guizot himself described it as the civil liberty of Constant's 'moderns' (Mill, 'Guizot's Essays', pp. 273–4). But, as we have seen, Mill thought that civil liberty was already enjoyed by the 'ancients'. It is likely that Mill referred instead to Locke's right of resistance and revolution (see ibid., p. 286), seen as the ultimate guarantee of the preservation of freedom.
[84] Ibid., p. 273.

In his apologia for the Athenian freedoms, written almost eight years after his review of Guizot, Mill refers explicitly to this distinction in order to excuse the one defect of the Athenian constitution: Greek religion, imbued with all sorts of superstition and tinged with fanaticism, exercised an increasingly deleterious influence as Greek civilisation progressed.[85] And, in *On Liberty*, the 'Socrates affair' is described more or less in the same terms – not as a violation of a constitutional liberty or an invasion of the 'self-regarding' sphere of action, but as a consequence of a pre-Christian definition of the 'other-regarding' one.[86] Thus, the affirmation that the Athenian citizen enjoyed full liberty in all 'self-regarding' actions is not contradicted by the episode of Socrates – or by the similar conviction of Anassagoras, Protagoras and Aristotle – because, by criticising religion, these men had entered a sphere decidedly 'other-regarding' according to the law of the time. They had breached one of the fundamental laws of the state.

V

Thus, according to Mill, a free and democratic society ought to be characterised, first, by the greatest possible popular participation in public life; second, by the greatest individual freedom in the sphere of 'self-regarding' actions (a sphere which is historically relative); and third, by the fullest possible development of free discussion, both as a habit of inquiry and as a method of government founded on persuasion rather than coercion. Classical Athens – at least the one of Pericles' speech and of Grote's *History* – was to Mill an unparalleled model because it possessed all these characteristics in the highest degree. Such a conviction undergirded the 1853 review and was also present in his most systematic exposition of the theme of democracy: the *Considerations on Representative Government* published in 1861. The latter – which abounded in examples taken from the classical world[87] – involved a comparison between Athenian and 'modern' democracy.[88] Clearly, Mill's ideal was still a direct democracy in a socio-political environment of the dimensions of the *polis*.[89] However, since this was unfeasible in large modern states, the problem that Mill tried to solve in the *Considerations* was how to render representative government not only

[85] Mill, 'Grote's *History of Greece*', p. 332.
[86] Mill, *On Liberty*, pp. 235–8.
[87] Cf. J. S. Mill, *Consideration on the Representative Government*, in *Collected Works*, vol. XIX, Tome 2, *Essays on Politics*, pp. 4, 431 and 438.
[88] *Ibid.*, p. 411. D. F. Thompson, *John Stuart Mill and Representative Government*, Princeton, 1976, pp. 13, 43–52.
[89] *Ibid.*, p. 412; cf. Bradley, *The Optimists*, London, 1980, p. 159.

democratic, but also as functionally equivalent as possible to that of the 'ancients', with their abundance of popular magistracies. In this sense, Mill was already formulating Thomas Hill Green's problem of 'how to realise under modern conditions that organic union between the citizen and civic institutions which made Athens great and free',[90] given the fact that 'the moral salvation of the individual lies in the life of citizenship'.[91]

Aristotelian civic virtues and direct democracy on the lines of the *polis* provide the framework necessary for understanding the proposals of institutional reform – and, sometimes, of institutional conservation – supported by Mill. For example, his enthusiasm for the 'liability to be placed on juries and to serve parish offices' was a reflection of his boundless admiration for 'the practice of the dycastery and ecclesia'.[92] Likewise, his hostility to the introduction of the secret ballot sprung from an 'Athenian' understanding of civic virtue, since he conceived of the vote as a public function or popular magistracy, not as personal right. Dennis Thompson has compared his concern for the general will and for the creation of a public-regarding spirit to that of Rousseau:[93] indeed, to Mill the vote 'ha[d] no more to do with [the voter's] personal wishes than the verdict of a juryman. It [wa]s strictly a matter of duty; he [wa]s bound to give it according to his best and most conscientious opinion of the public good'.[94] Citizens ought to be open to censorship from their peers regarding the use they made of this public magistracy, in the same way that MPs were liable to pressure from their constituents as to the use they made of their vote in the Commons. When a citizen was called to hold a public office:

He is called upon, while so engaged, to weigh interests not his own; to be guided, in case of conflicting claims, by another rule than his private partialities; to apply, at every turn, principles and maxims which have for their reason of existence the common good ... He is made to feel himself one of the public, and whatever is for their benefit to be for his benefit. Where this school of public interest does not exist, scarcely any sense is entertained that private persons, in no eminent social situation, owe any duties to society, except to obey the laws and submit to the government. There is no unselfish sentiment of identification with the public. Every thought or feeling, either of interest or of duty, is absorbed in the individual and in his family. The man never thinks of any collective interest, of any objects to be pursued jointly with others, but only in competition with them, and in some measure at their expense.[95]

[90] J. MacCunn, *Six Radical Thinkers*, New York, 1965, p. 246.
[91] *Ibid.*, p. 253.
[92] Mill, *Considerations*, p. 411.
[93] Thompson, *Mill and Representative Government*, pp. 46–7.
[94] Mill, *Considerations*, p. 302.
[95] *Ibid.*, p. 412.

To Mill the ideal citizen in a free *res publica* was – we could say – a modern Athenian and a philosopher of the Socratic school,[96] and his understanding of the role of the intellectual in a democratic system must be seen in the light of this conviction. As already indicated above, ever since his mental crisis, Mill had seen in Socrates a model 'public moralist'. In the same way he admired Themistocles, Aristides, Pericles and Demosthenes, all of whom had exercised their intellectual and moral gifts on behalf of the commonwealth. A society based on free discussion and direct democracy allowed intellectual minorities to emerge as the guides of public opinion. That depended on the fact that:

The multitude have often a true instinct for distinguishing an able man, when he has the means for displaying his ability in a fair field before them. If such a man fails to obtain at least a portion of his just weight, it is through institution or usages which keep him out of sight. In the old democracies there were no means of keeping out of sight an able man: the bema was open to him; he needed nobody's consent to become a public adviser.[97]

This passage is revealing on three accounts at least. First, it shows that – curiously enough – one of the reasons why Mill preferred direct to representative democracy was his notion that the former was much more open to the influence of intellectual elites. In the context of the *polis* elitism and participatory democracy coincided. By contrast, *chez les modernes* electoral corruption, control of the media and other obstacles to popular participation made things more difficult: 'the best friends of representative democracy can hardly be without misgivings, that the Themistocles or Demosthenes whose counsels would have saved the nation, might be unable during his whole life ever to obtain a seat'.[98]

Hence, the moderns required special legislative devices – such as proportional representation and plural votes for the educated minority – to ensure that the philosophers could get a fair hearing. If to Mill the vote was a popular magistracy comparable to the jury system, plural votes could be seen as a sort of 'special magistracy' to which citizens would accede through an exam. In this way educated and intellectually gifted people would recover part of that influence that they had enjoyed on the ancient *agora*.[99] Mill hoped that he would live to see a sizeable group of 'philosophers' returned to parliament.[100] In the legislative assembly they would have only one vote each, but

[96] A. Ryan, *J. S. Mill*, London, 1974, p. 202.
[97] Mill, *Considerations*, p. 458.
[98] *Ibid.*
[99] *Ibid.*, pp. 459–61.
[100] *Ibid.*, p. 458.

as a moral power they would count for much more, in virtue of their knowledge and of the influence that would give them over the rest. ... Modern democracies would have their occasional Pericles, and its habitual group of superior and guiding minds.[101]

Though his dream never came true, Mill himself had the chance of playing 'Pericles' in the Westminster assembly in 1865–8, and Collini, Kinzer and the Robsons[102] agree that in parliament his influence was indeed based on his intellectual prestige and moral eminence. Like the philosophers in the ecclesia, he played the role of the 'public moralist'.

As an MP and radical leader, both in and out of parliament, Mill revealed unsuspected sides of his personality and thought, for a further reason for the importance of the quotation above[103] is Mill's *populism*. As we have seen, he was convinced that 'the multitude have often a true instinct for distinguishing an able man' – a motto Gladstone would have fully endorsed, especially during his post-1876 career. Both as a radical MP in 1865–8 and as an extra-parliamentary agitator in 1869–73, Mill demonstrated that he did not fear the competition of professional politicians. Far from eschewing the challenges of mass politics, he was from the beginning a fervent admirer and supporter of Gladstone, then undergoing his first metamorphosis into what A. J. P. Taylor has described as 'the demagogue statesman'. But this is not all, for, as Collini has observed, Mill's own public speeches ' show him to have been adept at modifying the pitch and style of his reasoning when addressing larger and more enthusiastically partisan audiences [than the Westminster assembly]'.[104] He could be an effective platform speaker. Indeed, during the agitation for the Second Reform Act, Mill became the most popular liberal leader after Bright and Gladstone. His name was frequently linked with those of the two tribunes of the people on the banners of the London Working Men's Association and the Reform League – an achievement paralleled by no other major British intellectual, either before or since. After his defeat in November 1868, Mill did not seek re-election and declined the offer of other constituencies, but, as Collini puts it, he 'appeared as a yet more "extreme" radical in his popular speeches on those topics which most stirred him in his last phase, especially non-sectarian education, the enfranchisement of women, and land reform'.[105]

---

[101] *Ibid.*, p. 460.
[102] Cf. B. L. Kinzer, A. P. Robson, and J. M. Robson, *A Moralist In and Out of Parliament. John Stuart Mill at Westminster, 1865–1868*, Toronto, Buffalo and London, 1992, pp. 218–96; S. Collini, *Public Moralists. Political Thought and Intellectual Life in Britain, 1850–1890*. Oxford, 1991, pp. 163–9.
[103] See above, footnote 97.
[104] Collini, *Public Moralists*, p. 167.
[105] *Ibid.*

By 1870 Mill was in great demand as a popular speaker, and held important positions in a number of radical reform organisations, including the Jamaica Committee, the Land Tenure Reform Association, the Commons Preservation Society and the National Society for Women's Suffrage.[106] Like Gladstone from 1876 to 1880,

As his disillusion with the Liberal party and its leaders increased ... he explicitly appealed beyond them to an implied popular constituency in the country at large where, uniquely, right-mindedness could be expected to outweigh the habitual selfishness of the comfortable classes. In this vein he could evidently be an effective platform orator ... The land question, which disturbed the sensibility of the propertied classes so profoundly, particularly lent itself to this more populist style. In the last recorded speech of his life, made at a meeting of the Land Tenure Reform Association in March 1873, Mill explicitly allied the LTRA with Joseph Arch's new Agricultural Labourers' Union, looking forward to 'concerted organized cooperation'. Appropriately, the final words in the report of his last speech were '(*Loud Cheers*)': Mill had become an accomplished public speaker, and this was the 66-year-old philosopher on the stump, threatening to out-Gladstone Gladstone.[107]

Kinzer and the Robsons agree with this assessment, and further develop the Gladstonian parallel in their consideration of Mill's emphasis on morality in international relations, almost precursory to Gladstone's approach to the 1876 Bulgarian Agitation. They also observe how much Mill the stump orator anticipated Gladstone's Midlothian style, sharing both the expository rationalism of the political preacher and the appeal to the 'masses' against the 'classes', to 'England' against parliament.[108]

These considerations help us to place Mill's community-centred liberalism in context for they provide a key to understanding the relationship between liberalism and the rise of charismatic leadership, the 'Caesaristic-plebiscitical element' which Max Weber has described as characteristic of the period. Despite the fears later entertained by the idealist philosophers, mid-Victorian liberalism did not operate 'the substitution of individualism for a sense of community'. Rather, while community remained the crucial concept in the political system, there was a gradual change in the 'conception of the range of man's organic connections', so that the 'social union of the ancient *polis* [was] replicated by establishing new dimensions to modern social relations and relationships'.[109]

In *Liberty, Retrenchment and Reform* I have outlined the way in which 'community politics' often generated charismatic leadership at the local

---

[106] *Ibid.*, p. 169.
[107] *Ibid.*, pp. 167–8.
[108] Kinzer and the Robsons, *A Moralist In and Out of Parliament*, pp. 184–217.
[109] Turner, *Greek Heritage*, p. 367.

level – a phenomenon exemplified by men such as Cowen in Newcastle, Burt in the Morpeth district and 'Mabon' in the Rhondda.[110] Following Colin Matthew, I have also suggested that at the same time the particular stage of development of the mass media and the household franchise system allowed the formation of an integrated political community at a national level as well.[111] This was precisely the kind of constituency that Mill was beginning to address in the early 1870s, and that Gladstone successfully cultivated between 1876 and 1893. The fact that after shunning electoral canvassing he became a convert to platform speech-making is not surprising: he had realised that *this* was the most effective way in which the modern 'philosopher' could address the national 'ecclesia' of public opinion, fully exploiting both the press and the suggestibility of rousing mass demonstrations.[112] To him this had nothing to do with demagogy: the contemporary liberal conviction was that rhetoric was the midwife of truth and the counterpart of logic,[113] an Aristotelian view perfectly consistent with Mill's understanding of active citizenship.

Indeed, Matthew has shown that the success of the national political preaching or 'expository' speech-making of the Midlothian kind depended largely on the 'training' of the public provided by the 'intermediate bodies' which Mill praised as essential vehicles of the citizens' education. These included a multitude of local government councils whose countries' members and continuous elections almost realised Mill's ideal of a permanently deliberating *demos*. But they also included the debating societies, the local 'Houses of Commons' flourishing in Britain in the years between 1860 and 1914.[114] These 'local parliaments' encouraged discussion of public affairs and the hearing of both sides of a case, while 'guides to public speaking, such as the many editions of G. J. Holyoake's *Public Speaking and Debate*, directed the electorate into appropriate canons of behaviour'.[115] As *The Times* observed in 1873, 'we have become a nation of public speakers ... We are now more than ever a debating, that is, a Parliamentary people'.[116] Such was the context and ideological background of Mill's and Gladstone's conversion to popular speech-making, a kind of revivalistic political preaching which

---

[110] Biagini, *Liberty, Retrenchment and Reform*, pp. 346–56.
[111] H. C. G. Matthew, 'Rhetoric and Politics in Great Britain, 1860–1950', in P. J. Waller (ed.), *Politics and Social Change*, Oxford, 1987, p. 39; Biagini, *Liberty, Retrenchment and Reform*, pp. 369–425.
[112] There is a certain parallelism with Carlyle's 'Hero as Man of Letters': cf. *On Heroes, Hero-Worship, and the Heroic in History*, pp. 140–1.
[113] Matthew, 'Rhetoric and Politics', p. 34.
[114] *Ibid.*, p. 37.
[115] *Ibid.*, p. 38.
[116] *Ibid.*

offered a remarkable solution to the problem of marrying a representative system to a large-scale franchise. Within the context of the given materials – the nature of the franchise and the nature of the media – Gladstone had squared the circle: he had formulated a politics that was both charismatic and rational. ... Given the difficulties of expanding the complexities of an intricate series of principles, policies and events, the Midlothian speeches were of international importance in encouraging a new and high standard of political awareness, discussion and citizenship. The concept of the active citizen, so central to the ethos of Liberalism, was given fresh life and a larger definition by the new means of political discussion and communication.[117]

VI

In *Liberty, Retrenchment and Reform* I have implicitly questioned the often-quoted assumption that classical liberals followed Thomas Hobbes in believing that 'liberty is the absence of restraint'.[118] Instead I have suggested that *popular* liberals held quite a different concept of liberty – one characterised by an emphasis on 'civic virtue' and participation and indistinguishable from what is commonly described as the 'republican tradition'. In the present chapter I have investigated the intellectual background to this 'republican' current of liberalism.[119] Like the ideal

---

[117] H. C. G. Matthew, 'Introduction' to *The Gladstone Diaries*, vol. IX, Oxford, 1986, p. lxix.

[118] J. A. Colaiaco, *James Fitzjames Stephen and the Crisis of Victorian Thought*, pp. 127, 138.

[119] One possible objection to this 'republican' interpretation is that Victorian liberalism was characterised by an optimistic expectation of 'progress' very different from that of the republican tradition, which was usually pessimistic about historical trends. However, such an objection does not apply to Mill, who lived in the conviction that the phase of capitalist growth would soon come to an end (Ryan, *Mill*, pp. 180–1). To Mill the 'stationary state' foretold by Adam Smith was not a utopia, but a historical situation whose onset lay in the immediate future. It was being brought about by – among other factors – movements which Mill strongly supported, such as trade union action for higher wages and shorter hours, and the establishment of comparatively uneconomic, but socially attractive, forms of organisation for rural societies, such as peasant proprietorship in Ireland.

Under the 'stationary state' concern for the production of wealth would gradually be replaced by that for the quality of life – including environmentalism, culture, women's emancipation, social justice and human solidarity. From his posthumously published *Chapters on Socialism* it would appear that the forms of collectivist experiments that Mill was prepared to consider were based on this strategy, and amounted to an extension to the social and economic world of attitudes and procedures originated in the political sphere, and inspired by the ethos of the *agora*. These experiments would be based on producers' cooperatives, which would achieve the goal of 'unit[ing] the greatest individual liberty of action, with the common ownership of the raw material of the globe, and an equal participation of all in the benefit of combined labour' (*Autobiography*, cited in Ryan, p. 184). Such a project would seem wildly utopian nowadays, but we should remember that it became one of the main themes in the programme of the left over the succeeding fifty years – just a further reminder of 'how little the historical Mill resembled that figment created by twentieth-century textbooks in the history of political thought' (Collini, *Public Moralists*, p. 168).

commonwealth of popular liberals, Mill's 'Athenian' model – entailing government by public discussion and the right to dissent – was based on the equality of all citizens. There was no plural voting for the philosophers in Pericles' ecclesia, nor was there any legal device to protect 'orthodoxy' from the uneducated masses except 'the direct persuasiveness of gifted orators', as C. S. Meier puts it.[120] While Meier emphasises the role of the 'tribune-like qualities' of modern leaders such as Woodrow Wilson, Lloyd George, Roosevelt and Churchill in reinvigorating democracy,[121] Mill – like Gladstone – exemplifies the awareness shared by nineteenth-century Anglo-American liberals that:

Instituting democracy required ... the mobilization of the crowd [through] ... the magic of direct rhetoric. ... Without such interaction between orators and masses ... political systems become stratified, elitist, with their members preoccupied by their private needs and consumption ... democracy also seemed to require some aspects of charisma – not to redress the bureaucratic encroachment that Max Weber believed to threaten political decision-making, but to engage mass opinion.[122]

In this connection it is interesting to observe that – though modern scholars have often criticised Mill for being an elitist – his contemporary James Fitzjames Stephen attacked him for opening the gates to that very 'tyranny of the majority' that he intended to prevent. Stephen, like Matthew Arnold and Walter Bagehot, 'held that democracy must be reconciled with culture', and argued that the 'one very simple principle' of *On Liberty*

[if] allowed 'to govern absolutely', in Mill's words, all relations between society and the individual ... would ... supply a justification for the uneducated multitude to run roughshod over all institutions, and destroy the good along with the bad. He believed that in an age of democratization, authority and order need to be safeguarded more than liberty.[123]

In particular, despite his own personal agnosticism, Stephen feared that the emancipation of the ordinary intellect from the sanctions of religion would result in the subversion of all morality[124] – a position which could be summarised as Anglicanism *minus* Christianity. Moreover, he feared that Mill's emphasis on equality was conducive to social democracy and saw him as a dangerous pioneer of what to a later generation became known as 'new liberalism'.[125]

[120] Maier, 'Democracy since the French Revolution', in Dunn (ed.), *Democracy*, p. 149.
[121] *Ibid.*
[122] *Ibid.*, p. 150.
[123] Colaiaco, *James Fitzjames Stephen*, pp. 128–9.
[124] *Ibid.*, p. 129.
[125] *Ibid.*, p. 147.

Whether Stephen's analysis was correct or not, it is significant that the main exponent of classical liberalism in its classical period displayed many traits usually regarded as quintessentially 'republican'. The emphasis on civic virtue did not vanish in lateral liberal thought, but rather – under the influence of T. H. Green and the idealist philosophers – became even more marked.[126] This fact raises important questions about the nature of late nineteenth-century liberalism and its relationship with other democratic traditions, including the Labour one. Attempting to answer some of these questions is the main aim of the present book.

[126] Cf. MacCunn, *Six Radical Thinkers*, pp. 216, 246–53; see Turner, *Greek Heritage*, pp. 358–68 for the influence of Greek ideals on the idealists' conception of active citizenship and self-fulfilment; and W. H. Greenleaf, *The British Political Tradition*, vol. II, *The Ideological Heritage*, London, 1983, p. 95 (for the case of E. S. P. Haynes), and more in general pp. 110ff.

2   The limits of liberalism: Liberals and women's suffrage 1867–1914

Martin Pugh

For the cause of female enfranchisement British liberalism has provided a complete spectrum from heroism to villainy. In the 1860s John Stuart Mill gave the cause a crucial respectability at a point when it seemed likely to be buried in derision. But, at the other extreme, a Liberal Prime Minister, H. H. Asquith, saw fit to adopt an extraordinarily illiberal method of dealing with the suffragettes – the notorious 'Cat and Mouse' Act of 1913–14. To say the least, relations between Victorian liberalism and the women's movement were complicated. In this essay we will begin by considering the common ground between the two and the successes achieved; secondly, we will analyse the difficulties and obstacles to cooperation; thirdly we will consider how political developments during the later 1880s and 1890s further undermined Liberal sympathy for suffragism; and finally we will examine the role of local government in helping to put women's enfranchisement into the mainstream of liberalism in the years before 1914.

1

Much of the original momentum behind early Victorian feminism derived from female involvement in a range of moral causes including anti-slavery, temperance, peace and anti-vivisection.[1] Prior to 1832 a number of women became active participants in reform associations and subsequently in the Chartist movement where their presence was considered by some to be advantageous precisely because of their known association with moral crusades.[2] Women also proved themselves by their success in collecting funds, their contribution to the social life of the movement and their ability to practise exclusive dealing against shopkeepers.[3] A similar view emerges from the role of middle-class ladies in

[1] See the discussion in Jane Rendall, *The Origins of Modern Feminism*, London, 1985, and Olive Banks, *Faces of Feminism*, Oxford, 1981.
[2] Jutta Schwarzkopf, *Women in the Chartist Movement*, London, 1991, pp. 97, 187.
[3] Schwarzkopf, *Chartist Movement*, p. 176.

45

the Anti-Corn Law League where they helped with recruitment, social organisation and the moral appeal of the campaign. As early as 1845 Richard Cobden declared his sympathies over women's suffrage:

But although they cannot vote, it is a very singular fact – and it will be looked upon at some future time when the world has grown wiser and better, as an anomalous circumstance – that although ladies cannot vote, they may qualify as many blockheads and dunces to vote as they choose to confer property upon![4]

Thus, by the middle of the nineteenth century, women had established at least a limited presence in the mainstream of popular liberalism in the country. It was during the 1850s that the women's movement began to acquire a formal structure just as the parliamentary Liberal Party was being hammered into shape under Palmerston's leadership.[5] Amid the multitude of radical pressure groups loosely associated with the Liberal Party and increasingly looking for a further instalment of parliamentary reform under the aegis of liberalism, the 'Ladies of Langham Place' were not especially conspicuous; but they shared the same optimism that franchise reform would be the key to wider success for radical causes. The leading woman activist, Barbara Leigh Smith, was the daughter of Benjamin Leigh Smith, a Unitarian radical, Liberal MP and Anti-Corn Law League activist. Under her aegis emerged a network of pressure groups working for women's education, female employment and reform of the law on married women's property as well as the franchise. Their approach followed the typical pattern of established radical Liberal causes which pursued their ends by a combination of laborious extra-parliamentary propaganda and *ad hoc* alliances with sympathetic back-bench MPs. Even under Palmerston's somewhat hostile rule it proved possible to achieve limited reforms. For example, 1857 brought a major reform of the divorce law and 1858 saw the abolition of the property qual-ification for MPs, the first success for Chartism, albeit posthumously.

In this context contemporary feminists' expectations of progress for their cause were not wholly unrealistic; it seemed feasible to achieve their objectives by instalments just as the other radical groups did by making use of the parliamentary Liberal Party as the best available vehicle. Up to a point this was borne out by the controversy over franchise reform in 1866–7. After the defeat of the Russell–Gladstone Bill, the radicals perceived that they stood to gain more by exploiting the weakness of the minority Conservative government. As Disraeli accepted a succession of amendments from Liberal backbenchers anything seemed possible for a

[4] *The League*, 11 January 1845, p. 245.
[5] Sheila Herstein, *A Mid-Victorian Feminist: Barbara Leigh Smith Bodichon*, New Haven, 1986; Candida Lacey (ed.), *Barbara Leigh Smith Bodichon and the Langham Place Group*, London, 1987.

time. In these circumstances, John Stuart Mill's women's suffrage amendment, debated on 20 May 1867, was not altogether unrealistic. Disraeli was already on record as a supporter of women's suffrage.[6] However, tactics dictated that he should accept enough to please the Liberals without unduly provoking his own backbenchers, and he was no doubt right to see Mill's proposal as a bridge too far.

Yet Mill's supporters were far from discouraged at gathering only seventy-three votes in support of his amendment. At least the issue had begun to attract public interest and the campaign seemed to gather pace. Moreover, the 1867 Reform Act was clearly not the end but the beginning of a major phase of parliamentary reform. The more the new electorate strengthened radical liberalism, the more the women's cause seemed likely to benefit. After all, in the 1860s the case for women's suffrage was invariably expressed in the language of contemporary, radical liberalism. Harriet Taylor had argued that if nature had intended women purely for marriage, motherhood and domesticity it would hardly have been necessary to erect so many legal, political and social obstacles to exclude them from other roles.[7] Removing the artificial barriers which impeded the individual's development formed the unifying theme of Liberal rhetoric and much of the legislation of the post-1868 Gladstone government. More specifically, mainstream liberalism sought to extend the parliamentary vote to those who paid rates and taxes, respected the laws, and demonstrated their capacity for responsible citizenship by self-help strategies.[8] Women's enfranchisement could be articulated in precisely these terms.

In fact, Mill's approach to the female suffrage in 1866–7 seems to reflect the continued influence of utilitarianism on the one hand, and his wish to keep in step with Gladstone on the other. Hence he took it for granted that in the British system representation was accorded not to individuals but to classes or communities; and if a whole class such as working men or women suffered exclusion this was a just grievance. He avoided demanding the women's vote on grounds of natural rights but, rather, posed the utilitarian question as to whether society would benefit from their enfranchisement.[9] In a shrewd, tactical speech in the Commons in 1867 Mill based the claim largely on expediency not on abstract rights:

[6] House of Commons Debates, vol. XCIX, 20 June 1848, c. 950.
[7] Harriet Taylor, 'The Enfranchisement of Women', *The Westminster Review*, 60 (July 1851), pp. 289–311.
[8] Eugenio Biagini, *Liberty, Retrenchment and Reform*, Cambridge, 1992, pp. 274–5, 286–7.
[9] B. L. Kinzer, A. Robson and J. M. Robson, *A Moralist In and Out of Parliament: John Stuart Mill at Westminster 1865–1868*, Toronto, 1992, pp. 91, 130; Joseph Hamburger, *Intellectual in Politics: John Stuart Mill and the Philosophic Radicals*, New Haven, 1965, p. 81.

To lay a ground for refusing the suffrage to anyone, it is necessary to allege either personal unfitness or public danger. Can it be pretended that women who manage an estate or conduct a business – who pay rates and taxes, often to a large amount, and frequently from their own earnings – many of whom are responsible heads of families, and some of whom, in the capacity of school-mistresses, teach much much more than a great number of male electors have ever learnt – are not capable of a function of which every male householder is capable?[10]

In this period the most active parliamentary advocates of female suffrage comprised a group of radical intellectuals mostly associated with Mill, though most with rather longer parliamentary careers: Henry Fawcett, Jacob Bright, James Stansfeld, Professor James Stuart, Auberon Herbert, Leonard Courtney, William Woodall, Duncan MacLaren, Walter MacLaren and Charles MacLaren. Though most of these men remained backbenchers, Fawcett became Postmaster General and Stansfeld president of the Local Government Board in Gladstone's 1868–74 administration. In 1884, when the third reform bill was being debated, Fawcett defied the government whips over women's suffrage as did Courtney and Sir Charles Dilke. This brought a reprimand from Gladstone, but not dismissal from office.[11]

Another feature of Liberal suffragism was the prevalence of husband-and-wife teams, including the Mills, Fawcetts, Dilkes and MacLarens. Higher up the social and political scale the Earl and Countess of Aberdeen, close if uncomfortable acquaintances of Gladstone and Rosebery, consistently backed the suffrage and other women's causes. Lord Amberley, the son of Lord John Russell, also helped promote suffragism in concert with his wife Kate, the daughter of another Liberal minister, Lord Stanley of Alderley. It was her decision to start addressing public meetings on women's suffrage in 1870 that seems to have provoked Queen Victoria's memorable outburst to the effect that 'Lady Amberley ought to get a GOOD WHIPPING'.[12] Her outrage reflected not simply her anti-suffragism but the fact that someone of Lady Amberley's social standing had been prepared to be associated with it.

At least until the 1880s the women's suffrage cause continued to rely heavily upon alliances with Liberal members. Although Mill's own parliamentary career ended in 1868, Liberal backbenchers regularly agreed to promote suffrage bills, and Liberals invariably comprised two out of every three of those members who voted for women's suffrage bills,

---

[10] House of Commons Debates, vol. CLXXXVII, 20 May 1867, c. 818.

[11] S. Gwynn and G. Tuckwell, *The Life of Sir Charles W. Dilke*, London, 1917, pp. 6–9.

[12] Helen Taylor to Lady Amberley, 30 May 1870, in B. and P. Russell (eds.), *The Amberley Papers*, vol. II, 1937, pp. 345, 353; Sir T. Martin, *Queen Victoria As I Knew Her*, London, 1908, p. 69; Marjorie Pentland, *A Bonnie Fechter: the Life of Ishbel Marjoribanks, Marchioness of Aberdeen and Temair*, London, 1952, p. 100.

Table 1   *Votes cast by Liberal members on women's suffrage*

Year	For	Against	Year	For	Against
1870	90	51	1867	62	78
1875	75	67	1870	61	133
1878	90	70	1871	96	117
1879	66	63	1872	103	112
1883	81	50	1873	103	117
			1876	77	82

sometimes as many as three out of four. On the other hand, an examination of the record of the parliamentary Liberal Party as a whole gives a slightly different impression. Of those Liberal members who actually voted between 1867 and 1883 a majority supported women's suffrage on five occasions and a majority opposed it on six as shown in table 1.

These divisions suggest that suffragist support had reached a plateau and that the party as a whole had not yet been converted. The anti-suffragists enjoyed a somewhat larger reserve of support which was not always drawn upon, perhaps because members simply preferred to keep their heads down on bills that seemed unlikely to make progress.

Yet the failure to make dramatic progress on the suffrage question may be partly explained by the diversion of effort into other women's causes by Liberal members. Their first success followed close upon Mill's intervention in the Second Reform Bill. The leading suffragist at this stage, Lydia Becker, evidently regarded local government as the natural route to parliamentary franchisement.[13] By 1869 three backbenchers, G. Hodgkinson, A. Herbert and J. Candlish, had promoted a bill to grant female ratepayers a local government vote, and Becker briefed Jacob Bright to propose an amendment to the government's own Municipal Franchise Bill in that year. This measure amended the 1865 Act by shortening the occupation period for qualified electors from two and a half years to one. When H. A. Bruce, the Home Secretary, accepted Bright's amendment late at night it was incorporated into the bill with little discussion.

The local government franchise for female ratepayers enjoyed support from several sources. It reflected Mill's notion of responsible, participatory citizenship in small communities. One traditional expression of this was the vestry meeting at which every ratepayer enjoyed the opportunity to make decisions. In the 1890s the Liberals extended this idea by creating parish, rural district and urban district councils; in such small

[13] Lydia E. Becker, *The Rights and Duties of Women in Local Government*, 1879.

communities the inhabitants were likely to be known to one another so that decision-making could be a relatively open affair and the issues fell within the understanding of the citizenry.

But the reform of 1869 also reflected conventional ideas about women's domestic skills and interests. As local government formed an extension of existing female concerns about the poor, children, health and education, so the incorporation of women into the system could be regarded as consolidating rather than undermining the notion of the separate spheres for the two sexes. Moreover, the evidence generated by surveys of the weekly budgets of working-class families created a vivid impression of the financial skill and responsibility shown by women in their capacity as household managers. When the Municipal Franchise Bill reached the House of Lords, where it might have suffered damage, Lord Lichfield expressed the fashionable view that female ratepayers had 'the same interest in an economical administration of municipal affairs as any other inhabitant'.[14] For the government Lord Kimberley chose to present the reform as a matter of *restoring* the right enjoyed before the 1835 Act which had followed the example of the 1832 Reform Act by referring to 'male persons' for the first time.[15]

The municipal vote proved to be timely since it put women in a position to benefit from a remarkable extension of elective local authorities between 1870 and 1894. In 1870 W. E. Forster's Education Act allowed female ratepayers not only to vote in the new school board elections, but also to stand for election themselves. In the event the special advantage conferred on them by the cumulative voting system enabled women to be conspicuously successful; by 1900 around 270 women had been elected to school boards.[16]

On the whole, however, the promotion of women's causes by backbench Liberal members involved much more protracted effort. For example, a succession of Married Women's Property Acts in 1870, 1874, 1881 and 1882 eventually secured wives in the possession of both income and property acquired before and after their marriage. In his 1867 speech Mill had specifically drawn attention to this issue to justify his claim that the vital interests of women were liable to be neglected as a result of their exclusion from the electorate.[17]

Another long-running cause – the Contagious Diseases Acts – was debated in the Commons in 1870, 1873, 1875, 1876, 1882 and 1883 when the suspension of the legislation was finally approved, prior to complete

[14] House of Lords Debates, vol. CXCVII, 13 July 1869, c. 1417.
[15] House of Lords Debates, vol. CXCVIII, 19 July 1869, c. 145.
[16] After 1902 the school boards were abolished, but women were co-opted on to the county education committees; this brought their total representation to 641 in 1910.
[17] House of Commons Debates, vol. CLXXXVII, 20 May 1867, c. 828.

abolition in 1885. Liberal members evidently comprised the substantial majority of the abolitionists – 98 out of 126 in the 1875 division, for example. Success on this issue depended heavily upon the support of James Stansfeld who almost destroyed a promising ministerial career by his persistence. In the period between 1871 and 1874 when he was a minister, Stansfeld enjoyed a higher status as a radical leader than Chamberlain and Dilke; but after 1880 when Gladstone returned to office, he was not offered a post; his career only briefly flickered into life again in 1886 when he was promoted following Chamberlain's resignation from the cabinet.

In view of the immense and sustained effort required to achieve success over the Married Women's Property Acts and the Contagious Diseases Acts the women's movement had good reason to appreciate that a sympathetic minister working within his own departmental sphere could obtain easy gains for feminism. As Postmaster General, Fawcett presided over the department that became the first large-scale employer of women.[18] In his capacity as president of the Local Government Board Stansfeld first appointed a woman as a poor law inspector in 1872, an innovation that was deeply resented by the existing staff.[19] There was also a surprising conclusion to the campaign over the inadequate enforcement of factory legislation for women led by Sir Charles and Lady Dilke and the Women's Trade Union League. This led to a royal commission on the subject in 1891. Its report coincided with the appointment of a sympathetic, if anti-suffragist, Home Secretary, H. H. Asquith, who decided to appoint the first female factory inspectors in 1892.[20]

II

Liberal anti-suffragism naturally shared a good deal with Conservative anti-suffragism, notably the emphasis on the idea of separate spheres. But some Liberal antis chose to articulate it in terms of divine influence. In Gladstone's words: 'A permanent and vast difference of type has been imposed upon women and men respectively by the maker of both.' A variation on this theme recurs in the speeches of Asquith who argued that while liberalism properly attacked unearned or artificial privileges and distinctions, it should not interfere with the indelible differences imposed by 'nature herself'.[21]

[18] J. Manners, 'Employment of Women in the Public Service', *Quarterly Review*, 151 (1881).
[19] J. L. and Barbara Hammond, *James Stansfeld: A Victorian Champion of Sex Equality*, London, 1932, pp. 112–13.
[20] Mary Drake McFeely, *Lady Inspectors*, Athens (Ga.), 1991, pp. 13–14.
[21] Brian Harrison, *Separate Spheres: the Opposition to Women's Suffrage in Britain*, London, 1978, pp. 52, 57.

Other strands of anti-suffragism were more distinctively Liberal. For example, the anti-clericalism of John Bright and John Morley seems to have coloured their perception. Starting from the assumption that women were emotional and thus susceptible to the spread of ritualism, they looked to education as a remedy. But they grew disillusioned about the prospect of emancipating women from priestly influence and became increasingly anti-suffragist. Other radicals including Henry Labouchere, Joseph Chamberlain and Randall Cremer, reflected the influence of positivist thinking in their approach to the suffrage. This strengthened their highly conservative emphasis on the centrality of family life and the role of women as the civilising force within the family. Cremer went as far as to claim that the law recognised woman's key role by giving her a privileged position, for example, by relieving wives of responsibility for their debts.[22]

However, the immediate cause of much Liberal suspicion towards women's suffrage in the 1860s and 1870s is to be found in the broader evolution of radical liberalism. From the perspective of Gladstone and the party managers, liberalism presented a dismaying spectacle; it was a kaleidoscope of pressure groups all perpetually clamouring for attention. Enthusiasm for 'fads' and 'crotchets' seemed, to the leaders, to lead Liberals into attaching an exaggerated importance to marginal issues and into sacrificing loyalty to the party in order to secure immediate objectives. The results were only too plain during 1871–4 when the parliamentary party began to dissolve into a morass of pressure groups; increasingly the Conservatives argued that liberalism represented minority causes not the national interest.

Inevitably, the women's movement appeared to be yet another symptom of this phenomenon, and indeed its advocates were archetypal faddists. In the short run Gladstone tried to deal with the problem by 'chopping off the heads' of the radicals, that is by giving office to their abler leaders. However, the example of Fawcett and Stansfeld suggests that such tactics had limited success. In the longer run he manufactured a series of great crusades designed to impose some discipline upon the party's supporters. But the single-issue strategy sometimes worked too well; for example, women activists felt attracted by the moral overtones of Gladstone's campaign over the Bulgarian Atrocities, but this only led them to expect more from him over other moral issues. Meanwhile, the association of liberalism with faddism began to appear an electoral drawback, for it allowed the Conservatives to characterise the party as unfit to govern because it was too subject to the influence of extreme, minority groups.

[22] Howard Evans, *Sir Randall Cremer: His Life and Work*, London, 1909, p. 342.

The dilemma was encapsulated in the relationship between Gladstone and Henry Fawcett. Essentially a disciple of Mill, Fawcett adopted a critical, independent attitude towards most established institutions and he vigorously opposed restrictions upon individual opportunity and all forms of unearned privilege. He rejected protective legislation, condemned the hereditary House of Lords, advocated proportional representation and supported the opening of university courses and degrees to women. His feminism has rightly been described as a corollary of his brand of individualistic liberalism.[23] He must have been a most uncomfortable colleague, for he repeatedly exposed the limitations of Gladstone's own laboriously acquired liberalism. Moreover, he carried his principles to the point of refusing on several occasions to vote with the government of which he was a member, and helped to secure the defeat of the Irish Universities Bill in 1873. In the Prime Minister's opinion Fawcett was 'totally unable to work in concert with others'.[24]

This view of Fawcett was corroborated by his enthusiasm for promoting the cause of proportional representation, an idea developed in Britain by Thomas Hare in the 1850s and refined during the 1860s.[25] It was no accident that four of those who were most convinced about women's suffrage – Fawcett, Mill, Courtney and Herbert – also comprised the parliamentary core of the pressure for proportional representation. Mill, in fact, had tried to introduce it into the 1867 Reform Bill ten days after his suffrage amendment. At this time proportional representation was not regarded, as it has commonly been in the twentieth century, as a means for ensuring the fair representation of *parties*; those Victorian Liberals who advocated this reform usually did so on the grounds that it would enable independently minded MPs to secure election against the wishes of their party machines or their parliamentary leaders.[26] This seemed feasible because in a multimember constituency the candidate would have to win only the appropriate quota of votes to be elected, not the simple majority required under the first-past-the-post system.

On the other hand, to its Liberal critics proportional representation appeared almost calculated to exacerbate the party's existing propensity for faddism. It seemed by no means impossible that every fanatical enthusiast for women's suffrage, the local veto, the Deceased Wife's Sister's Bill, the repeal of the Contagious Diseases Acts and a plethora of similar

23 Lawrence Goldman (ed.), *The Blind Victorian: Henry Fawcett and British Liberalism*, Cambridge, 1989, p. 13.

24 David Rubinstein, 'Victorian Feminists: Henry and Millicent Fawcett', in Goldman, *Blind Victorian*, p. 86.

25 Proportional Representation Society, *First Annual Report*, 1885.

26 *A Plea for Real Representation*, Proportional Representation Society (revised 1909), p. 6.

causes might mobilise sufficient votes to guarantee the return of members pledged to a single issue. During the 1880s proportional representation also suffered from its perceived association with the Irish Question. Liberal opponents of Home Rule like Leonard Courtney argued that the polarisation of opinion between Unionism and Home Rule was squeezing moderate Liberals out of the Irish constituencies altogether.[27] They advocated proportional representation as an expedient for saving such moderates, or rebels, from extinction, and in effect offering another obstacle to Gladstonian policy. Clearly such an innovation would have exacerbated the Prime Minister's already frustrating task of keeping a parliamentary majority intact for a full term by protecting the electoral base of rebels and enthusiasts of all kinds. 'What we want in this House', declared Gladstone, 'is to have the prevailing sense of the community. We do not want to have represented in miniature particular shades of opinion that may at the moment prevail in it.'[28]

Like all the radical pressure groups, the women campaigners had to decide how far to pursue their goals by attacking the Liberal Party and how far by working within it. In time many of the nonconformists became completely absorbed into the party establishment. But at the other end of the spectrum some temperance reformers maintained a militant stance.[29] They provided a model for those feminists who were prepared to make a nuisance of themselves by, for example, intervention in by-elections, aimed at securing the defeat of government candidates.[30]

This form of militancy was applied with some success by Josephine Butler, the leading figure in the campaign for the abolition of the Contagious Diseases Acts during the 1870s and 1880s.[31] As a good Liberal herself Mrs Butler found little difficulty in exploiting the 'nonconformist conscience' of provincial England, both in middle-class and working-class communities. Her National Association organised 17,000 petitions containing two and a half million signatures, and employed sympathetic MPs, notably James Stansfeld, to ensure that repeal was regularly raised in the House of Commons throughout the 1870s and 1880s.

But although Gladstone voted in favour of repeal from 1875, he characteristically managed to alienate Mrs Butler, by generally refusing her requests for a meeting he gave her the impression that, although

---

[27] Sir Horace Plunkett to Leonard Courtney, 15 June 1911, Electoral Reform Society Records.

[28] House of Commons Debate, vol. CCII, 15 June 1870, c. 147, quoted in Jennifer Hart, *Proportional Representation*, Oxford, 1992.

[29] D. A. Hamer, *The Politics of Electoral Pressure*, Oxford, 1977, pp. 165–99.

[30] Harrison, *Separate Spheres*, pp. 36, 74, 127.

[31] Josephine Butler, *Personal Reminiscences of a Great Crusade*, London, 1898.

sympathetic, he lacked any real understanding of the importance of the issue.[32] Her supporters attempted to step up the pressure by means of guerrilla campaigns against Gladstone's candidates in by-elections. They achieved notable success at Newark in 1870 where the Liberal candidate was Sir Henry Storks, whose return the Prime Minister was particularly keen to achieve because of his role in assisting with Cardwell's army reforms. However, as a general in Malta, Storks had been responsible for implementing the Contagious Diseases Acts. He was therefore an attractive target for the National Association, and was in fact obliged to stand down in favour of a candidate who supported repeal.[33] When Storks tried again at Colchester in the same year the abolitionists ran their own candidate against him, split the vote and secured his defeat.[34] However, subsequent attempts proved less successful. At Pontefract in 1872, H. C. E. Childers, who had had responsibility for the Contagious Diseases Acts in Plymouth and Portsmouth, survived a split vote. The fact was that as the electorate grew and the party machines developed, by-election interventions became increasingly anachronistic; nonetheless, the tactic did enable small pressure groups to obtain national publicity as the Edwardian campaigns of the WSPU were to demonstrate.

III

In the period between the mid-1880s and the turn of the century the relationship between liberalism and women's suffrage was greatly complicated by major political developments. The first problem lay simply in the changing significance of parliamentary reform in Liberal politics. 'There is no more unwelcome fact to Liberals', observed one backbencher in 1884, 'than that popular institutions have not always and everywhere been a success.'[35] Certainly the shock defeat of 1874 and the rather narrow victory of 1880 reminded Liberals of their dwindling popular support, and this helped to focus attention upon the defects of the electoral system as far as it affected *men*. The debates on the reform bill of 1884, when another Liberal backbencher, William Woodall, proposed a women's suffrage amendment, underlined the difficulty. Woodall's amendment was heavily squashed by Gladstone who contended, with some reason, that such a clause would be a gift to the Tory majority in the House of Lords which was only too anxious to find excuses to reject the bill.[36]

[32] Hammond, *James Stansfeld*, pp. 179.
[33] Butler, *Reminiscences*, pp. 107–8; Hammond, *James Stansfeld*, p. 151.
[34] Butler, *Reminiscences*, pp. 121–3; Hammond, *James Stansfeld*, p. 178.
[35] House of Commons Debates, vol. CCLXXXIX, 12 June 1884, c. 102.
[36] House of Commons Debates, vol. CCLXXXVIII, 10 June 1884, c. 1959.

Yet Liberal anti-suffragism by this stage was more than merely tactical. Attitudes had been changing and the vague doubts expressed in the 1860s had begun to take on concrete form. A number of the intellectual radicals who had been enthused by reform in the 1860s had already grown disillusioned with the whole question, partly because of the propensity of many of the new voters to support traditionalist causes and right-wing leaders, and partly because of the emergence of the 'caucus' and the more rigid partisanship it entailed.[37] Among these erstwhile radicals Thorold Rogers admitted in the 1884 debate that he had developed doubts about women's suffrage. James Bryce now began to repudiate the no-taxation-without-representation line of argument hitherto used to support the women's claim.[38] Similarly, E. A. Leatham argued that 'it is not because men pay rates and taxes, or even occupy property, that they have votes, but because they are men'.[39] To some extent this reaction was the price to be paid for the *progress* women's suffrage had made since the 1860s. No longer an abstract question of principle, it had increasingly to be considered in terms of the tangible political consequences. Was it desirable to enfranchise *single* women? Would it be possible to stop at such a limited measure of enfranchisement? What policies would women vote for? Would the granting of a vote inevitably mean allowing women to stand for election as it had in local government?

In the event, although Conservative members rallied to support Woodall's amendment, in order to make mischief, the clause was defeated. The obvious reluctance of many supposedly suffragist Liberals to defy Gladstone over this clearly antagonised some of the women. Moreover, since no further electoral reform was enacted until 1918 it began to appear that a major opportunity had been lost through Gladstone's obstructionism and that the suffrage cause was destined to languish for some years. The significance of 1884 lies in the fact that although it incorporated only six out of every ten adult men into the electorate, it did in fact give representation to large numbers of poor people. The system discriminated largely against men who were young and single – and thus less likely to be householders – rather than against the working class.[40] The effect of this was to destroy much of the momentum behind the parliamentary reform question for the next twenty years; as a result women were left somewhat isolated as the outstanding section of society without the vote.

[37] Christopher Harvie, *The Lights of Liberalism*, London, 1976, p. 195.
[38] House of Commons Debates, vol. CCLXXXIX, 12 June 1884, c. 166.
[39] House of Commons Debates, vol. CCLXXXIX, 12 June 1884, c. 103.
[40] Duncan Tanner, 'The Parliamentary Electoral System, the "Fourth" Reform Act and the Rise of Labour in England and Wales', *Bulletin of the Institute of Historical Research*, 61 (1983), p. 134.

For Liberals the ramifications of reform went considerably deeper, for the 1884 reform led to their limited victory in the election of 1885 and thus to the split over Home Rule in 1886. That crisis inevitably had implications for relations with the women's movement. It clearly reduced the friction between the parliamentarians and the National Liberal Federation which had been such a feature of the 1860s and 1870s, and allowed the radical pressure groups to occupy a much more central role in the diminished Liberal Party. However, this was not particularly helpful because before 1886 the women's groups had not made much progress within the NLF. This was partly because the activists simply made use of the connections and allies they already had in parliament, and also because the extra-parliamentary organisations did not seem to stand in great need of women's support since they enjoyed a comfortable advantage over their Conservative rivals in the constituencies. Moreover, the unofficial leader of extra-parliamentary radicalism, Joseph Chamberlain, was notoriously hostile to women's suffrage and, indeed, to any signs of independent-mindedness on the part of women.[41] Thus the strategy of integration into the party via the NLF which could be pursued by the National Education League or the Liberation Society, was not so obviously feasible and appealing to the women. After 1886 the faddists were left in a much more dominant position and the programme of the NLF was taken rather more seriously even by Gladstone. But this left both working-class radicals and feminists somewhat marginalised.

This became clear after the Liberals' heavy defeat in 1886 when the NLF adopted an electoral reform policy calculated to improve the party's position: a three-month qualifying period for voters, successive occupation between constituencies, withdrawal of the requirement that candidates pay the expenses of returning officers, one-day polling and the abolition of plural voting. Resolutions along these lines were passed in 1888, 1889, 1890, 1891, 1895, 1897, 1898, 1899 and 1901. Women's suffrage was raised only occasionally by Stansfeld and Woodall and failed to be adopted as NLF policy.[42] In fact not until 1905 was an official resolution for women's suffrage considered by the NLF's annual conference; it was simply not a priority.[43]

This reflected the judgement of the experienced constituency organisers and candidates as to which innovations were likely to restore the party's fortunes; it was not obvious that women represented part of the solution. As a result the party proved to be slow to mobilise its female support in a formal or systematic way. A number of women's Liberal

---

[41] Carole Seymour-Jones, *Beatrice Webb*, London, 1992, p. 102.
[42] National Liberal Federation, *Annual Report*, 1889, p. 137.
[43] National Liberal Federation, *Annual Report*, 1905, p. 66.

Associations sprang up spontaneously, but it was not until 1887 that a national Women's Liberal Federation was launched under the presidency of the seventy-five year old Mrs Catherine Gladstone – no friend of women's rights.[44] For the leadership this represented a calculated risk. On the one hand the party now needed all the constituency organisation it could get. The Conservatives' success with the Primrose League and the withdrawal of the Liberal Unionists had largely destroyed the Liberals' advantage at the local level. On the other hand, Gladstone feared giving the women greater leverage within the party; he had some reason to think that there was an underlying drift towards women's suffrage – even his daughter, Mary, had become a convert in 1884.[45]

Up to a point the experiment appeared to work satisfactorily. By 1888 the new Women's Liberal Federation had already enrolled 20,000 members, and claimed 43,000 by 1893, though there were only 133 local branches. By the time of the 1892 general election a regular pattern of electoral work on behalf of the party had been developed. When an election was called each women's association placed itself under the orders of the local Liberal agent; it usually became responsible for running one of the committee rooms and conducted the canvass for that area.[46] In addition a few of the leading figures such as Lady Aberdeen toured the country as platform speakers supporting Liberal candidates.

However, the advocates of women's suffrage naturally regarded the WLF, filled as it was with the wives and daughters of Liberal MPs and peers, primarily as a recruiting ground for the cause; it might serve as a Trojan horse within the Gladstonian citadel. During 1888–90 the Countess of Carlisle began to orchestrate the pressure for the adoption of a women's suffrage policy on the part of the WLF. In order to avert a confrontation with the party, Lady Aberdeen, who was anxious to be loyal both to the women's cause and to the party, attempted to persuade Gladstone to address the WLFs annual meetings. He, however, proved rather stubborn and eventually failed to retain control over the WLF, just as he had failed with the NLF. By 1892 the issue had come to a head for three reasons. First, the suffragists felt angry about the large number of Liberal members who had voted against a suffrage bill in that year following another public intervention by Gladstone.[47] Second, they suspected that after the Liberals' success at the general election the women's work was in danger of being taken for granted. Third, the

[44] Pat Jalland, *Women, Marriage and Politics 1860–1914*, Oxford, 1986, p. 200.
[45] Jalland, *Women, Marriage and Politics*, p. 215.
[46] Emlyn Boys to M. G. Fawcett, 26 September 1892, Millicent Fawcett Papers, M50/2, 26/29, Manchester Central Library.
[47] W. E. Gladstone to Samuel Smith, 11 April 1892, in P. Hollis (ed.), *Women in Public 1850–1900*, London, 1979, pp. 319–21.

suffragists had established a number of new WLF branches and consequently won a majority of places on the executive committee. As a result Catherine Gladstone stepped down as president at the end of 1892 to be replaced briefly by Lady Aberdeen and subsequently by the more militant Lady Carlisle. Thereafter the WLF adopted women's suffrage as its official policy, whereupon the minority of members who were unwilling to antagonise the party leadership withdrew to form the Women's National Liberal Federation.

However, even this split merely led to another controversy over how far the WLF should be prepared to go in putting pressure on the Liberal Party to take up the women's suffrage policy. Millicent Fawcett was among those who urged the WLF to withhold its support at elections from any Liberal candidates who opposed women's suffrage.[48] However, it was not until 1902 that the WLF decided to refuse its endorsement to anti-suffragists, though even then it remained for each branch to decide how to pressurise its local candidates. In some constituencies the Liberal Associations responded to this by simply absorbing the loyal Liberal women into their own organisation and leaving the resolute suffragists outside the fold. However, by 1893 at least sixty-three Women's Liberal Associations had affiliated to the Central Committee of the National Society for Women's Suffrage.[49] In short, the effect of the whole controversy was to divert much of the energy of the Liberal women into suffragism and thus to diminish their contribution to the party.

To some extent these internal controversies in the Liberal ranks reflected the impact of external pressure, for during the late Victorian period feminism, in some ways, acquired a more Conservative tone. Historians have scarcely begun to give full recognition to the fact that even among the first generation of feminists many of the key figures, including Emily Davies, Frances Power Cobbe, Isabella Tod, Helen Blackburn and Lilias Ashworth Hallet, were Conservatives.[50] Other suffragists were in the process of moving to the right, notably Millicent Fawcett who abandoned her original loyalty to the Liberal Party for Liberal Unionism, and eventually adopted a strident Tory position over such questions as Ireland and South Africa. In her frequent appearances on Conservative platforms Fawcett went out of her way to depict women as:

[48] 'Private and Confidential' circular, quoted in Rosamund Billington, 'Women, Politics and Local Liberalism: from Female Suffrage to "Votes for Women"', *Journal of Regional and Local Studies*, 5 (1985), p. 7.

[49] Billington, 'Women, Politics and Local Liberalism', p. 6.

[50] Barbara Caine, *Victorian Feminists*, Oxford, 1992, pp. 127, 144–5.

an immense and very valuable Conservative force ... There were many things which tended to make women a force for the preservation of order ... and which brought home to them the fact that order was essential to liberty.[51]

Such claims only served to reinforce Liberal fears engendered by the Conservatives' success in establishing the Primrose League, a mass organisation almost half of whose membership was female.[52] In 1887, 1889, 1891 and 1894 the National Union of Conservative and Unionist Associations endorsed women's suffrage resolutions at its annual conferences. This was backed up in parliament by backbench Tory MPs (Sir Albert Rollit, F. Faithfull Begg, Algernon Borthwick and Sir James Agg-Gardner) who were all involved in the Primrose League and promoted women's suffrage bills in the 1890s. In fact, during the later 1880s and 1890s the Conservative MPs, originally the core of anti-suffragism, markedly changed their behaviour in favour of women's suffrage.[53]

The inevitable consequence of all this was that the National Liberal Federation increasingly viewed the women's question in terms of the likely electoral advantage for the political parties. This forced the Liberal suffragists on to the defensive. One finds them pleading that 'women would not vote Tory to the extent that was generally supposed'.[54] Clearly the party's declining electoral fortunes had deprived Liberal suffragism of much of the confidence it had enjoyed in Mill's heyday.

IV

Yet in spite of the deterioration in the formal relationship between liberalism and the suffrage during the 1890s, the women's cause nonetheless managed to make progress, but more by indirect means, notably through participation in local government. This proved to be significant partly because it offered scope for women to demonstrate their competence in public life, but it also enabled Liberal and socialist women to make a substantial contribution to the wider field of social reform and thereby to chart a new route towards national politics.

Many Victorian women approached local government as a result of traditional philanthropic activity. A classic example was the workhouse visiting promoted by Louisa Twining, which had first established that women could play a useful role. But after 1870 the more consciously feminist and politically aware women saw in local government an oppor-

[51] David Rubinstein, *A Different World for Women: the Life of Millicent Garrett Fawcett*, Oxford, 1991, p. 139.
[52] Martin Pugh, *The Tories and the People 1880–1935*, 1985, pp. 48–51.
[53] Pugh, *Tories and the People*, pp. 60–1.
[54] National Liberal Federation, *Annual Report*, London, 1889, p. 137.

tunity to advance the wider case for parliamentary enfranchisement.[55] For example, despite her resounding triumph in the first school board elections in London, Elizabeth Garrett admitted to being somewhat uninterested in working-class education, and she proved to be an infrequent attender at meetings.[56]

Naturally enough, the suffragists felt very anxious to ensure that women took advantage of their opportunities in local government lest their opponents should claim non-participation as proof that women were not really interested in politics. To this end both the Women's Local Government Society and the National Union of Women Workers attempted to promote the adoption of female candidates. In some cases this meant persuading local party caucuses to allow women into their team, which created more difficulty for the Liberals since most of the ambitious women were of Liberal or socialist views. However, many women did not wish to be tied to a party label, and others were in any case refused a nomination. They often ran successfully as Independents as did Helen Taylor, the step-daughter of Mill, in Southwark. On the whole, the party competition tended to be stronger in large boroughs, and the poor law boards were generally regarded as less political in character. Thus from 1875 there was a rapid increase in the number of female guardians: 893 by 1895 and 1,310 by 1910. School boards also proved to be an attractive venture for women. Where the competing interests fielded teams of candidates it made sense to include a woman so as to broaden their appeal.[57] But even where this was not an option, the cumulative voting system proved to be advantageous for independent female candidates because it allowed the elector to concentrate all his, or her, votes on a single candidate. This sometimes resulted in spectacular victories. Elizabeth Garrett headed the St Marylebone poll of 1870, in which there were twenty-two candidates, with nearly 48,000 votes compared to 13,000 for the second candidate. At the same election Emily Davies led the field in Greenwich.

In the context of Liberal politics women's local government activities were important largely for the contribution they made to the party's changing agenda. The women frequently stood in the poorest wards and with the backing of working men's organisations. Consequently, they adopted radical social policies. As poor law guardians, for example, they often supported the boarding out system for children, the employment of professional nurses in poor law hospitals and greater reliance on outdoor relief for certain applicants like the elderly. On school boards women

---

[55] Patricia Hollis, *Ladies Elect*, 1987, pp. 47–8.
[56] Hollis, *Ladies Elect*, pp. 72–7.
[57] Hollis, *Ladies Elect*, pp. 78–9.

became involved in pressing for subsidised milk, the feeding of needy schoolchildren and the abolition of fees. Annie Besant, for example, scored a notable success in persuading the London school board to experiment with school meals. On other local authorities the women interested themselves in sanitation, housing and 'good labour practices' which meant respecting trade union rates of pay and using a direct labour department.[58]

The most prominent Liberal women candidates in this period were Jane Cobden and Lady Margaret Sandhurst who won elections respectively in Bow and Bromley and in Brixton for the first London County Council in 1889. After the election the victorious Progressives selected a third woman, Emma Cons, to serve as an alderman. These women enjoyed the backing of their local Liberal and Radical Associations. In Bow the association secretary, George Lansbury, managed Cobden's campaign and the parliamentary candidate spoke on her behalf.[59] These candidates represented a more advanced or 'constructive' brand of radicalism than that of many conventional Liberal parliamentarians. Their programme included a number of national issues such as the payment of MPs, but chiefly comprised social policies including municipal housing, the equalisation of the poor rate and the introduction of minimum wages in the sweated trades.

In this context the absence of a woman like Millicent Fawcett from local government is entirely explicable. Her liberalism closely reflected the narrowly political radicalism of Henry Fawcett who had opposed interventionism such as factory legislation and consistently criticised the 'tendency to over-legislation' in Gladstone's government. Throughout her life Millicent Fawcett resisted the trend towards collectivism on essentially individualistic grounds; as late as the 1920s she waged a rearguard action against the proposal for family allowances which was then attracting feminist support.[60] In this sense she must be regarded as a somewhat marginal figure during the 1890s.

The more radical women involved themselves in local government and social reform the more they became part of the new liberalism which in the 1890s seemed to younger Liberals the future programme for their party. This is not to suggest that the women themselves changed the course of the party, rather that the practical work of experimentation with social policies complemented the work of revising liberalism by Herbert

---

[58] Sue Millar, 'Middle Class Women and Public Politics in the Late Nineteenth and Early Twentieth Centuries: A Study of the Cobden Sisters', Sussex University MA thesis, 1985, pp. 45–6.

[59] Jonathan Schneer, *George Lansbury*, Manchester, 1990, p. 72.

[60] Martin Pugh, *Women and the Women's Movement in Britain 1914–1959*, London, 1992, p. 239.

Samuel, L. T. Hobhouse, J. A. Hobson and others around the turn of the century. Several of the innovations of the 1880s and 1890s, especially those affecting children, were to become the subject of Liberal legislation after 1906. In other respects experiments at municipal level simply helped to establish what was beyond the capacity and resources of local authorities, thereby paving the way for nationally imposed and financed solutions, designed, for example, to break up the traditional responsibilities of the poor law authorities. In effect social reform served as a bridge linking national and local government; thereby it offered a route by which women might make their way from one to the other without fundamentally challenging conventional notions about the separate spheres. Suffragists like Stansfeld had begun to appreciate this: 'the enfranchisement of women', he claimed, 'would have the effect of concentrating the mind of the public and our legislators upon the great social reforms ... it would tend to moralise politics'.[61] Not surprisingly, when the Liberals created new elective authorities in 1894 they expressly granted women the right to serve as councillors on the new parish, rural district and urban district councils. James Stansfeld and Walter MacLaren intervened in the legislation, against the government's wishes, to widen the electorate for these new authorities by incorporating *married* women. This carried some implications for the parliamentary franchise debate, for by 1900 Liberal and Labour suffragists had become convinced that in order to obviate the danger of increasing the representation of property, and thereby of Conservative support, any measure of female enfranchisement ought to include the wives of working men.[62]

These developments in local government forced anti-suffragism on to the defensive. For example, Asquith and Bryce, though content for women to participate in school and poor law boards, tried to draw the line at membership of the county councils which they considered to be too parliamentary in style.[63] Yet such a distinction could hardly be maintained for long. The Conservative legislation to set up county councils had left it unclear whether a woman enjoyed the right to serve as a councillor, though giving her the right to vote. Subsequently when the election of Cobden and Sanderson was challenged in the courts the judges ruled that they were not eligible.[64] Attempts were made to correct this in backbench bills introduced in both Houses by MacLaren in 1889, by Lord Meath in 1889 and 1890, by James Stuart in 1891, by Lord Aberdeen in 1901 and by Lord Beauchamp in 1904.

[61] National Liberal Federation, *Annual Report*, 1889, p. 137.
[62] D. Lloyd George to the Master of Elibanl, 5 September 1911, Alexander Murray Papers, vol. v, National Library of Scotland.
[63] Hollis, *Ladies Elect*, p. 41.
[64] Miller, 'Cobden Sisters', pp. 47–51.

By 1907, when the new Liberal government intervened to give women the right to become county councillors, the proposal was no longer regarded simply as a modest tidying up exercise. As a result of Balfour's 1902 Education Act the law now *required* female representation on county education committees; the 1905 Unemployed Workmen's Act made the same stipulation for local distress committees. Attitudes had changed since 1869 when it had been possible to regard women's local government role simply as an extension of female domesticity. In 1907 both the supporters and the opponents of the Liberal bill repudiated any suggestion that local government reform had no implications for the parliamentary franchise for women. 'There is hardly any subject matter which parliament can deal with which a county council cannot', claimed Lord Halsbury.[65] The comments made in both Houses reflected an appreciation – still not sufficiently recognised by historians of women's suffrage – that the parliamentarians had already been converted to women's suffrage. Even the Conservative-dominated House of Commons had voted for a suffrage bill by 230 to 159 votes in 1897, and by 184 to 70 in 1904. In each case the Liberal anti-suffragist vote fell, and in 1905 the NLF at last overwhelmingly carried a women's suffrage resolution. In 1908 the new House of Commons voted by 273 to 94 votes in favour of women's enfranchisement.

This shift coincided, however, with a tightening up of pressure by the Women's Liberal Federation which, in 1902, officially decided to withhold all assistance from anti-suffragist Liberal candidates, though local branches remained free to help if they wished, Thus, during 1903–5 some Liberal by-election candidates were denied help while others felt obliged to give written pledges before canvassing was done for them by WLF.[66] This situation helps to explain the excessively severe attitude adopted by some leading Liberal politicians around 1905 when they encountered what was very mild pressure from the newly formed Women's Social and Political Union. Clearly by-election interventions against the Liberals pre-dated the use of such tactics by the Pankhursts by several years, and it was tempting to vent upon them the anger already provoked by the Liberal Party's own women members. However, the continued failure to enact a franchise bill soon resulted in a series of resignations by Liberal women activists from 1906 onwards. They felt that their only ultimate sanction against Asquith was the threat of a complete withdrawal of electoral support. The crisis engendered by Lloyd George's budget during 1909–10 postponed this dilemma. But between 1912 and 1914 some

---

[65] House of Lords Debates, vol. CLXXV, c. 1353, 1361.
[66] Claire Hirshfield, 'Fractured Faith: Liberal Party Women and the Suffrage Issue in Britain, 1892–1914', *Gender and History*, 2 (1990), p. 2.

sixty-eight WLF associations withdrew and 18,000 members were lost.[67] 1912 was the year in which an electoral pact was forged between the National Union of Women's Suffrage Societies and the Labour Party in which Liberal and ex-Liberal women were instrumental.[68] By this stage the arguments of substance about women's enfranchisement had been exhausted; the question had become one of tactics, pride and political advantage. Once faced with a realistic bill in 1917 the Liberals voted emphatically by 184 to 12 to enfranchise over eight million women. This was acceptable because it included wives along the spinsters and widows. The victory underlined what Mill and almost all suffragists had been slow to see in the 1860s, namely, that a bold, democratic measure of enfranchisement often proves easier to attain than a very limited one.

[67] Hirshfield, 'Fractured Faith', p. 187.
[68] See Leslie P. Hume, *The National Union of Women's Suffrage Societies 1897–1914*, New York, 1982; Sandra Holton, *Feminism and Democracy*, Cambridge, 1987; Martin Pugh, 'Labour and Women's Suffrage', in K. D. Brown (ed.), *The First Labour Party 1906–1914*, London, 1985.

3   Women, liberalism and citizenship, 1918–1930

Pat Thane

I

The women's movement from the late Victorian period to the 1930s should be seen, more than it has been, as part of the broad ferment of discussion among radicals about how a viable democracy was to be achieved and practised in advanced industrial society; how the growing body of individuals who were acquiring or demanding rights of full citizenship could actively participate in the decision-making of an increasingly powerful and centralised state; and how that power and centralisation could be controlled.

For women such issues took on greatest saliency after 1918 when most women over thirty gained the national vote. They had now to face the question of the roles women could and should play within the political system and how women were to be mobilised to play them. This imagining of a democratic political system in which women participated fully, and attempts to bring it into being, were widespread over a range of women's organisations, yet its language, concepts and ideals have hardly begun to be explored.[1]

In general women's achievements, if not their efforts, have been judged negatively. Pugh recognises some of the effort and enthusiasm with which some women sought to embrace their new opportunities, at least in the 1920s, but is inclined to believe that their impact was dissipated by the division of effort across a range of causes and organisations. Harrison gives more positive stress to the large amount of legislation which activists regarded as favourable to women which was passed in the ten years after 1918. He is also more positive about the political effectiveness of the inheritors of pre-1918 moderate suffragism as against the dismissiveness of their tactics which historians have adopted a little

---

[1] Though it has begun to be opened up by B. Harrison, *Prudent Revolutionaries. Portraits of English Feminists between the Wars*, Oxford, 1987; Joanna Alberti, *Beyond Suffrage. Feminists in War and Peace, 1914–18*, London, 1989; H. L. Smith (ed.), *British Feminism in the Twentieth Century*, Aldershot, 1991; Martin Pugh, *Women and the Women's Movement in Britain 1914–1959*, London, 1992.

uncritically from the contemporary comments of some of the inheritors of the militant tradition, in particular Lady Rhondda, founder of *Time and Tide* and the Six Point Group, and Dora Russell.[2]

This chapter focuses upon the suffragist inheritance in the 1920s, in particular upon an aspect of it that has been noted[3] but little explored – that a significant number of its leading and publicly influential activists were committed Liberals and determinedly remained so even in the 1930s and beyond, despite the disintegration of their party. Their liberalism was a central and explicit component of their feminism.

II

The close theoretical association between feminism and liberalism is well known and was most clearly expressed by J. S. Mill, though their compatibility has been questioned recently.[4] There have been excellent studies of the important contribution of Liberal women to the party and to suffragism before 1914,[5] but it has been concluded that, after the vote was partially gained in 1918, women who had been active Liberals were either so disillusioned by the long resistance of the leadership to the campaign for the vote that they deserted the party, or if they did not they were rendered impotent by the decline of the party.

Hirschfield, whose study of the Liberal women and suffragism ends in 1918, concludes:

With the passage of enfranchising legislation in 1918, the suffrage issue was defused as a source of conflict among Liberals. The resolution of the matter, however, came too late for the W[omen's] L[iberal] F[ederation] which had been fatally fractured by years of internal strife and survived the war only to experience the ignominy of near-total irrelevance in the 1920s.[6]

Pugh similarly stresses the decline in membership of the WLF after 1920 and their continuing lack of influence upon their party's male

---

[2] Harrison, *Prudent Revolutionaries*, pp. 301–24.

[3] For example, by Harrison, *Prudent Revolutionaries*, pp. 13, 309.

[4] For example, C. Pateman, *The Disorder of Women: Democracy, Feminism and Political Theory*, especially the essay 'Women and Consent', Cambridge, 1989. See also Susan James, 'The Good-enough Citizen: Citizenship and Independence' in G. Bock and S. James, *Beyond Equality and Difference. Citizenship, Feminist Politics and Female Subjectivity*, London, 1992.

[5] Linda Walker, 'Party Political Women: A Comparative Study of Liberal Women and the Primrose League, 1890–1914', in Jane Rendall (ed.), *Equal or Different. Women's Politics 1800–1914*, Oxford, 1987; Sandra S. Holton, *Feminism and Democracy: Women's Suffrage and Reform Politics in Britain, 1900–1918*, Cambridge, 1986; Claire Hirschfield, 'A Fractured Faith: Liberal Party Women and the Suffrage Issue in Britain, 1892–1914', *Gender and History*, 2, (Summer 1990), pp. 173–97.

[6] Hirschfield, 'Fractured Faith', p. 188.

Table 2 *WNLF membership*

1914	150,000
1921	74,633
1922	76,000
1923	71,040 [a]
1924	71,000
1925	88,000
1928	100,000 +

[a] The figures as reported are contradictory. The *Annual Report*, as quoted in the *Liberal Women's News*, gives 71,040 in April 1923. A year later it gives 71,000, commenting that this compares with 64,000 in the previous year.
Source: Federation News, Liberal Women's News; Walker, 'Party Political Women', p. 169; Hirschfield, 'Fractured Faith', p. 188. In the 1920s not all local WLF branches chose to affiliate to the WNLF, though an active campaign to persuade them to do so may account for the increased membership numbers reported.

leaders. He comments that several leading feminists of the 1920s were Liberals but that 'much of their effort was diverted into non-party women's pressure groups'.[7]

In fact, after an initial decline, membership of the Women's National Liberal Federation, as the party women's organisation was known from 1918,[8] rose – surprisingly, in view of the party's national decline. This is shown in table 2.[9]

It is true that a number of prominent feminists who were active Liberals are better known to historians for their activities in women's organisations outside the Liberal Party. Margery Corbett Ashby was secretary of the leading suffragist organisation, the National Union of Women's Suffrage Societies (NUWSS), in 1907. She succeeded Eleanor

[7] Pugh, *Women and the Women's Movement*, pp. 139–41.
[8] When the WLF and the WNLF, which had split in 1892 over the issue of loyalty to a party leadership which resisted women's suffrage, were reunited. See Hirschfield, 'Fractured Faith', p. 188.
[9] The figures in table 2 were reconstructed from the sources available to me at the British Library and the Manchester Central Reference Library, neither of which possesses a complete set of *Annual Reports* of the WNLF. The WNLF's monthly journal was inconsistent in its reporting of membership numbers. The *Federation News* throughout its existence from 1921 to 1923 printed the *Annual Report* which included membership figures. The *Liberal Women's News* did not do so and reported irregularly and, as the table suggests, sometimes confusingly. The report of numbers in 1928 (*LWN*, Feb. 1928, p. 20) may be due to euphoria at the rise in membership. Numbers were not quoted in succeeding years and there are frequent hints that they were falling in the early 1930s. The figures quoted here differ from those quoted by Pugh, *Women and the Women's Movement*, p. 140. He appears to have confused the numbers for the years 1922, 1923, 1924 and 1926 and he gives none beyond 1926.

Rathbone as president of the National Union of Societies for Equal Citizenship (NUSEC) which NUWSS became in 1918. She became president of the Townswomen's Guilds (TGs) from 1930. These were initiated by NUSEC from 1928, for 'ordinary', politically uncommitted urban women, 'to encourage the education of women and to enable them as citizens to make their best contribution towards the common good'.[10] They had 54,000 members by 1939.[11] She also presided over the Women's Freedom League in the 1930s. This had been founded as a radical suffragist organisation before the war and continued to work for gender equality in common with other groups such as NUSEC, with whom its membership seems greatly to have overlapped.

Ashby was best known for her passionate internationalism and devotion to the cause of peace.[12] From 1923 until the Second World War she was president of the International Women's Suffrage Alliance (IWSA), later the International Alliance of Women for Suffrage and Equal Citizenship. This stood for: 'equal pay and equal opportunities for all women, including the right to work for married women and is of [the] opinion that future labour regulations should tend towards equality for men and women'. It also stood for such welfare issues as the needs of widows and fatherless children.[13] Ashby praised it equally because it brought together women from over forty countries 'with a splendid spirit of friendly co-operation which over-rode all difficulties of race, colour, religion and language'. The British branch of the Commonwealth League, over which she, indefatigably, also presided, had similar virtues in her eyes. She saw such organisations as contributing to the overriding objective of world peace. To this end also, like many others, she placed much faith in the League of Nations and was an early and active member of the League of Nations Union. In 1932 she was one of the official British representatives to the disarmament conference at Geneva, the only female in the British delegation and one of only five women delegates in all. She was an early and outspoken opponent of fascism.

She was also a devoted Liberal. She was president of the WNLF until 1928 when she had to resign on taking up the presidency of the, formally non-political, NUSEC, though she remained very active in it. She stood

[10] E. McCarty, 'Attitudes to Women and Domesticity in England c. 1939–1955', Oxford University D.Phil. thesis, 1994, p. 271.

[11] McCarty, 'Attitudes to Women', p. 306.

[12] Alberti, *Beyond Suffrage*, p. 201ff.

[13] Mrs Corbett Ashby, 'The Rome Congress', *Federation News*, June 1923. The monthly journal of the WLNF underwent several changes of name: the *British Liberal Women's News* from its foundation in 1919 until Feb. 1920; the *Women's Liberal Magazine* (*WLM*) until Jan. 1921; the *Federation News* (*FN*) until April 1924 when it became the *Liberal Women's News* (*LWN*).

for parliament eight times as a Liberal, between 1918 and 1944, always unsuccessfully. She came from a strongly Liberal and democratic family, brought up to simple living, high thinking and a sense of public responsibility. Her father was a Liberal MP between 1906 and 1910. Both parents encouraged her to acquire education (classics at Newnham, Cambridge), skill at public speaking and a professional training (teaching, which she hated and soon abandoned for voluntary social work and public activism). She married a supportive husband and had, to her regret, only one child.

Ashby's mother was a pioneer female poor law guardian who took Margery to the International Council of Women in Berlin in 1904. She helped to launch Women's Institutes (WIs) in Britain and these provided the model for Townswomen's Guilds. The WIs were founded from 1915 by suffragists with the aim of assisting country women to improve their lives and their self-esteem by, among other things, encouraging them to use their civil rights. Each branch was theoretically a model of participatory democracy, with an elected committee. Members were encouraged to learn about, debate and campaign publicly for issues important to their lives, such as improved water and electricity supplies and maternity services, to improve and to value their rural and domestic skills whilst, equally importantly, meeting and socialising with other women. The National Federation of Women's Institutes (NFWI) became the largest women's organisation in inter-war Britain, with 250,000 members by 1925, and did not decline thereafter. Its leadership collaborated with NUSEC and other organisations on various campaigns, though it would be a mistake to assume that the mass of its membership was highly politicised, nor should we underestimate the WIs' contribution to the empowerment, on a number of levels both public and private, of women who were apparently previously uninvolved in politics; or interpret it as simply dissipating feminist energy and splitting a potentially effective women's movement.[14]

When Ashby died in 1981, her obituary in *The Times* commented that 'probably no-one has done more for the emancipation of women during this century'.[15] She embodied the close links among the apparently divided women's organisations and her range of interests was held together as much by her Liberalism as by her feminism.

Better remembered, though probably not more influential, was her

[14] Maggie Morgan, 'The Women's Institute Movement – The Acceptable Face of Feminism?' in S. Oldfield, *This Working Day World. Women's Lives and Culture(s) in Britain 1914–45*, London, 1994, pp. 29–40; M. Morgan, 'The Women's Institute Movement, 1915–1960', University of Sussex D. Phil. thesis, 1993.
[15] Harrison, *Prudent Revolutionaries*, p. 205.

associate, Eleanor Rathbone. Rathbone similarly grew up in the world of late Victorian liberalism, public service, austerity and nonconformity (Quakerism and Unitarianism)[16] which thoroughly formed her ideas and actions. Her father, to whom she was close, was a long-serving Liberal MP. She was educated at Somerville, Oxford, which she followed by voluntary work in her native Liverpool and election as the first woman member of Liverpool City Council. She was an early activist in NUWSS and the first president of NUSEC.

Rathbone always had close personal links with Liberals but operated publicly through complementary non-party institutions such as NUSEC and was an Independent MP for the Combined English Universities' seat from 1929 to her death in 1946. She is best known for campaigning for and achieving, just before her death, family allowances, in a more attenuated form than she hoped. However, a keynote of her career was a pragmatic recognition that it is better to achieve something than nothing and that this was to be expected of real politics: 'not the optimum but the achievable optimum' as she put it – as distinct from what she saw as the rhetorical impossibilism of such critics as Lady Rhondda. She spoke in parliament against female circumcision in Kenya, for Gandhi and the emancipation of Indian women, and she was another early anti-fascist and strong supporter of the League of Nations.[17]

Rathbone worked closely with Eva Hubback, who is less well remembered, but who was at least as influential in her lifetime. Hubback also worked for NUWSS before the war, after an initial attraction to the suffragettes was repelled by their mounting militancy. She was parliamentary secretary of NUSEC until 1927, through the peak of its campaigning for equal rights legislation and she was a key figure in setting up the Townswomen's Guilds. In the late 1920s and 30s she was influential in the Children's Minimum Council, which was formed to combat child malnutrition, and the National Birth Control Association (later the Family Planning Association), both important and effective campaigning bodies, and she was also active in the campaign of the 1930s for widening the franchise for Indian women. British women saw this as a legitimate concern of theirs, since the British government was engaged in negotiating a new constitution for India which would give it dominion ('Home Rule' within the empire) status. They believed that they could assist Indian women in their demands for equal representation in the new

---

[16] Though Ashby appears to have been a life-long Anglican.

[17] Information on Rathbone is drawn mainly from Harrison, *Prudent Revolutionaries*, pp. 99–124, and Susan Pedersen 'Eleanor Rathbone. The Victorian Family Under the Daughter's Eye', in S. Pedersen and P. Mandler, *After the Victorians. Private Conscience and Public Duty in Modern Britain*, London, 1994, pp. 105–26.

constitution[18] by exerting such influence as they had upon the British government.

From 1927 Hubback was principal of the innovative Morley Adult Education College in Lambeth, London. She was also strongly committed to peace and was an early opponent of fascism.

Hubback grew up in a wealthy Liberal Jewish family which socialised her into a strong sense of public duty. Her mother, Gertrude, founded the Union of Jewish Women in 1902 and remained active in it until 1946. Her father, Meyer Spielman, was a stockbroker who moved into the world of voluntary action. Eva gained a first in economics at Newnham, where she later taught, but she initially returned home and took up voluntary work, becoming a poor law guardian in Paddington in 1910. In 1917 she was widowed with three young children and had to work for survival, despite support from her family.

Among her many activities, one that she valued highly was her work for the Association for Education in Citizenship (AEC) which she founded in 1933 with her close friends Ernest and Shena Simon. The Simons were prominent Liberals in the Liberal city of Manchester. Ernest, from 1947 Lord Simon of Wythernshawe,[19] was the Liberal MP for Withington, Manchester in 1923–4 and 1929–32, long a city councillor, and was Lord Mayor of Manchester in 1921. Shena Simon was a Manchester city councillor from 1934 to 1970 and as active in public service and on women's issues as other women described here. The final drafts of the Liberal Yellow Book emerged from a holiday taken by the three of them and Walter and Eleanor Layton.

Hubback believed that:

the most fundamental of all our problems is ... how to evoke civic consciousness. The accumulation of knowledge and the development of reasoning power will by themselves be useless if an active motive force be not first generated.

The aim of the AEC was particularly to educate young people in democracy, seeking:

to advance the study of and training in citizenship by which is meant training in the moral qualities necessary for the citizens of a democracy; the encouragement of clear thinking in everyday affairs; and the acquisition of ... knowledge of the modern world.[20]

---

[18] Aparma Basu and Bharati Ray, *Women's Struggle. A History of the All India Women's Conference 1927–1990*, New Delhi, 1990.

[19] I am grateful for his bequest to Manchester University which endowed the Simon Fellowship which I held in the academic year 1993–4 and which enabled me to carry out the research for this chapter.

[20] Harrison, *Prudent Revolutionaries*, pp. 285–6. For the emphasis on citizenship in the British Liberal tradition, cf. above, chapter 1, pp. 21–44.

She was seeking to keep alive in the world of the wider franchise, among people from different backgrounds from her own, the 'public spirit and private conscience' which had animated progressives of her own and previous generations.

For all her close association with liberalism, Hubback resisted pressure from friends and relatives in the late 1920s and early 1930s to stand as a Liberal in either national or local elections. She first stood as a Labour candidate for Hendon Borough Council in 1932 and was a Labour member of the LCC from 1946 to 1948. Like many progressive inter-war intellectuals, she hovered between liberalism, in which she had grown up and which was her intellectual home, and Labour, which was evidently the rising party of progress. She made the break without evidently changing her political ideas; she called herself a Lib–Lab.[21]

Another child of enthusiastic late-Victorian Liberals, who was early imbued with the commitment to public service in the complementary worlds of voluntary action and public welfare, was Violet Markham. She differed from her Liberal contemporaries in being initially anti-suffragist. She attributed this to the influence of her strong-minded, and publicly very active, mother. She justified it in terms she shared with many other women who were both pro- and anti-suffrage – that women's domestic skills and experience gave them a special capacity to improve the deplorable social conditions which centuries of male rule had allowed to continue, and that this was most effectively achieved within the sphere of local government where responsibility for much social policy lay. Women, therefore, should have the local but not the national vote. Probably more influential, however, was Markham's quintessentially Liberal belief that most women, like very many men, were insufficiently educated and politically knowledgeable to use the vote responsibly. When she changed her view in 1916, she still expressed her wish that it might be possible to change the whole basis of the franchise from property and age to 'service, citizenship and education'.[22] An important complement to this view was her active and lasting commitment to the education of working-class girls. Her change of mind in 1916 was a result of her observation of women's responsible commitment to the war effort.

She continued to believe broadly in the different contributions men and women could make to public life, but espoused a robust definition of gender difference which by no means confined women to the home. Her address in the local elections in Chesterfield in 1925 stated:

[21] Information on Hubback is mainly drawn from Harrison, *Prudent Revolutionaries*, pp. 273–300.
[22] Jane Lewis, *Women and Social Action in Victorian and Edwardian England*, Stanford (Ca.) Aldershot, 1991, p. 290.

as women now share the privileges of equal citizenship with men, they should not shirk the responsibilities of that new status, but be prepared to pull their full weight in the boat. Municipal affairs, it should be remembered, fall very largely within a woman's special province. A woman's first job is homemaking and the great activities of a Municipality, Health, Housing, Education are concerned with the nation's homemaking on a public scale. The day is long past when men and women could be cooped up in separate pens; a few ladylike, philanthropic duties being left to the women, while men do the rest.

I look on a sound education as being the master key to citizenship.[23]

She was elected to Chesterfield School Board in 1897 and remained actively involved with Chesterfield Education Committee for thirty years. In 1927–8 she was Liberal mayor of Chesterfield.

Markham explicitly did not think domesticity woman's sole goal, married late and took her husband's name only in private whilst continuing to be very active in public. Her political interests were certainly wider than the domestic and municipal. She was a committed Liberal imperialist, writing three books on South Africa, the last of which, in 1913, argued for better educational opportunity for black Africans as good in itself and a necessary preparation for their participation in the desirable eventual Home Rule.

She became active on the national scene during the First World War when she was appointed to a number of public bodies mainly concerned with the employment and training of women, due to her connections with prominent Liberal men; her views on the suffrage strained her relationship with Liberal women, though this was to recover after the war. She liked to work with men. When in the bleak days of 1923 she wrote 'Liberals Awake!', an article urging the establishment of study circles on key questions such as housing, health, education, taxation, foreign relations, etc. to keep Liberal thinking alive, she wanted 'to see the study circles composed jointly of men and women having personally no use for sexes penned in separate preserves'.[24] She defined herself as a feminist, but not 'one of those rampant feminists, the type of woman who exasperates me more and more each day'.[25]

For the remainder of her life, Markham campaigned for improved opportunities and conditions of employment for women of all backgrounds. With many Liberal contemporaries she was an early campaigner for equal pay, not just for 'equal work' – which it could too easily be claimed that women and men rarely actually did – but for work of 'equal value'. She was a reluctant Liberal candidate in the general election of

---

[23] Helen Jones (ed.), *Duty and Citizenship. The Correspondence and Papers of Violet Markham, 1896–1953*, London, 1994, p. 110.
[24] *FN*, Jan. 1923, pp. 2–3.
[25] *Ibid.*

1918 in the seat of her recently deceased brother and had little interest in a parliamentary career. She was a member of the executive of the WNLF in the 1920s and chaired its education sub-committee. In 1925 she was one of two women who subsidised an improved format for the federation's journal, as they sought to compete for women's support with Labour and Conservatives, after the shock of another poor Liberal performance in the election of December 1924.

She supported the League of Nations[26] and developed an especially strong interest in Germany, after living there with her soldier husband after the war, urging moderate treatment of the defeated nation.[27]

Indeed, like many women, she was active in many complementary causes with impressive energy and commitment. Markham, however, knew her limits. She resisted the demands of the 'birth control enthusiasts' to join their committees:

because I make it an absolute rule never to give my name to any committee for which I am not working and I *can't* take on a difficult and controversial subject like Birth Control, not from any lack of sympathy with the aim but because I literally haven't the time to devote to it.[28]

She remained in public life until her death in 1953, still a Liberal.[29]

Lady Cowdray was married to a wealthy Liberal MP, the engineer Weetman Pearson, who was elevated to the peerage in 1910. She joined the WLF executive in 1910 and gave time and money generously to it and to suffragism. She also helped to found the Liberal Woman's Suffrage Union. She was president of the WNLF in 1921, when she was described as 'an advanced Liberal with a well-thought-out political creed in which she firmly believes'.[30] She was active in voluntary welfare, especially in relation to health and education, and in supporting state social reforms such as old age pensions. She and her husband also enabled the League of Nations Union to survive its first difficult years with generous donations.

Much of the Cowdray wealth was inherited by their daughter Lady Denman. She was not active in the WLF but was a close associate of its most active members and encouraged its links with the WIs, which she helped to found and which she chaired from 1917 to 1946. She was also a founder member of another organisation of which the WNLF approved, the National Birth Control Association, from 1930. This was

---

[26] V. Markham, 'The Scandal of Corfu', *FN*, Oct. 1923.
[27] *FN*, Feb. 1923.
[28] *LWN*, 1925, p. 110.
[29] The best study of Markham is Jones, *Duty and Citizenship*; Lewis, *Woman and Social Action*, deals mainly with her career before World War I.
[30] *FN*, Dec. 1921.

founded to coordinate the growing demand to make birth control information as readily accessible to working-class as to better-off women. Denman gave considerable sums of money to voluntary clinics which supplemented local authority effort by providing birth control and other forms of health care to poorer women. She became director of the Women's Land Army from 1939 to 1945.

Denman was brought into the leadership of the birth control movement by another Liberal woman, Margery Spring Rice. One aim of the movement was to draw clients into the democratic running of the clinics, to make them one further example of the Millite aspiration to informed consumer control. Also on the committee were Eva Hubback and Eleanor Acland, a leading pre-war Liberal suffragist from a prominent Liberal family who was an active member of the WNLF in the 1920s.

The second woman to enter parliament, Margaret Wintringham, the Liberal MP for Louth in 1921–4, was typical in her range of interests. A schoolteacher before her marriage, education remained one of her chief interests, 'followed closely by housing, peace, temperance, agriculture and the welfare of women'. In her home county of Lincolnshire she was a JP, honorary secretary and organiser of the local WIs, founder of a girls club, member of the rural district housing committee and closely involved in a variety of voluntary and statutory welfare activities. She helped to pilot a succession of equal franchise bills through parliament. 'She fought for the retention of women police, for improved factory conditions, and an increase in the number of women factory inspectors, for the Legitimacy Bill and for all legislation to improve the conditions of women's life both in the home and in the labour world.' Yet, 'her work was never confined to so-called "women's questions". A keen internationalist, she took part in debates on foreign affairs; a keen Free Trader, she fought ... every form of Protection.'[31] She was president of the WNLF in 1925.

III

There was a similar pattern to the lives of all these women and they, with others, made a significant and lasting contribution to public life, mainly – though not exclusively – with the aim of improving the relative position of women. Though much of the historiography stresses discontinuities created by the war and the partial attainment of the vote, they exemplify continuity: in their determination to achieve gender equality; in carrying into the inter-war years, and in many cases beyond, the late-Victorian

[31] *LWN*, Jan. 1925.

commitment to public service, which some have also seen as dying around the time of the war[32]; and in their commitment to liberalism.

The latter is the most mysterious continuity. Why should women who could and did devote themselves to so many causes which had some prospect of success have remained to varying degrees so long committed to and often very active in a party which was evidently in decline and whose leaders they knew to be resistant to the issues which concerned them most? It has been argued that by clinging to the party some women had less successful public careers than they might have had, and in particular that it diminished their chances of election to parliament.[33] Such chances were poor for women in all parties and it is in any case questionable whether a backbench MP had more power or influence than the leading pressure group activists many of these women became. By standing even in hopeless constituencies they could provide a role model for women and had a platform for their favourite causes.

Liberal women behaved like the men who stuck by organised liberalism despite its decline, most notably Keynes and Beveridge.[34] They occupied spaces in public service which the Conservative-led democracy of the inter-war years left open for them. They stayed with liberalism because it provided them with a set of principles and ideals in which they believed and which they did not wish to die. It gave coherence to the range of their activities and aspirations, including their feminism, as no other available theory did. Violet Markham expressed this with characteristic clarity in a letter to Elizabeth Haldane in 1922:

I cling, like yourself, to the party, for great though its weakness at the moment and deplorable though the lack of vision in our unsatisfactory leaders, Liberalism as a *faith* and a *principle* is what I cannot give up.[35]

The Women's Liberal Federation and liberalism provided a supportive environment and network for committed middle- and upper-class women as they sought means for themselves and other women to use their new citizenship rights and to play new roles in public life; who shunned the Conservative Party and felt uneasy in the Labour Party. The content of their 'faith' and 'principle' we will see, if we examine the ideas the Liberal women expressed and their activities.

---

[32] This continuity is the theme of Pedersen and Mandler, *After the Victorians*.
[33] Harrison, *Prudent Revolutionaries*, pp. 130–1.
[34] Pedersen and Mandler, pp. 6–12.
[35] Jones, *Duty and Citizenship*, pp. 106–7.

Women and liberalism: the WNLF

The principle objectives of the WNLF were:

(a) to promote the adoption of Liberal principles in the government of
the country;
(b) to promote just legislation for women and the removal of all their
legal disabilities as citizens and to protect the interests of children;
(c) to advance political education by meetings, lectures and the distribution of literature.[36]

The WNLF continued to play an important part in campaigning for
the party. Its members' skill in bringing out the female vote was given
much of the credit for Asquith's victory at Paisley in 1920. Indeed they
gave Asquith devoted support which he had done little to deserve and
certainly did not return. They held determinedly to their independence
within the party whilst seeking more influence within it.[37]

One of their central purposes after 1918 was to encourage and assist
women to make use of their new rights by voting and standing for election at local and national level, taking up offices newly opened to them
such as that of JP[38] and putting pressure on local and national politicians
on issues they considered important. They demanded equal representation of women on government committees and commissions and international delegations. This was an aspiration shared with many other
organisations, though the leading role in monitoring women's progress in
public life, and demanding more, was taken by the National Council of
Women, guided by its parliamentary secretary, Bertha Mason, Liberal
and ex-suffragist.[39]

The WNLF worked closely with other women's organisations, locally
and nationally. Women Liberals were urged to cooperate locally with
organisations such as WIs, Women's Citizens Associations and Women's
Cooperative Guilds, for 'it is important to make each MP feel there is
public opinion in each constituency watching him'.[40] They provided
training for women in the skills of committee work and public speaking
and encouraged branches to read about and debate issues of importance.
Their policies, for example on housing, were often constructed on the
basis of questionnaires sent to branches. There was a strong underlying
assumption that women were generally uninterested in politics and
needed to be awakened to their new role. However, when she stood in the
general election of December 1923, Corbett Ashby thought that 'the

[36] *WLM*, July 1920, p. 126.
[37] *WLM*, May 1920, p. 94.
[38] 'How to become a JP', *WLM*, May 1920, p. 88.
[39] *WLM*, June 1920.
[40] *Ibid.*

woman elector is settling down seriously to her duties and responsibilities as an elector' and was better informed than at the previous election.[41]

The WNLF had a largely middle- and upper-class membership. Seventeen out of thirty-five candidates for election to the executive in 1920 were titled and others belonged to titled families.[42] Some efforts were made to attract working-class members but there is little sign that the WNLF could compete with Labour for their allegiance.[43] Branch meetings were serious minded, hearing lectures on a range of issues, such as 'Women's responsibility as a citizen',[44] though lightened by entertainment. For example, in 1920, Eleanor Rathbone gave the Birkenhead branch a fierce speech on how women's opportunities had been disappointingly knocked back since the war and urging the fight for equality of opportunity, focusing upon equal franchise and equal occupational opportunities. Then 'after refreshments Mrs H. Graham White sang two solos in a delightful manner and Miss Gladys New gave two violin solos with exceptional ability'.[45]

The role of the woman voter was defined explicitly in terms of 'citizenship' and service to the 'community', of the responsibility of each individual not only for herself but to serve the collectivity. In 1920, Norwich WLF was told:

Women had not sufficiently realized their opportunities and how closely they were concerned with the problem of citizenship: the housing problem, the care of mothers, the children, the sick, the aged and mentally deficient, the cause of education, the moral cleansing of our streets and the seeing that adequate wages were paid for good work done well were all largely women's problems.[46]

Women Liberals did not expect gender equality, on any definition, to flow naturally from gaining the vote. Those who did not realise it from the start, learned from experience that they would have to work for it.

'Why I am a Liberal'

The monthly journal of the WNLF and reports of its annual council (conference) meetings express an explicit commitment to Liberal theory and principles. They returned repeatedly to the question of the meaning of liberalism and of their commitment to it, in common with many Liberals at this time of decline and doubt. A prize essay 'Why I am a

[41] *FN*, Jan. 1924.
[42] *WLM*, June 1920, p. 119.
[43] *WLM*, June 1920, p. 111.
[44] *WLM*, Oct. 1920, pp. 1301–2.
[45] *WLM*, June 1920, p. 106.
[46] *WLM*, May 1920, p. 94.

Liberal' appeared in *Liberal Women's News* in 1925 written by Mrs Penberthy, president of Exeter Free Church Council. She had grown up in a Liberal family and wrote:

I am a Liberal because I wholeheartedly believe in Free Trade, in the League of Nations, in drastic Temperance Reform, Equal Suffrage, Religious Equality, Disestablishment, Revision of the Land Laws and Divorce Laws with a host of kindred reforms which can only become possible when better housing obtains.[47]

She shared these classic Liberal beliefs with other members of the Federation.

The WNLF continually defined liberalism against their main rival, Labour: 'We believe in individual effort and that is where we differ from our socialist friends' as Hilda Runciman, their (highly orthodox and not noticeably feminist) president put it in 1920. When the annual council discussed the 'policy of the Liberal Party' in the same year it insisted upon 'making it perfectly clear that the Liberal Party will have no share or part in a class war'.[48]

When Mrs Eleanor Cadbury (a Quaker, president of NCW and of the Free Church Council, convenor of the Peace Section of IWSA and Birmingham city councillor) stood, hopelessly, as candidate for King's Norton, Birmingham, in December 1924, she confessed that due to her strong interest in social reform she had often felt tempted to join the Labour Party. She did not, because in the election they had:

appealed largely to self-interest, with such placards as 'Vote for Labour and do the best for yourself.' Many of the reforms for which both we and Labour stand are similar, but the antagonism and class feeling that are fostered throughout their ranks, the suspicion and distrust, the absence of a really wide, all-embracing vision, block the road to real progress.

She believed:

there is a place for a strong rejuvenated Progressive Liberalism ... there is more scope for individual responsibility, thought and action ... still the old watchword of Liberal reformers holds good that our aim is to work for 'the greatest good of the greatest number'.

Miss Sydney Brown, BA, told Leicester WLF in 1920:

in the development of the nation, the Liberal aim had been to keep liberty for the individual without encroaching on the liberty of others.[49]

They believed that liberalism was still developing and was capable of further change in response to new conditions.

---

[47] *LWN*, April 1925.
[48] *WLM*, May 1920, p. 90.
[49] *WLM*, Oct. 1920, p. 141.

Catherine Alderton (the first woman mayor of Colchester in 1923, a JP, a member of the WNLF executive since 1912, a Congregationalist, active in voluntary as well as local government, and unsuccessful Liberal parliamentary candidate in 1922) wrote shortly before becoming the first woman to be elected to Essex County Council:

If we live up to the noble ideals of Liberalism, we cannot help at once being involved in a deep concern for the whole community, particularly for those members of it who are least able to look after themselves. Liberalism means 'loving one's neighbour as oneself' and 'doing to others as one would be done by' and Liberals, at any rate, should believe that it really is possible to govern our towns and cities on these principles.[50]

Liberalism and feminism

The WNLF were convinced of the consistency of liberalism with feminism. Feminism was a term that women Liberals were unafraid to adopt, in contrast to Labour women.[51] They could feel secure with the term in view of the long association between liberalism and feminism. By contrast, Labour and socialist women had always to face within their parties the challenge that the claims of class took precedence over those of gender.

They were explicit about the meaning of Liberal feminism. A eulogy in 1922 in memory of Eva McLaren, a founder member of the WLF, and later of the Liberal Women's Suffrage Union, by her young associate in the latter, Eleanor Acland, stated:

Although she was one of the most ardent feminists, there was no trace in her of that rather bitter 'anti-man' spirit which warped some women suffragists in the days of our fight for the vote. A fighter she was and a hard fighter too, but with her feminism was the outcome of love of justice and love of the human race. She strove for the rights of women as citizens and human beings; and she challenged the Liberal party to make that fight its own because it was essentially a Liberal movement in the direct line of Liberal progress toward democracy ... she felt the two causes were essentially one.[52]

Individuals varied in their emphases and interests, but the Liberal women do not readily fit the binary paradigms which dominate histories of feminism: 'old' or 'new', 'equal rights' or 'welfare', 'equality' or 'difference' feminists.[53] An unequivocal statement that:

---

[50] *LWN*, April 1928, p. 43.
[51] Pat Thane 'The Women of the British Labour Party and Feminism, 1906–1945', in H. L. Smith (ed.), *British Feminism in the Twentieth Century*, Aldershot, 1990; Pamela Graves, *Labour Women. Women in British Working-Class Politics, 1918–1939*. Cambridge, 1994.
[52] *FN*, May 1922.
[53] For example, O. Banks, *Faces of Feminism*, Oxford, 1981.

As women our prime interest is rightly and inevitably children and the home ... it is no out-of-date truism that the family is the backbone of the country.[54]

was countered by quite different statements and actions and by the range of issues to which Liberal women were committed. Winifred Le Sueur, the honorary secretary of Open Door International (established to campaign for gender equality in employment including after marriage) and chair of Slough WLA asked:

What reforms on feminist lines are most needed by the women of 1929? The answer may be summed up shortly as the attainment of equal status, equal liberties, equal opportunities.[55]

She gave most prominence to equality in the labour market. The WNLF campaigned against the 'marriage bar' to the employment of married women. In 1933 their journal published balanced articles for and against 'Should a Married Woman Work?' In general, they saw the domestic and the political spheres as complementary rather than opposed; experience formed in the former should be used for the benefit of the latter.

In common with other organisations including the WFL[56] they very actively participated in the campaign coordinated by NUSEC for a fully equal franchise. Branches were constantly urged to petition the Prime Minister[57] and their MPs and to join the regular demonstrations. They were determined supporters of equal rights for women to inherit peerages and sit in the House of Lords. WNLF used female auditors, Ethel Watts and Co.

They worked closely with other organisations such as NUSEC, the League of Nations Union, The Women's International League for Peace and Freedom (WIL) and the WFL. Liberal women were urged:

Be interested in women's movements and causes; even if various women's organizations are 'non-party' it is foolish to allow members of the opposite parties to do all their work and monopolize all places on their committees. Liberal influence is needed in all movements ... women voters are interested in a wide field, in the so-called women's questions, health, housing, education, child welfare and maternal mortality and also in the great questions of peace, unemployment, free trade.[58]

[54] *LWN*, Dec. 1928. From the prize-winning essay in a competition: 'What I Expect from the Next Liberal Government'.
[55] Winifred Le Sueur, 'Feminist Problems of Today', *LWN*, Oct. 1929, p. 305.
[56] *FN*, Feb. 1924.
[57] *FN*, May 1921.
[58] *LWN*, Nov. 1928.

Reform

The WNLF did place great emphasis upon welfare issues because they believed that the need was urgent and had been conspicuously neglected by male politicians. They sought to extend the New Liberal reform programme, supporting growth of the sphere of state action, provided that it enabled people to improve their lives and did not coerce them and that it encouraged cooperation between state and voluntary action. Nor did they see welfare as women's only political goal.

The case that welfare should be the first priority of enfranchised women was trenchantly put by Commandant Allen, a former suffragette, pioneer policewoman and member of the WNLF executive in the 1920s:

Perhaps one of the most urgent needs of the day is that work applying to women should be done by women ... No-one today entirely visualizes all that men doing women's work has meant of unnecessary suffering and discomfort for women in the old days before the great fight that ended in the parliamentary representation of the female citizen in England.[59]

Like other women of the time they sought, with some success, to push welfare to the centre of the political stage, to rank equally with the conventional stuff of high politics. As Mrs Scott Anderson of the Cambridge WLA told the Grantham branch in 1920:

She had a vote. She hoped to make use of that vote. They [the WNLF] put purity, temperance, housing, maternity and child welfare as high as the question of the state of Poland and the sooner those who stood for Parliament realized they had got to give more attention to these matters the better.[60]

Many of the issues on which they campaigned with some successes in the 1920s had been embodied in the 'Women's Charter' which had been put to the WLF annual conference in 1910. This called upon the Liberal government to introduce: equal divorce and inheritance laws, equal rights to guardianship of children, stiffer penalties for assaults against women and children, 'measures for improving the condition of married women of the working classes', 'equal payment to men and women for equal service', equal job opportunities and access to training, equal protective legislation in the workplace, free milk and free baths and play-rooms for working-class children. In 1910 this mix of equal rights and welfare demands had alarmed Liberal women loyal to the party leadership as 'purely feminist ... extravagances of policy' and it was narrowly defeated.[61] By 1920 it was generally accepted in the WNLF, except for divisions on the issue of protective legislation, and it provided the core of their reform programme.

59 Commandant Allen, 'Work for Women Police', *FN*, June 1923.
60 *Women's Liberal Magazine (WLM)*, Feb. 1920.
61 Hirschfield, 'Fractured Faith', pp. 192–3.

About 'endowment of motherhood' (family allowances), a newly important issue in the 1920s, they had initial reservations, preferring to support higher wages to enable men and women to provide for their family needs, quoting favourably a 'sailor's wife':

We know what all these government allowances for children mean. We've had it with the separation allowance: INTERFERENCE! (with intense bitterness). Let them pay our men proper money and we'll get it for the children all right.[62]

Their enthusiasm grew in later years, partly under pressure from Eleanor Rathbone,[63] though they still preferred to minimise the role of the state, advocating a scheme administered by employers and financed by redistribution from childless employees to those with children.

The WNLF believed that the 'first aim of Liberal social legislation should be to establish security of livelihood'.[64] The conference unanimously resolved in 1920 and continued to hold that:

the worker is entitled to a fair share in the product of industry and [we believe] that a minimum rate of wages sufficient to support an average family, leaving a reasonable margin for comfort and leisure should be fixed for all workers. It [the conference] urges that effect should be given to the principles of self-government and partnership in industry on the lines of the proposals contained in the Whitley Reports.[65]

They opposed 'nationalisation of all forms of industry' while supporting that of 'certain monopoly services' and recognising that unemployment 'and the existing control of industry and distribution of its rewards' was causing 'unrest and dissatisfaction'. They supported trade unions when they acted peaceably, expressing pride in the Liberal Party's record of advancing trade union rights, but opposed the General Strike as political rather than industrial in intent.[66]

They showed increasing concern about unemployment as it mounted, especially stressing that it was a real but neglected problem among women. One immediate solution was improved training for domestic work. Margaret Corbett Ashby betrayed the *de haut en bas* quality, which could characterise their entirely serious desire to improve the conditions of poorer women, when she commented:

No woman proud of her own housecraft can see, without dismay, the suggestion that any untrained woman, perhaps from the roughest quarters, and hitherto engaged in some very simple, strenuous but straightforward factory work, can be

---

[62] *Ibid.*
[63] *LWN*, March 1925, April 1925.
[64] *LWN*, July 1924.
[65] *WLM*, June 1920.
[66] *FN*, May 1921.

immediately taken to live with us in our homes, be in daily touch with our children or our invalids when our standards of life and speech and our customs differ so greatly.[67]

Ashby herself made no attempt to perform 'housecraft' until the last ten years of her life, in the 1970s. The dedicated public service of all of these women was possible because they employed servants. However, in reality, many women urgently needed paid work in the 1920s and domestic service was all that was readily available. A key element in Liberal demands, which they shared especially with the WIs and TGs, was that training in domestic service should be designed not merely to increase efficiency but to raise its status and to achieve recognition that it was a highly skilled occupation comparable with male skilled work.[68]

The women Liberals joined other organisations in the campaign for widows' pensions. When these were introduced in 1925, Margaret Wintringham commented from the chair at the annual council that this 'was directly attributable to women's votes and women MPs', though it gave them less than they wanted.

The WNLF also shared in the broad campaign for reforms of family laws.[69] The Matrimonial Causes Act 1923 (the outcome of a bill drafted by Hubback) equalised grounds for divorce between the sexes.[70] In 1925 women acquired equal rights in the guardianship of children, a much attenuated version of a bill drafted by Wintringham. In the same year, the level of maintenance which a separated wife could claim was raised and she acquired rights to retain possession of the matrimonial home and to a share of the household possessions. Children born to unmarried parents were enabled to be legitimised when their parents married. Adoption of children was legalised. On all of these issues, members of WLF branches harried their MPs whilst their leaders lobbied in London. The legislation which resulted often fell short of what women sought and in the absence of detailed studies of the background to the legislation it is difficult to establish how influential their campaigns were. It is hard, however, to believe that the co-existence of the campaigns for women's acquisition of the vote and the legislation was entirely coincidental.[71]

Another important campaign they shared with other groups was for the employment of women police. Women's voluntary patrols had formed during the war, mainly to protect women and children from harassment

---

[67] *FN*, Feb. 1923.
[68] 'What is wrong with domestic service?' (unsigned), *LWN*, April 1930.
[69] Pat Thane, 'Women in the British Labour Party and the Construction of State Welfare, 1906–1939', in S. Koven and S. Michel, *Mothers of a New World. Maternalist Politics and the Origins of Welfare States*, London, 1993, pp. 356–7.
[70] Harrison, *Prudent Revolutionaries*, p. 279.
[71] *FN*, Feb. 1923.

in public places. Commandant Allen was leader of one such group, the Women's Auxiliary Service. They were energetic volunteers in the General Strike, to the approval of the WNLF executive. The aim was not just to extend the range of occupations open to women but to improve protection and care for female and child victims of physical and sexual abuse, which was acknowledged to be a major problem.[72] As Allen informed women Liberals:

one fact alone ought to convince us of the necessity for their service, that it should not need to be a policeman to whom statements from the victims of assault have to be made. These, one only has to think for a moment to understand why, should only be made by a woman or a little girl to another woman, the police-woman.[73]

It was proposed that they should also be in charge of women in police cells, accompany female prisoners in transit and patrol parks.[74]

In 1923 twenty women patrols were established in the metropolis with – following some resistance in the force – equal powers with male constables. A battle continued to prevent erosion of their numbers and powers and for their establishment elsewhere: 'in no way to take the place of men but to do the work that only women can do', as Allen put it.[75]

Advised by the Women's Auxiliary Service, WNLF branches were urged to put strong pressure on their local authorities. In 1926 there were still only 137 policewomen in England and Wales compared with 53,734 men.[76] By 1928, there were 147 in thirty-eight towns, 50 of them in London.[77]

The new female magistrates also worked hard for the protection of women. The first resolution of their first annual conference in 1921 was for abolition of the death sentence for infanticide immediately after childbirth. This became law in 1922. Mrs Dowson, JP, told Liberal women:

In cases of indecent or criminal assaults on little girls it is of immense importance that evidence should be taken by women, and that women should always be present in the courts, near the child, to minimize the strangeness and fear she is bound to feel.[78]

In some courts this was already the practice, in others there was opposition. Women Liberals were urged to check on practice in their district and urge reform where it was not carried out.

---

[72] *WLM*, May 1920, p. 88.
[73] *FN*, April 1923.
[74] *LWN*, Nov. 1928.
[75] *FN*, April 1923, p. 44.
[76] *FN*, June 1923; *LWN*, Feb. 1926, April 1926.
[77] *LWN*, Nov. 1928.
[78] *FN*, February 1924, p. 22.

There were demands also that women on trial should face a jury made up of at least 50 per cent of females;[79] and for the extension of the rights of women to sit on juries, which were restricted by a property qualification which excluded most married women.[80]

There were also unsuccessful demands to raise the age of consent, for both sexes, to eighteen. There was a thin line between the need to protect the vulnerable from abuse and illiberal social puritanism. A similar tension between what was assumed to be good for the community and the freedom of the individual arose concerning the sterilisation of the mentally handicapped. This was advocated by a number of otherwise humane reformers at the time and the WNLF conference approved it, in the interests of 'the future quality of the race', subject to assurances that it would be performed only with informed consent.

With greater energy, enthusiasm and effectiveness, the WNLF supported the campaign for birth control. The executive felt that 'every woman was entitled to the best medical knowledge available, whether she obtains it from private sources or public welfare centres'.[81]

Retrenchment and peace

Liberal women were in favour of welfare but not of 'waste'. They were for minimising state expenditure wherever this was compatible with the desirable improvement of services; hence the proposal to place the cost of administration of family endowment upon employers. After the onset of unemployment they consistently supported low taxation of business to facilitate recovery. In 1920 they supported a levy on 'war fortunes' to help pay off the national debt and consistently and strongly advocated cuts in arms expenditure. Thus, as in Gladstone's days, 'peace' was the first requisite for true 'retrenchment': but it was also an end in itself.

Welfare issues were as high on the WLNF agenda as others but not higher. In the early 1920s they made repeated pleas for the humane treatment of Germany,[82] and against the occupation of the Ruhr;[83] for 'reconstruction not destruction' of central Europe.[84] They condemned the government's role in Russia[85] and opposed the Turkish government's treatment of Armenians and Christians.[86] Above all they opposed

---

[79] *WLM*, June 1920.
[80] Ownership of land of at least £10 value or a ratepayer on property valued at at least £20 p.a., £30 in Middlesex. *FN*, June 1921, p. 29.
[81] *LWN*, April 1926, p. 52.
[82] *WLM*, Feb. 1920, p. 59.
[83] *FN*, Feb. 1923.
[84] *WLM*, May 1920, p. 87.
[85] *WLM*, May 1920, p. 91.
[86] *WLM*, Feb. 1920, p. 59.

government coercion in Ireland – 'this infamous policy which is reducing Britain to the level of Turkey which overshadows the whole political horizon';[87] and supported Irish 'Home Rule',[88] as a self-governing dominion within the empire. In October 1920 Margaret Buckmaster urged women Liberals:

The women of England who after years of struggle have won for themselves the rights of citizenship should now be prepared to bear the burden of responsibility that those rights entail ... In Ireland the blackest form of coercion is being carried out by a government which draws its authority from the people of this country.[89]

All branches were asked to pass resolutions on the issue and make them known to their MPs[90] and in May 1921 to attend a women's protest meeting in London.[91] In June it was reported as the 'overwhelming concern' of the branches.[92] In December the executive expressed its thankfulness at the prospect of a settlement in Ireland.

The WNLF supported campaigns against slavery, 'white' or other, and for the rights of aborigines, a cause they shared with women's organisations in Australia and elsewhere. Above all, they supported the League of Nations as the main hope for world peace[93] and demanded that Britain's representatives be democratically elected and include a just proportion of women.[94] Their annual council resolved in 1924 to make the League 'the basis and instrument of our foreign policy'.[95] Throughout the world women saw the League of Nations as an institution through which they could press for gender equality and other desirable changes, with considerable and underestimated effect.[96] In 1932 Kathleen Courtney, the honorary secretary of the Women's Peace Crusade, reported to the WNLF on the recently concluded thirteenth session of the League:

Are there two Leagues of Nations? In all the non-political spheres the success of the League is amazing. Wherever self-interest and selfish political motives do not intrude international co-operation can work miracles for the benefit of the human race.[97]

In combating epidemics and disease, controlling slavery and traffic in women and children, influencing labour and social security standards, all

[87] Leader, 'Ireland', *WLM*, Nov. 1920, p. 134.
[88] *WLM*, Feb. 1920, p. 59.
[89] *WLM*, July 1920, p. 110.
[90] *WLM*, Oct. 1920, p. 125.
[91] *FN*, May 1921.
[92] *FN*, June 1921.
[93] *WLM*, Feb. 1920, p. 59.
[94] *WLM*, June 1920, p. 118.
[95] *LWN*, July 1924.
[96] Carol Miller 'Lobbying the League: Women's International Organizations and the League of Nations', Oxford University D.Phil. thesis, 1992.
[97] *LWN*, November 1932, p. 834.

issues on which women were active and on which their voices were heard, there had been real successes. In the male-dominated sphere of international politics it had been largely ineffective.

The WNLF actively supported internationalism and the wider women's peace movement, sending official representatives to meetings and demonstrations such as that organised by the League of Nations Union in London on Armistice Day 1921.[98] Their journal noted with pride in June 1923 that two 'lifelong and enthusiastic Liberals', Corbett Ashby and the Marchioness of Aberdeen, were presidents of the Women's International Suffrage Association (WISA) and the International Council of Women simultaneously.

Empire

The WNLF were committed Liberal imperialists, immediately critical of imperial coercion, as in Ireland, or the use of forced labour in British colonies in Africa.[99] In 1928 Margaret Wintringham reminded Liberal women that:

the Empire is a Liberal Empire and without Liberalism would have been lost a hundred years ago, if indeed it had ever been gained.

The Liberal policy is based on the principle that self-government should be granted as a right to advanced and responsible peoples.

Liberals have always believed in binding the Empire together by mutual trust and affection and not by the application of force.

The problem however throughout the formation of the Empire has been a particularly difficult one in the case of backward people, and the Liberal policy was that they should be governed in their own interest with protection and development and without exploitation. Sometimes however we see the principle of self-government for the colonies has come into conflict with the equally strong Liberal principle of protection for the native, as when the slave trade was abolished against the will of the colonists.

But the Liberal statesmen, seeing that justice was due to all, set up Crown Colony Government where the predominance of backward peoples prevailed. They realized that self-government can only be carried out when native and colonist jointly share in its administration.[100]

The WNLF executive in 1926 put a series of resolutions to dominion premiers attending the Imperial Conference in London. They deplored:

the retrograde steps taken by the Government of His Majesty's Dominion of South Africa regarding the treatment and status of native races, believing that

[98] *FN*, Nov. 1921.
[99] *WLM*, April 1920, p. 77; June 1920, p. 106–7.
[100] *LWN*, April 1928, p. 51.

such action runs counter to the British traditional spirit of trusteeship of native peoples.

They urged:

the vital importance of preserving in the Mandated Territories both the letter and the spirit of trusteeship for native inhabitants and the necessity for providing adequate facilities for hearing petitions from the people themselves for redress of substantial grievances.[101]

They recognised that the empire was changing, re-printing the Marquess of Lothian's address to the Liberal Summer School of 1930:

The Empire in its old form, bound together under the authority and control of Great Britain is ceasing to exist. The passionate demand for independence and self-government that is sweeping through India today will be shared by Africa tomorrow. Public opinion is replacing 'authority' as the dominant force within the British Commonwealth and its races and peoples will only continue as members of a single commonwealth if a new basis of unity can be found in the agreement of public opinion that the Empire serves common purposes such as peace, justice and equality which are implicit in the British constitution.

He pointed out that there were now many small nations in the world. Europe had begun 'to see that it must have some common form of government' and

If the British Empire is dissolved it will merely add some twenty or thirty new nations to the existing national chaos. In the conception of Dominion status which must form the basis of the new British Commonwealth, we have the greatest creative idea of modern time – the idea of national liberty combined with an Imperial unity within which each nation is equal and autonomous while yet belonging to the larger commonwealth ... perhaps the most valuable function of the British Commonwealth is to form a bridge between the continents ... the intimate association of races within the British Empire may prevent the racial war which so many pessimists predict for the future.[102]

The WNLF took increasing interest in the women of India as the independence movement gathered strength. This could take the form of condescension which measured Indian progress by the speed with which it abandoned 'native superstition' for western practices. Lady Simon, wife of Sir John and a leading member of the WNLF, reported from India in 1929 that 'a country cannot be great when its women are not free', and India was held back while 'the old customs of Purdah and child marriage are traditions that die hard'. Some of these 'traditions' were recent inventions – child marriage and suttee (immolation of the widow on the death of her husband) – but not purdah,[103] which Indian women nationalists

---

[101] *LWN*, Nov. 1926.
[102] 'The British Commonwealth of Nations', *LWN*, Sept. 1930.
[103] Basu and Ray, *Women's Struggle*.

themselves opposed. But some Indian women resented the failure to pay attention to what they were actually demanding and some Liberals at least learned an important lesson from their protests.[104]

More commonly, the concern was that the women of India 'should play their part in the national life of that country when it attained self-government' and to help combat famine and poverty in the country-side.[105] *Liberal Women's News* reprinted a speech given by Miss R. M. Fleming to the British Commonwealth League attacking race prejudice. She began:

> The western European long thought of his civilization as something so far superior to anything that the world has ever seen that it hardly occurred to him that any detail of its routine might not be suitable for infliction on other groups living in different environments and accustomed to different traditional ideas and customs. And in many ways our civilization is something of which we may legitimately feel proud ... but our civilization has also many failures and many aspects suitable to our own environment and traditional conditions but doubtfully suitable for others ... None so far as I know has ever proved or even attempted to prove that the skin is the seat of the intellect or the moral character ... the temples of Egypt, the temples of India, the earliest systems of writing, the first artistic contribution, some of the greatest philosophies have been contributed to the sum total of human achievement by people with pigmented skins ... It must be remembered that Africans have their own, sometimes highly complex, systems of education.[106]

Free trade

Binding together the commitments of the women Liberals to reform, peace, empire and Home Rule were their parallel commitments to liberty, democracy and free trade. The latter was a matter of passionate, consistent and wholly unquestioned conviction. It was put not in terms of appeal to Liberal tradition but as practical policy to reduce the cost of living and increase the chances of world peace. Protection, it was argued, would further increase unemployment by slowing world trade and would increase the potential for conflict among nations.

In June 1932 Wintringham stressed that:

> International co-operation is what Liberals have always stood for and it is certainly what we Liberals must work for now ... there is no better definition of Liberalism than the old one: trust in each other tempered by prudence ... we must work for the abolition of this narrow cramping nationalism in trade that has recently been imposed upon us ... ours is the cause of hope as against despair; of

---

[104] Pederson, *Eleanor Rathbone*, pp. 110–11.
[105] *LWN*, June 1932.
[106] *LWN*, Jan. 1933.

trust as against suspicion; of persuasion as against coercion; of freedom as against restraint; of peace, whether in politics or in economics, as against war.[107]

Perhaps the last achievement of the Victorian Liberal party was to provide the post-1918 women's movement with a theoretical and practical framework and set of concepts used by an influential section of the first generation of women to acquire formal citizenship as they sought to define their new roles, and give them practical expression. If they did not wholly succeed in overturning millennia of gender inequality, it should not be assumed that they wholly failed.

[107] *LWN*, June 1932.

4   Democracy and popular religion: Moody and Sankey's mission to Britain, 1873–1875

John Coffey

I

The mission of the American evangelists, D. L. Moody and Ira D. Sankey, was one of the great public events of mid-Victorian Britain. Between June 1873 and August 1875, the Congregationalist preacher and his Methodist singing partner filled the largest public halls of England, Scotland and Ireland, with audiences of up to 20,000. In these two years several million people heard the revivalists, and Moody and Sankey established themselves as the greatest mass communicators of their generation.[1] In London alone, it was estimated that the aggregate attendance at their meetings was two and a half million,[2] and according to the *Daily Telegraph* they had converted the capital's largest building, Islington's Agricultural Hall, 'into an open church'.[3] Sankey's hymn book – later to sell between fifty and ninety million copies worldwide[4] – earned the evangelists £7,000 in royalties while they were still in Britain, though it sold for only sixpence.[5] Even the messenger boys were singing Sankey's songs in the streets,[6] and the title of one of his most popular pieces entered the language as a common expression: 'Hold the fort'.[7] The popularity of the evangelists was so great that continental newspapers commented on the phenomenon,[8] whilst the provincial and

---

[1] For accounts of the vast crowds at these meetings see *Irish Times*, 10 November 1874, p. 3; *Liverpool Mercury*, 8 February, 1875, p. 6; *Daily Telegraph*, 16 March 1875, p. 9; W. R. Moody, *The Life of D. L. Moody*, New York, 1930, pp. 179–81. Bernard Weisberger estimates that the aggregate audience addressed by the revivalists in Britain at this time was between three and four million. See his *They Gathered at the River: The Story of the Great Revivalists*, Boston, 1958, p. 201.

[2] Moody, *Moody*, p. 225.

[3] *Daily Telegraph*, 16 March 1875, p. 9.

[4] S. Tamke, *Make a Joyful Noise unto the Lord: Hymns as a Reflection of Victorian Social Attitudes*, Athens (OH), 1978, pp. 4, 143.

[5] Benson, *The English Hymn: Its Development and Use in Worship*, New York, 1915, pp. 486–87.

[6] *Liverpool Mercury*, 8 March 1875, p. 6. See also the *Congregationalist*, March 1875, p. 176.

[7] J. Pollock, *Moody without Sankey*, London, 1983, p. 150.

[8] See the *Pall Mall Gazette*, 17 June 1875, p. 2282; 21 June 1875, p. 2325.

national press in Britain devoted hundreds of columns to reports of the revival meetings. People as diverse as George Bernard Shaw, Matthew Arnold and Friedrich Engels criticised the American visitors and their audiences, and even Queen Victoria was not amused by their antics. The *New York Times* concluded that 'the Moody and Sankey fever' could only be accounted for 'on the theory of the gravedigger in *Hamlet*, that in England everybody is mad'.[9]

This chapter seeks to explain the appeal of Moody and Sankey in terms of their 'moral populism'.[10] It argues that their revivalism was connected with popular radicalism in two specific ways. In the first place, the Americans symbolised the possibility of a more democratic social order. Their populist style was widely interpreted as providing a typically American affirmation of the value of the common people and their culture, and a radical challenge to aristocracy and privilege. Secondly, the religious zeal and moral earnestness of the revival was infused into contemporary political protest, inspiring both nonconformist radicals and the 'Grand Old Man' of British politics, William Gladstone.

II

This interpretation of Moody and Sankey's social and political significance differs sharply from the conventional one. American scholars have generally regarded Moody as a forerunner of reactionary fundamentalism. Instead of accepting the 'social gospel', they claim, Moody preached that the world was rapidly deteriorating and would only be changed by the Second Coming of Christ. 'I look upon this world as a wrecked vessel', he famously opined. 'God has given me a lifeboat and said to me, "Moody, save all you can".' This message of individual salvation failed to attract the working class, these historians suggest, and by the late nineteenth century it was no longer socially or intellectually credible. Moody and his supporters were in retreat from the modern world, already far down the road to reactionary fundamentalism.[11]

British historians have not devoted as much attention to Moody and

---

[9] *New York Times*, 22 June 1875, p. 6.

[10] See Patrick Joyce, *Visions of the People: Industrial England and the Question of Class, 1840–1914*, Cambridge, 1991.

[11] See, for instance: W. McLouglin, *Modern Revivalism*, New York, 1959, pp. 167–8, 179–81, 252–9, 267–70, 278; J. Findlay, *Dwight L. Moody: American Evangelist*, Chicago, 1969, pp. 274–85; M. Marty, *Righteous Empire: the Protestant Experience in America*, New York, 1970, pp. 163, 180–4; S. Sizar, *Gospel Hymns and Social Religion*, Philadelphia, 1978, pp. 148–53; and G. Marsden, *Fundamentalism and American Culture: The Shaping of Twentieth-Century Evangelicalism*, Oxford, 1980, pp. 32–9.

Sankey as have their American colleagues.[12] However, in *Holding the Fort* John Kent has advanced an interpretation of Moody's British mission largely in line with that of American historians. Kent claims that Moody and Sankey failed to reach the working classes, and that their popularity was really confined to 'the evangelical sub-culture', whose members attended the meetings again and again. This helped to conceal the reality that the religion Moody and Sankey preached had already had its day. By the 1870s it was 'anti-modernist, anti-materialist, anti-democratic and often anti-intellectual', and although it would be 'unfair' to describe Moody as 'one of the fathers of later right-wing extremism', his political significance clearly lay right of centre.[13]

At first glance, some parts of this analysis seem plausible. The charge that the evangelists failed to attract the working classes, for instance, can be found in some contemporary accounts. 'The saints are not fighting the devil on his own ground', reported the *Liverpool Leader*. 'The common people and our social Ishmaelites do not hear Moody and Sankey gladly.'[14] Moreover, establishment figures could be friendly towards the evangelists. In the United States, they enjoyed the patronage of wealthy businessmen like Andrew Carnegie, and in Britain their campaign was supported by Conservatives like Lord Shaftesbury and Disraeli's Lord Chancellor, Cairns. To them, Moody and Sankey were reaching the 'lower orders' and might be expected to save them from socialism and anarchy.[15] Their brand of revivalism was acceptable because it was respectable and orderly, quite unlike the hysterical enthusiasm associated with the American camp meeting.[16] As a Primitive Methodist minister sadly pointed out, 'the holy shout was vetoed' in Moody's meetings.[17]

---

[12] Kitson Clark noted in 1962 that recent books had 'little on Moody and Sankey' (*The Making of Victorian England*, London, 1962, p. 22). Since then a number of historians have drawn attention to their importance in Britain: O. Chadwick, *The Victorian Church*, vol. II, London, 1970, pp. 184, 286–7, 471; C. Binfield, *And So Down to Prayers: Studies in English Nonconformity 1780–1920*, London, 1977, pp. 8, 76, 97, 139, 224; A. L. Drummond and J. Bulloch, *The Church in Late Victorian Scotland 1874–1900*, Edinburgh, 1978, pp. 9–18; P. J. Waller, *Democracy and Sectarianism: A Political History of Liverpool 1868–1939*, Liverpool, 1981, p. 27; I. G. C. Hutchinson, *A Political History of Scotland: Parties, Elections and Issues*, Edinburgh, 1986, pp. 136–8; G. Parsons (ed.), *Religion in Victorian England*, vol. I: *Traditions*, Manchester, 1988, pp. 218–22, 230–2; D. W. Bebbington, *Evangelicalism in Modern Britain: A History from the 1730s to the 1980s*, London, 1989, pp. 162–4.

[13] J. Kent, *Holding the Fort: Studies in Victorian Revivalism*, London, 1978, pp. 132–235, 356–68.

[14] *Liverpool Leader*, 13 February 1875.

[15] See the *Saturday Review*, 20 March 1875, pp. 311–12; *Bee-Hive*, 26 June 1875, p. 10.

[16] For comments to this effect see *Nonconformist*, 15 April 1874, p. 841; *Irish Times*, 2 November 1874, p. 5; *Manchester Guardian*, 2 December 1874, p. 5; *Graphic*, 17 April 1875, p. 379.

[17] *Primitive Methodist Magazine*, May 1875, pp. 336–7. See also the *Pall Mall Gazette*, 26 April 1875, p. 1562.

Moody was also careful to avoid criticising the clergy or the established churches as other revivalists had done.[18] Instead he cultivated their support and declared that 'This spirit that always says "Come out" is from Satan'.[19] His ecumenism brought together evangelical Anglicans and nonconformists,[20] and avoided sectarianism in a way that was gratifying to social conservatives.

However, as we shall see, the vulgar and disruptive tendencies of Moody's revivalism were frequently more obvious to critics than its respectable and ecumenical features. In the United States, Moody may have seemed almost sophisticated and urbane compared to his wilder predecessors, but in Britain both conservative journals and radical working-class publications agreed that the populist evangelist presented a radical alternative to conventional elitism. In order to understand the cultural significance of Moody and Sankey's mission, therefore, we must place them in the right context and not fall into the anachronistic trap of reading 1920s American fundamentalism back into the entirely different situation of Britain in the 1870s. To do so is to be blinded by hindsight and to ignore what Moody and his supporters actually stood for at that time.[21]

In these early days, at least, Moody was far from being a reactionary pietist. As president of the Chicago YMCA in the 1860s, he was something of a social activist,[22] and he did not hesitate to attack employers who paid 'starvation wages'.[23] It is true that he was not a full-blown collectivist, but then neither were most working-class radicals in this period.[24] The pessimism about social reform which later characterised Moody's preaching was not evident in the 1870s, and the social gospel

---

[18] 'Not the least allusion to controversial matters mingles with their services' stated the *Irish Times*, 10 November 1874, p. 3.

[19] P. Morgan, 'A Study of the Work of Four American Evangelists in Britain from 1873 to 1905, and the Effect upon Organised Christianity of their Work there', Oxford University B. Litt. thesis, 1958, p. 463. Morgan points out (p. 468) that in Ireland even Catholic newspapers were favourable towards Moody because of his refusal to use his platform to attack their church.

[20] Of the 501 clergymen who attended Moody and Sankey's farewell meeting in London in July 1875, 188 were Anglicans, and the rest were nonconformists. A common evangelical theology bound together low-church Anglicans and Dissenters. Historians who stress the conflict between the two groups often overlook this.

[21] James Findlay is almost the only historian to note the vital difference in the contexts of Moody's British and American missions: 'The popularity of the two American evangelists in England was partly tied to a rising spirit of democracy, a factor which was absent in the United States' (*Dwight L. Moody*, p. 302n and also pp. 181–2).

[22] See Pollock, *Moody without Sankey*, pp. 55, 61.

[23] D. L. Moody, *On the Ten Commandments*, Chicago, 1977 (1896), p. 93.

[24] See A. J. Reid, 'Old Unionism Reconsidered: the Radicalism of Robert Knight, 1870–1900', in E. Biagini and A. J. Reid (eds.), *Currents of Radicalism: Popular Radicalism, Organised Labour and Party Politics in Britain, 1850–1914*, Cambridge, 1991, pp. 214–43.

advocate, George Adam Smith, declared that 'in the seventies, there was no preacher more civic or more practical among us'.[25] The preacher made an impact too, for he provided the inspiration for many organisations working among the poor and deprived.[26] Indeed, as Ian Sellers has argued, Moody's revivalism should be linked to the heyday of the nonconformist conscience: 'none of the great names of late nineteenth century nonconformity ... escaped the influence of the Moody and Sankey revival – several, in fact, first discovered their passion for personal evangelism and social service through this very agency'.[27] Many of these nonconformists were dedicated Liberals who hardly fit with the stereotype of the apolitical pietist often said to form the bulk of Moody's support: men like R. W. Dale, Hugh Price Hughes, Edward Baines, Alexander Maclaren, Samuel Smith, F. B. Meyer and Principal Rainy.[28] Even the tory Anglicans who backed Moody's London campaign were deeply committed to social reform.[29] So to suggest, as Kent does, that Moody's mission marked the withdrawal of evangelicals from involvement in society is simply incorrect.

Moreover, Moody and Sankey did reach the British working classes. *The Times* reported that 'it is an error to say that they have not reached the lower strata of the life of London and of our large towns generally. It is no opinion but a fact that they have done so'.[30] In Sheffield a special service for the unchurched was attended by a crowd of 5,000, whom the *Independent* described as 'unmistakeably composed of the class for which the service was intended'.[31] The *Nonconformist* described a similar service in Liverpool: 'Rough, ill-clad working men were there, and in the motley assemblage were sailors, dock labourers, and many horny handed artisans, whom it was presumed had never been reached by clergyman or minister'.[32]

Moody and Sankey's appeal transcended barriers of gender, age and class. The Congregationalist minister, R. W. Dale, wrote that at the Birmingham meetings 'the people were of all sorts, young and old, rich

[25] G. A. Smith, *The Life of Henry Drummond*, London, 1899, p. 57.

[26] See K. Heasman, *Evangelicals in Action*, London, 1962, p. 27; Hutchinson, *Political History of Scotland*, pp. 136–8.

[27] I. Sellers, *Nineteenth Century Nonconformity*, London, 1977, pp. 95, 33.

[28] For evidence of the political stance of these men see J. Parry, *Democracy and Religion: Gladstone and the Liberal Party 1867–75*, Cambridge, 1986, ch. 4, and D. Bebbington, *The Nonconformist Conscience: Chapel and Politics, 1870–1914*, London, 1982.

[29] Lord Shaftesbury is the most eminent case, but the two major organisers of the London mission also illustrate the point; Quentin Hogg became the founder of the polytechnic movement, and Arthur Kinnaird was active in women's campaigns.

[30] *The Times*, 23 June 1875, p. 9.

[31] *Sheffield Independent*, 1 January 1875, p. 3.

[32] *Nonconformist*, 17 February 1875, p. 171.

and poor, keen tradesmen, manufacturers, merchants, and young ladies who had just left school, rough boys who knew more about dogs and pigeons than about books, and cultivated women'.[33] Nor was geography a barrier to success; Moody and Sankey's popularity in nonconformist Newcastle may have been understandable, but they then went on to take Presbyterian Edinburgh by storm, to preach to crowds of 20,000 in Roman Catholic Dublin, and to sustain a four-month campaign in London itself. As one historian of revivalism has said, Moody and Sankey had 'a well-nigh universal appeal in the eighteen-seventies'.[34] This has been obscured by the tendency to assume that Victorian society was sharply divided along class lines, and that something popular with the bourgeoisie could not have been popular with the proletariat. Yet it is now becoming clear that the working and middle classes generally thought of themselves as 'the people', united against 'privilege and aristocratic "monopoly"'.[35]

The importance of Moody and Sankey lay in the fact that to contemporaries they were highly visible representatives of 'the people', and their populist style was (to use Rohan McWilliam's phrase about the Tichborne cause) 'gently subversive and evocative of an alternative society'.[36] The heart of this chapter explains why this was so by analysing the language, ritual and ceremony of Moody and Sankey's meetings, and teasing out their symbolic meanings.[37]

III

Any explanation of Moody and Sankey's great popularity must necessarily begin with the publicity for their services. Before they ever arrived in a town, the evangelists had been heralded from the pulpit and in the local press. They cultivated the support of clergy and laity alike, for advertising the meetings involved a great participative effort. Supporters held prayer meetings, organised committees, formed choirs, raised funds

---

[33] *Congregationalist*, March 1875, p. 139. See also the *Daily Telegraph*, 10 March 1875, p. 5.

[34] Weisberger, *Gathered at the River*, p. 176.

[35] E. F. Biagini, *Liberty, Retrenchment and Reform: Popular Liberalism in the Age of Gladstone, 1860–80*, Cambridge, 1992, pp. 11–12; and P. Joyce, *Visions of the People*, pp. 1–84.

[36] R. McWilliam, 'Radicalism and Popular Culture: the Tichborne Cause and the Politics of "fair play", 1867–1886', in Biagini and Reid (eds.), *Currents of Radicalism*, p. 45.

[37] This approach follows the example of a number of scholars, F. O'Gorman, 'Campaign Rituals and Ceremonies: the Social Meaning of Elections in England 1780–1860', *Past and Present*, 135 (1992), pp. 79–115; J. Sperber, 'Festivals of National Unity in the German Revolution of 1848–49', *Past and Present*, 136 (1992), pp. 114–38. For an older study which also pays close attention to political symbolism, see G. L. Mosse, *The Nationalisation of the Masses*, New York, 1975.

and visited every household in the locality. It was hard to avoid knowing about the evangelists. The secularist *National Reformer* complained of the 'large posters, seven feet broad, the patrols of sandwich men and the unlimited advertising'.[38] Traditional Calvinists felt that this betrayed reliance on human method not on divine grace,[39] but Moody was unapologetically pragmatic: 'Some ministers think it undignified to advertise their services. It's a good deal more undignified to preach to empty pews, I think'.[40] The quotation sums up the Moody approach: he valued the masses more than the gentility or culture of a refined church ceremony. The ubiquity of the advertising demonstrated his desire to reach the people, wherever they lived, and whatever their situation in society.

The fact that Moody's meetings were held not in churches, chapels or cathedrals but in great agricultural and city halls is also important. These secular buildings signified that revivalist religion was not to be confused with traditional, intellectual and institutionalised Christendom. They promised a simple, genuine and unencumbered service, and symbolised the plain style of democratic Protestantism.[41] They also offered a great spectacle. To see such vast auditoriums lit by gas chandeliers hanging from the roof, decorated by scarlet banners emblazoned with biblical texts and filled with 10–20,000 people must have been a remarkable sight.[42] Yet more powerful than the spectacle was the ecstasy of community song which turned the audience into a congregation. 'Melody from thousands of human voices sweeps individuals into its swell like the walls of the sea', reported *The Times*.[43] The *Daily Telegraph* used the same imagery: 'the wave of sound rolls round and round the building, forming a very ocean of melody such as may scarcely be imagined'.[44]

This congregational singing was just one feature of the varied and fast-moving programme offered at Moody's meetings. 'There is never any hitch, any awkward pause, any long-drawn monotony in the entertainment', reported the *National Reformer*. 'Solos and choruses, brief prayers,

---

[38] *National Reformer*, 13 June 1875, p. 378.
[39] Two Calvinist ministers wrote critiques of the Moody and Sankey revival stressing this point: J. K. Popham, *Moody and Sankey's Errors versus the Scripture of Truth*, London, 1875; J. Kennedy, *Hyper-Evangelism, 'Another Gospel' though a Mighty Power*, Dingwall, 1875.
[40] Moody, *Moody*, p. 368.
[41] Paul Gifford suggests a similar interpretation of the social meaning of great tents in evangelism. See his '"Africa shall be Saved": An Appraisal of Reinhard Bonnke's Pan-African Crusade', *Journal of Religion in Africa*, 17 (1987), p. 66.
[42] For vivid descriptions of the Agricultural Hall see *Illustrated London News*, 20 March 1875, p. 278; *Graphic*, 20 March 1875, p. 275.
[43] *The Times*, 16 March 1875, p. 9.
[44] *Daily Telegraph*, 10 March 1875, p. 5.

short Bible readings, with racy comments, keep the attention alert.'[45] As another observer pointed out, Moody 'never began to preach until he had gathered his audience into almost perfect rapport with himself. From the time he came before his vast audiences, to the moment when he rose to preach, he kept the entire body absorbingly occupied with something interesting.'[46] Sometimes this could take novel forms. In an Edinburgh meeting a group of black American singers were concealed in the gallery, and at the given signal they rose to surprise the audience with the refrain, 'There are angels watching over you.'[47] The American organ used by Sankey was an equally startling innovation for a staid Edinburgh population who had only recently begun to sing hymns, never mind popular songs. It was too much for one old woman, who rushed out of a meeting shouting, 'Let me oot! Let me oot! What would John Knox think of the like of you?'[48]

Moody's rationale for this approach lay in his belief that the audience was sovereign.[49] Their tastes and values determined the presentation of his message, if not the message itself. 'Men are crying out for variety', he said. 'Well let them have variety; they want it, in everything else they get it; why not in this?'[50] Such faith in the masses is the first article of the populist's creed. A major factor in Gladstone's popularity was his ability to develop a strong rapport with his audiences based on mutual respect.[51]

Yet Moody started out with an advantage Gladstone never had; the revivalist was himself a man of the people. Although contemporaries were often astonished that someone who lacked eloquence, learning and position in society could be so popular,[52] it was precisely because of his ordinariness that Moody had such a wide appeal. He was seen as a plain and unsophisticated man speaking directly and earnestly from the heart. Like his contemporary, William Booth, Moody rarely used words which a child could not understand.[53] He reduced his style to the lowest common denominator. This was highly effective when speaking to groups of working men; as the *Irish Times* commented, 'it is useless to speak in ornate diction' to rough and uncultivated men.[54] The simple language

---

[45] *National Reformer*, 16 May 1875, p. 305.
[46] Quoted from Moody, *Moody*, p. 428.
[47] Kent, *Holding the Fort*, p. 162.
[48] Ira D. Sankey, *Sankey's Story of the Gospel Hymns*, Philadelphia, 1906, p. 26.
[49] On the concept of the sovereign audience see N. Hatch, *The Democratization of American Christianity*, New Haven, 1989, ch. 5.
[50] *Nonconformist*, 27 January 1875, p. 76.
[51] On Gladstone's populism, see R. T. Shannon, *Gladstone and the Bulgarian Agitations*, London, 1963, p. 164.
[52] See for instance *National Reformer*, 21 March 1875, p. 241.
[53] See F. E. Longley, *The Great Revival*, London, 1875, n.p. On Booth see R. Collier, *The General Next to God*, London, 1965, p. 242.
[54] *Irish Times*, 17 November 1874, p. 5.

also served to reinforce Moody's image as a trustworthy, down-to-earth character. The radical working-class *Reynolds News* appreciated Moody because he was 'a rough and ready preacher, who cares not to study the dulcet phrases by which to win over the souls of the rich, but who calls a spade a spade in the plain, honest and straightforward work of preaching the stern teachings of the Gospel.'[55] This commonsense realism appealed to a mass audience which would have been left untouched by a more academic style.[56]

The impression that Moody was a sturdy and reliable chap was reinforced by his physical appearance. The *Graphic* reported: 'Mr. Moody stood forth, a strong-made man of quite John Bull girth of chest, with handsome features and immense brown beard – full of energy, straightforward commonsense, and a momentum that bore down all before it'.[57] Moody was a muscular Christian, the model of mature masculinity. His physical presence obviously had a similar effect to that of the Liberal demagogue, John Bright, whose 'powerful features gave you at first sight an impression of singular force and firmness of character'.[58]

Sankey – though more fashion-conscious – also won people over by the simplicity of his singing. 'Everything is calculated to charm a simpleminded audience', lamented the *National Reformer*. 'The words and tunes are immediately accessible for the songs run and skip to a sort of simple lilt, which the most uncultivated can at once catch and appreciate. There is no depth or subtlety in the simpleness; all that it has to reveal is revealed at first hearing'.[59] Sankey was not concerned to elevate the masses culturally, or to cultivate their aesthetic tastebuds. But his willingness to take the tunes of the music hall and use them for religious worship earned him the affection of millions all over the English-speaking world. Nigel Scotland tells us that 'Sankey's hymns were great favourites with many agricultural labourers', whose union marches through the streets were accompanied by songs like 'God speed the plough' and 'God save Joseph Arch', sung to the tunes of *Sacred Songs and Solos*. They were particularly suited to the working masses because their short choruses were easily memorised by those unable to read.[60]

---

[55] *Reynolds News*, 30 May 1875, p. 4.
[56] On this point see Drummond and Bulloch, *Church in Victorian Scotland*, pp. 10–11. On Moody's meagre formal education see Findlay, *Moody*, pp. 39–41.
[57] *Graphic*, 29 March 1875, p. 275.
[58] See A. Briggs, *Victorian People: A Reassessment of Person and Themes 1851–67*, London, 1954, p. 206.
[59] *National Reformer*, 25 April 1875, p. 261.
[60] N. Scotland, *Methodism and the Revolt of the Field*, Gloucester, 1981, pp. 104–5, 177. For further evidence of Sankey's hymns among farm labourers, see J. W. Robertson Scott, *The Day Before Yesterday: Memories of an Uneducated Man*, London, 1951, p. 92.

The simplicity of the evangelists' approach made them seem natural and homely. Sankey's songs were brimming with domestic imagery, and to John Kent they suggest 'a Heaven which is an everlasting Festival of the United Family'.[61] Like Gladstone and Bright, Moody relied on a minimum of notes and spoke fluently and extempore so that, as R. W. Dale remarked, he talked to thousands 'just as he would to a dozen old friends at the fireside'.[62] His sermons were said to be 'full of Yankee humour',[63] and he had mastered the full range of oratorical techniques:

Argument, satire, ridicule and laughter-provoking fun and frolic, the homeliest of illustrations, the most daring of paradoxes, or the tenderest of pathos, and the most terrible of invective are used unsparingly, as occasion suits, to drive home and to clench the nail of conviction.[64]

Like Sankey, Moody constantly employed imagery and anecdotes from everyday life, particularly such stories about the family 'as would touch the tenderest feelings', as *Reynolds News* put it.[65] Moody reminded Samuel Smith, later to become a Liberal MP, of Abraham Lincoln, another 'home spun genius'.[66]

A vital aspect of this genius was Moody's ability to spin a good yarn. His great repertoire of stories made his preaching fascinating. One of his typical sermons had the following subheadings: A Touching Chicago Story, The Loss of a Child, the Poor Drunkard, Rowland Hill and Lady Erskine, The Boy and the Dark Mountain.[67] He had the gift of telling these stories with great vividness. When relating a tale of a preacher who was searching for his runaway son, he had the crowd following the preacher's every move with bated breath, and when the preacher finally found his son in San Francisco, there was 'a sigh of relief amongst the ladies'. Moody brought his sermon to a climax by pointing to the crowd and calling in a high voice on backsliders to 'come home to God'.[68] He had translated Christ's parable of the prodigal son into modern idiom. 'The Oriental drapery was stripped off', said Dale, 'and he told stories as if they had happened in Chicago just before he had left home, or in Birmingham an hour or two before the service began'.[69] Moody brought the stories of the bible down to earth and up to date, often taking great

---

[61] Kent, *Holding the Fort*, p. 230.
[62] *Congregationalist*, March 1875, pp. 139–40.
[63] *Vanity Fair Album*, 3 April 1875.
[64] *Graphic*, 17 April 1875, p. 379.
[65] *Reynolds News*, 21 March 1875, p. 2.
[66] S. Smith, *My Life Work*, London, 1902, pp. 92–3. Lincoln had visited Moody's Sunday School in Chicago in 1860 (Weisberger, *Gathered at the River*, p. 187).
[67] Moody, *London Discourses*, London, 1875, pp. 18–25.
[68] *Reynolds News*, 21 March 1875, p. 2.
[69] *Congregationalist*, March 1875, p. 142.

liberties with the text. He treated his audience to an imaginary conversation between Bartimaeus and Zaccheus, introducing them to 'Mrs Bartimaeus'[70] and assuring them that Moses was given a blank cheque on heaven by the Lord.[71]

To critics this blurred the distinction between the sacred and the profane, secularising and vulgarising religion. The assumption lying behind the criticism was that only classical art could properly express the sublime and the transcendent; vulgar commercial images, homely anecdotes, and popular music only cheapened spirituality. Yet, as Malcolm Bull has argued with reference to American evangelicalism, 'the paradoxical union of the inconsequential and the theological ... can be seen, not as a trivialisation of traditional Christianity by consumerism, but as a sacralisation of popular culture'.[72] Sankey's singing took the tunes of the music hall and devoted them to a religious purpose and Moody proudly affirmed the dignity of the plain, simple and unornamented things of life. He rejected the idea that Samson should have used 'a more polished and finished weapon' than the jawbone of an ass, and reminded his listeners that the Israelites marched round Jericho with rams' horns, not horns of gold or silver.[73]

None of this was, of course, completely novel. Moody's sermons were described as 'pseudo-Spurgeonesque',[74] or in the words of *Punch*, 'an exaggeration of that jocular species of pulpit oration' brought into vogue by the great Baptist preacher, C. H. Spurgeon.[75] As David Bebbington has recently shown, Spurgeon was one of the most articulate English defenders of the claims of the people against the elite. The parallels with Moody are numerous: Spurgeon celebrated the qualities of the common man, despised high culture, praised robust manliness, denounced the Church of England and the Conservative Party, admired the egalitarianism of the United States, and was attacked for his vulgarity by Matthew Arnold.[76] He stood consciously in the tradition of the greatest of seventeenth century 'mechanick preachers', John Bunyan, a man to whom Moody was also compared.[77] Both Spurgeon and Moody tapped into a

[70] *Birmingham Daily Post*, 19 January 1875, p. 8.
[71] *Daily Telegraph*, 10 March 1875, p. 5.
[72] M. Bull, 'Hot Dogs', *London Review of Books*, 14 June 1990, pp. 24–5.
[73] *Daily Telegraph*, 10 March 1875, p. 5.
[74] A London Physician, *Emotional Goodness, or Moody and Sankey Reviewed*, London, 1875, p. 23.
[75] *Punch*, 20 March 1875, p. 173. On his first visit to England Moody had heard Spurgeon preach at the Agricultural Hall, little knowing that he would one day preach there himself. See C. Ray, *Life of C. H. Spurgeon*, London, 1903, p. 401.
[76] See D. W. Bebbington, 'Spurgeon and the Common Man', *Baptist Review of Theology*, to appear.
[77] See for example the *Liverpool Mercury*, 3 February 1874, p. 6.

long and venerable British–American tradition of popular preaching, and their style resonated deeply with listeners who had been raised on *The Pilgrim's Progress*.[78] Both men stood as contemporary champions of the Puritan 'plain style' over against the Laudian 'beauty of holiness'. They favoured a religious form that was democratic and egalitarian, as opposed to one which was hierarchical and sacerdotal.

This is not to deny that the evangelicalism of Moody and Spurgeon was an irreducibly religious phenomenon. The deepest motivation of these preachers came from their belief that through their preaching people would come to believe in Christ and gain eternal salvation. Yet the way in which this spiritual message was presented had social significance. Moody's theology, like his style, was simple and anti-intellectual. Someone once told him that they did not believe in his theology. 'My theology', Moody retorted, 'I didn't know I had any!'[79] He always claimed to stick by the three R's: 'Ruin by Sin, Redemption by Christ, and Regeneration by the Holy Ghost.'[80] This stripped-down kerygma was proclaimed by Moody with great earnestness, the characteristic most often attributed to him. 'Mr Moody is successful in drawing the people', declared *Reynolds News*, 'because he has something to say which he believes for himself, and the people will always listen to an intensely earnest man'.[81]

No doubt the people also listened because the doctrines of original sin and redemption by grace had an attractively egalitarian thrust. 'There is no difference', Moody declared, 'none between lords, dukes or beggars. The ministers present and the greatest drunkards that walk the streets of London [are] the same. It is only through Christ that they [can] be saved'.[82] The *Daily Telegraph* felt that Moody's message of Christ's love for each individual brought home to every listener 'a sense of personal worth, and proclaimed the equality of the poor with the rich'.[83]

This message – in contrast to its form – was traditional, even old-fashioned. Moody continued to teach that on the cross Christ had borne the punishment which sinners deserved, even though this doctrine was widely regarded as outmoded. John Kent argues that such doctrinal traditionalism fitted with the social conservatism of people who 'recoiled at the sight of the new democracy, urban, multitudinous, industrialized',

---

[78] On Bunyan's importance to working-class radicals see Biagini, *Liberty, Retrenchment and Reform*, p. 37.
[79] R. Hofstadter, *Anti-intellectualism in American Life*, London, 1964, p. 108.
[80] W. S. Hudson, *Religion in America*, New York, 1965, p. 223.
[81] *Reynolds News*, 21 March 1875, p. 1.
[82] *Daily Telegraph*, 23 March 1875, p. 3.
[83] *Daily Telegraph*, 26 May 1875, p. 5.

and denounced 'the vulgarity, lack of standards, and materialism of the new mass civilisation'.[84] But, as David Martin points out, religion which is theologically 'backwards' can also be sociologically advanced.[85] Moody may have recoiled at intellectual modernity, but his revivalism fitted perfectly with the age of mass democracy.[86] He succeeded precisely because of his dogmatic certainties and stark polarities. He preached sermons with titles like 'Saved or Lost: The One Alternative'.[87] Critics believed that as a result 'Truths of wide and mysterious import are narrowed and hardened'.[88] Yet Moody's dogmatism, like that of Bright – whom mid-Victorian intellectuals also found distasteful – lay at the heart of his popularity.[89] 'Mr Moody calls unhesitatingly to this struggling, confused mass to follow him', reported *The Times*, 'and he is obeyed'.[90] Those who did adapt their theology to modern intellectual trends, by contrast, were often incapable of reaching the proverbial man in the street, because their love of paradox and ambiguity made them appear 'wishy-washy'. As *Reynolds News* expressed it, 'Milk and water expounders of Christianity are undesirable at the present crisis'.[91]

Moody's old-fashioned dogmatism rested on biblical literalism. He was hostile to modern biblical criticism, believing wholeheartedly in the literal nature of Noah's universal flood. A letter to *The Times* remarked that he seemed to hold to the verbal inspiration of the present English translation of the Bible.[92] Behind this biblicism lay a populist logic. If, as scholars claimed, Scripture was a highly complex and ambiguous text, its interpretation would need to be placed in the hands of experts who possessed the requisite linguistic and exegetical skills. Moody was utterly opposed to this. For him the meaning of Scripture was plain and accessible to all. He worried that biblical criticism was taking the Bible away from the people. It certainly added unnecessary complications. 'Many Americans don't know there's one Isaiah', he was fond of saying in his later years, 'why bother them about two?'[93] Such fundamentalist liter-

---

[84] Kent, *Holding the Fort*, pp. 222–4, 204.

[85] D. Martin, *Tongues of Fire: The Explosion of Protestantism in Latin America*, London, 1990, p. 107.

[86] Ironically it is Kent himself who recoils from 'the new mass civilisation', for he clearly deplores Moody and Sankey's vulgarity, their attempt to democratise religious experience and their 'materialistic picture of heaven' (see *Holding the Fort*, pp. 178, 212–14, 225).

[87] Moody, *London Discourses*, pp. 18–25.

[88] *The Times*, 16 March 1875, p. 9.

[89] Asa Briggs writes: 'Mid-Victorian intellectuals could forgive anything except unbounded self-confidence; they liked doubt, for doubt was evidence of subtlety. They profoundly distrusted Bright, who appeared never to have had a doubt in his life' (*Victorian People*, pp. 206–7).

[90] *The Times*, 16 July 1875, p. 4.

[91] *Reynolds News*, 30 May 1875, p. 4.

[92] *The Times*, 19 July 1875, p. 4.

[93] Quoted by J. Harries, *G. Campbell Morgan*, New York, 1930, p. 160.

alism may have been anti-intellectual, but it was also anti-authoritarian. As Nathan Hatch suggests, it allied to the Protestant doctrine of *sola scriptura* a 'popular hermeneutics' which asserted the right of every layman or woman to read and interpret Scripture for themselves.[94]

Thus although the form of Moody and Sankey's revivalism was strikingly modern, and its content traditional, both can be seen as populist. Moody and Sankey were backing the masses against the classes. They suggested to listeners a society in which popular tastes were esteemed and respected, one which was not dominated by the genteel and sophisticated aristocracy. It was for this reason that popular publications often portrayed Moody and Sankey as champions of the common people, and compared their plain style with the obfuscations of elites. *Lloyd's Weekly* contrasted the 'plain speaking from the heart' of Moody with the 'vast array of scholarly precedents, instances and syllogisms' employed by Gladstone.[95] Moody was also contrasted with the learned clergy. Although he cultivated clergy support for his campaign, he also inadvertently encouraged anti-clericalism.[96] With a carnivalesque delight in the inversion of social order, *Reynolds News* declared: 'There are two men in London now who are doing the work of fifty bishops. The old, old truth which Mr Moody the evangelist comes to proclaim, attracts thousands of people who are tired of the feeble, inane services of the Church'.[97] This anti-clericalism was particularly evident in Scotland, where the simple theology of Moody was contrasted to the labyrinthine complexity of Calvinist orthodoxy,[98] and the evangelist's use of lay Christians was compared with the clerical domination in the Presbyterian establishment. One letter to the *Glasgow Herald* suggested that clerical attacks on Moody and Sankey were simply 'the old cry raised long ago at Ephesus, "Our craft is in danger"'.[99]

To these laypeople, Moody was a type of the common man, unlearned and unordained, but more effective than the religious experts. It was only to be expected that the American evangelists would be sneered at by 'the

---

[94] N. Hatch, *The Democratization of American Christianity*, pp. 179–83. As Alister McGrath explains, the 'magisterial' reformers emphasised the importance of church tradition in order to minimise the radical democratic implications of the *sola scriptura* principle (McGrath, *Reformation Thought: an Introduction*, Oxford, 1988, pp. 106–9).

[95] *Lloyd's Weekly*, 4 April 1875, p. 6. Had *Lloyd's* been comparing the two men a year later during the Bulgarian Agitations, it may have pointed out the similarities between their styles.

[96] Even Kent and McLoughlin, who stress Moody's conservatism, concede this point. See Kent, *Holding the Fort*, p. 162 and McLoughlin, *Modern Revivalism*, p. 207.

[97] *Reynolds News*, 21 March 1875, p. 1.

[98] *Scotsman*, 18 December 1873, p. 6.

[99] *Glasgow Herald*, 3 March 1874, p. 7. See also 28 February 1874, p. 3. This runs counter to Biagini's claim that in Scotland anti-clericalism was 'much less pronounced' than south of the border (*Liberty, Retrenchment and Reform*, p. 218).

excruciatingly aristocratic journals hired to sneer at everything which comes from or concerns the people'.[100] 'The high class ungodly' and 'West End sinners' disliked Moody's 'vigorous style of exposing hateful hypocrisy and open vice', thought *Reynolds News*, 'because they did not want the nature of their misdeeds laid bare'.[101] In a similar vein the *Sheffield Independent* reported that 'hundreds of dainty young men' had stopped coming to Moody's meetings because they were 'shocked by the Yankee slang, and aghast at the lack of refinement' in the preacher.[102] The rhetoric used here is revealing. Moody is 'vigorous', the young gentlemen 'dainty'. He 'exposes' and 'lays bare' sin, whereas the young men presumably want a gospel dressed up to suit their delicate tastes. He is bold and direct, they are fastidious. Moody, in short, is a real man, his critics decidedly effeminate.

The ultimate proof of the genteel classes' aversion to the vulgar Moody was the storm provoked by the revivalists' proposed visit to Eton College. When the matter was debated in the Lords, the Labour *Bee-Hive* attacked the 'superannuated fogies' who were shocked by the evangelists' audacity.[103] *Reynolds News* was equally dismissive of 'the old ladies – we beg pardon, the noble Lords'.[104] *The Times* felt that a revivalist service at Eton would be seen as 'imprudent', something to 'boast of in the lower ranks of the religious world', and 'printed with a sneer against learned and sleepy dignitaries'.[105] This is precisely what happened in the United States, where the press portrayed the evangelists 'as plain men ... to whom eventually even the upper classes had to listen – a victory for people's religion, so to speak, over the "dead forms" of high churchmen and nobles'.[106] In Britain, too, as the evidence above suggests, Moody and Sankey were regarded by many plebeian radicals as champions of popular culture against aristocratic privilege and control.

IV

Moody and Sankey's elite critics also saw the radical social implications of the revival movement, but for them this was a source of concern, not of delight. We should, of course, be aware of an element of polemical exaggeration in their criticisms; opponents of evangelical religion traditionally stressed its radical and disruptive elements and ignored its

---

[100] *Reynolds News*, 21 March 1875, p. 1.
[101] *Reynolds News*, 30 May 1875, p. 4.
[102] *Sheffield Independent*, 18 January 1875, p. 3.
[103] *Bee-Hive*, 26 June 1875, p. 10.
[104] *Reynolds News*, 27 June 1875, p. 5.
[105] *The Times*, 22 June 1875.
[106] Sizer, *Gospel Hymns and Social Religion*, p. 215.

socially conservative side.[107] Nevertheless, when set alongside the support given to Moody by a radical republican newspaper like *Reynolds News*, the critics' worries do not seem so unfounded. Both friend and foe regarded the evangelists as representatives of a new kind of society, and challengers of the traditional order. The rhetoric of the revivalists' critics reveals a fear of both fragmentation and levelling. We shall deal with each of these in turn.

Critics believed that revivalism would result in fragmentation and disruption in the lives of individuals, the church and the nation. At the core this was a concern about the fissiparous enthusiasm for which revivalism was notorious. 'The sensational style of excitement like the revivals is not the religion that can last', thought Queen Victoria, 'and it is not, I think, wholesome for the mind or heart'.[108] Others went further, portraying the revival meetings in utterly hyperbolic terms as veritable Bacchanalian feasts. The *Daily Telegraph* claimed that Moody and Sankey knew how 'to stir a mass of people into a frenzy',[109] and the *Saturday Review* talked of 'blatant orgies of ignorant zeal'.[110]

Such enthusiasm was thought by critics to lead to irrationalism. Moody and Sankey were 'abbots of unreason', 'crack-brained American evangelists'.[111] It was said that the board of guardians in charge of a Salford lunatic asylum were so used to cases of religious mania following the evangelists' meetings in Manchester, that when confronted by a new victim they exclaimed: 'What, another Moody and Sankey!'[112] Women were felt to be particularly susceptible to the emotional and mental instability caused by enthusiasm. Revivalism 'appealed more strongly to the more impressionable sex', said the *Pall Mall Gazette*,[113] and according to the *World* magazine, the evangelists had had 'the satisfaction of throwing females into convulsions'.[114]

Such accusations had been made against many previous revival movements.[115] But as the Jacobs have pointed out, 'The tumult that horrified

---

[107] This point has been made by James Henretta in M. Jacob and J. Jacob (eds.), *The Origins of Anglo-American Radicalism*, London, 1984, pp. 270–1.

[108] Queen Victoria, *Letters 1862–78*, vol. II, edited by G. E. Buckle, London, 1926, p. 386.

[109] *Daily Telegraph*, 22 June 1875, p. 5.

[110] *Saturday Review*, 6 March 1875, pp. 311–12.

[111] These quotations are from Moody, *Moody*, p. 210.

[112] *Pall Mall Gazette*, 1 March 1875, p. 804. Individual instances of this 'religious mania' were reported in *Lloyd's Weekly*, 14 March 1875, p. 10, and the *National Reformer*, 9 May 1875, p. 299.

[113] *Pall Mall Gazette*, 20 July 1875, pp. 267–8.

[114] Quoted in Moody, *Moody*, p. 29. Moody's friends may have contrasted his manliness with the effeminacy of his 'gentlemen' opponents, but his critics saw themselves as guardians of male rationality against female enthusiasm.

[115] They were raised in the 1859–60 revival and during the Great Awakening in the United States for instance. See J. E. Orr, *The Second Evangelical Awakening*, London, 1949, p. 177, and D. Lovejoy, '"Desperate Enthusiasm": Early Signs of American Radicalism', in Jacob and Jacob (eds.), *Origins of Anglo-American Radicalism*, pp. 231–9.

conservatives betokened a strategic shift in the centre of control rather than a breakdown of order'.[116] Moody and Sankey's revivalism, whilst more restrained than earlier varieties, seemed to signify 'a strategic shift in the centre of control' from traditional elites to the ordinary people.

Anti-intellectualism was another feature of Moody and Sankey's religious style which worried critics. As *The Times* noted, Moody appealed to the heart rather than the head.[117] The *Spectator* felt that revivalists considered lack of learning 'a positive advantage in the region of faith'.[118] Liberal churchmen sought a *via media* between evangelical fervour and secular scepticism. 'The maintenance of old dogmas will make men fanatical revivalists or mere atheists', suggested one Unitarian. 'Is there no hope for rational religion?'[119] Yet liberal theologians were to find themselves caught in a no man's land between secular culture and popular Christianity, dismissed by the former as irrelevant and by the latter as compromised. While they sought unsuccessfully to make Christianity credible to 'modern man' (that is, to other intellectuals), evangelists like Moody demonstrated that religion could still be popular with the modern masses.

Added to the claim that revivalism emphasised the heart above the head was the charge that it stressed grace at the expense of law. By emphasising that divine grace and faith in Christ could work instantaneous conversion it seemed to be downplaying the importance of a lifetime of ethical endeavour. To his critics, Moody seemed to be presenting conversion as a 'temporary outbreak of excited feeling'.[120] One London minister drew attention to the antinomian chorus of a Sankey song: '"Doing" is a deadly thing/"Doing" ends in death'.[121] Ireland's Cardinal Cullen circulated a pastoral letter condemning the 'itinerant preachers or singers who have endeavoured to do away with good works and the necessity of baptism, promising to save men by leaning on the Lord and by a foolish sensationalism without requiring them to be sorry for their sins'.[122]

Moody's evangelical conversionism was, therefore, perceived as a threat to the moralism and sacramentalism of more traditional Christianity. 'I care nothing for baptism', Moody had declared, 'nothing for mere churchgoing. These are all right as far as they go, but you must

[116] Jacob and Jacob, *Origins of Anglo-American Radicalism*, p. 10.
[117] *The Times*, 16 March 1875, p. 9.
[118] *Spectator*, 13 March 1875, p. 334.
[119] *Glasgow Herald*, 7 March 1874, p. 3.
[120] *Saturday Review*, 6 March 1875, pp. 311–12.
[121] Letter to *The Times*, 22 June 1875, p. 8.
[122] Quoted in the *Liverpool Mercury*, 16 February 1875, p. 8.

go beyond them for the new birth'.[123] Such pronouncements led the *Saturday Review* to state that if Moody was right, then ordinary church services were a 'melancholy delusion', and ought to be at once 'superseded by something more lively and stimulating in the new style'.[124] Others urged that since Moody and Sankey were actually quite misguided, religious life should be restored as quickly and quietly as possible to 'its normal condition under the faithful exercise of pastoral oversight'.[125] But supporters of Moody and Sankey hailed them for breaking 'the neck of old Formality';[126] the churches had seen 'their traditions broken into and their forms thrown to the wind'.[127] To use Weberian terminology, the charismatic, sect-type religion of Moody and Sankey was challenging the traditional, bureaucratic and hierarchical church-type religion of the Anglican establishment.

In their worst nightmares critics feared that if it became too popular, revivalism could fragment the religious life of the nation, turning Britain into an American-style religious supermarket, characterised by the absence of an established church and a vast plurality of sects. Lord Bath disparagingly labelled the evangelists 'unlicensed vendors of religious wares',[128] displaying typical aristocratic contempt for unordained preachers and the unregulated free market in religion which produced them. The *World* envisaged a full-scale invasion of Britain by an army of American Moody and Sankeys peddling their hard-sell Gospel:

> If the clerks in American stores, and nigger minstrels who have lost their voices, are once taught that they have only to come over to England, and profess themselves to be 'evangelists' in order to be feted and adulated, the whole country will be overrun by these pestilential vermin. We shall have 'experiences' and convulsions in every village.[129]

The aversion to American revivalistic pluralism was most clearly seen in the Eton College case. Moody and Sankey's plan to visit the college was seen as a presumptuous challenge to the monopoly of the established church over religious education there. Contemporaries were concerned that if the two evangelists were allowed to preach, then there would be no good reason to refuse any group which felt it had an important message for the boys.[130] *Punch* caricatured the concern by printing a Public

---

[123] Quoted in Kent, *Holding the Fort*, p. 179.
[124] *Saturday Review*, 20 March 1875, pp. 374–5.
[125] *Glasgow Herald*, 27 February 1875.
[126] Quoted in the *Saturday Review*, 6 March 1875, p. 311.
[127] *The Times*, 16 July 1875, p. 4.
[128] *Daily Telegraph*, 22 June 1875, p. 4.
[129] Quoted in A London Physician, *Emotional Goodness*, p. 22.
[130] *The Times*, 21 June 1875, p. 9.

Schools Mission Calendar which listed as the speakers for the month of July, the Cardinal Archbishop of Westminster, Rabbi Moses Aaron Ben Israel Solomons, Brigham Young, Mr Bradlaugh, a prophet of the Peculiar People and a deputation from the Free Lovers.[131] The caricature was not amusing to many upper-class Englishmen loyal to the Church of England. Nonconformity was bad enough, but the prospect of England becoming like the United States was unthinkable.

The fear of fragmentation and disruption was joined in the minds of Moody and Sankey's critics with an antipathy to the levelling consequences of American populism. Cultured despisers of popular religion accused it of dragging religion down to the level of the common crowd, instead of using religion to elevate and educate the masses. The *Saturday Review* labelled the revival, 'this movement for the degradation of religion'.[132] A letter in the *Pall Mall Gazette* claimed that Moody and Sankey had to 'stoop to conquer', and were willing to do so because they 'deem that what is sacred can only affect a crowd when degraded to their level'.[133] To put it in one word, the evangelists were 'vulgar'.

Central to their vulgarity was their readiness to juxtapose the sacred and the profane. The Anglican *Record* found Moody's story of 'the man who lost his dog and found his Saviour', 'so painfully revolting as to border on blasphemy'.[134] *Punch* also commented on this paradoxically earthy treatment of the heavenly:

> Their manner seems strangely at odds with their matter,
>   The former grotesque, most serious the latter,
> They proclaim Gospel truths, spite of grave prepossessions,
>   In colloquial slang and commercial expressions,
> State Scriptural truths in American phrases,
>   And interpolate jokes twixt their prayers and their praises.
> The intent is sincere – let us trust in all charity –
>   But religion they cloak in the garb of vulgarity,
> And, under a guise of seeming profanity,
>   As comic evangelists preach Christianity.[135]

The puzzlement of Moody and Sankey's elite critics over the expression of religious truths through the medium of popular culture was symptomatic of their low opinion of the masses themselves.[136] Bernard Shaw

---

[131] *Punch*, 3 July 1875, p. 283.
[132] *Saturday Review*, 22 June 1875, p. 809.
[133] *Pall Mall Gazette*, 11 March 1875, p. 947.
[134] Quoted in Kent, *Holding the Fort*, p. 143.
[135] *Punch*, 20 March 1875, p. 123.
[136] As John Carey has observed, intellectuals have a tendency to believe that religious feeling can only be expressed in high cultural forms. See his *The Intellectuals and the Masses: Pride and Prejudice among the Literary Intelligentsia, 1880–1939*, London, 1992, pp. 82–90.

wrote that 'the unreasoning mind of the people' only appreciated Moody because he had 'the gift of the gab'. As one of his biographers notes, Shaw was already sounding 'the aristocratic and anti-democratic note which is to be found in all his work'.[137] The hymn-writer John Ellerton was equally disparaging about the preferences of the masses: 'Is our chief care to be that the tunes are pretty and popular, and the words something that will go with a swing? Are we thus to sanction the trash which, alas, will find its way even into good hymn books?'[138]

Ironically, similar remarks are also to be found in the secularist *National Reformer*, read mainly by men from the working and middle classes. The revivalists' audiences were said to be composed of 'the most ignorant, the most superstitious, the weakest and the most credulous; the hysterical and the unthinking'.[139] Sankey's hymns were 'jumping choruses, full of the repetitions which children and negroes and the like underdeveloped creatures love'. It was hardly surprising that these tunes were so popular since 'the mass of the public is just about on a level with the child and the negro'.[140] Freethinkers clearly regarded themselves as independent rationalists who had raised themselves above the level of the superstitious mass of mankind. Moody's religion degraded men whilst rationalism elevated them. Charles Bradlaugh disagreed with Mill's belief that religion could have an elevating and poetic effect on men: 'Where is the elevation or poetry of a Moody and Sankey revival?'[141]

The contrast between Moody and Sankey's populist conception of religion and the elitist views of their critics was particularly evident in the debate over the 'Inquiry Room', in which anxious souls were counselled after Moody's meetings, usually by laymen. Archbishop Tait felt that this counselling must often be 'crude'; 'the delicate and difficult duty of this ministry' ought not to be left to laypeople.[142] Perhaps he was right, but as David Martin has remarked, vulgarity is 'the price of religious democracy'.[143] The Inquiry Room was another example of the way in which Moody's revivalism empowered the common people and dethroned religious elites.

---

[137] St J. G. Ervine, *Bernard Shaw: His Life, Work and Friends*, London, 1956, pp. 51–3. John Carey has recently described Shaw as 'a sentimental pseudo-Nietzschean who disparaged the democratic electorate' (*The Intellectuals and the Masses*, pp. 62–3).

[138] *Church Congress Report*, London, 1875, p. 588. More recently Erik Routley has dismissed Sankey's songs as the 'crude ... music of backwoodsmen' (*The Music of Christian Hymnody*, London, 1957, p. 132).

[139] *National Reformer*, 18 April 1875, p. 241.

[140] *National Reformer*, 25 April 1875, p. 261.

[141] *National Reformer*, 9 May 1875, p. 301.

[142] *Daily Telegraph*, 26 May 1875, p. 5.

[143] Martin, *Tongues of Fire*, p. 41.

V

Moody and Sankey's critics and supporters, therefore, did not regard the evangelists as social conservatives. On the contrary, they were widely seen as disruptive populists who presented a challenge to the British *status quo*. That this was so should not really surprise us. In the first place, there had been a long alliance in Britain between enthusiastic popular religion and political radicalism, stretching back to the Scottish and English Revolutions of the seventeenth century. In a pamphlet like *The Scotch Presbyterian Eloquence* (1692), an Episcopalian attack on Presbyterianism, we find exactly the same charges as were levelled at Moody – emotionalism, irrationality, antinomianism, vulgarity and political radicalism. Biagini has demonstrated the importance of the seventeenth-century heritage to plebeian radicals,[144] and it seems that part of Moody and Sankey's attraction derived from these historical associations.

Added to this was the evangelists' association with the United States, where 'the dynamics of unopposed revivalism'[145] had resulted in what Nathan Hatch calls 'the democratisation of American Christianity'.[146] Daniel Walker Howe has observed that 'In both the eighteenth and nineteenth centuries, revivalism and democracy were interrelated phenomena. Each asserted popular claims against those of the elite, pluralism against orthodoxy, charisma against rationalism, competitiveness against authority, an innovative Americanism against European tradition'.[147] Moody and Sankey were part of this revivalist tradition, and it is for this reason above all that the British saw them as bearers of democratic promise. Radical liberals in the 1870s still looked to the United States for inspiration.[148] *Reynolds News*, for instance, published an article on 'American independence and English snobbism', hailing the American Revolution as 'perhaps the greatest event in the political history of mankind', and condemning the aristocratic snobbishness which it

---

[144] Biagini, *Liberty, Retrenchment and Reform*, pp. 41–6.

[145] The phrase is George Marsden's ('Fundamentalism as an American phenomenon: a comparison with English Evangelicalism', *Church History*, 46 (1977), p. 225).

[146] Hatch, *The Democratization of American Christianity, passim*. See also the important statistical studies of R. Stark and R. Finke, 'How the Upstart Sects Won America', *Journal for the Scientific Study of Religion*, 28 (1989), pp. 27–44; and R. Finke, 'Religious Deregulation: Origins and Consequences', *Journal of Church and State*, 32 (1990), pp. 609–26.

[147] D. W. Howe, 'Religion and Politics in the Antebellum North', in M. Noll (ed.), *Religion and American Politics: from the Colonial Period to the 1980s*, Oxford, 1990, pp. 125–6.

[148] See H. Pelling, *America and the British Left from Bright to Bevan*, London, 1956, pp. 1–48; and Biagini, *Liberty, Retrenchment and Reform*, pp. 69–83. For the development of a more critical attitude towards the United States see H. A. Tulloch, 'Changing British Attitudes towards the United States in the 1880s', *Historical Journal*, 20 (1977), pp. 825–40.

believed had a crippling effect on British national life. To *Reynolds News* Moody and Sankey exemplified the virtues of that democratic and egalitarian society: 'They powerfully illustrate the kind of individual confidence that renders the American Union what it is'.[149] The debate over Moody and Sankey was not merely about the merits of populism in religion, but also about the future direction of British society.

The revivalists' critics feared that Britain was moving in the direction of the United States, where pluralism and vulgarity seemed to reign supreme. It was Matthew Arnold who presented the most persuasive critique of the fragmentation and levelling which were thought to be characteristic of Moody and Sankey's American revivalism. As a Coleridgean, Arnold was a firm believer in the value of an elite – the 'clerisy' – who could raise the masses to 'sweetness and light' and bring cultural homogeneity to society. Moody and Sankey's populism undermined elitism, their vulgarity did nothing at all for 'sweetness and light', and the fissiparous nature of revivalistic religion threatened cultural homogeneity. Arnold had been concerned about populism since the 1840s, when he wrote: 'I see a wave of more than American vulgarity, moral, intellectual and social, preparing to break over us'.[150] Moody and Sankey were prime examples of this vulgarity. Their biblical literalism turned the Bible into a 'materialistic fairy tale',[151] and rather than elevating the tastes of the masses, revivalism uncritically endorsed their present position. 'Our people are very good at following their conscience', Arnold wrote. 'Where they are not so good is in ascertaining whether their conscience tells them right'.[152] The clear implication was that 'our people' needed guidance from wise souls like Arnold himself.

The *Saturday Review* wholeheartedly agreed, and made a direct connection between the American revivalists and the Americanisation of politics which Britain had been experiencing since the 1867 Reform Act ushered in the age of mass politics: 'it is possible that even some of those who are not indisposed to see our political institutions Americanised may find it prudent to hesitate before subjecting the religious habits and traditions of this country to a similar transformation'.[153]

The culprits hinted darkly at here were nonconformist politicians like Joseph Chamberlain and John Bright who both wished to see Britain conform to the American model in religion and politics. Chamberlain

---

[149] *Reynolds News*, 14 March 1875, p. 5.
[150] Matthew Arnold, *Letters: 1848–1888*, vol. I, edited by G. Russell, London, 1895, p. 4.
[151] Arnold, 'God and the Bible', in his *Complete Prose Works*, vol. VII, Ann Arbor, 1970, p. 372.
[152] Arnold, 'Emerson', in his *Complete Prose Works*, vol. X, Ann Arbor, 1974, p. 179.
[153] *Saturday Review*, 6 March 1875, p. 312; also 20 March 1875, p. 374.

was aware that 'cultured persons find the society there is vulgar; less agreeable to the delicate tastes of delicately trained minds', but as Peter Clarke writes, 'he judged it preferable for the ordinary worker, and his earnest hope of moving along similar lines in Britain was undeniable'.[154] However, as a Unitarian, Chamberlain was no supporter of the evangelicals Moody and Sankey, criticising their revivalism as 'theological dram-drinking'.[155] This aversion to evangelical fervour was to render him incapable of wooing the nonconformist conscience. He shared with academic liberals an anti-populism which saw mass enthusiasm as dangerously irrational and vulnerable to authoritarianism.[156]

John Bright – who once had lunch with Moody[157] – was by contrast a full-blooded populist and an ardent admirer of the United States. In January 1875, Moody vacated the Bingley Hall in Birmingham for one evening to allow Bright to address his constituents. Rather appropriately, Bright spoke in praise of disestablishment, which he claimed had allowed true religion in America to blow freely like the wind.[158] According to Asa Briggs, Bright 'had no respect for the traditional deference structure of English society' and 'appeared to be anxious to substitute in its place a society not unlike America. Democratising English parliamentary institutions was merely one aspect of a bigger assault on English society'.[159]

Moody and Sankey, therefore, came to Britain at a time when radicals were still attacking the evils of hierarchy and aristocratic privilege, and when the nonconformist conscience was at its most sensitive. Their earnestness, egalitarianism and enthusiasm resonated deeply with mid-Victorian crowds. As Patrick Joyce points out, the great political agitations of the 1860s and 1870s were characterised by a 'moral populism' infused with religious zeal.[160] Eugenio Biagini's chapter in this collection (chapter 1 above) shows that even the sceptical philosopher, J. S. Mill, was an exponent of populist politics. This was not a new phenomenon, of course. Ian Bradley has argued that the significance of William Wilberforce lies partly in the fact that he taught politicians to see campaigns as righteous crusades against the powers of darkness. Richard Cobden learned from the anti-slavery movement that if 'a moral and even

[154] P. Clarke, *A Question of Leadership*, London, 1991, pp. 63–5.
[155] A. Mackintosh, *Joseph Chamberlain: an Honest Biography*, London, 1906, p. 385.
[156] Cf. Parry, *Democracy and Religion*, p. 224.
[157] K. Robbins, *John Bright*, London, 1979, p. 220.
[158] *Daily Telegraph*, 27 January 1875, p. 4.
[159] A. Briggs, *Victorian People*, p. 207.
[160] P. Joyce, *Visions of the People: Industrial England and the Question of Class, 1848–1914*, Cambridge, 1991, ch. 3. On the moral populism of the Tichborne cause see M. Roe, *Kenealy and the Tichborne Cause: A Study in Mid-Victorian Populism*, Melbourne, 1974, esp. ch. 7.

a religious spirit' could be infused into his campaign against the Corn Laws, it would be 'irresistible'.[161] In the United States too, as the recent work of Richard Cawardine has demonstrated, there was an intimate connection between evangelicalism and the forms of political election-eering. Politicians were well aware that the moral earnestness and religious enthusiasm of the revivalist tradition could be channelled into political campaigning to powerful effect.[162]

It is hardly surprising, then, that contemporary critics of Moody and Sankey's revivalism recognised its affinity with political agitations. When Samuel Plimsoll was roused to righteous indignation in parliament over Disraeli's decision to drop the bill to introduce safety legislation for merchant shipping, the Prime Minister dismissed him as 'a Moody and Sankey in politics', due to his 'enthusiasm' and lack of decorum.[163] The American evangelists were condemned along with the spokesmen of the Tichborne cause for exciting their followers 'to abandon sober reason for the pleasures of violent emotion'.[164] Matthew Arnold's criticisms of Gladstone's populist campaigns in the late 1870s also clearly echoed his condemnation of Moody and Sankey. The comparison made by these critics was a valid one, for the evangelists were doing for religion what Bright and Gladstone were doing for politics; they were taking it from its sacred buildings and offering it to the urban masses.

However, the parallels run deeper, for many of those who supported Moody and Sankey were often also involved in the great political agitations of this period. Three of Moody's most prominent supporters, C. H. Spurgeon, R. W. Dale and Lord Shaftesbury, also backed the Plimsoll campaign.[165] Samuel Smith, later to become a Liberal MP, first became politically involved when he joined the Bulgarian Agitations after helping to organise Moody's Liverpool meetings.[166] The Agricultural Labourers Union set its songs to the tunes of Sankey,[167] and Plimsoll himself was moved to tears when his cousin sang to him the singularly appropriate Sankey number, 'Will Your Anchor Hold in the Storms of Life?'[168]

---

[161] I. Bradley, 'William Wilberforce: the Saint', *History Today*, 33 (1983), p. 43.

[162] See R. Cawardine, 'Evangelicals, Whigs and the Election of William Henry Harrison', *Journal of American Studies*, 17 (1983), pp. 47–75; *Evangelicals and Politics in Antebellum America*, New Haven, 1993, pp. 50–4, 60. See also R. Hofstadter, 'William Jennings Bryan: the Democrat as Revivalist', in his *The American Political Tradition*, New York, 1948, ch. 8.

[163] G. H. Peters, *The Plimsoll Line: The Story of Samuel Plimsoll, Member of Parliament for Derby from 1868 to 1880*, London, 1975, pp. 104–16.

[164] Roe, *Kenealy and the Tichborne Cause*, pp. 188–9.

[165] Peters, *The Plimsoll Line*, pp. v, 73.

[166] R. T. Shannon, *Gladstone and the Bulgarian Agitations*, p. 28.

[167] See *The Labourers Union Chronicle*, 6 Feb. 1875, p. 5; 13 March 1875, p. 2; 3 April 1875, p. 2; 29 May 1875, p. 4.

[168] Peters, *The Plimsoll Line*, pp. 94–5.

But, most significantly of all, it seems that William Gladstone – himself raised in an evangelical family – was energised by his experience of the revivalists' meetings.[169] Gladstone was to become the greatest exponent of 'moral populism'. His extra-parliamentary speech-making tours from the Bulgarian Agitations onwards did more than anything else to introduce the American presidential style into British electioneering. He declared that when it came to the great ethical issues, those concerning truth, justice and humanity, 'there, gentlemen, all the world over, I will back the masses against the classes'.[170] Matthew Arnold saw this populism as irresponsible; Gladstone was letting the lower and middle classes determine the programme of the Liberal party and then devoting himself to ensuring its success.[171] Arnold believed in the 'hard doctrine of the unsoundness of the majority' – that many were called but few were chosen.[172] The worship of size and numbers found among English nonconformists and Americans was dangerous and vulgar, for opinions ought not to be counted, but to be weighed.[173]

Gladstone, however, had far greater respect for nonconformity. In 1876, he launched himself into the agitations against the Turkish massacres of Christians in Bulgaria. R. T. Shannon, in his classic study of the Bulgarian Agitations, suggested that the evangelical revival – and in particular the campaigns of Moody and Sankey – was one of the major sources of inspiration for the agitations. Shannon describes them as 'semi-religious, semi-political' events, and writes that 'the Blackheath demonstration had about it much of the character of a great revivalist rally'.[174] Colin Matthew agrees that conviction of evangelical intensity lay behind the campaign[175] and, to Peter Clarke, Gladstone was 'the prophet as statesman, the Ayatollah of Victorian Christianity'.[176]

The new political style adopted by Gladstone from 1876 had complex roots, but it was inspired, at least in part, by his experience of the revivalism of Moody and Sankey the previous year. At first Gladstone seems to have been worried that the excitement of the services could

---

[169] On Gladstone's evangelical upbringing see H. C. G. Matthew, *Gladstone, 1809–1874*, Oxford, 1986, pp. 6–8.

[170] Quoted in Clarke, *A Question of Leadership*, pp. 34–5.

[171] Arnold, 'The Nadir of Liberalism', in his *Complete Prose Works*, vol. XI, Ann Arbor, 1977, p. 65.

[172] Arnold, 'Numbers, or the Majority and the Remnant', in his *Complete Prose Works*, vol. X, pp. 144, 159.

[173] Arnold, 'A Letter to *The Times*', in his *Complete Prose Works*, vol. XI, pp. 82–3.

[174] Shannon, *Bulgarian Agitations*, pp. xi, 115.

[175] H. C. G. Matthew, 'Introduction' to *Gladstone Diaries*, vol. IX: January 1875–December 1880, Oxford, 1986, p. xlvii.

[176] P. Clarke, *A Question of Leadership*, p. 32. See Biagini, *Liberty, Retrenchment and Reform*, ch. 7, for a detailed discussion of Gladstone as a charismatic leader.

produce no deep lasting effects. His friend, Arthur Kinnaird, who was one of the organisers of Moody's meetings, wrote to the politician on 12 April to reassure him that this was not so: 'it is folly not to admit that the outward manifestations of excitement produce very real effects'.[177] Two weeks later, on 25 April, Gladstone wrote in his diary: 'Islington Hall 7½ PM with A. K[innaird]. The sight was wonderful, & touching in a high degree: also the earnestness of Mr. M[oody] whom I saw for a moment'.[178]

It is hardly coincidental that in the Bulgarian Agitation a year after Moody and Sankey's meetings, Gladstone – in Shannon's words – 'found he could employ mass enthusiasm in a righteous cause'.[179] According to Matthew, Gladstone only came back to politics after 1875 because of 'exceptional circumstances'; the normality of politics was suspended and there was a new millenarian tone.[180] Kinnaird had written to Gladstone to provide 'a justification of resorting to extraordinary means to arouse this nation'. He referred his friend to the thirtieth chapter of the second book of Chronicles, in which we read of Hezekiah leading the people in a festival of national repentance and renewal.[181] By late 1876 Gladstone was acting like a latter-day Hezekiah, reproducing in the political sphere the evangelical earnestness which he had seen in Moody and Sankey's revival meetings. His diary entry for 28 December 1879 reveals a politician as much fired by a sense of divine mission as Moody himself:

For the past 3½ years I have been passing through a political experience which I believe is without example in our Parliamentary history. I profess to believe it has been an occasion when the battle to be fought was a battle of justice humanity freedom law, all in their first elements from the very root, and all on a gigantic scale. The word spoken was a word for millions, and for millions who cannot themselves speak. If I really believe this then I should regard my having been morally forced into this work as a great and high election of God.[182]

VI

The revivalism of Moody and Sankey, therefore, was both symptomatic of the moral populism of late Victorian British politics and an intensifying influence upon it. Through its impact on nonconformity and Gladstone it indirectly shaped the campaigning style of political radicals. Moreover,

---

[177] Letter from Arthur Kinnaird to Gladstone, 12 April 1875, in the Gladstone papers, vol. CXLV, British Library Add. ms. 44,230.
[178] Matthew (ed.), *Gladstone Diaries*, vol. IX, p. 32.
[179] Shannon, *Bulgarian Agitations*, p. 12.
[180] Matthew, Introduction to the *Gladstone Diaries*, vol. IX, pp. xxiv–xxv.
[181] Letter from A. Kinnaird to Gladstone, 12 April 1875.
[182] Matthew (ed.), *Gladstone Diaries*, vol. IX, p. 471.

the new revivalism offered an alternative cultural vision which challenged elitism in the name of the people. Just as the campaign against vaccination challenged the monopoly of doctors, and the Tichborne cause attacked the corruption of lawyers, so revivalism presented a challenge to the traditional clericalism and aristocratic gentility of much British religion. Of course, unlike these political movements, the element of social protest in Moody and Sankey's mission was implicit and unspoken. Yet for all this it was quite clear, and beneath the evangelists' obvious civility there ran a strong undercurrent of dissidence. Liberal radicals had long believed that the people's religion – just as much as the people's food – should be free from the control of the state and social hierarchies. The revivalism of Moody and Sankey provided an example of a religious form shaped not by sophisticated clerical elites, but by the preferences and aspirations of the common people.

The success of Moody and Sankey also suggests that the evangelical influence upon British society was still considerable in this period. Historians tend to miss this by projecting twentieth-century secularisation back into the nineteenth century. Yet, as the work of Jonathan Parry and the chapters by Machin and Scotland in this book remind us, religion was a powerful political force in Victorian Britain.[183] A more secular future lay ahead, of course, and evangelical Christianity was soon to enter into decline.[184] At this stage, however, evangelicals were not yet retreating into their sub-cultural ghetto, as historians like Kent suppose. Moody and Sankey's campaign marked a high point of evangelical self-confidence and influence on British social and political life. One might even speak of the mid-1870s as 'the evangelical moment'.

[183] See Parry, *Democracy and Religion, passim*. On the importance of Protestant dissent to political radicalism see also Biagini, *Liberty, Retrenchment and Reform*, pp. 15–16.
[184] See D. W. Bebbington, *Evangelicalism in Modern Britain*, pp. 141–50.

5   Disestablishment and democracy,
        c. 1840–1930

Ian Machin

I

The questions of disestablishment of religion and of spiritual independence from the state do not necessarily coincide, but both have been
important features of the movement towards democratic freedom in the
United Kingdom. As agents of democracy they have accompanied electoral reform, constitutional change, nationalism and legal freedom of
action for trade unions. These different questions overlapped with each
other. For example, the desire for voluntary, non-established religion or
spiritual freedom depended on franchise extension for its more effective
expression in politics and its greater hope of realisation. This connection
helped to bear out Max Weber's contention that non-established denominations made a special contribution to the evolution of democracy.[1]

   In the 1860s Richard Masheder, a Fellow of a Cambridge college, was
fearful that steps towards democracy, such as had been urged in the
'People's Charter', would directly encourage disestablishment. He
wrote: 'It is by annual Parliaments, equal electoral districts, and "a
reasonable remuneration to members of Parliament", that Dissent calcu-
lates upon reaching the goal proposed – the separation of Church and
State'.[2] Churchmen who wished to uphold their established status
should therefore defend the existing constitution as eagerly as they championed the church establishment. He proceeded to depict the dangers
which he thought would follow disestablishment:

I believe that the downfall of the aristocracy and monarchy will follow close upon
the downfall of the Established Church ... we will suppose that the dust of the
Established Church is given to the four winds of heaven ... about AD 2000. Well,
soon after that event, I doubt not, an agitation would be commenced against the
aristocracy and monarchy.[3]

[1] M. Weber, *The Sociology of Religion*, trans. E. Fischoff, London, 1965, p. 84.
[2] R. Masheder, *Dissent and Democracy: Their Mutual Relations and Common Objects*,
   London, 1864, pp. 5–4, also 312ff.
[3] *Ibid.*, pp. 24–5.

The desire to liberate religion from the control of a secular state, or from the inequalities caused by the possession and exercise of constitutional privilege, stemmed from Constantine the Great's adoption of the Christian faith as the imperial Roman religion in the fourth century. This event led, in the course of time, to controversy over whether it was good for churches to be established and patronised by the state. The Free Churchmen argued that the church was essentially a voluntary group of people, holding beliefs in common and generally wishing to conduct its religious affairs without the intervention of secular government. The latter might sometimes wish to intervene, especially if it regarded a sect as potentially subversive. But from the strictly religious point of view a church could never be simply a branch of the state. One of the reasons for disestablishment listed in a political handbook of 1903 ran as follows:

it is contrary to religion that the secular power should have any voice at all in religious matters; a Church ought in no way to be placed under the control of the State, which is, thereby, as likely to be fostering error as to be upholding the true form of religion ... the connection of Church and State causes, not the spiritualisation of the State, but simply the secularisation of the Church ... as long as the Church is bound up with the State it must be controlled in every particular by the State, i.e. by Parliament; and Parliament, being increasingly composed of members of divers sects and creeds, many of them hostile to the Establishment, or even to religion, is a body eminently unfit to govern the Church, or to legislate on religious questions ... so long as the Church is connected with the State, its higher ecclesiastical rulers must be appointed on the advice of the Prime Minister, who is not necessarily a member of the Church of England, and is possibly not even a Christian.[4]

These arguments, when suitably modified, were also applied by those who wanted self-government for a church which would continue to enjoy state endorsement through the possession of established status – a church, that is, which would be self-governing and established at the same time. For such a church, spiritual self-government would be achieved by allowing it as much religious freedom as a non-established church. The force of the desire for ecclesiastical self-government in established churches, assisted by the secular democratic urge, has been such that today the Church of Scotland has complete religious self-government and the Church of England has progressed a long way towards it.

Arguments in favour of disestablishment, however, have certainly not been limited to this demand for spiritual independence. Another argument given in the political handbook of 1903 reads as follows:

---

[4] Sydney Buxton, *A Handbook to Political Questions of the Day, and the Arguments on Either Side*, London, 1903, pp. 107–8.

while the State should be tolerant of all religious sects, it ought not to support any special Denomination. In so doing, the State outstrips its field of work, and trespasses on freedom of religious thought and on the principle of religious equality ... State recognition of a special Church, by taking her under protection, by ensuring her the possession of vast prosperity, by placing her ministers in a position of superiority, places those who do not belong to her communion ... in a position of exceptional pecuniary and social disadvantage ... a State privileged Church divides the community and accentuates religious differences ... if dissenters were relieved from an irritating injustice, and Churchmen were deprived of a position of superiority, religious differences would lose much of their sting, social exclusiveness would be diminished, and the artificial barriers which now keep men apart would be broken down.[5]

As this quotation shows, the argument for disestablishment could be secular in nature as well as religious, combining claims for social equality with claims for religious equality. The earliest broad and co-ordinated argument for disestablishment in nineteenth-century Britain was put forward in *Ecclesiastical Establishments Considered*, a pamphlet of 1829 by Andrew Marshall, a minister of the Scottish United Secession Church. This publication gave five reasons for disestablishment which were purely religious in nature, and five which were more secular. Among the latter, Marshall said that established churches created and maintained social distinctions because of the privileges they possessed; and (as a radical writing in a period when the demand for free trade was developing) that churches, like commerce, needed free, unhindered rivalry in order to flourish.[6]

Both the secular and the religious arguments for Voluntaryism (the advocacy of 'voluntary', non-established religion) were frequently heard – calling on the one hand for 'free trade in religion', and on the other for acknowledgement of 'the Crown rights of the Redeemer' rather than state control of a church. The two approaches often coalesced, if not always very comfortably. The outright claim for Voluntaryism could be seen as both a reinforcement of and a hindrance to the lesser and more practical claims of nineteenth-century dissent. The Voluntary claim was a natural accompaniment to demands for equal rights in regard to marriage, burials and university education, and to release from the payment of church rates. But it was also a hindrance to these claims, because it raised a much larger question which aroused more heat and passion and caused more determined efforts to defend established church

---

[5] *Ibid.*, pp. 106–7.
[6] A. Marshall, *Ecclesiastical Establishments Considered*, Glasgow, 1829; A. B. Montgomery, 'The Voluntary Controversy in the Church of Scotland, 1829–43', University of Edinburgh, unpublished Ph.D. thesis, 1953, pp. 9–23; G. I. T. Machin, *Politics and the Churches in Great Britain, 1832 to 1868*, Oxford, 1977, pp. 25–6, 100–2.

privilege. It is possible that, if effectively organised Voluntaryism had not existed from 1844, when Edward Miall and other nonconformists formed the Anti-State Church Association (re-named in 1853 the Liberation Society, or 'the Society for the Liberation of Religion from State Patronage and Control'), nonconformists would not have had to wait until 1880 before their main practical grievances were removed. On the other hand, the political pressure arising for disestablishment in Ireland and Wales (on account of their majority religious complexions) might have ensured that disestablishment occurred in those countries if the London-based Liberation Society had never come into being.

Among the arguments against a state-controlled religious system, it was contended that a dual and perhaps conflicting allegiance occurred among members of an established church who were called on to be loyal to both religious doctrines and state decrees. The actions of a temporal government, in exercising its control of the church, might infringe on religious conscience. If this occurred, a conscientious church member might feel compelled to put loyalty to conviction before submission to the state. In extreme circumstances this could lead to martyrdom, as it did on numerous occasions in the era of the Reformation, for example in the cases of More and Cranmer. In more liberal and relaxed circumstances the demands of conscience could lead to a call for spiritual self-government in the church, which would remain officially established but would no longer be subject to religious control by the state.[7] Alternatively, the problem of conscience could become so strong that it produced a demand for complete Voluntaryism by members of an established church, which showed readiness to abandon any constitutionally privileged position for the sake of obtaining perceived doctrinal purity and liturgical freedom. An example of this development occurred when a determined High Church clergyman, the Revd Alexander Mackonochie, who was anxious for legal freedom to carry out certain acts of ritual and hence for freedom from state control, joined the heavily nonconformist Liberation Society for a short period, and thereafter became president of a 'Church League for promoting the separation of Church and State', founded in 1877.[8]

Those who were outside an established church, on the other hand, already possessed spiritual freedom from the state. For their part, the desire for disestablishment was a wish to realise general principles of

[7] As was proposed by Thomas Chalmers in his *Lectures on the Extension and Establishment of National Churches*, Glasgow, 1838, pp. 11–12. See also Stewart J. Brown, *Thomas Chalmers and the Godly Commonwealth in Scotland*, Oxford, 1982, pp. 269–71, 337.

[8] G. I. T. Machin, *Politics and the Churches in Great Britain, 1869 to 1921*, Oxford, 1987, pp. 85–6; M. Reynolds, *Martyr of Ritualism: Father Mackonochie of St Alban's, Holborn*, London, 1965, pp. 206–9.

religious equality. This approach was fundamentally idealistic, but could nevertheless be accompanied by the allurements of material gain which would come from abolishing the pecuniary privileges of establishment – notably the requirement to pay church rates in order to maintain the parish churches. The desire for both disestablishment and spiritual independence could also, and sometimes did, have a purely secular motivation, and did not need religious belief to provide sufficient justification for it.[9]

As has been said, the aims of achieving spiritual independence and disestablishment by no means invariably went together. Members of non-established churches might favour both objectives, regarding ecclesiastical self-government as an essential part of religious equality; on the other hand, they might oppose self-government within an establishment as being, compared with disestablishment, an inadequate manifestation of religious freedom. Members of established churches who wanted self-government usually, though not invariably, clung to the establishment principle, and (to quote Thomas Chalmers in 1843) were 'not Voluntaries'. The attitude of Chalmers, who led the Scottish secession of 1843 and the formation of the Free Church on the grounds of spiritual independence, differed widely from the attitude of Voluntaries such as Edward Miall, John Bright, Joseph Chamberlain, John Morley or Charles Bradlaugh.

Some denominations which had seceded from an established church – such as the Congregationalists, Baptists and Quakers, and (in Scotland) the dissenting groups which formed the United Presbyterian Church in 1847 – were opposed on principle, at least officially, to religious establishments. But some other nonconformist denominations maintained the ideal of a 'pure', self-governing establishment without the intervention of secular state control. Wesleyans and the Calvinistic Methodists of Wales respected this principle, though their commitment to it had markedly weakened by the later nineteenth century.[10] The Scottish Free Churchmen, who seceded from the Church of Scotland in 1843, also adhered to this viewpoint (as mentioned); but for the majority of them the adherence was an increasingly loose one, and most Scots Free Churchmen campaigned for disestablishment in the period 1874–86.[11]

[9] See E. Royle, *Radicals, Secularists and Republicans: Popular Free Thought in Britain, 1866–1915*, Manchester, 1980, pp. 65, 187, 202.

[10] R. Davies, A. R. George and G. Rupp (eds.), *A History of the Methodist Church in Great Britain*, vol. III, London, 1983, pp. 142–3, 263; G. I. T. Machin, 'A Welsh Church Rate Fracas, Aberystwyth, 1832–3', *Welsh History Review*, 6 (1973), pp. 462–8; Machin, *Politics and the Churches in Great Britain, 1832 to 1868*, pp. 247, 345–6.

[11] J. Kennedy, *The Disestablishment Movement in the Free Church*, Edinburgh, 1882, pp. 11–13, 26; R. Rainy, 'Disestablishment in Scotland', *Contemporary Review*, 41 (1882), pp. 431–44; P. Carnegie Simpson, *The Life of Principal Rainy*, 2 vols., London, 1909, vol. I, pp. 277–8; I. Machin, 'Voluntaryism and Reunion, 1874–1929', in N. Macdougall (ed.), *Church, Politics and Society: Scotland, 1408–1929*, Edinburgh, 1983, pp. 221–2.

The Roman Catholic Church was neither a secession church nor, with respect to principle, a Voluntary church. If it was the established church of a country, it would not oppose the establishment principle. But the Catholic Church in Ireland, on account of its own political and constitutional position, wanted disestablishment of the Church of Ireland. For the same reason the Catholic Church in Great Britain probably favoured disestablishment of the Churches of England and Scotland, though it did not campaign for it.

Thus the desires for spiritual freedom and for disestablishment were both uneven in the United Kingdom of the nineteenth and early twentieth centuries. Their contributory factors did not coalesce easily together. Protestant dissenters and Roman Catholics could unite only temporarily, in support of Irish disestablishment, in the later 1860s. Other issues, especially the national education controversy from 1870, soon drove them apart. The Education Act of 1870 did not grant rate aid to the 'voluntary' (mainly Anglican and Roman Catholic) schools. Roman Catholics, like Anglicans, wanted to receive rate aid for their schools on the same basis as the new state board schools, but this desire was opposed by most nonconformists. The latter were also against the grants which voluntary schools obtained from central government funds, seeing this as an example of state bestowal of money, and hence of privilege, on some religious bodies. But the lasting division between nonconformists and Catholics over education was partly counteracted by a large degree of common support for Irish Home Rule from the mid-1880s. In 1886 most (though by no means all) nonconformists were able to support the desire of the great majority of Catholics for Irish Home Rule.

II

A link between the demand for democracy and the demand for disestablishment had existed for a long time, having been clearly present in the English revolutionary upheavals of the mid-seventeenth century. The two demands emerged in harness in the late eighteenth century, stimulated by the French Enlightenment and the 1789 Revolution. An international dimension of both democracy and disestablishment is also indicated by the encouragement given to both of them by the American Revolution, which itself derived a good deal of encouragement from the British example of revolt in the seventeenth century. The government of the newly independent United States adopted a policy of federal disestablishment in the years 1787–91.[12] But it was left to the legislatures of the

---

[12] E. R. Norman, *The Conscience of the State in North America*, Cambridge, 1968, pp. 31–2 (and the references in this book to other sources).

different states to decide whether they would maintain or abolish religious establishments. The last religious establishment in the United States (ironically a Congregational one, in Massachusetts) was not terminated until 1833.[13] This event no doubt encouraged the call for disestablishment which was rising in the United Kingdom in the 1830s. Only in 1868, however, did the passage of the Fourteenth Amendment to the American constitution bind the individual states to commit themselves against instituting a church establishment.[14]

Overseas influences on disestablishment in Britain did not end with the American connection, which had a powerful effect on different kinds of nineteenth-century British radical movements. In a newly-independent Italy, Cavour's unsuccessful demand for 'a free Church in a free State' had a marked effect on British aspirations for disestablishment;[15] though by no means so clearly on Ireland, where the disestablishment cry came mainly from pro-papal Catholics. Cavour perhaps derived his much-debated idea of *libera chiesa in libero stato* partly from the American example and from British claims. He was also strongly influenced by the work of a Protestant (Waldensian) pastor, Alexandre Vinet, who published in 1841 a noted *Essai sur la manifestation des convictions religieuses et sur la séparation de l'Eglise et de l'Etat.*[16] Cavour held that the freeing of a church from the control of the state was indispensable to a general acceptance of liberty. One of his political collaborators, Marco Minghetti, who was later a premier of Italy and a noted literary vindicator of the separation of church and state, had published opinions in 1866 which might have influenced those developed by Gladstone at a later date, holding that church and state could co-exist more harmoniously when separated than when united.[17] Moreover, Cavour's own wish for 'a free Church in a free State' was couched in broad terms which a British radical could equally have expressed:

[We desire] to imbue all sections of society, both civil and religious, with the ideal of liberty. We desire economic liberty, we desire administrative liberty, we desire full and absolute liberty of conscience. We desire all the political liberties that are compatible with the maintenance of public order. And therefore, as a necessary consequence of this order of things, we deem it essential ... that the principle of liberty should be applied to the relations between Church and State.[18]

---

[13] *Ibid.*, pp. 42–7.
[14] *Ibid.*, pp. 47–8.
[15] E. F. Biagini, *Liberty, Retrenchment and Reform: Popular Liberalism in the Age of Gladstone, 1860–80*, Cambridge, 1992, p. 229.
[16] S. W. Halperin, *The Separation of Church and State in Italian Thought from Cavour to Mussolini*, Chicago, 1937 (reprinted New York, 1971), pp. 8–9 and ff.
[17] A. C. Jemolo, *Church and State in Italy, 1850–1950*, trans. D. Moore, Oxford, 1960, pp. 17–20.
[18] *Ibid.*, pp. 23–4; S. W. Halperin, *The Separation of Church and State*, pp. 15–16.

Another continental contribution, if a much smaller one, was later given to the hopes of British Voluntaries. When the disestablishment cause was flagging in Britain at the beginning of the twentieth century, some encouragement was obtained from the enactment of a French law in December 1905 separating church and state. This arose from strong anti-clerical developments in French society and politics.[19] The attention of committee members of the Liberation Society was drawn to this law, which was greeted approvingly.[20] It gave a slight boost to Voluntary hopes, and a considerable amount of favourable legislation was expected in Britain (at least in regard to education and Welsh disestablishment) after the Liberal landslide victory in the general election of January 1906. But hopes of a reversal of the Education Act of 1902, which had given rate aid to the voluntary schools, were disappointed. There was a frustrating delay over Welsh disestablishment until, after a constitutional crisis between the government and the Lords, a bill was finally carried in 1914 to disestablish the church in Wales, but then suspended in its operation until 1920 because of the First World War and subsequent negotiations over the issue. The force of French anti-clericalism found little reflection in Britain, where militant Voluntaryism (in itself, by this time, not very obviously anti-clerical) was on the wane.

III

Theoretical justifications and overseas influences were important to the development of the disestablishment question. But probably more important than either of these factors was the extent of numerical support, actual or potential, for the Voluntary cause. The relative numerical strength of churches (in terms of members and attenders) was a central factor in explaining the success or failure of attempts at disestablishment. On the basis simply of the number of members belonging to non-established churches, it could be claimed that Voluntaryism had a majority in its favour in the population of the United Kingdom. But the strength of this argument was reduced by the fact that many of these members showed no obvious interest in supporting the Voluntary demand.

Both Protestant dissent and Roman Catholicism expanded rapidly in the United Kingdom in the first half of the nineteenth century – and the

[19] M. Larkin, *Church and State after the Dreyfus Affair: The Separation Issue in France,* London, 1974, especially 130ff. The separation law of 1905 is printed on pp. 227–41. Cf. K. Robbins, *History, Religion and Identity in Modern Britain,* London, 1993, p. 119.
[20] Liberation Society Executive Committee Minutes, 1905 (Greater London Archives); Machin, *Politics and the Churches in Great Britain, 1869 to 1921,* p. 271.

latter, though not the former, continued expanding rapidly until the second half of the twentieth. The sharp and steady fall of population in Ireland for several decades after the Famine of 1845 caused the number of Roman Catholics in the 'southern' Irish counties (which later formed the Republic) to drop from about four million in 1861 to under three million in 1901. Nevertheless the Catholic majority in this area remained constant in size during this period.[21] Based on this majority, a constitutional political organisation was formed in 1865 (the National Association) aiming at disestablishment and other reforms. Gladstone and the Liberal Party responded positively to these desires in 1868–9, and disestablishment of the Church of Ireland was enacted. The force of numbers was similarly important in Wales, the only other country in the United Kingdom where disestablishment occurred. There, at the time of the religious census of 1851, nonconformists comprised about three-quarters of the church-going inhabitants and probably over half the entire population.[22]

In both Ireland and Wales, disestablishment took place in response to a majority of the population being outside the established church. In Scotland also a clear majority of the population (about 60 per cent) was, from the evidence provided by the 1851 religious census, attached to non-established denominations.[23] This was at the root of the increasing success of the disestablishment movement in Scotland up to 1886. But after that date, partly on account of political changes caused by the Irish Home Rule crisis, there was a significant narrowing of the differences between Scots Presbyterians inside and outside the established church. Through this development, the demand for disestablishment lost support, and it was replaced by moves, from 1907, to bring about a reunited and enlarged Church of Scotland grounded on spiritual independence and self-government. This movement to reunite was eventually successful in 1929.

England was the only country in the United Kingdom where members of non-established denominations did not increase sufficiently to become a clear majority of the population. The religious census of 1851 indicated, when its results were published in 1854, that just under half the church-goers in England (the church-goers comprising about half the population) attended the services of non-established churches.[24] The number of nonconformists was still growing at that time, so England might have

[21] R. Currie, A. Gilbert and L. Horsley, *Churches and Churchgoers: Patterns of Church Growth in the British Isles since 1700*, Oxford, 1977, p. 220.

[22] Kenneth O. Morgan, *Wales in British Politics, 1868–1922*, 3rd edn, Cardiff, 1980, pp. 12–13.

[23] Currie, Gilbert and Horsley, *Churches and Churchgoers*, p. 219.

[24] *Report on the Religious Census of 1851*, Parliamentary Papers 1852–3 (1969), vol. LXXXIX, pp. clviii and ff.; Machin, *Politics and the Churches in Great Britain, 1832 to 1868*, pp. 8–10.

seemed to be preparing to join Ireland, Wales and Scotland in attaining a non-established majority. But this prospect slowly receded. The lack of any further national religious census after 1851 hinders efforts to chart the relative numerical progress of denominations. But the scattered evidence of regional investigations suggests that nonconformists in England declined in proportion to the population from about 1880.[25] Membership figures show that an absolute drop in numbers, amazingly uniform across the major nonconformist denominations, commenced within one or two years of 1906, the *annus mirabilis* when the greatest nonconformist electoral victory occurred, nearly 200 dissenters being returned to the House of Commons. Wesleyans reached their highest annual peak of membership in England in 1906, Congregationalists their highest annual membership level in Wales in 1905, and in England in 1908. Baptists attained their highest membership in Wales in 1906, and in England in 1907; Primitive Methodists were at their peak of British membership in 1908.[26]

The numerical decline of nonconformity was of central significance in explaining the decline of the Voluntary cause in England. Because of the highly contentious nature of this cause, nonconformity itself had been far from providing a clear majority of its members in favour of it; and it was unlikely that a majority in favour could be provided by any other source. The numbers of Roman Catholics were increasing rapidly in Great Britain, but they did not campaign for disestablishment there even though they probably favoured it. A sizeable number of Anglicans (especially amongst Anglo-Catholics) and probably all secularists favoured disestablishment, but these groups were not large enough to compensate for the attrition of numbers caused by the decrease of dissent.

IV

Nationalism was another potent factor in the combination of influences which promoted disestablishment. The role of nationalism was obviously important in campaigns to disestablish churches which were seen as symbols of external domination. This was the case with the Church of Ireland, which was constitutionally joined with the Church of England in the Union Act of 1800; also with the Church in Wales, which was incorporated with the Church of England as part of the province of Canterbury.[27]

[25] Machin, *Politics and Churches, 1869 to 1921*, pp. 11–14.
[26] Currie, Gilbert and Horsley, pp. 142–3, 149–50, 163.
[27] E. R. Norman, *The Catholic Church and Ireland in the Age of Rebellion, 1859–73*, London, 1965, pp. 1–4; Morgan, *Wales in British Politics*, pp. 6–18, 297–304.

There were, as already mentioned, strong non-established majorities in both Ireland and Wales, and feelings of nationalism helped to motivate them.[28] Irish nationalism was already flourishing in the early nineteenth century, and its continuance became linked to the desire for disestablishment. In Wales nationalism developed, for cultural and political reasons, in the course of the nineteenth century.[29] Language gave Welsh nonconformity part of its appeal as an agent of nationalism. Preaching in Welsh was usual in the chapels, while in the church in Wales no Welsh-speaking bishop was appointed between 1715 and 1882 (though one or two nineteenth-century bishops learned Welsh while in office). Nationalist feeling, displayed in the 1880s by the rising radicalism personified by Tom Ellis and Lloyd George, made Welsh Voluntaries want to conduct their own campaign by 1887, independent of the mainly English-led Liberation Society.[30]

In Scotland there was also some nationalist feeling, but it was generally less developed than in Wales until at least the 1920s. The established Church in Scotland did not, of course, represent outside domination, because it had originated within the country and was different in doctrine and organisation from the Church of England. In Scotland, therefore, unlike Ireland and Wales, disestablishment did not have a nationalist element. Its cause in Scotland was opposition to lay patronage and the consequent Voluntary theory or practical support, found especially in the non-established Presbyterian denominations and in other dissenting groups.

Within the United Kingdom, England was the only country where the sentiment of national separatism did not (and could not) exist, as there was no outside domination to protest against. Consequently disestablishment in England, as in Scotland, was a claim based on aspirations for religious liberation and democracy, but not for nationalist freedom. On the other hand, in Ireland and Wales, though in the former much more than in the latter, nationalist feeling accompanied a similar desire for democracy and religious freedom.

V

The relationship between disestablishment and the social structure also showed differences between one country and another in the United

---

[28] Cf. D. W. Bebbington, 'Religion and National Feeling in Nineteenth-Century Wales and Scotland', in S. P. Mews (ed.), *Religion and National Identity* (*Studies in Church History*, vol. XVIII), Oxford 1982, pp. 489–503.

[29] Morgan, *Wales in British Politics*, pp. 6–20 and ff.; D. G. Evans, *A History of Wales, 1815–1906*, Cardiff, 1989, pp. 314–17.

[30] Morgan, pp. 77–8; Machin, *Politics and Churches, 1869 to 1921*, p. 192.

Kingdom. The demand for disestablishment probably ran deeper in the social structure in Ireland than in other parts of the United Kingdom. This was because the demand came mostly from Roman Catholicism, which had the allegiance of most Irish peasants as well as of many members of higher social classes. In Wales, also, support for disestablishment penetrated deeply into society, on account of the nonconformity of many agricultural and industrial workers, as well as of many middle-class (but very few upper-class) persons. But the lack of any obvious church attachment among many of the Welsh unskilled workers, especially in the towns, restricted the social influence of the Voluntary cause, which was usually spread through nonconformist societies and newspapers (and perhaps, to some extent, through chapels).[31] A similar social extension and limitation occurred in both England and Scotland.[32] Most of the rapidly growing number of industrial workers in nineteenth-century Britain did not attend a church (except perhaps on rare occasions), in contrast to Ireland, which remained largely non-industrialised and where most of the peasantry were church-going Catholics. Hence an issue like disestablishment, which was mainly denomination-based, was restricted in its support by the limitations of denominational outreach.

The leaders of the Voluntary claim throughout the United Kingdom were largely middle class. They were usually politicians, ministers of religion, and lay professional and business men. Their followers were other middle-class people and a large number of skilled workers.[33] Added to these was a certain number of unskilled labourers, especially amongst agricultural workers who might (in England) be Primitive Methodists or Bible Christians. An attempt was made in the 1870s to extend Voluntary support and organisation among working men by developing the use of trade union leaders for this purpose. Although the prominent trade unionist George Howell was noted for his efforts in this respect, addressing audiences in different towns, the plan did not have lasting success and petered out.[34] The Voluntary movement was not taken up by the working classes when they became more politically organised. Some individual trade unionists and Labour politicians were in favour of disestablishment, but Voluntaryism did not gain a secure or permanent hold

---

[31] Cf. Morgan, p. 13.
[32] K. S. Inglis, *Churches and the Working Classes in Victorian England*, London, 1963, pp. 1–20; S. Mayor, *The Churches and the Labour Movement*, London, 1967, p. 25ff.; A. Drummond and J. Bulloch, *The Church in Victorian Scotland, 1843–74*, Edinburgh, 1875, pp. 36–7.
[33] K. D. Brown, 'Nonconformity and Trade Unionism – the Sheffield Outrages of 1866', in E. F. Biagini and A. J. Reid (eds.), *Currents of Radicalism: Popular Radicalism, Organised Labour and Party Politics in Britain, 1850–1914*, Cambridge, 1991, p. 90.
[34] S. M. Ingham, 'The Disestablishment Movement in England, 1868–74', *Journal of Religious History*, 3 (1964), pp. 38–60.

in either the parliamentary or the trade union wing of the twentieth-century Labour movement.[35] This movement spanned too wide a section of society, and was too concerned with matters which it saw as more important, for Voluntaryism to gain a notable place within it. The social sources of Voluntaryism had not spread widely or deeply enough among the working classes for this to happen.

Disestablishment in Britain as a whole never became a widespread popular movement because nonconformity did not extend far enough among the population (having always to contend with established churches which remained persistently flourishing) and had a mainly middle-class or artisan membership. Moreover, even a wider spread of nonconformity would not necessarily have meant that more dissenters could have been persuaded to support disestablishment. The limit of most nonconformists' interest in politics, purely as nonconformists, was the removal of any aspect of practical inequality.

The Voluntary movement was receding in strength by the opening years of the twentieth century, when the Labour Party (or its predecessor, the Labour Representation Committee) had appeared. Voluntaryism became less powerful still by 1918, when the Labour Party began to emerge as a large, entirely independent party. Trade unions – which, while chapel membership was declining, grew from two million to eight million in membership between 1900 and 1920[36] – were far more effective representatives of working-class strength than were nonconformist denominations. For much of the twentieth century, social class differences played a particularly notable part in British politics. Trade unions were concentrated class organisations, including unskilled as well as skilled workers in their ranks, and they had specific class objectives in view. Denominations, on the other hand, were not distinct class organisations and did not have distinct class aims.

There was, however, no necessary connection between the decline in chapel membership and the rise in trade union membership in the early twentieth century. It was not necessary to leave one organisation in order to join the other. Indeed, trade unions were to some degree extensions of the denominations (on a generalised basis) rather then replacements for them. The same people could belong to a church or a chapel and a trade union, and often did. Therefore, trade unionists could have urged the cause of disestablishment simultaneously with the cause of better pay and working conditions. On the other hand, trade unionists came from a variety of denominations (and from none), and most of them were prob-

---

[35] Machin, *Politics and Churches, 1869 to 1921*, p. 283; R. A. Bray, *Labour and the Churches*, London, 1912, pp. 52ff.
[36] J. Lovell, *British Trade Unions, 1875–1933*, London, 1977, pp. 45–6, 58.

ably not interested in Voluntaryism.[37] Moreover, their interests as trade unionists lay in matters of pay, employment and welfare. These questions became more and more central to society, especially when, in the 1920s and 1930s, employment became hard to obtain and concern with welfare payments became more pressing. In these developing circumstances in the inter-war years, Voluntaryism – rapidly dwindling in any case after most Scottish dissenters had swung their attention to finding means of reuniting with the Church of Scotland, and after Welsh disestablishment had been finally put into operation in 1920[38] – became more and more marginal to society. A further reason for this was that Voluntaryism was unlikely to impinge a great deal on the working class when the established churches could no longer be effectively represented as organs of oppression or even, in anything like the degree they had been, as symbols of inequality.

VI

The disestablishment movement, like other pressure groups such as the Chartists, the Anti-Corn Law League, the Reform League, the National Education League and the trade unions, had to gain support in parliament if it was to succeed in obtaining the measures it desired. More and more nonconformists gained the vote in successive parliamentary reform acts, and more and more of them entered parliament, rising from about 35 MPs after the general election of 1852 to a peak of nearly 200 after the election of 1906.[39] But the degree of interest in, and desire for, disestablishment varied between one nonconformist MP and another, and they were influenced substantially by the strength of the cause in the country. Except in Wales, support for disestablishment was declining after 1886. After 1895 it increasingly appeared that disestablishment in Wales might be, when time and conditions were ripe, the only viable parliamentary proposition in regard to the realisation of Voluntaryism.

The urging of nonconformist aims affected all political parties, but no political party could be the perfect medium for realising them. No British political party was tied to one religious point of view. Unlike some continental parties, all British political parties were undenominational and 'non-confessional', and sought support from people of all religious bodies and of none.

[37] Machin, *Politics and Churches, 1869 to 1921*, p. 281.
[38] R. Sjölinder, *Presbyterian Reunion in Scotland, 1907–21*, trans. E. J. Sharpe, Edinburgh, 1962, p. 105ff.; P. M. H. Bell, *Disestablishment in Ireland and Wales*, London, 1969, pp. 297–315.
[39] Machin, *Politics and Churches, 1832 to 1868*, p. 248 and n.; S. Koss, *Nonconformity in Modern British Politics*, London, 1975, pp. 177, 228.

Nineteenth-century conservatism was too wedded to defence of the established churches to acquiesce in disestablishment. But consent to the other claims of dissent was no stranger to Conservative policy in an age when both parties tended to pursue rival liberal ends. Wellington's government had agreed to the repeal of the Test and Corporation Acts in 1828; Peel's ministry in the mid-1830s gave some encouragement to the claims of dissent; and Disraeli's government in 1868 agreed to the abolition of compulsory church rates. Moreover, Welsh disestablishment was finally implemented in 1920 by a Conservative-dominated coalition.

The Liberal Party, however, was the more hopeful political vehicle for dissenting aims in the nineteenth and early twentieth centuries. In spite of the running friction between Whigs and radicals in this party over nonconformist and other reforms, a partnership of some kind was usually (but by no means invariably) maintained between nonconformity and the Liberal Party. Voluntaryism, however, did not find a great deal of favour in the Liberal Party. Although a Liberal government disestablished the Church of Ireland in 1869, subsequent attempts by Edward Miall to carry Voluntary motions in the early 1870s were firmly rebutted by Gladstone on account of the need for party unity, and were heavily defeated in the Commons. It was only after the Liberal split of 1886, when most of the Whigs had left the party, that Gladstone (himself an anti-Erastian Anglo-Catholic, and therefore having some sympathy with Voluntaryism) declared his support for disestablishment in Wales and Scotland. The English case he left aside as it did not have very strong pressure behind it. In an important speech of June 1889, in which he gave a fairly clear indication that he would support disestablishment in Wales and Scotland when these questions were next raised in parliament, he said (no doubt with relief) that it seemed that the English matter would not have to be taken up in his lifetime: 'naturally at my time of life such a subject is placed beyond all reasonable possibility of contact with myself'.[40] During the brief period of Liberal government from 1892 to 1895, ministers tried without success to carry a bill for Welsh disestablishment in 1894 and 1895, and got no further than expressing positive intentions in regard to Scotland. After the considerably successful Liberal ministries of 1905 to 1915 (which carried Welsh disestablishment), the Liberal Party suffered, in the years 1916–18, a split far more disastrous than that of 1886. The consequent decline of the Liberal Party removed the major political support from residual Voluntary hopes.

The Labour Party did not provide a promising alternative home for disestablishment. The first major step in Labour parliamentary expan-

[40] *Annual Register*, vol. CXXXI (1889), pp. 134–6; Machin, *Politics and Churches, 1869 to 1921*, pp. 193–4.

sion, the return of twenty-nine MPs in 1906, occurred when disestablishment was losing momentum and could not greatly recommend itself to Labour Party attention as a vital and promising policy. Another factor contributing to Labour reluctance to take up the question was that the Labour Party, like the Liberals and Conservatives, looked for support from members of all denominations and of none. So, like the Liberals before it, Labour preferred, for the sake of party unity, to avoid a divisive question like disestablishment.[41] The Labour Party concentrated instead on aims of social welfare. One of the socialist groups at the turn of the century, the Social Democratic Federation, did include disestablishment amongst its aims in a programme of 1900, but gave it a comparatively low priority. Keir Hardie and some other members of the Independent Labour Party favoured disestablishment, but it was not among their major political concerns.[42] Voluntary objectives did not appear in Labour Party manifestos. This situation might have been different if disestablishment had maintained its previous political force well into the twentieth century. But, since powerful factors had already combined to weaken the disestablishment aim, a political party had no need to concern itself with a comparatively minor issue which did not coincide with its own major preoccupations and which was likely to divide its supporters.

VII

Thus far we have discussed the main factors influencing Voluntaryism. No more than a brief outline of the actual development of the disestablishment issue need be given here, as it has been covered in considerable detail in published works.[43] Voluntary views were occasionally expressed in print before the nineteenth century, but the Voluntary controversy really began in Scotland in the 1820s. A prolific pamphlet warfare

---

[41] Machin, *Politics and Churches, 1869 to 1921*, p. 283.

[42] *Ibid.*, pp. 283–4.

[43] See I. G. Jones, 'The Liberation Society and Welsh politics, 1844–68', *Welsh History Review*, 1.2 (1961), pp. 193–244; S. M. Ingham, 'The Disestablishment Movement in England, 1868–74', *Journal of Religious History*, 3 (1964), pp. 38–60; P. M. H. Bell, *Disestablishment in Ireland and Wales*, London, 1969; W. H. Mackintosh, *Disestablishment and Liberation: The Movement for the Separation of the Anglican Church from State Control*, London, 1972; D. M. Thompson, 'The Liberation Society, 1844–68', in Patricia Hollis (ed.), *Pressure from Without in Early Victorian England*, London, 1974, pp. 210–38; D. A. Hamer, *The Politics of Electoral Pressure: A Study in the History of Victorian Reform Agitations*, Hassocks, 1977, pp. 91–121, 139–64; Machin, *Politics and the Churches in Great Britain* (both volumes); D. W. Bebbington, *The Nonconformist Conscience: Chapel and Politics, 1870–1914*, London, 1982, especially chapter II; J. P. Parry, *Democracy and Religion: Gladstone and the Liberal Party, 1867–75*, Cambridge, 1986, especially pp. 200–28.

developed there after Andrew Marshall laid down his challenge to church establishments in 1829. In Scotland the dissenters' claims were more concerned with theory than they were elsewhere, for in Scotland the practical grievances of dissent were comparatively few. For example, while Scottish university chairs were not opened to dissenters until 1853, the absence of any restriction on granting university degrees to dissenters caused many nonconformists from England and Wales to take degrees at Scottish universities.

During the 1830s support for the Voluntary principle was also spreading amongst English and Welsh dissenters;[44] though their political efforts in their own causes were more concerned with relief from their marriage, university, church rate and other inequities. Before the 1860s only one of these claims was met, when in 1836 the marriage question was considerably, but not wholly, settled by the Dissenters' Marriage Act of 1836.[45]

In the meantime the more politically militant nonconformists took up the attack on what seemed to be the root of their practical disabilities, the maintenance of established religion. A Religious Freedom Society and an Evangelical Voluntary Church Association were formed in 1839 to advocate disestablishment.[46] The *Nonconformist* newspaper, dedicated to the entire separation of church and state, commenced publication in 1841 under the editorship of Edward Miall; and the Anti-State Church Association was founded in 1844, becoming known as the Liberation Society in 1853.

The Voluntary cause also received indirect assistance from outside nonconformity. The Tractarian movement in the Church of England was impatient with ecclesiastical control by a secular and partly non-Anglican parliament.[47] Some Tractarians began to favour a Voluntary religious system, sympathising in this respect (though not at all over theology) with nonconformists. Gladstone had imbibed High Church doctrines before the Oxford Movement began in 1833, and he found that Tractarian views, not least their inclination to support church independence from the state, coincided with his own developing opinions from the 1840s. Influenced by joining the Liberal Party in 1859, Gladstone merged to a considerable degree the Tractarian view on this matter with the noncon-

---

[44] R. G. Cowherd, *The Politics of English Dissent: The Religious Aspects of Liberal and Humanitarian Reform Movements from 1815 to 1848*, London, 1959, pp. 153–9; Machin, *Politics and Churches, 1832 to 1868*, pp. 107–10; R. Brent, *Liberal Anglican Politics: Whiggery, Religion and Reform*, Oxford, 1987, pp. 257–260.

[45] R. G. Cowherd, *The Politics of English Dissent*, pp. 92–4; O. Chadwick, *The Victorian Church*, part I, London, 1966, pp. 142–5.

[46] Cowherd, *The Politics of English Dissent*, p. 154.

[47] Machin, *Politics and Churches, 1832 to 1868*, pp. 85–6.

formist outlook. He began to give political support, and in some instances even leadership, to nonconformist causes such as the burials claim in the 1860s, when he helped to develop an alliance with dissenters by holding important private meetings with leading ministers and laymen.[48] Nevertheless Tractarianism, and its off-shoot of Ritualism, had a dual effect on disestablishment. For while dissenting Voluntaries welcomed the support of some Ritualists for their campaign, they also regarded the growth of Ritualism as one of the main reasons to disestablish the Church of England, on the grounds that the latter was abandoning its original Protestantism by harbouring Ritualism.[49]

Some liberal Anglicans also favoured disestablishment, as did secularists.[50] Nonconformists had, moreover, obtained a victory in 1843 when they persuaded the Conservative government to abandon the education clauses of a Factory Act which would have extended the authority of the Church of England, and another victory (though partial and indirect) in the same year through the disruption of the Church of Scotland. Even though Chalmers and his associates who led the secession of the new Free Church from the Scottish establishment proclaimed that they were not Voluntaries, they were at least dissenters in practice; and, later, many Scots Free Churchmen came to advocate disestablishment of the Church of Scotland.[51] In 1846 the repeal of the corn laws gratified the many dissenters campaigning for it; and in 1847 the United Presbyterian Church, which upheld Voluntaryism on principle, was formed through a religious union in Scotland.[52] Thus Voluntaryism seemed to be on an encouraging course by the later 1840s, and it appeared to be established as a significant section of radical and democratic opinion.

But it was a long time before Voluntary hopes received any fulfilment. When Voluntaryism did receive its first legislative success, this proved to be the biggest gain which it ever obtained – the disestablishment of the Church of Ireland in 1869. Following this, the disestablishment

---

[48] G. I. T. Machin, 'Gladstone and Nonconformity in the 1860s: The Formation of an Alliance', *Historical Journal*, 17 (1974), pp. 347–64; C. Newman Hall, *Autobiography*, London, 1898, pp. 167ff., 267–8, 272.

[49] J. Guinness Rogers, *The Ritualistic Movement in the Church of England, a Reason for Disestablishment*, London, 1869; Machin, *Politics and Churches, 1869 to 1921*, pp. 6–7, 94, 237.

[50] Machin, *Politics and Churches, 1832 to 1868*, p. 102; E. Royle, *Radicals, Secularists and Republicans: Popular Freethought in Britain, 1866–1915*, Manchester, 1980, pp. 304, 331.

[51] I. G. C. Hutchison, *A Political History of Scotland, 1832–1924*, Edinburgh, 1986, p. 143; J. G. Kellas, 'The Liberal Party and the Scottish Church Disestablishment Crisis', *English Historical Review*, 79 (1964), pp. 31–46; P. Carnegie Simpson, *The Life of Principal Rainy*, 2 vols., London, 1909, vol. II, pp. 21–4.

[52] Machin, *Politics and Churches, 1832 to 1868*, pp. 114, 145; D. Woodside, *The Soul of a Scottish Church, or the Contribution of the United Presbyterian Church to Scottish Life and Religion*, Edinburgh, 1918.

campaign was at its most prominent in society and politics from then until 1895. But this period was far from being one of uniform strength for Voluntaryism. The enfranchisement of large numbers of workers in 1867 and 1884, and the increase in their influence on parliamentary returns caused by the Distribution of Seats Act of 1885, did not in the long run have the effect of satisfying Voluntary hopes, partly because many of the enfranchised workers were not interested in disestablishment. The removal of the remaining nonconformist grievances, mainly by the Burials Act of 1880, almost eliminated the practical issues which had given material support to Voluntary attitudes. Roman Catholics did not give active support to Voluntaryism after their success over Irish disestablishment, and Catholics and nonconformists, having been politically united in 1868–9, divided thereafter because of radically differing attitudes to education policy.

The disestablishment issue, moreover, promoted disunity in the Liberal Party. After their reluctant concession of Irish disestablishment (they would have preferred a policy of concurrent endowment, meaning government financial support of the Catholic Church in Ireland), the Whig old guard in the party were opposed to further Voluntary progress. With the aim of preserving party unity, which was being gravely weakened by conflict over the Education Act and other matters, Gladstone pointedly opposed Miall's attempts to pass motions in the early 1870s for the disestablishment of the Churches of England and Scotland.[53] Relations between dissent and the Liberal leadership reached a lower ebb than ever before. The alliance, however, revived in the later 1870s through Gladstone's issue of his best-selling pamphlet against the atrocities in Bulgaria, giving a strong call for moral protest which enabled nonconformists to rejoin him. They helped to carry him into a second premiership in 1880.[54]

Joseph Chamberlain urged disestablishment as part of his radical programme in the early 1880s. But Gladstone maintained his discouraging attitude to Voluntaryism until the Liberal split over Irish Home Rule in 1886. The departure of most of the Whigs from the party on account of opposition to this policy, and consequently the greater weight in the party obtained by radicalism and nonconformity, caused Gladstone to indicate, in a speech in 1889, his support for disestablishment in Scotland and Wales.

[53] J. P. Parry, *Democracy and Religion: Gladstone and the Liberal Party, 1867–75*, Cambridge, 1986, pp. 210ff., 307, 311–12, 333ff.; Machin, *Politics and Churches, 1869 to 1921*, pp. 44–6, 48–52, 55–6.

[54] R. T. Shannon, *Gladstone and the Bulgarian Agitation*, London, 1963, pp. 160–71; D. W. Bebbington, *The Nonconformist Conscience*, pp. 115–16; Machin, *Politics and Churches, 1869 to 1921*, pp. 104–5.

In Scotland there was a strong and popular disestablishment campaign from 1874 to 1886, stimulated by an Act of 1874 removing patronage in the Church of Scotland, which was condemned by United Presbyterians and many Free Churchmen as being unsatisfactory as a reduction of state power.[55] But this upsurge of interest in the disestablishment question in Scotland did not persist very strongly beyond 1886. This was initially because the political split over Irish Home Rule substantially reduced the Liberal strength in Scotland. There was growing support for an alternative church policy in that country, based on a compromise solution of the long-standing division over Voluntaryism. This policy aimed to reunite the non-established Presbyterian denominations with the Church of Scotland, on the basis of guaranteed spiritual independence and self-government within a continuing framework of establishment.[56] On account of this growing development, disestablishment in Wales was left increasingly as the only practical proposition out of the wide Voluntary aims put forward by the Liberation Society. But bills for Welsh disestablishment failed twice, in 1894 and 1895, before the Liberals were defeated and went out of office for ten years.

The question may be considered whether disestablishment would have occurred in England or Scotland if the split among the Liberals in 1886, followed as it was by Conservative ascendancy for most of the next twenty years, had not occurred. In England the situation would probably not have been different, for the question depended on social and demographic developments, especially the relative strength of denominations, which were of longer-term significance than an event – albeit an important event – in political party fortunes. In Scotland also, if less clearly, developments would probably have been the same as actually occurred; for moves to reunite dissenting Presbyterians with the Church of Scotland commenced before the Home Rule crisis of 1886.[57] Thus it would seem that the Liberal split of 1886 did not have a decisive effect on the long-term developments and results of church issues in England and Scotland. The basic reasons which eventually produced these results had already begun to operate before the political division of 1886.

Democratic advance had not been working consistently to the advantage of disestablishment. The restricted franchise extensions in the Reform Acts of 1832 and 1867 had given more political opportunity to nonconformity, and the Voluntary cause had advanced in the twenty years or so after each of these measures. But the same effect did not

[55] I. G. C. Hutchison, *A Political History of Scotland*, pp. 143–75; Machin, 'Voluntaryism and Reunion, 1874–1929', pp. 221–2.

[56] Machin, 'Voluntaryism and Reunion, 1874–1929', pp. 224, 226, 228, 231–3.

[57] *Ibid.*, pp. 224–6.

follow the electoral changes of 1884–5. The important redistribution of seats in 1885, which established much more equal numbers of electors in constituencies, gave increased power to working-class voters. Since many of these voters were not dissenters, this change reduced the comparative weight of the middle-class radical vote which was probably the most important ingredient in support for Voluntaryism. Moreover, the middle-class radical vote was itself contracting in the later nineteenth century as more middle-class electors – fearful of actual or potential statutory inroads on the freedom of property ownership – turned from Liberal to Conservative in their voting behaviour. This tendency included some nonconformists, not least those who were opposed to Irish Home Rule.

As the political weight and effectiveness of working-class voters increased, other issues, which did considerably more than disestablishment to arouse working-class interest, came increasingly to the fore. These were issues of social improvement such as the introduction of old age pensions (continuously debated from 1886), the establishment of an eight-hour working day, and extensions of the legal rights of trade unions. These matters were the chief concerns of the unions and of the growing number of Labour political groups. Many of the Labour and trade union leaders were nonconformists, and, as already mentioned, some early published programmes of the Labour groups included disestablishment (as a fairly low priority). But this Labour interest in Voluntaryism grew weaker rather than stronger. By 1914 it must have been abundantly clear that the Labour Party did not contain as strong an element of support for disestablishment as the Liberal Party had previously done.[58] This was the result not only of the beginning of nonconformist numerical decline and of increasing interest in social reform questions, but also of lessening interest in disestablishment among nonconformists themselves, who were becoming more absorbed in social issues – the leading domestic question of the day.

The turn of the century did not bring revival for the Liberation Society. This was losing membership and financial support, and relying on well-experienced and hoary-headed veterans to lead it – such as John Carvell Williams, who had been prominent in its activities since the 1860s – rather than attracting much in the way of new blood.[59] Lloyd George became a member of its committee, but, as an increasingly prominent politician, he played little more than the role of guest speaker and presti-

---

[58] Machin, *Politics and Churches, 1869 to 1921*, pp. 280–4; K. D. Brown, 'Nonconformity and the British Labour Movement: A Case Study', *Journal of Social History*, 8 (1975), pp. 113–20.
[59] Machin, *Politics and Churches, 1869 to 1921*, p. 223; the address of Revd Dr Joseph Parker to the assembly of the Congregational Union of England and Wales, April 1901 (*Congregational Year-Book*, 1902, p. 19).

gious embellishment. However, some occurrences did sustain the hopes of Voluntaries, not least a movement since the early 1890s to establish Free Church councils, which had developed rapidly at both national and local levels.[60]

Some revival of interest in Voluntaryism also arose from reaction against the spread of Ritualism in the Church of England.[61] A largely unsuccessful parliamentary attempt to restrain ritualistic practices had been made when the Public Worship Regulation Act had been passed in 1874. The continued growth of Ritualism caused a strong movement in opposition to it, which began about 1895 and continued for many years. The nonconformist role in this movement was shown partly in dislike of the Education Act of 1902. This not only, as it was said, 'put Rome on the rates' (by giving rate aid to Roman Catholic schools), but also encouraged Ritualism by giving rate aid to Anglican schools which might be under Ritualist influence. To Voluntaries, fear about the strengthening of the church establishment by granting a new widespread source of funding for its schools was also very much at issue. The bill's 'complete public endowment of denominational schools', said Asquith, 'was nothing more nor less than a fresh endowment of the Church of England'.[62] James Guinness Rogers, a leading Congregational minister and Voluntary, wrote that 'the practical issue of the Government policy has been not only to grant a new endowment to the State Church, but also to give a fresh legislative sanction to the State Church principle'. Nonconformists regarded 'the establishment of a State Church School as an annexe to the existing State Church'. The Liberation Society hoped that the Education Act would 'convince the electorate in increasing numbers of the necessity for the disestablishment and disendowment of the State Church'.[63] In the midst of the reaction to the Education Act there occurred an evangelical revival in Wales in 1904–5, led by Evan Roberts, which drew many new members into the dissenting denominations and considerably enlarged them, though this effect was only temporary.[64] Finally, in January 1906 there was a nonconformist electoral landslide within the Liberal land-

[60] E. K. H. Jordan, *Free Church Unity: A History of the Free Church Council Movement, 1896–1941*, London, 1956, pp. 20–51; Bebbington, *Nonconformist Conscience*, pp. 61–74.

[61] Machin, *Politics and Churches, 1869 to 1921*, p. 251.

[62] J. A. Spender and C. Asquith, *Life of Herbert Henry Asquith*, 2 vols., London, 1932, vol. I, p. 166.

[63] J. Guinness Rogers, *An Autobiography*, London, 1903, pp. 289–90; Liberation Society Executive Committee Minutes, 22 Dec. 1902, vol. IX, pp. 270–2.

[64] C. R. Williams, 'The Welsh Religious Revival, 1904–5', *British Journal of Sociology*, 3 (1952), pp. 242–59; B. Hall, 'The Welsh Revival of 1904–5: A Critique', in G. J. Cuming and D. Baker (eds.), *Popular Belief and Practice* (*Studies in Church History*, vol. VIII) Oxford 1972, pp. 291–301; *The Religious Revival in Wales, 1904, by Awstin and Other Special Correspondents of the Western Mail*, London, 1905.

slide, returning to parliament a larger number of dissenting MPs than either before or since (though six of them were returned as Conservatives). The largest denominational contribution was provided by the Congregationalists, and the next largest by the Wesleyans.[65]

But after these events came anti-climax. The Liberal government, obstructed by determined Conservative action operating through the House of Lords, was unable to change the terms of the 1902 Education Act. After the Lords' veto powers had been reduced in the Parliament Act of 1911, the government did not try very hard to change educational policy. It had lost its large majority of 1906. From 1910 it practically depended on maintaining the support of the Irish Home Rule party in order to stay in office, and this made it more politic than ever not to infringe on Roman Catholic educational desires. In order to retain the support of Catholics, and of many Anglicans, nonconformist hopes of changing the educational policy of 1902 had to be disappointed.

The government had also thought it politic to delay introducing a Welsh disestablishment bill until 1909, and in that session the bill was dropped through lack of parliamentary time.[66] Another Welsh disestablishment bill was introduced in 1912, after the passage of the Parliament Act had made it seem very likely that it would pass. The bill was enacted in 1914, after receiving the full delaying treatment (in excess of two years) from the Lords under the provisions of the Act of 1911. However, the outbreak of the First World War intervened to cause a much longer delay. The new Act (along with the Irish Home Rule Act) was declared to be suspended until the armed conflict had concluded. When Welsh disestablishment was finally implemented in 1920, this was done by a government which, although led by Lloyd George, consisted mostly of Conservatives. After the armistice of November 1918, negotiations had taken place which resulted (through the passing of an Amending Act, or Welsh Church Temporalities Act, in 1919) in more generous financial provision for the disestablished church in Wales than had been made in the Act of 1914.

Long before this, it had become likely that there would be no further acts of disestablishment in the United Kingdom, at least for the foreseeable future. The prospect of disestablishment, except in Wales, was not strengthened simply by the return of a large number of nonconformist MPs in 1906. Many of these were not primarily interested in disestablishment (it was no longer the case, for example, that Lloyd George was

[65] S. Koss, *Nonconformity in Modern British Politics*, London, 1975, p. 228. Seventy-three Congregationalists were returned, thirty-five Wesleyans, seventeen Baptists, seventeen Unitarians, and smaller numbers of other nonconformists; *ibid.*
[66] Machin, *Politics and Churches, 1869 to 1921*, pp. 298–302.

mainly interested in Welsh disestablishment),[67] and the Voluntary cause in England and Scotland could only have been revived by a large upsurge in popular support for it. Not only did this fail to occur, but nonconformist membership numbers began to decline, and the Liberal split of 1916–18 further weakened the party political prospects affecting the success of dissenting causes. The Labour Party rose to displace the Liberals after the First World War; and, as we have seen, while there was much nonconformist influence in this party there was little pressure on it to take up disestablishment, a matter which would have caused division in the party as it had already done among the Liberals.

VIII

While disestablishment was rapidly declining by the 1920s, the alternative policy of religious self-government within an establishment obtained some important victories. In both Scotland and England, where pressure for disestablishment had declined, pressure for spiritual independence increased. In Scotland discussions had been taking place since 1907 on reunion between the established church and the United Free Church, the main non-established Presbyterian body.[68] The First World War delayed these proceedings. But in 1921 the Lloyd George coalition passed a bill which had to go through if the United Free Church was to agree to join the establishment. This measure, entitled the Church of Scotland Act, provided for complete religious self-government within the Scottish establishment. On this basis most United Free Churchmen were able to agree to unite with the Church of Scotland. After the passage in parliament of a temporalities measure in 1925, settling the question of endowments, union between the Church of Scotland and most of the United Free Church formally occurred in 1929 (a minority in the latter church, being unable to accept the terms on Voluntary grounds, continued as a separate body with the same title).[69]

Many members of the Church of England had envied the greater degree of spiritual independence in the Church of Scotland well before 1921, including its freedom from patronage in ministerial appointments since the Patronage Act of 1874. At the end of the nineteenth century,

[67] S. Koss, *Nonconformity in Modern British Politics*, pp. 78, 88; J. F. Glasier, 'English Nonconformity and the Decline of Liberalism', *American Historical Review*, 80 (1957–8), p. 361.

[68] R. Sjölinder, *Presbyterian Reunion in Scotland, 1907–21*, trans. E. J. Sharpe, Edinburgh, 1962, 163ff.

[69] Machin, 'Voluntaryism and Reunion, 1874–1929', pp. 229–33; A. Muir, *John White*, CH, London, 1958, pp. 214–67; A. I. Dunlop, 'The Paths to Reunion in 1929', *Records of the Scottish Church History Society*, 20 (1980), pp. 163–78.

desire for greater self-government in the Church of England was voiced by the Church Reform League, founded in 1895, which wanted to establish representative bodies at all levels from parish councils to a national assembly.[70] The league also wanted the abolition of patronage, appointment of the clergy by an elected board in each diocese, and the election of bishops exclusively by cathedral chapters, replacing episcopal appointment by the crown.[71] A Benefices Bill was passed in 1898, but this was only a partial measure of patronage reform which by no means satisfied those who had been campaigning for twenty-eight years for a stronger measure. Similarly, the formation of a Representative Church Council of bishops, clergy and laity in 1904 only whetted the appetites of reformers for a greater degree of church self-government.

So the demand for autonomy remained, and gathered strength. On 4 July 1913 the Representative Church Council passed a resolution which said that there was 'no inconsistency between a national recognition of religion and the spiritual independence of the Church'.[72] On the request of this council, the archbishops agreed to appoint a Committee on Church and State. The report of this committee, published in July 1916, stressed the difficulty of getting church legislation through a parliament that, taken as a whole, had not enough interest in it to give it sufficient time. The Church of England needed more liberty to decide on reforms for itself, though it would be content (at least initially) with considerably less liberty than the Church of Scotland, which had traditionally been freer from state control. Some members of the committee wanted to go as far as recommending disestablishment, but the majority did not support this view. The committee proposed that a new representative Church Assembly be established, having the power to adopt laws for the church which would be subject to parliamentary veto. In order to give parliamentary recognition to this body an Enabling Bill, drafted in the committee's report, would need to be passed. There was strong campaigning for this bill, and the demand for it overlapped with a desire for more church involvement in the appointment of bishops. The Enabling Bill passed through parliament in 1919 against opposition from various quarters, including Voluntaries who said that the church could only be sufficiently liberated by disestablishment, not by the compromise which the bill represented.[73] The National Assembly of the Church of England,

---

[70] Minutes of the Council of Church Reform League, 27 Nov. 1895, 10 Jan. 1896 (CRL/1, Church House, Westminster); Machin, *Politics and Churches, 1869 to 1921*, pp. 224, 232–3.

[71] Machin, *Politics and Churches, 1869 to 1921*, p. 224.

[72] *Ibid.*, p. 317.

[73] D. M. Thompson, 'The Politics of the Enabling Act, 1919', in D. Baker (ed.), *Church, Society and Politics* (*Studies in Church History*, vol. XII), Oxford, 1975, pp. 383–92; Machin, *Politics and Churches, 1869 to 1921*, pp. 319–20.

which was created under the new Act and which had legislative powers subject to parliamentary veto, lasted until 1970 when it was succeeded by the General Synod.[74]

Thus, within three years of the ending of the First World War, the ecclesiastical position of Great Britain was transformed through the adoption or implementation of these measures – Welsh disestablishment, the Church of Scotland Act, and the Enabling Act for the Church of England. Only one of these, however, represented the application of Voluntaryism. The other two rather illustrated the way in which spiritual independence within an establishment had replaced Voluntaryism as the practical means of winning religious freedom.

In the Church of England, moreover, religious freedom had been only very partially attained. Parliament could still reject its measures, and this happened, in a notable clash of church and state legislatures, when parliament threw out the Revised Prayer Book (which sought to accommodate some Ritualist procedures) in 1927 and 1928.[75] Much later, after the General Synod had replaced the National Assembly, more authority in self-government was attained by the church. Notably, in 1977, more church participation was gained in the appointment of bishops – though today the Prime Minister still retains a place in recommending names to the crown for appointment.[76]

A. V. Dicey said that the Enabling Act of 1919 heralded 'the approaching disestablishment of the Church of England'.[77] He appears to have been wrong. Even at the time he made this statement, the call for disestablishment from outside the church had notably declined in strength, and it did not revive. From within the church, however, the call for disestablishment has become rather more vocal in recent years than it was in 1919; but it seems to remain the desire of a small minority of members. Altogether, while disestablishment remains today a matter of interest and debate, it does not bulk large among questions of controversy.

IX

The moves to establish a democratic society have been reflected not only in the partial attainment of disestablishment but in the achievement of

[74] R. Lloyd, *The Church of England, 1900–65*, London, 1966, p. 243ff.

[75] G. K. A. Bell, *Randall Davidson, Archbishop of Canterbury*, 2 vols., London, 1935, vol. II, p. 1335ff.; W. Joynson-Hicks, *The Prayer Book Crisis* (London, 1928).

[76] Machin, *Politics and Churches, 1869 to 1921*, pp. 233–4, 317–20; B. Palmer, *High and Mitred: Prime Ministers as Bishop-Makers, 1837–1977*, London, 1992, pp. 279–88; K. Medhurst and G. Moyser, *Church and Politics in a Secular Age*, Oxford, 1988, p. 141ff.

[77] Dicey to Lord Balfour of Burleigh, 7 May 1920; Balfour of Burleigh Papers, vol. XLVII (courtesy of Scottish Record Office).

substantial religious self-government. Democratic advance has also, incidentally, influenced changes in ecclesiastical organisation and policy – notably (and topically) the adoption of an ordained female ministry, first in the Congregational Church in 1917, followed soon afterwards by the Baptists and later by other nonconformist churches, and subsequently by the Church of Scotland in 1968 and the Church of England in 1992.

Democratic power and extension sometimes worked in support of disestablishment, and sometimes against it. The electoral reform of 1867 encouraged the Voluntary cause by enfranchising many more of its potential supporters, but the electoral redistribution of 1885 weakened it by increasing the voting power of the working class, most of whose members were not very interested in disestablishment. Churches were disestablished in Ireland and Wales basically because of the existence of a large majority in both countries which did not belong to the establishment, and because national feeling gave additional force to the demand. The fact that in Scotland eventually, and in England throughout, a majority of the population did not support disestablishment, helps to explain why Voluntaryism did not succeed in those countries.

Another contributory factor was the removal or diminution of established church privileges. As legal inequalities were abolished, disestablishment was no longer backed up by more practical grievances and was left depending on the more tenuous support of theoretical justification. This was an inadequate basis on which to attract popular support, especially when rural anti-clericalism, which had lent support to Voluntaryism, was dying out by the end of the nineteenth century on account of the decline of clerical incomes obtained from agriculture.

Political change also added to the decline of support for disestablishment. The Liberal Party, the Voluntaries' chief hope of realising their aim, divided and began to decline in 1916–18, and the Labour Party did not replace it as a possible vehicle for disestablishment.

Altogether there seemed little hope of further disestablishment by the 1920s. In 1934 Philip Snowden, a leading Labour politician and a Methodist, was able to state: 'It is curious how a political question excites great interest for a time, and then becomes a dead issue. The present generation has never heard of the Disestablishment of the Church of England.'[78] Nineteen years later a report of a Free Church Federal Council commission, entitled *The Free Churches and the State*, gave the opinion that 'It would be easy by ill-considered proposals for disestablishment to jeopardize the existing valuable co-operation between Church and State, in which the Free Churches have come increasingly to

[78] Philip, Viscount Snowden, *An Autobiography*, 2 vols., London, 1934, vol. I, pp. 41–2.

share'.[79] However, as a substitute for disestablishment to a considerable extent, a large degree of self-government has been achieved by the established churches, especially in Scotland but increasingly also in England. This development, and the demise of an active Liberation Society by the late 1950s, have not prevented occasional calls still being made for disestablishment in England. But none of these has gained much support or lasted any length of time. The effects of democratic demand have been shown in the attainment of disestablishment in some countries in the British Isles, and the gain of spiritual independence in others.

[79] *The Free Churches and the State*, Free Church Federal Council publication, London, 1953, p. 62.

Part II

Economic democracy and the 'moral economy' of free trade

6 The National Agricultural Labourers' Union and the demand for a stake in the soil, 1872–1896

Nigel Scotland

I

The year 1871 had witnessed the passage of a government bill into law which gave legal recognition to trade unions and enabled them to protect their funds under the Friendly Society Acts. No difficult provisos regarding the division of funds for benefit and funds for strike purposes remained, although unions were still liable to criminal prosecutions under the 1825 Act for picketing and obstruction. Despite the passing of the Act, very little agitation occurred until the winter which followed. The harvest of 1871, which proved to be a bad one, and caused prices to rise, also contributed to the sudden upsurge of activity in the opening weeks of 1872.

The initial focus of attention was in Warwickshire at Wellesbourne where on 14 February the celebrated union meeting was held on the village green under the great chestnut tree. Yet, almost simultaneously, scattered villages from all over the southern counties where agricultural wages were lower, began to join the action as the down-trodden workers started to take to their feet. In the first weeks of February and March 1872, the picture was one of numerous small local unions springing to life. These were often clustered around one of the larger market towns.

By the spring of 1872 these local unions had become so numerous that some kind of umbrella organisation was called for in order to facilitate coordinated action and protest. The Warwickshire Union led by Joseph Arch (1828–1919), a champion hedge-cutter and a sturdy independent individual who was also a Methodist local preacher, proved to be the most influential among these local unions. On 19 May, Arch's union called a conference of delegates representing twenty-six counties. The result of this was the formation of the National Agricultural Labourers' Union with its headquarters in Leamington. By the end of 1873 the new union had over 1,000 branches and a membership of 71,835. At its peak there were 80,000 labourers in the ranks and the union's newspaper, the

Labourers' Union Chronicle, was selling 30,000 copies an issue.[1] From the early 1880s onwards the National, like other agricultural unions, went into a decade and a half of gradual but steady decline. Although there were one or two brief revivals in membership, the National was a spent force in 1895. By the end of 1896 all traces of its existence had finally disappeared. Hence 1896 is the terminating point of this study.

In 1874 the newly formed union published a rule book[2] which also contained a statement of its objectives. Two of these relate to the question of land and a stake in the soil. They read as follows: 'to provide them with gardens or allotments; and to assist deserving and suitable labourers to migrate and emigrate'. The right to a stake in the soil for the labourers was thus a union objective from its inception. Because land could only be rented by labourers at the pleasure of the owner until 1894, the National was involved in a campaign of 'land for the labourer' for virtually the entire duration of its existence.

An early instance of this concern for the provision of land for the labourer was seen at Littlemore in Oxfordshire. There, a union branch secretary advocated the acquisition of land for allotments in a speech at a meeting in September 1872. Three years later the Oxfordshire district committee began to make plans for a society to acquire land for its members to cultivate.[3]

Early speeches on the part of Joseph Arch and other prominent leaders raised the theme of land for the labourers. Typical of these was Arch's own appearance at the annual conference of the union's Cirencester district which was held at the 'British Workman' in Cheltenham. In his speech he said that 'it would be the object of the union, as soon as possible, to devise means to obtain small plots of land in every district to be cultivated by members of the union'.[4] In these early speeches Arch often put the blame for the depressed state of agriculture on the land laws which allowed wealthy families to monopolise large tracts of land without any commitment to cultivate them. Arch maintained that were the labourers given the right to own and cultivate such land the state of English agriculture would be greatly improved. He did not appear to recognise the impact of cheap imports of foreign wheat which were driving prices down.

The year 1875 witnessed a traumatic conflict within the National Union and a rival group emerged under the leadership of Matthew

---

[1] N. A. D. Scotland, *Agricultural Trade Union in Gloucestershire*, Cheltenham, 1991, p. 18.
[2] 'Constitution and Rules of the National Agricultural Labourers' Union Revised at the Annual May Council 1874', Howell Collection, Bishopsgate Institute, ms 116.
[3] P. R. L. Horn, 'Agricultural Trade Unionism in Oxfordshire' in J. P. D. Dunbabin, *Rural Discontent in the Nineteenth Century*, London, 1973, p. 111.
[4] *Labourers' Union Chronicle*, 16 January 1875.

Vincent who was the owner and editor of the union newspaper.[5] Vincent's rival organisation, which only lasted for a little over two years, took the title of the National Farm Labourers' Union. Significantly it laid particular emphasis on land policy. One of its stated aims was:

to accelerate the solution of the land question by the purchase and hire of land so as to promote small holdings for the occupation and ownership of farm labourers, and thus secure to them a participation in the profits of the soil, improve the rate of wages and increase the proper independence of the labourer.[6]

The rival union sought to achieve this goal by forming a land company which would be able to hold land in trust. Members paid ½d subscription towards a land share.[7] The union's newly titled paper for 24 June 1876 announced that its capital holding amounted to £25,000 in shares of £1 each and £9,000 in shares of £2 10s. each. It was further stated that the new organisation intended to supersede strikes and lock-outs among labouring classes by 'promoting the garden allotment system throughout the villages and towns of the kingdom'.[8] Typical of the advertisements which appeared in the new union paper was the following:

LAND! LAND! LAND!
Wanted to HIRE on long lease, SMALL FARMS or PLOTS OF LAND for division into Small Holdings or Allotment for tillage by Agricultural Labourers.
– Apply to J. W. Lake, Honorary Secretary, National Farm Labourers' Union, 1 Priory Terrace, Leamington.[9]

Despite the union's brief existence, the land company continued. By 1879 the company had branches in twenty-five counties all told, 689 shares at £1 had been taken up, and 15 at £2 10s.[10]

By 1878 most of those who had defected to Vincent's schismatic organisation had returned to the fold of the old National Union, still led by Arch, and a campaign of land for the labourers continued. Arch's land proposals, it should be said, were for the most part rather more modest than his rival's had been. In the main he campaigned for greater

[5] One reason for the dispute was that some of Arch's main leaders, including the general secretary, Henry Taylor, felt that Vincent was altering reports which were handed to him for publication in the union's newspaper. Pamela Horn, 'Agricultural Trade Unionism', pp. 100–1 suggests that Vincent's main complaint was the ending of support to the lock-out men.
[6] *Labourers' Union Chronicle*, 28 August 1875.
[7] *National Agricultural Labourers' Chronicle*, 17 June 1876.
[8] *Ibid*, 24 June 1876.
[9] *Labourers' Union Chronicle*, 18 March 1876.
[10] Horn, 'Agricultural Trade Unionism', p. 63.

availability of small holdings at modest rents, the provision of allotment lands in every village and much greater security of tenure for the tenant. The union's paper which carried the subtitle 'An Independent Advocate of British Toilers' Rights to Free Land', continued to advocate the cause and frequently carried adverts requesting land for rent at modest prices. In the early 1880s it also urged on the labourers the possibility of emigrating to the new lands of the empire where there was the promise of four to six acres of land per man.[11] Part of the union thinking behind this strategy was that by reducing the population of the villages in this way more land would be available for those who remained.

In one sense, it has always been the case that radical movements among the peasantry and later the working classes have demanded greater shares in the soil. The National Union's campaign for land was therefore predictable. Yet there were several other significant influences which emerged in the nineteenth century and which fed into the union land reform objectives.

II

There were a number of earlier nineteenth-century radical movements with aspirations of land for the people and it was inevitable that they would impact themselves in varying degrees on Arch's union platform. Some of Arch's chief lieutenants had been youngsters in the 1830s and their parents had witnessed the rising tide of opposition to high bread prices and low wages. This was particularly so in East Anglia where the large field gangs were always more prone to riot or rick-burning. Nevertheless there were protests on the part of the farm labourers in Buckingham, Dorset, Norwich, Ipswich, Gloucester, Oxford and Winchester in the 1830s. It was in the wake of these that an Essex Labourers' Petition of 1837 had requested 'small allotments of land to labourers to be cultivated with a spade'.[12] It is significant that a number of strong National Union branches developed in towns and villages where there was a previous history of agrarian protest.

Owenism had propounded the idea of a cooperative community on the land and the Chartists had conceived of a land company with the objective of providing land and cottages for the labourer. It is significant that at the inaugural meeting of the National Union one of those who shared

[11] See *Boston Guardian*, 7 February 1874, 'Free Emigration to New Zealand!! Free Passages are Granted by the Government of New Zealand To married and single Agricultural Labourers etc.'; in the *Norwich Argus*, 18 May 1872; Henry Gibson promised free land to any Swaffham district agricultural union members who would emigrate to Canada.

[12] E. P. Thompson, *The Making of the English Working Class*, London, 1963, p. 229.

the platform was the Reverend Arthur O'Neill, a Birmingham Baptist minister, who had been imprisoned for Chartist activities in 1842.[13] There were occasional references to the Chartists in the speeches made at some union branch meetings. For example, at a meeting at Dumbleton in Gloucestershire, a labourer named Smith, who took the chair, showed how he 'with four acres of land upon the O'Connor allotments could and did make a living for his family, and was better off than when he worked for a farmer at 12s. a week'.[14]

Generally speaking, however, there is little in the speeches of the union branch officials by way of quotation or inspiration from radical individuals. The most frequent references seem to have been to the parliamentary speeches of Cobden and Bright, Liberals of a previous generation. In Norfolk, for example, there were six references to Cobden and Bright in a twenty-year survey of the union newspaper.[15] A typical instance is contained in the speech given by Thomas Burnett at a union meeting in Lissington Primitive Methodist chapel in which he commended 'the work of Cobden and Bright as agitators for the peoples' bread'.[16] It is perhaps not without significance that Joseph Arch's own father 'steady as Old Time – a plodding man' had been victimised for anti-corn law sympathies.[17]

The point being made here is simply that these earlier kindred radical movements fed into the land programme of Arch's National Union. There are clear similarities between the Chartist allotment schemes and the Allotment and Small Holdings Association of which he became an executive committee member.[18] Again, it is apparent that Arch drew inspiration from the Liberal radical tradition epitomised by Cobden and Bright. One of his biographers noted that, along with Wesley's commentaries and Spurgeon's sermons, his favourite books were Bright's and Cobden's speeches.[19] Cobden had in fact declared in his own last speech at Rochdale in November 1864: 'If I were five-and-twenty or thirty, instead of unhappily twice that number of years, I would take Adam Smith in hand, and I would have a league for "free trade in land" just as we had a league for "free trade in corn."'[20]

---

[13] Horn, 'Agricultural Trade Unionism', p. 63.
[14] *Gloucester Journal*, 1 March 1873.
[15] See N. A. D. Scotland, *Methodism and the Revolt of the Field*, Gloucester, 1980.
[16] *English Labourers' Chronicle*, 24 May 1879.
[17] Horn, 'Agricultural Trade Unionism', p. 63. See also *English Labourers' Chronicle*, 23 January 1886.
[18] *English Labourers' Chronicle*, 16 January 1886.
[19] *Ibid.*, 23 January 1886.
[20] J. Morley, *Life of Cobden* (1903 edition), cited in J. Butt and I. F. Clarke, *The Victorians and Social Protest*, Exeter, 1973, p. 196.

One impact of these earlier radical movements was to impress upon the labourers the fact that they had been robbed of their age-long rights to the land by the enclosure schemes. They also instilled in them the motivation to fight for the recovery of their rights. Certainly it was the case that some of the National Union's prominent leaders had either witnessed enclosure schemes themselves or learned of them at first hand.

The land question was one of the favourite themes of William Yeats, the leader of the National's Gloucester district. He gave a lengthy address at a somewhat stormy union gathering at the village of Dumbleton in the spring of 1873. Despite being interrupted several times by the local rector, Yeats maintained that the land and the labourer should be inseparable, instead of which 'scarcely a labourer could be found that had the slightest interest in the land'. The same speaker went on to argue that many of those who were in possession of land 'came into possession of it by direct confiscation'. The only hope, he maintained, of gaining a stake in the soil for tens of thousands of poor labourers, 'is what can never be prevented, about seven feet of space to cover him when he ceased to exist!' (great cheering and cries of 'That's true', and 'Shame' resounded upon all hands).[21]

Union supporters John and Henry Cox were among the early vehement opponents of enclosure. In their *Rise of the Farm Labourer*, which was published in 1874, they wrote:

These lords of the manor accepted with eagerness Acts by which they were enabled to fence round the clump of fern and furze that had previously afforded fuel free of all charge, to the poor cottagers of the District; yet instead of making them fertile and productive of food and employment, they have but converted them into nurseries of legal crime.

Society, and not the individual landowner, was the original owner of land, and every licence to enclose has been a surrender by society of its rights ... But if society is forced to give up its rights without the compensation of an increased food supply, then the action of these law-making landowners can only be regarded as legalised robbery.[22]

In July 1874 Arch's *Union Chronicle* printed a full-length front-page article entitled: 'The commons of England belonged to the peasantry and were stolen by the landlords'.[23] The writer claimed that the commoners had the common lands prior to the growth of the manorial system, and that since the lords of the manor did not purchase their rights from the commoners, they can only have taken possession by fraud: 'for any Act of Parliament which takes the land from one class for whom it is the staff

[21] *Gloucester Journal*, 1 March 1873.
[22] J. C. Cox and H. Cox, *The Rise of the Farm Labourer*, London, 1874, p. 67.
[23] *Labourers' Union Chronicle*, 25 July 1874.

of life, and gives it to another class that requires it only from greed, envy, and monopoly, is not a law, but only a memorandum of iniquity'.[24] The writer then cited, with obvious approval, Blackstone's distinction that human laws are of no validity if they contravene the law of nature. Commending 'this authoritative statement to that stupid dolt the Marquis of Bristol' the article vigorously asserted:

An Act of Parliament ... cannot sanctify or justify iniquity ... what is contrary to the law of nature, and at enmity with society, and menacing the prosperity of the people, we demand loudly and authoritatively shall be destroyed.[25]

The *English Labourers' Chronicle* did much to encourage the union members to regain their rights to the soil. In April 1881 it reprinted a passage from a little book entitled *The Laws of God versus the Laws of Man*. Written in the form of a catechism, it made a vigorous attack on the greed of those landlords who deprived the labourer of his age-long rights to the soil. The narrative which is couched in the language of the Old Testament, enunciated the familiar theme that land is the property of the whole community.

THE SHORT CATECHISM

Question   Who created the land?
Answer   God.
Question   Who then has the sole right to order its disposal?
Answer   God.
Question   And what has He declared in His will respecting it?
Answer   That it should be divided among all people, to every man his portion.
See Numbers 26, verses 51–56 to prove that God designed the land to be the common property of the people! Yet the aristocracy and large landed proprietors of this country, by means of corrupt feudal laws ... monopolise most of the land in this country; and thus the common people have been robbed of their just share in the possession of the land of their birth. Why should the people of this country be thus deprived of their rights?[26]

George Ball (b. 1832), who became the National's vice president, wrote to the *English Labourers' Chronicle* in June 1883 and urged labourers 'to unite as one man and never rest until we regain our lost inheritance'. Union hymns and songs also gave vent to these same aspirations.

Lord Reginald
Lord Reginald wants to get more land still –
If he lacks the power, he don't [sic] lack the will;
He'll steel [sic] our commons, if ever he can,
For he doesn't believe in the rights of man.

[24] *Ibid.*, 25 July 1874.
[25] *Ibid.*, 25 July 1874.
[26] *English Labourers' Chronicle*, 30 April 1881.

But the time is near, when he'll have to be taught,
That the land wasn't made to furnish his sport;
That the down-trodden peasants, the children of toil,
By their labour and sweat, *have their rights in the soil.*
Oh the wrongs of the poor![27]

Another song from Howard Evans' collection entitled *Songs for Singing at Agricultural Labourers' Meetings* included the following lines:

God opens wide his mighty hand
And showers his blessings wide,
He never made this glorious land
To pamper rich men's pride
Give back the rights upon the land
Our fathers had of yore
We'll be content with nothing less,
We ask for nothing more.[28]

Edward Richardson, the Buckingham district official, produced another volume of songs under the title *The National Agricultural Labourers' Union Melody Book*. Some of his collection expressed the same demands. A typical instance is 'The Father's Song' which contained the following stanza:

Deliver me from the serfdom of the toil,
From laws made to please the few;
Give me an interest, a share in the soil,
Let me try what I can do.[29]

Even in the 1880s the reversal of enclosure was still a recurring theme of National Union speeches. In an address at Wickham Market on the subject of 'The Labourers and the Franchise', Arch touched on the land issue. Referring to the Commons Enclosure Bills, Arch wondered:

whether the democracy would not demand these eight million acres should be disgorged and given to the people again [Hear, Hear and cheering]. He did not wish to interfere with the rights of property if property did not interfere with the rights of the people, but if he had 10,000 acres of land which the Creator had provided for the sustenance of all and he were to turn off the labourers, let the land go to waste and convert it into deer forest, he would be acting contrary to the Divine Will [Hear, hear].[30]

Other union activists argued against enclosure on the ground that it had not delivered its stated objective which was to make land available for

---

[27] H. Evans, 'Lord Reginald', *Songs for Singing at Agricultural Labourers' Meetings*, London, 1875, p. 22 (italics mine).
[28] H. Evans, 'We ask for Nothing More', *ibid.*, p. 22 (italics mine).
[29] E. Richard, *The National Agricultural Labourers' Union Melody Book*, Coventry, 1873.
[30] *English Labourers' Chronicle*, 13 January 1883.

improved farming and hence the production of cheaper food as a benefit to the poorer classes. In fact the reverse was the case and much of what had been enclosed in the name of progress had merely become hunting grounds and gaming parks for the wealthy. A frequent ploy of union agitators was therefore to inform the labourers that they had been hood-winked, indeed robbed, by the rich. Constant attacks were made and resolutions were passed against enclosure. For example, speaking at a National Union meeting at Aldborough in Norfolk in September 1876, James Ayton (1821–1883) moved 'a resolution, in the form of a petition praying the Government to defer legislation in further enclosure of commons, believing such legislation would be unjust to the rural popula-tion while deprived of their political rights'.[31]

III

Researches have shown that most of the significant leaders of the National Agricultural Labourers' Union were office-holding Method-ists.[32] That is, they were more than nominal Methodists or those who happened to express the opposition to the parson and farmers by atten-dance at a Methodist chapel on a Sunday. It is significant, therefore, that during the time of the National Union's struggle for land for the labourer, the various branches of methodism were by no means neutral in the stance which they adopted. As early as 1873 the *United Methodist Free Churches Magazine* pronounced in favour of land for the labourer: 'It would surely be no great thing if large farmers would allow each of the married labourers half an acre of land, on which they might grow pota-toes for their own family, and sufficient to keep a couple of pigs'.[33] The writer went on to state that, according to the current way of thinking, farmers are not bound to adopt such a policy. Nevertheless, a Christian spirit would surely prompt action of this kind.

Later in the same year, the *Primitive Methodist* attacked England's land system as a root cause of national impoverishment:

One reason doubtless, why so much fertile land is lying waste is the system which places the land in the hands of the few. One hundred years ago there were 250,000 land-owners in England, but now there are not 30,000. We do not advo-cate the French system of compulsory division, but we have a decided objection to the tying up of the land in the family of 'TOMKINS'.[34]

[31] *Norfolk News*, 1 April 1876.
[32] See, for example, N. A. D. Scotland, *Methodism and the Revolt of the Field*, pp. 55–74.
[33] 'Our Monthly Chronicle', *UMFC Magazine*, January 1873.
[34] *Primitive Methodist*, 24 July 1873.

The writer opposed the law of entail on the ground that it prevented land flowing into the market when there was a necessity for it: 'Such a system is an insult to common sense, an outrage to humanity, and the sooner Parliament alters this law and does justice to a country they are called upon to govern, the better'.[35] The article concluded:

the land-owning class must either rise to a just appreciation of the moral duties which the situation imposes upon them, or else await in silence the gradual awakening of the nation to the idea that a land system, in which the cultivation of the soil is not the primary object of its ownership, is one which public policy can no longer consent to maintain.[36]

It is almost uncanny to observe the parallel between what the Methodist periodicals were writing and what the union activists were advocating. For example, a Mr W. Gause who presided at a meeting of Arch's union in April 1881 at Guyhirn in Cambridgeshire, referred to the land question in his introductory remarks. He maintained that 'the land must be put within the reach of the labouring man, and until that is done England will not prosper, no matter what Government is in power'.[37] Gause went on to develop one of the union's recurring themes but couched in markedly biblical phraseology:

God gave the land to man to till and enjoy its fruits, but unjust laws have been passed which forbid a great portion of mankind enjoying the fruits of the land, and whilst the land brought forth in abundance many have starved and died. When we as a nation, work to carry out justice one to another, God will work in harmony with us, and bless our land again.[38]

In the 1880s Primitive Methodists were still attacking the country's land system in similar fashion. In an article entitled 'The Duty of the Church in Relation to the Present Social Movements' the Reverend J. Welford maintained that:

God never intended the land to be in the hands of a few men that were no better than others. The land was made for the people, the people must live on it ... What was wanted was not nationalisation of land, but the unmonopolising of it ... They must instil into the mind of the landowners that the land was not absolutely theirs, but a trust held for the common good, and that in the use of it they are not simply to study their own pleasure and profit, but the public weal.[39]

In 1885 the *Primitive Methodist Magazine* printed an article by Robert Bryant entitled 'Land Tenure'. This is a discussion of some depth in

---

[35] *Ibid.*, 24 July 1873.
[36] *Ibid.*, 24 July 1873.
[37] *English Labourers' Chronicle*, 30 April 1881.
[38] *Ibid.*
[39] *Primitive Methodist*, 23 October 1884.

which the writer argued that land is a trust given by God to the whole community. Thus Bryant wrote:

The pervading principle of such tenure is, that landed possessions or holdings are a trust granted by the community or state, and the tenant or person holding it becomes a trustee or public functionary pledged to certain duties or responsibilities. And that this is the fundamental principle of land-tenure as set forth in the Bible will appear on examination.[40]

At a later point in his article, Bryant argued this principle on the basis of Leviticus 25, verses 23 and 24. His main point was that 'the land is the Lord's' and that 'He gave the nations their inheritance ... and the land was held for the good of the entire community, and all individual rights and interests were subordinate'. Bryant's position was substantially that expressed by many of Arch's National Union delegates and officials who grounded the rights of labourers on this Old Testament principle that the land was a trust for the good of the whole of society. George Edwards of Kenninghall in Norfolk, for example, made the same point that the land belongs to the people as a whole. At the beginning of his speech to unionists of the Diss district he said: 'the land should belong to the people, especially to the agricultural labourers who were born on the soil. Why Adam was born to the soil ...'[41]

In the early part of 1894 Arch's *Chronicle* printed a number of letters on the subject of land tenure of which the two following written by Norfolk union officials are typical examples. Arthur Munford of Winfarthing in Norfolk, a fairly frequent contributor to the *Chronicle* in the 1890s, wrote:

the future cry must be 'Land for the People'. The only system of land tenure which has the sanction of God was the Mosaic, wherein arrangements were made that the poor should never be driven from the soil ... The scriptural ideal is that every man should sit under his own vine and fig tree, none daring to make him afraid.[42]

In the following month William Gray of Runton wrote on the same theme and concluded 'that nothing but abolishing our present land system and giving all men an equal right to use the earth will ever deal effectually with the vexed question of the unemployed'.[43] 'The idea that a few people have absolute right to the use of earth', he concluded, 'is not in accordance with divine teaching'.[44]

It is clear that Methodist social and political thinking on matters connected to the land not only ran in parallel with the union platform but

[40] R. Bryant, 'Land Tenure', *Primitive Methodist Magazine*, n.s., 3 (1885).
[41] *English Labourers' Chronicle*, 17 January 1880.
[42] *Ibid.*, 12 May 1894.
[43] *Ibid.*, 2 June 1894.
[44] *Ibid.*

often fed into it and indeed reinforced it. The Methodist ethos of many union villages also ensured a more receptive response and commitment to the union pleas of land for the labourers.

IV

Yet if it is true that there was a strong point of correspondence between the union's land reform policy and Methodist ideology there was an even stronger convergence with Liberal Party reform proposals. Arch was a free trader through and through. His first significant publication was *Free Trade Versus Protection or Fair Trade, weighed in the Balances and Found Wanting*.[45] Although he believed free trade in food was the most important aspect of free trade, he saw the principle must also include free land, free church, free schools and free labour. Jesse Collings (1831–1920), MP for Ipswich, had been on the union's executive committee since its inception and Arch, George Ball and other leading district officials were all active in the Liberal Party cause. Arch's very first public appearance in London was at a meeting on land tenure reform presided over by John Stuart Mill. Arch was also reported to have 'powerfully aided Mr Mill's association' by forceful speeches at Bradford, Huddersfield and other great towns.[46] When Sir Charles Dilke (1843–1911) brought forward his Allotment Extension Bill in 1874 he was supplied with background information by the union's Howard Evans.[47] In the 1880s the National Union began to throw all its efforts into helping the labourers to secure the vote, sensing that in achieving this they would have a better hope of achieving their union objectives including a stake in the soil for the farm workers.

On 28 February 1884, Gladstone introduced his Representation of the People Bill into the House. Although union membership was waning at the time, Arch was resolved that the National should make a good showing. So on Easter Monday 'a vast multitude' paraded through the streets of Leamington headed by the town band and carrying a new silk banner inscribed with the words 'Franchise Bill 1884'.[48] Finally in December the bill became law and the labourers had achieved the vote. One immediate result of this was that the agricultural labourers, grateful for the gift of the vote, began to throw themselves wholeheartedly in support of the Liberal Party candidates in the forthcoming general election. In many union branches and districts, meetings were organised

[45] J. Arch, *Free Trade Versus Protection or Fair Trade, weighed in the Balances and Found Wanting*, Coventry, 1884.

[46] *English Labourers' Chronicle*, 23 January 1886.

[47] *Ibid.*, 1 May 1886. See also J. Collings, *Land Reform*, London, 1906, p. 179, and R. Jenkins, *Sir Charles Dilke: A Victorian Tragedy*, London, 1958, p. 97.

[48] See P. L. R. Horn, *Joseph Arch: Farm Workers' Leader*, Kineton, 1971, p. 162.

explaining to the labourers how to vote and how to get their names on the electoral roll. They also made it clear to the labourers that the secret ballot meant that there was no way by which their employers could tell which way they had voted. Arch himself suggested the setting up of mock elections in as many places as possible to explain voting procedures to the men. One of many such meetings was that held at the village of Crondal in Wiltshire in January 1885. After very full information regarding procedures had been gone through, voting papers were handed to the twenty-six labourers who were present. They were asked to decide between Sir Stafford Northcote and William Gladstone. The result of the ballot was pleasing with William Gladstone receiving all twenty-six votes![49]

The campaign in support of the Liberals in Gloucestershire typifies the National's general strategy. In the east of the county where the union was strongest the branches gave vigorous support to the newly adopted candidate Arthur Brend Winterbotham (1837–92). Although by 1885 the union was virtually a spent force in the north and west of the county, the agricultural labourers did what they could to muster support for Godfrey Samuelson in his bid to win Tewkesbury for the Liberals.

The prospect of the election certainly acted as a fresh spur to the Cirencester district officials of the union to try and rekindle the men's enthusiasm. The district delegate, Thomas Boulton, wrote: 'Now you have your votes, there is ten times more need for you to combine, and to send men to properly represent you.'[50] From the very first weeks of January, district secretary Henry Hemming (1830–1909) flung himself into a campaign of support for Winterbotham. Writing in his district column, Hemming informed his readers that 'Our Liberal friends in the county are forwarding literature which is suitable to inform labourers on political matters.'[51]

Winterbotham stated, amongst other things, that 'if he won the seat it would be principally by the votes of the labourers in the front rank'.[52] His main election platform was continuing free trade and an urgent campaign of land for the labourer in the form of small holdings. Winterbotham strongly advocated Joseph Chamberlain's 'unauthorised programme' and the promise of 'three acres and a cow'.[53]

Hemming was energetic in the Liberal cause and during the year his district column in the *English Labourers' Chronicle* gave details of many branch meetings which he organised to explain the use of the ballot box

---

[49] *Ibid.*, p. 164.
[50] *English Labourers' Chronicle*, 31 January 1885.
[51] *Ibid.*, 31 January 1885.
[52] *Ibid.*, 18 April 1885.
[53] *Cheltenham Free Press*, 5 December 1885.

to the labourers.[54] Later in June and July several public gatherings were organised, some of which were addressed by Arthur Winterbotham himself.[55] Later in August, Hemming invited George Ball, the union's vice president and district secretary for West Suffolk, to come and generate further support for the cause.[56]

In November Hemming wrote careful instructions to all the labourers on the value of their vote and the technicalities of voting:

Let me urge on one and all of you the value of your vote ... Be sure and make your cross on the right hand side opposite the name of the man you vote for. Mr Winterbotham's name will be the lowest on the voting paper. As you are aware the poll will be open until 8 o'clock but all of you try and get there as soon as you can and record your votes.[57]

All this huge expenditure of energy on the part of Hemming and the union in support of the Liberal cause paid rich dividends, as Winterbotham was returned with a majority of seventy-four votes. It was the first time the Tories had been dislodged for forty-three years.

Once the labourers were enfranchised the Liberal Party began to articulate a programme which gave much more forceful support to the labourers' demands for land. Arch himself was elected to parliament for the Liberals in 1886 for the North-West Norfolk constituency. This considerably strengthened the bond between the union and the Liberal Party. On his adoption as a candidate Arch spelt out his objectives to the electorate. These included a number of specific commitments on land issues. Among them were 'a complete Reform of the Land Laws including abolition of the system of Primogeniture, Entail and Settlement' and a further 'Reform in the Agricultural Holding Acts' which covered 'greater protection for their capital expended in the land'. Arch also listed the following specific commitment to secure 'the power to Government or Local Boards to acquire land in every village, at reasonable purchase value, and re-let or sell it in small portions to any person requiring the same'.[58]

Arch's maiden speech inevitably addressed the land question from the labourers' perspective. He urged that the labourer should have the right to more than a rood of ground:

I do not find any human or Divine law which would confine the labourer to one rood of God's earth. If I have any energy, tact, and skill by which I could

[54] See, for example, *English Labourers' Chronicle* 14 and 28 February 1885 and 7 and 14 March 1885.
[55] See *Stroud Journal*, 12 September 1885, *Wilts and Gloucester Standard*, 30 June 1885.
[56] *English Labourers' Chronicle*, 15 August 1885.
[57] *Ibid.*, 21 November 1885.
[58] P. L. R. Horn, *Joseph Arch*, pp. 234–5.

cultivate my acre or two, and buy my cow into the bargain, I do not see just reason why my energies should be crippled and my forces held back.[59]

Arch's motivation for this demand was clearly rooted in his Methodist upbringing and his radical Liberal convictions. He does not appear to have been influenced by socialist land theory. Indeed he declared:

We are not Socialistic, not in the offensive meaning of the word; but to a certain extent we are socialists because we are social beings. We would like social comforts and social society; but we have a great aversion to social policy paid for out of the poor rates.[60]

Arch concluded his speech by pointing out that though many of the new Liberal members in the House were there on account of the farm labourers' votes, he had 'never heard any Liberal candidate promise the labourers three acres and a cow'.[61]

The Liberals did much for the labourers in helping them to improve the extent of their rights to the land. 1883 had seen the passing of Jesse Collings' Allotment Extension Act. This bill required the trustees of certain charities to announce every year that they were prepared to let out their lands in parcels of not more than an acre to labourers and others. All disputes were to come before the county courts which were easily approached, and therefore relatively cheap for the labourers. Much of the ground work for this bill was undertaken by Howard Evans, a leading adviser and executive official in Arch's union.[62] The bill was weakened during its passage through the Lords. The Upper House replaced the county court as the centre of appeal by the Charity Commission, a body which had little sympathy with the bill. The Lords also succeeded in smuggling in a further provision which stated that the trustees need not let 'unsuitable land' for allotment purposes.

Arch, together with other Liberals, saw that land monopoly was the root of the Irish problem. He was a warm supporter of both of Gladstone's proposed solutions: the granting of Home Rule and the plan to buy out the landlords to the tune of fifty million pounds.[63] Howard Evans in his notes and queries column in the English Labourers' Chronicle reported that Arch had 'spoken strongly on Mr Gladstone's side, so far as Home Rule is concerned'.[64] Evans himself was a warm supporter of Gladstone's proposals. He wrote: 'To buy out the Irish landlords is a good object in itself. The Irish are a nation of tenant farmers. What Mr

[59] Ibid., p. 242.
[60] Ibid., p. 243.
[61] Ibid., p. 243.
[62] W. Hasback, A History of the English Agricultural Labourer, London, 1908, p. 306.
[63] English Labourers' Chronicle, 3 April 1886.
[64] Ibid., 24 April 1886.

Gladstone wants to do is to enable the Irish tenants to buy their own farms by paying a certain fixed rent for a term of years'.[65]

In 1887 Collings brought forward another bill which was designed to increase the number of allotments, and also make available small holdings; a small holding being of sufficient size to provide a man with full employment. Again Collings' efforts were foiled, his bill being replaced by another of far milder quality.

The labourers' access to the land was thus not facilitated until the Local Government Act of 1894 which extended democratic self-government to the local level by the creation of district and parish councils. The parish councils were given the right to rent land compulsorily for allotment purposes with the proviso that no person might receive more than four acres.

It is clear that the Liberal Party did a great deal to reinforce and underpin the National Union's land aspirations. More than this, the Liberal Party also helped to generate a revival of union interest in the later 1880s and early 1890s particularly in Gloucestershire, Oxfordshire and East Anglia.[66] However, in so doing the Liberals also contributed to the demise of the union itself. Henry Hemming, the Cirencester district secretary, was one of several prominent officials who sensed the problem. He felt that his members were losing their motivation and slipping away from membership. 'Politics just now', he wrote in August 1885, 'seem to be the principal topic of the day, and we are glad to find the men much in earnest about exercising their political rights'. He went on, however, to urge the men not to dispense with the union:

You will want the union quite as much now as you have in the past, and unless you stand well together you will not be in a position to demand a fair share of the profits of the soil.[67]

The labourers, however, seemed unable to heed Hemming's word and in Gloucestershire, as elsewhere, there was a steady drift away from union membership in the later 1880s and early 1890s. By the close of 1896 the National was no more.

---

[65] *Ibid.*, 24 April 1886.
[66] For the revival in Oxfordshire see Horn, 'Agricultural Trade Unionism', pp. 113–18. For the revival in Norfolk see N. A. D. Scotland, 'Zacharias Walker (1843–1900), Norfolk Radical Trade Unionist', *Norfolk Archaeology*, 37, 2 (1979).
[67] *English Labourers' Chronicle*, 15 August 1885.

V

In the event, the progress which the National Union achieved had been painfully slow and it was not until 1882 that the labourers gained any legal rights to the use of a plot of land with security of tenure. The goal which the National had set itself of 'the land for the people' was thus in the end largely unrealised. Even when he came to write his autobiography, Arch was still forced to write: 'The land for the people is the goal the labourers are working for ... I want to see ... a labourer ... grow fruit, vegetables, and keep a pig for himself'.[68]

In their campaigning, by and large, the National Union did not espouse a policy of land nationalisation. There were occasional pleas for land nationalisation and during the latter years of the union campaign some activists derived encouragement from the Land Restoration League. At a branch meeting at the village of Finmere in Oxfordshire, for example, a motion was passed in favour of land nationalisation.[69] Similarly at Old Buckenham, following a union procession, George Mitchell (1827–1910) moved a resolution for the nationalisation of land.[70] Generally speaking, however, these were isolated instances. Arch himself did not join the Land Nationalisation Society which was formed in 1881. He committed himself rather to the less extreme Free Land League which was inaugurated in 1885 and which directed its energies to demanding leasehold enfranchisement.[71]

It seems clear that the overriding motivational factors in Arch's union's land campaign were those of the progressive wing of the Liberal Party linked in with a growing politically orientated Methodist nonconformity. Perhaps the major reason why the National's land aspirations were unfulfilled was that Arch and his branch and district officials had become too closely entwined with the Liberal Party's equivocations over the land question both in England and in Ireland. This may also help to explain why in the early twentieth century the new agricultural unions switched their allegiance away from the Liberals to the Labour Party agenda.

[68] J. Arch, *The Story of His Life*, London, 1894.
[69] Horn, 'Agricultural Trade Unionism', p. 118.
[70] *English Labourers' Chronicle*, 13 January 1883.
[71] J. Butt and I. F. Clarke, *The Victorians and Social Protest*, pp. 200, 204.

7   Free trade, protectionism and the 'food of the people: the Liberal opposition to the Cattle Diseases Bill of 1878

Jonathan Spain

I

At the close of the parliamentary session of 1878 Joseph Chamberlain wrote to a Birmingham political ally: 'I am glad to see that the session's work has not been altogether fruitless ... Dilke and I together have had the real triumphs of the session', primarily, Chamberlain considered, 'in forcing the government to entirely change the cattle bill'.[1] Why should the parliamentary Radicals see political advantage in attacking a bill designed to check the spread of cattle disease – a measure one might naturally assume to be the preserve of veterinary scientists and public administrators?

In fact, cattle disease legislation occupied a highly contentious position within the mainstream of political debate and party conflict throughout the mid- to late-Victorian period. Successive attempts at legislation, caused by recurrent outbreaks of cattle disease between the mid-1860s and the mid-1880s, provoked a vociferous clash between powerful and vested interests. On the one side were farmers, landlords and their county representatives who argued for a complete ban on the trade in imported livestock for domestic consumption as the only effective means to eradicate disease and enable an increase in domestic meat supplies. On the other side was the urban borough interest, comprised of groups directly connected with the foreign livestock trade – butchers, wholesalers and importers – and the wider community of poorer working-class consumers and their borough representatives, who interpreted the demand for prohibition of the trade as a return to protectionism and higher meat prices.[2]

---

[1] Chamberlain to J. T. Bunce, 8 August 1878, Joseph Chamberlain Papers, Birmingham University Library (JC5/8/39).

[2] There is no systematic treatment of this issue by historians of Victorian party politics, although H. J. Hanham, *Elections and Party Management. Politics in the Time of Disraeli and Gladstone*, Hassocks, 1978, pp. 33–6, surveys the issue as a factor in county politics without reference to the 1878 bill. The economic aspects of the question have been dealt

By the mid-1880s the contest had swung decisively in favour of the agricultural lobby. By then the question was losing much of its political dimension as a result of the substitution of the foreign livestock trade by imports of refrigerated and frozen meat from North America, Argentina, Australia and New Zealand – thus securing an alternative source of cheaper meat for the urban working classes.[3] However, prior to the full emergence of the frozen meat trade in the 1880s attempts at legislative restriction of the trade in foreign livestock saw parliament as the focal point for an emotive and symbolic conflict between consumers and producers, town versus country, with the revival of the old political battle between 'free trade' and 'protectionism' over the question of the 'food of the people'. The Cattle Diseases Bill of 1878 is a notable example.

Chamberlain was one of a group of parliamentary Radicals or 'advanced Liberals' as they were also described, which included Sir Charles Dilke, A. J. Mundella, Joseph Cowen, Henry Fawcett and Jacob Bright, who all took a prominent part in the campaign mounted against the bill. Their willingness to attack the measure as a protectionist conspiracy for the narrow benefit of the landed interest; their acceptance of the 'revealed truth' of the Cobdenite equation of free trade with cheap and abundant food and universally shared prosperity amongst the community of consumers – the 'moral economy' of free trade – illustrated the enduring influence of Cobdenite radicalism and the politics of the Anti-Corn Law League upon late-Victorian popular liberalism.[4]

The 'triumph' to which Chamberlain referred 'in forcing the government to entirely change the cattle bill' was not, however, the sole preserve of the Radicals: a number of Tory borough members voiced their opposition to the bill; by the same token a group of Liberal county members

with by W. D. Zimmerman, 'The Live Cattle Trade between the United States and Great Britain, 1868–1885', *Agricultural History*, 36, 1 (1962), pp. 46–52 and more fully by R. Perren, 'The North American Beef and Cattle Trade with Great Britain, 1870–1914', *Economic History Review*, 24, 3 (1971) pp 430–44. See also A. B. Erickson, 'The Cattle Plague in England, 1865–67', *Agricultural History*, 35, 2 (1961), pp. 94–103. The medical aspects are dealt with by S. A. Hall, 'The Cattle Plague of 1865', *Medical History*, 6 (1962), pp. 45–58; also Lise Wilkinson, *Animals and Disease. An Introduction to the History of Comparative Medicine*, Cambridge, 1992. On the economics of food supply, see R. Scola, *Feeding the Victorian City; the Food Supply of Manchester*, Manchester, 1992. Finally, for the philanthropic critique of the live cattle trade which emerged in the 1880s, see Samuel Plimsoll, *Cattle Ships*, (1890).

[3] See Perren, 'The North American Beef and Cattle Trade', pp. 430–5, Zimmerman, 'The Live Cattle Trade', pp. 46–52; also R. C. K. Ensor, *England, 1870–1914*, Oxford, 1966 (reprint), pp. 119–20 and J. T. Mitchell and J. Raymond, *History of the Frozen Meat Trade*, London, 1912.

[4] Regarding the rise of popular Liberal support for Cobden in the 1860s and 1870s see below, chapter 8, pp. 193–218; for a general survey of this theme, see E. F. Biagini, *Liberty, Retrenchment and Reform; Popular Liberalism in the Age of Gladstone 1860–1880*, Cambridge, 1992, pp. 95–102.

voted with the government, indicating the borough/county split evoked by the question; more significantly, the radical campaign against the bill was fully supported by the leadership and front bench of the Liberal party. The most prominent parliamentary opponent of the bill was W. E. Forster, whilst Ripon in the Lords, Hartington, the party leader in the Commons, Gladstone – supposedly in 'retirement' – Harcourt, James and Herschell were also active opponents of the measure.

The combined achievement of the front bench and advanced wing of the Liberal Party, in successfully pressing Beaconsfield's government into a series of amendments which practically rewrote the bill, foreshadowed a return to domestic political concerns and a general rise in the political fortunes of the Liberal Party during 1879–80. The intense political absorption in foreign policy and the 'Eastern Question' between the summer of 1876 and the late spring of 1878, which was marked by open disunity between the front bench and the advanced wing of the party (and not least amongst Radicals themselves), has been well documented.[5] Yet, as the passage of the Cattle Diseases bill illustrates, the Liberal leadership and the parliamentary Radicals were able to find common ground where domestic issues were concerned. Free trade, let us be reminded, remained a focal point for Radical–Whig cooperation at Westminster. In opposition, it was evidently more important for the Whig leadership of Hartington and Granville to court the Radicals than bow to Liberal county members who supported the measure.

II

To understand why the bill of 1878 generated such vehement criticism and served to rejuvenate the parliamentary opposition, it is necessary to consider the framework of legislation and the underlying administrative principles laid down during Gladstone's first ministry. In the early 1860s attention was focused by the veterinary lobby and farmers on the need for tighter controls on the import of livestock from Russia and Central Europe, where rinderpest (cattle plague) was endemic. However, early legislative efforts were blocked by the free-trade lobby assisted by self-interested graziers, dealers and butchers. The cattle plague of 1865–7, which decimated domestic herds and was traced to livestock shipments from Eastern Europe, necessitated government intervention. Following a royal commission a temporary one-year Act was passed in 1866 which

---

[5] See P. J. Durrans, 'A Two-edged Sword; the Liberal attack on Disraelian Imperialism', *Journal of Imperial and Commonwealth History*, 10 (1981–2), pp. 262–79; also J. P. Rossi, 'The Transformation of the British Liberal Party; A Study in the Tactics of the Liberal Opposition, 1874–1880', *Trans. of the American Phil. Soc.* 68, 8 (1978), pp. 32–77.

introduced compulsory slaughter of infected herds with partial compensation from the local rate. Stringent controls were imposed on the importation and movement of cattle – orders in council prohibited the landing of livestock from infected countries. Such was the magnitude of the situation that counter-arguments from the free-trade lobby over higher meat prices were overruled.[6]

With the eventual suppression of the outbreak in 1867, consideration turned to the form and scope of permanent legislation, responsibility for which fell to W. E. Forster, Vice President of the Council in Gladstone's newly elected government. Forster's Contagious Diseases (Animals) Act of 1869 consolidated and formalised existing powers in one measure. Under the Act authority to deal with domestic outbreaks was committed in the first instance to local authorities, upon whom were devolved varying discretionary powers to control the movement of stock, to regulate markets and fairs, isolate infected herds and, in the case of cattle plague, order compulsory slaughter with partial compensation from the rates. The 1869 Act, in its approach to the control of domestic livestock, followed the established legislative model of permissive powers delegated to local authorities with an absence of strong central supervision.

Forster's approach to controls on foreign livestock was to lean heavily towards the continuance of the trade. Wholesale statutory prohibition, a policy favoured by the farming lobby, was rejected in favour of a regime of discretionary controls. The Privy Council retained a reserve power to prohibit the landing of livestock from countries where cattle plague was endemic. The Privy Council was also granted a further discretionary power of specifying other countries where there was deemed to be a risk of disease, from which importation was permitted subject to inspection and slaughter at the ports prior to movement inland. Special foreign animal wharves were built to handle this trade. With the exception of such 'scheduled' countries, the importation of livestock would be free and unrestricted. Thus the *presumption* of the law was in favour of the continuance of the trade unless the Privy Council saw fit to prohibit or impose restrictions. Forster's Act effectively balanced the need for controls on the spread of disease from abroad with his own party's adherence to the free-trade system, of which the trade in foreign livestock was recognised as an important and expanding part.[7]

---

[6] See Hall, 'The Cattle Plague of 1865', and Erickson, 'The Cattle Plague in England'; also E. J. Feuchtwanger, *Democracy and Empire, Britain 1865–1914*, London, 1985, p. 31.

[7] See Forster's letter on this subject to his wife of 10 January 1869, quoted in T. W. Reid, *Life of Forster*, London, 1888, vol. II, p. 2, and vol. I, pp. 458 and 529; also Forster's speech introducing the bill in the Commons, 4 March 1869, *Hansard*, 3rd series, vol. CXCIV, pp. 672–7.

During the 1860s and 1870s this trade became an increasing source of cheap meat for the expanding urban population. Imported livestock could not compete for price with prime quality English and Scottish beef; what it did offer was supplies of lesser quality beef, pork, mutton and offal – the poor man's food – at prices which undercut domestic suppliers.[8] In aggregate terms, contemporary estimates for the proportion of the domestic market met by foreign livestock vary between 7 and 12.5 per cent.[9] Yet, according to Perren, the trade was geographically concentrated in the centres of high-density population where there was an increasing demand for cheap meat – the markets of London, the midlands, and parts of Lancashire in the hinterland of Liverpool[10] – but this was also true of Yorkshire towns such as Sheffield as well as Newcastle and the north-east.[11] Between 1865 and 1869 45 per cent of cattle, 25 per cent of sheep and 22 per cent of pigs sold in the metropolitan markets of London was foreign in origin.[12] From 1868 a rapidly increasing proportion of this trade was from North America,[13] whilst the Scandinavian countries, Denmark in particular,[14] as well as northern Spain and Portugal,[15] became important sources of supply.

In accordance with the 1869 Act orders in council were issued prohibiting the landing of livestock from Russia and Eastern and Central Europe, where cattle plague was rife, whilst other countries such as France, Belgium and Germany were 'scheduled' – their livestock slaugh-

[8] See Perren, 'The North American Beef and Cattle Trade', pp. 440–1.
[9] Forster, quoting the view of the Veterinary Department, stated in the Commons that imported cattle made up approx. 12 per cent of total consumption: *Hansard*, vol. CCXIV, p. 523, 14 February 1873. In 1878 Forster stated the figure was 12.5 per cent: *Hansard*, vol. CCXLI, p. 148, 24 June 1878. This figure was disputed by farmers' representatives. See reports in the *Farmer's Magazine*, January 1873, p. 5 and May 1878, p. 344, which placed the figure for imported cattle at between 5.64 and 7.5 per cent.
[10] Perren, 'The North American Beef and Cattle Trade', pp. 440–1.
[11] A. J. Mundella stated that 27 per cent of the Sheffield meat market was supplied by foreign livestock imports: *Leeds Mercury*, 27 June 1878, p. 4. See also the report of Newcastle Council on the Tyne cattle trade: *Newcastle Daily Chronicle*, 23 February 1878, p. 4, which put the figure at approx. 50 per cent of the total livestock passing through the meat market every week. Scola, *Feeding the Victorian City*, pp. 48–51, states in the case of Manchester that imports of livestock from Ireland were the most significant factor, although foreign imports reached 10 per cent on occasions.
[12] Perren, 'The North American Beef and Cattle Trade', pp. 440–1.
[13] *Ibid.* and Zimmerman, 'The Live Cattle Trade', pp. 46–52.
[14] Imports of cattle had risen from 8,900 in 1866 to 50,000 in 1875. See 'Report of HM Consular officials in Europe and North America Regarding the Cattle Trade', *Parliamentary Papers*, vol. LXXXIV, 1877, p. 377 (Denmark); H. M. Jenkins, 'Report on Agriculture of Denmark', *Journal of the Royal Agricultural Society (JRAS)* 12 (1876), p. 309 and reports in the *Newcastle Daily Chronicle*, 12 January 1878, p. 4 and 18 February 1878, p. 4.
[15] See 'Report of HM Consular Officials', *Parliamentary Papers*, vol. LXXXIV, 1877, p. 431 (Spain); see also the *Daily News*, 26 June 1878, letter from Messrs Hope and Harrington, importers of Oporto cattle, p. 5.

tered at the port of landing. At the same time, Forster allowed the trade from Scandinavia, the Iberian peninsula and North America to continue and expand without restriction on movement from the ports, in the absence of reports of disease and the knowledge of better systems of veterinary inspection.[16] Perren has pointed to the price stability enjoyed by livestock importers over the dead meat trade which arose, principally, from the lesser urgency to sell on arrival and therefore the absence of short-term gluts in supply. Livestock from non-scheduled countries could be kept temporarily, then sold at market in a controlled manner at remunerative prices, whilst still undercutting domestic suppliers.[17]

A further, albeit less extensive, outbreak of cattle plague in 1872 provides an interesting study in Forster's approach to the operation of the 1869 Act. In July, when outbreaks of cattle plague in several east-coast ports were traced to shipments of German cattle from Hamburg, the most rigorous action taken by Foster was merely to rescind a special exemption granted to Schleswig-Holstein earlier that year to export cattle to inland markets without restriction. All German cattle would henceforth be subject to the rule of slaughter at the ports. Forster emphasised the current high price of meat, particularly in the London markets and recognised that 'Hitherto they had prohibited all imports from countries where cattle plague prevailed. But he hoped the German Government would take speedy and effectual steps to stamp out the plague ... by which means that serious inconvenience to the trade might be obviated'.[18] When put to the test Liberal policy erred in favour of continuance of the trade; the most rigorous powers available under the Act were not employed.

The legislation of 1869 came under parliamentary scrutiny in 1873. Forster's select committee successfully deflected demands from the farming lobby for compulsory slaughter of all imported livestock for immediate consumption by focusing upon inadequacies in controls on domestic livestock – the farming lobby's weak flank. Attention was directed at the weakness in powers granted to local authorities, lack of uniformity in their implementation, insufficient levels of compensation where slaughter was imposed and the exemption of Irish cattle from the same regime of domestic controls imposed elsewhere in the 'home' countries.[19] The correct balance between foreign and home restrictions was

---

[16] See 'Report of HM Consular Officials' which provides a country-by-country survey of the extent of the trade, local veterinary precautions and restrictions in place on importation into the British Isles.

[17] Perren, 'The North American Beef and Cattle Trade', pp. 433, 438–41.

[18] *Hansard*, vol. CCXIII, p. 214, 31 July 1873. See also Forster's reply of 3 August 1873, *Hansard*, vol. CCXIII, p. 379.

[19] 'Report of the Select Committee on the Operation of the Contagious Diseases (Animals) Act 1869', *Parliamentary Papers*, vol. XI, 1873, p. 189.

the key issue. Restrictions on importation without effective domestic controls amounted to protectionism, since home producers would be placed at an artificial price advantage. More rigorous domestic controls without adequate controls on foreign infection would not stamp out disease. These were the competing contentions when further legislation was considered in 1878.

III

The Liberal defeat at the general election of 1874 brought about the first effective transfer of power in a generation. The new Conservative administration came under almost immediate pressure from its supporters amongst the agricultural lobby to reverse the policy of its predecessor. In May a delegation from the Central Chamber of Agriculture pressed the Duke of Richmond, Lord President of the Council, to impose compulsory slaughter on all 'fat' cattle at the ports of landing. However the duke had also received deputations from the boroughs opposing such a change and his reply was a model of ministerial rectitude. Taking refuge behind the select committee of 1873, Richmond announced that the discretionary regime would remain, whilst leaving the question open for future consideration.[20] The government's caution can best be understood within the context of the new political map created by the Tory victory of 1874. The Conservative predominance in the counties was strengthened but it was in the boroughs that the most dramatic gains were made.[21] Sensitivity to borough opinion on the question forestalled any support for sudden change in the established policy. Moreover, old-style Tory protectionism had no voice in the cabinet and was scarcely represented on the back benches.[22]

The issue of controls on foreign livestock was pushed to one side during the next three years, largely as a result of the farming lobby's own concentration on the need for uniformity in the controls on 'home' livestock and, in particular, Irish cattle. Forster's order of 1873 extending compulsory slaughter to cases of pleuro-pneumonia had omitted Irish cattle – a source of concern to English graziers who received much of their long-term store cattle for fattening from Ireland. The matter was taken up by C. S. Read, who, despite his position as a junior government minister, became engaged in a running quarrel with the Privy Council

[20] 'Report of the delegation to the Duke of Richmond, 22 May 1874', *Farmer's Magazine*, June 1874.
[21] Chris Cook and Brendan Keith, *British Historical Facts, 1830–1900*, London, 1975, pp. 140–1.
[22] Paul Smith, *Disraelian Conservatism and Social Reform*, London 1967, pp. 303–8. Smith does not, however, consider the cattle diseases question during the 1874–80 parliament.

and the Veterinary Department over their continued failure to act. This culminated in the autumn of 1875 in an open attack by Read at a meeting of his Norfolk constituents which precipitated his resignation from the government.[23] The consequence was that Richmond spent much of his first two years in office dealing with the question of Irish cattle, but it was not until 1876 that he saw himself clear to support such a measure.[24]

In 1874 Richmond had accepted the recommendation of Forster's select committee that no additional restrictions on foreign livestock should be imposed – whilst granting himself a degree of latitude with regard to the future. Over the next three years the policy of selective action against specific countries was continued under the discretionary regime formalised by Forster. However, during the early months of 1877, outbreaks of cattle plague at Deptford and Hull, in both cases attributed to shipments from Hamburg, drew attention once more in a sudden and dramatic fashion to the issue, serving to revive the long-simmering demand for total prohibition of the foreign livestock trade.

A prominent position was now taken by the council of the Royal Agricultural Society (RAS).[25] Feeling within the farming community was evidently running high. On 7 March the council rejected a compromise resolution calling for universal slaughter at the ports of debarkation in a favour of a total ban on importation. 'Store' cattle brought in for longer-term fattening were omitted from the proposed ban, although it was proposed that they be subjected to quarantine and inspection at the ports. As a necessary counter-weight the council also called for further measures to tackle domestic outbreaks.[26] Professor Black, chief officer at the Veterinary Department, attended the council's meetings, arguing vigorously against a total ban on imported livestock; the present powers, he argued, met the exigencies of the case; and further, such a ban amounted to a serious breach of faith with the governments of non-infected foreign countries, who had acted assiduously to prevent disease.[27] Such arguments met with a stony reception. The very prompt-

---

[23] See Read's comments on behalf of the delegation to Richmond, 22 May 1874, *Farmer's Magazine*, June 1874; also Read's correspondence of 1874–6 with Corry, Disraeli's private secretary, Hughenden Papers (microfilm at Cambridge Univ. Lib.) B/XXI/R/52–55 and Richmond's criticism of Read, B/XXI/Le/87–88.

[24] See Richmond's correspondence with Corry and Disraeli, Hughenden Papers, B/XXI/Le/87, 94, 100. This was enacted as the Cattle Diseases (Ireland) Act, 1876, *Parliamentary Papers*, vol. I, 1876, p. 293.

[25] For a detailed account of the 1877 outbreak and the proceedings of the council of the Royal Agricultural Society (RAS) see 'The Outbreak of Cattle Plague', *JRAS*, 13 (1877), pp. 211–41. For an account of the role of the Chambers of Agriculture see A. H. H. Matthews, *Fifty Years of Agricultural Politics. A History of the Chambers of Agriculture*, London, 1915.

[26] *JRAS*, 'The Outbreak of Cattle Plague', pp. 220–9.

[27] *Ibid.* pp. 216, 226.

ness of the Veterinary Department in implementing its powers of isolation and slaughter at the ports had not prevented outbreaks in adjacent districts, with consequent financial loss and harassment to local farmers. The conclusion drawn by the majority of the council was 'to draw the line at the European ports'.[28]

The resolutions of the RAS were brought before the House of Lords by Lord Fortescue on 17 March. Given the Government's subsequent position on the question, it is interesting that at this stage Richmond placed great weight on free-trade counter-arguments – the sudden loss of 200,000 head of cattle, one million sheep and 50,000 swine from the 'supply of food for the people of this country'. Richmond went further, recognising the price advantage enjoyed by imported livestock over dead meat – not subject to quick sale at potentially unremunerative prices.[29] Such sensitivity to free-trade arguments countered opposition attempts to raise the spectre of protectionism; the Liberal front bench was fully aware of the political advantage to be drawn from the issue. In the Commons, Gladstone called for a full debate on the question of whether the prohibition of foreign cattle was to be introduced, 'the removal of which was one of the measures of free trade'. The Chancellor of the Exchequer, Northcote, denied the government had any such intention.[30] In fact, the government could reject the extreme policy adopted by the RAS, a total ban on importation, whilst leaving the question of compulsory slaughter at the ports privately under consideration.

The government, in time-honoured fashion, announced a select committee to consider the question and report. Its composition was announced on 24 April. The farmers were well represented and so too were the boroughs. The 'advanced Liberal' members Jacob Bright, Joseph Chamberlain, George Anderson, John Holms, A. J. Mundella, Joseph Pease and the architect of the 1869 Act, W. E. Forster were all nominated. The committee was given a wide remit to consider not only the recent outbreaks and the efficacy of current legislation but also the impact of the foreign livestock trade on the price of meat. Evidence was taken in May and a report was presented at the end of July.[31]

Despite the efforts of Forster and the advanced Liberals, the report came down in favour of further restrictions of the foreign livestock trade, particularly with European countries. The argument put forward by the agricultural lobby, that the key to stamping out disease lay in greater

---

[28] *Ibid.*, speech by Jacob Wilson, p. 233. See also the reports of Professor Black and Mr Druig, the RAS veterinary officer, pp. 211–16.
[29] *Hansard*, vol. CCXXXIII, pp. 98–103, 17 March 1878.
[30] *Ibid.*, pp. 1447–8, 19 April 1878.
[31] 'Select Committee Report on the Cattle Plague', *Parliamentary Papers*, vol. IX, 1877.

security from foreign contamination and that an increase in domestic supply would follow, was largely accepted. The report also considered the potential of chilled or frozen North American beef but concluded that the trade 'was at present in far too uncertain and experimental a condition to justify reliance upon [it] for an unfailing supply'.[32] For this reason, North American cattle were exempted from the report's recommendations. Instead, the report proposed the total prohibition of livestock from Russia, all cattle from Germany (excluding Schleswig-Holstein) and Belgium and that 'the rest of Europe as to all animals' should be added to the list of scheduled countries. Simply put, all continental livestock for immediate consumption would be scheduled for compulsory slaughter at designated ports, prior to shipment to inland markets. Store and dairy cattle were exempted from slaughter (but subject to extended quarantine and inspection prior to movement inland) and, as we have seen, livestock from North America.[33] Barring these exemptions, free importation of livestock into the interior was to be prohibited. The argument put forward by the free-trade lobby that such 'interference' would ruin the trade through the creation of supply gluts and sudden drops in price to unremunerative levels was discounted; the report urged that the creation of a fixed rule of slaughter at specified ports of debarkation would bring stability to the trade. The impact of such changes could not be foretold, since the late 1860s, imports from European countries such as France which had been placed on the schedule had steadily declined,[34] whilst imports from countries operating without restriction such as Denmark, Spain and Portugal had increased.[35] Much would depend on technological development in the transit of dead meat, still in its infancy in 1878.

The report recognised the need for tougher domestic controls and greater uniformity in their implementation, echoing Forster's select committee of 1873. In 1877, Forster was successful in adding a clause to the report linking further foreign restrictions to the introduction of the domestic proposals.[36] This was a damage limiting exercise – repeated attempts by Forster and the advanced Liberals to retain the existing discretionary regime were rejected by the committee. Advanced Liberal committee members now turned their attention to the boroughs.

[32] *Ibid.*, clause 34, p. viii.
[33] *Ibid.*, clause 27, p. vi.
[34] Richmond, in his reply to Fortescue in the Lords on 19 March 1877 had pointed to the case of France, which was placed on the schedule in 1869. In the following seven years, imports of cattle had declined from 112,618 to 24,094; *Hansard*, vol. CCXXXIII, p. 101. By 1877 this figure had dropped to 2,804; *Farmer's Magazine* (June, 1878), p. 418.
[35] See 'Report of HM Consular Officials in Europe and North America Regarding the Cattle Trade'.
[36] 'Select Committee Report on the Cattle Plague', clause 38, part 12, p. ix.

A. J. Mundella advised Robert Leader, the editor of the *Sheffield Independent*, not to overlook the matter: 'It is monstrous ... we shall have meat at a tremendous price if they legislate in the spirit of this report'.[37] But with a clear nod to further foreign restrictions, the Prime Minister informed a delegation from the RAS that a bill would be introduced in the new session, adding that they must look to the dead meat trade to maintain the price of meat.[38]

The Contagious Diseases (Animals) Bill, 1878, was introduced into the House of Lords on 12 February. The opening weeks of the session had been dominated by the Eastern Question, with the debates on the vote of credit and the sending of the fleet to the Dardanelles. The question of war or peace held precedence, yet even so the arguments for and against additional restrictions on the foreign livestock trade were formed and given public expression. During the autumn and winter of 1877–8 the RAS, chambers of agriculture and local farmers' clubs all took up the matter, stressing the long-term increase in domestic meat supply which would arise once the threat of foreign infection was removed. Fears of a short-term shortfall in supply and higher prices were met with expressions of optimism in the capacity of the dead meat trade to prevent any scarcity.[39] Such attempts by agriculturalists to create an identity of interest between domestic producers and consumers met without success.

The first expression on opposition came, not surprisingly, from those groups directly concerned with the foreign livestock trade. A meeting at Huddersfield of butchers' representatives from towns across Yorkshire agreed to memorialise the Privy Council against restrictions which, if carried into effect, amounted to a 'practical prohibition on trade'.[40] On 22 January, Jacob Bright, the advanced Liberal member, led a deputation of the Foreign Cattle Trade Association to the Duke of Richmond in further protest at the proposed restrictions.[41] Attention was beginning to be drawn to the question in certain port towns, such as Newcastle, where the trade in imported livestock was thriving. Joseph Cowen's *Newcastle Daily Chronicle* gave prominence to a report on 'the Tyne Cattle Trade' by 'A consumer', which detailed the potentially disastrous results of

[37] Mundella to Robert Leader, 27 July 1877, quoted in W. H. G. Armytage, *A. J. Mundella 1825–1897. The Liberal Background to the Labour Movement*, London, 1951, p. 187.

[38] 'Report of Delegation to the PM, 23 November 1877, *JRAS*, 14 (1878), appendix (v), Report to Council, p. ix.

[39] For example, 'Our Meat Supply', *Farmer's Magazine*, January 1878, pp. 27–30; report of meeting of Newcastle Farmer's Club, *Newcastle Daily Chronicle*, 7 January 1878, p. 4; petition of the Leicester Chamber of Agriculture to the House of Commons, *The Times*, 25 January 1878, p. 10, col. f. See also G. F. Turner, *Cattle Traffic and Cattle Diseases: Their Influence on the Price of Meat. An Appeal to the Public*, 1878.

[40] *The Times*, 17 January 1878, p. 4, col. b.

[41] *The Times*, 23 January 1878, p. 10, col. f.

compulsory slaughter upon this trade, a policy which, it was asserted, would create a protective system in meat similar to the corn laws, resulting in meat becoming a luxury item.[42]

Amid these signs of emerging contentiousness, the bill, which was introduced in the House of Lords on 12 February and given its second reading on 5 March, was broadly in line with the select committee's recommendations. The Privy Council retained the absolute power to prohibit the landing of foreign livestock, whilst, under clause 33 and schedule 5 of the bill, all livestock imported for immediate consumption was to be subjected to compulsory slaughter at designated ports of debarkation. The bill, as introduced, did *not* exempt North American livestock from this rule. Dairy and store cattle *were* exempted subject to quarantine and subsequent movement under special licence. The Act was to come into force in January 1878 to allow the trade to make the necessary adjustments.

The bill also consolidated and extended powers dealing with domestic outbreaks of rinderpest (cattle plague), pleuro-pneumonia and, for the first time, foot and mouth disease. The geographical area and period of isolation was extended and in the case of cattle plague the power of compulsory slaughter was transferred from local authorities to the Privy Council and compensation from the local rate to the Exchequer. The bill introduced compulsory powers of isolation in the case of foot and mouth disease with reserve powers to the Privy Council. Provisions were also set out to deal with herds in transit and at markets and fairs, although these powers were vaguely worded and permissive. Additional discretionary powers were granted to the Privy Council with respect to urban milk sheds and milk shops and the bill's provisions were extended to cover Scotland and Ireland.[43]

Yet whilst the bill looked to enhance the powers of the Privy Council and to ensure greater uniformity in implementation, many of the new powers (with the exception of the foot and mouth disease clauses) were volitional and permissive. By contrast, with regard to foreign livestock for immediate consumption, the bill laid down a statutory rule of compulsory slaughter at the ports, whilst favouring domestic dairy farmers and graziers, the latter importing store cattle for fattening, prior to sale at higher prices.

In the House of Lords, Richmond took up the arguments presented by the select committee and the farming lobby and, in contrast to his stated reservations of 1877, the duke now stressed the importance of the nascent

[42] *Newcastle Daily Chronicle*, 12 January 1878, p. 4, col. c.
[43] The Contagious Diseases (Animals) Act, 1878, *Parliamentary Papers*, vol. I, 1878, pp. 725–52.

trade in chilled and frozen meat. 'Properly considered', Richmond asserted the interests of consumers and producers were identical. In the long term the measure would render the country independent of foreign supply, increase the supply of meat and reduce its price for all classes.[44] Attempting to accommodate the conflicting parties, Richmond now argued that the enactment of further domestic powers was contingent upon the adoption of compulsory slaughter at the ports. The question remained: if the farming representatives were prepared to accept such a compromise, would borough members and, in particular, the new intake of Tory borough MPs be prepared to accept such a measure?

Ripon, former President of the Council in Gladstone's first administration, signalled the opposition's strategy. The bill would not be opposed outright; indeed, certain measures, such as the enhancement of the Privy Council's powers and the greater uniformity, were to be welcomed. However, Ripon objected wholeheartedly to clause 33 dealing with foreign animals and, in particular, the failure to exempt North American livestock from compulsory slaughter.[45] The select committee had been disregarded on this point, probably to establish a universal rule. Yet, when the bill was sent to a select committee of the upper chamber, the government, conceding to mounting pressure, restored this exemption. This action, which was clearly conceded to retain the measure in something like its original form, set in train a further series of concessions which undermined the principle of the bill, causing the legislation to be re-cast with considerable political embarrassment to the government.

The onset of this discomfort began in the Lords. On 27 May, when the bill returned to the whole House, Ripon widened the scope of his attack, focusing attention on the five countries (Denmark, Norway, Sweden, Spain and Portugal) which under the 1869 Act were allowed to import without restriction and where, according to consular reports, the incidence of disease was minimal. If North American livestock was to be exempt why not livestock from these countries? Ripon set down the core of the Liberal argument: trade was bad, wages low, and the present was no time for experimental legislation with the food supply. Ripon's amendment was defeated quite comfortably in the Lords.[46] However, trouble was brewing in the Commons, where there were signs of a gathering campaign of protest from borough constituencies.

February and March witnessed a deepening of this protest. Representatives of the cattle trade from the north of England set in train the

---

[44] *Hansard*, vol. CCXXXVIII, pp. 748–52, debate on second reading in the Lords, 5 March 1878.

[45] *Ibid.*, pp. 725–34.

[46] *Hansard*, vol. CCXL, 27 May 1878, Ripon's speech, pp. 725–32.

formation of deputations from across the country to express opposition to clause 33.[47] Borough councils in the port towns, notably Liverpool and Newcastle, began to criticise the measure.[48] On 26 March Richmond received a large deputation including representatives of towns across the north and west of England, some twenty Radical and Tory borough MPs and representatives of the cattle trade.[49] The group was led by W. E. Forster, now emerging as the most prominent opponent of the bill[50] and A. J. Mundella, who called for the exemption of North American live-stock. Richmond recognised the representative nature of the deputation but rejected the demand for retention of Forster's discretionary regime, although, as we have seen, the lesser demand regarding North American cattle was accepted.

Yet it was not all clear that the government as a whole was committed to the bill in its present form, prior to its passage through the Commons. The Foreign Office, in particular, appeared increasingly lukewarm towards the measure. In 1877, consular trade reports had provided evidence supporting the continuance of the trade, unrestricted, from Scandinavia and the Iberian peninsula.[51] From January 1878 onwards the Foreign Office was under pressure from European countries, in partic-ular Denmark and Sweden, to modify the bill further. A barrage of diplo-matic notes from the Danish court requesting the exemption of Danish livestock from compulsory slaughter was directed by Derby and Salisbury, his successor as Foreign Secretary, to the Privy Council for their lordships' 'attentive consideration', together with accompanying tabulated evidence of the absence of disease. There followed an increas-ingly terse exchange of letters between under-secretaries, in which the Foreign Office repeatedly called on the Privy Council for an adequate diplomatic response.[52]

On the domestic front, clear signs were emerging that a cry of 'protec-tionism' would be levelled against the government if it proceeded with the bill in its present form. A crowded meeting at Cannon Street in London was informed that 'the People's food would be seriously dimin-ished and the dial of Free Trade ... put back thirty-five years'.[53] This

---

47 *The Times*, 28 February 1878, p. 4, col. f.

48 The Liverpool MPs, Torr and Rathbone, led a deputation of the town council to Richmond: *The Times*, 15 March 1878, p. 5, col. f. See also 'Newcastle Council and the Cattle Trade Bill', *Newcastle Daily Chronicle*, 23 February 1878, p. 4, col. a.

49 *The Times*, 26 March 1878, p. 11, col. f.

50 Forster was chairman of a special sub-committee set up by the Cobden Club to defend the importation of foreign livestock. John Rylands and T. B. Potter also served on the committee. *Daily News*, 8 July 1878, p. 3; report of the AGM of the Cobden Club.

51 See footnote 14.

52 'Correspondence Respecting the Contagious Diseases (Animals) Bill', *Parliamentary Papers*, vol. LXI, 1878, pp. 141–51.

53 *The Times*, 22 February 1878, p. 4, col. e.

theme was taken up by the radical press, most prominently at this early stage by *Reynolds News* and the *Newcastle Daily Chronicle*.[54] Mainstream opinion, represented in a *Times* editorial, noted an 'arising popular suspicion' that the bill was a protectionist measure giving rise to 'a certain amount of excitement in the manufacturing districts of the North'.[55] The government's position was further undermined by James Caird, the respected apostle of 'high farming' who refuted the argument that any serious measure aimed at restricting the import of foreign livestock would not cause a rise in meat prices; that increase would be in proportion to the market share which foreign livestock formerly enjoyed.[56]

The issue was given added importance in the early summer of 1878 when rumours began to circulate of an early dissolution of parliament centred on a successful outcome to Beaconsfield's diplomacy at the Congress of Berlin. The advanced Liberals quickly came to see the Cattle Diseases Bill as an issue to be run at the Tories in the boroughs. In mid-June Mundella instructed his Sheffield supporters to begin preparations for a sudden election – the first step to be a public meeting on the cattle bill.[57] This took place on 26 June, during the extended second reading in the Commons. Mundella assured his audience that:

> during the ten years he had served them he had never met them on a question which seemed to him to come so nearly to the pockets of the community ... In Sheffield they knew something about the price of meat. Every man knew it was a great deal too high ... He would speak and vote against the bill and fight it inch by inch, clause by clause (applause). He believed it was an insiduous measure, in favour of one class and against another. It was a bid for the counties to obtain votes of farmers and get political power.[58]

The *Examiner*, a journal of advanced Liberal opinion, which switched support to the government during the 'Eastern crisis', commented somewhat dryly that even 'magnanimous Liberals might confess to a little satisfaction if the government passed this extraordinary bill and then appealed to the country'.[59]

[54] *Reynolds News*, reports by 'Northumbrian', 17 March 1878, p. 3 and 31 April 1878, p. 3; 'Protectionist Legislation', *Newcastle Daily Chronicle*, 14 February 1878, p. 2 and 'The Government and the Cattle Trade', 6 April 1878, p. 2.

[55] *The Times*, 16 May 1878, p. 9, col. e.

[56] *The Times*, 29 May 1878, p. 12, col. f. Caird estimated the foreign proportion at one-twelfth of total consumption. The impact on the price of butcher's meat was highlighted by the radical press: 'As the bill stands, it is a tax of a penny upon every pound of meat consumed by the family of a working man': 'Land and Beef', *Reynolds News*, 31 January 1878, p. 3.

[57] See Armytage, *A. J. Mundella, The Liberal Background to the Labour Movement*, pp. 187–8.

[58] See report carried by the *Leeds Mercury*, 27 June 1878, p. 3.

[59] 'The Cattle Bill', *Examiner*, 29 June 1878, p. 809. See also the editorial in *The Times*, 26 June 1878, p. 9, col. c for a similar comment.

However, prior to the second reading in the House of Commons, there is clear evidence that the government was preparing for further concessions on the bill. On 13 June, Northcote informed the Prime Minister, then at Berlin for the Congress, that 'trouble' was to be expected – the issue was being worked against the Tory candidate at a by-election at Southampton.[60] On 22 June, Northcote reported further, 'We shall have a great fight over the cattle bill next week', adding that although Richmond was 'very stiff, nearly all the rest of the Cabinet are for holding language which will not stop us from ultimately accepting Forster's (Lord Ripon's) compromise'.[61] Privately, the government's position would remain flexible and the vote on a second reading would not constitute a final decision on the scope of the measure.

The second reading began on 24 June, continuing through several lengthy sittings until 1 July. The advanced Liberal, Peter Rylands, had given notice of a motion rejecting the bill in its entirety. This was now withdrawn in favour of an amendment by Forster rejecting compulsory slaughter of foreign livestock 'under all circumstances by act of parliament' – a strategem designed to garner the votes of Tory borough members. Forster argued that although the bill was not in itself a 'protectionist' measure, its effect would be a return to protectionism; the home restrictions did not go far enough and would not stamp out domestic outbreaks; the foreign restrictions would reduce the supply and raise the price of meat. The disparity in the treatment of home and foreign producers placed the latter at a price disadvantage, protecting the former from foreign competition.[62]

Opposition to the bill was also expressed by Tory borough members, most stridently by Wheelhouse and Walker, the MPs for Leeds and Salford. Ritchie, the Tory member for Tower Hamlets, endorsed Forster's detailed criticism, calling for stronger powers over domestic herds to be introduced in committee.[63] Advanced Liberals offered the most vehement opposition. Joseph Chamberlain, speaking 'from the consumers' point of view', castigated the measure as 'a maximum of interference with trade combined with a minimum of protection from disease'.[64] George Anderson asserted: 'the bill was a tyrannical, arbitrary and oppressive measure ... There was no doubt that the price of meat would be raised'.[65]

Whilst the second reading proceeded, Northcote informed Beaconsfield, 'We shall have to consent to modifications on the cattle bill in

[60] Hughenden Papers, BXX/N/181.
[61] Hughenden Papers, BXX/N/184.
[62] Forster's speech, *Hansard*, vol. CCXLI, pp. 145–61, 24 June 1878.
[63] *Ibid.*, pp. 172, 180–1, 183.
[64] *Ibid.*, p. 351.
[65] *Ibid.*, p. 359.

committee and give the Privy Council power to admit cattle from Denmark, Sweden, Portugal, etc.', adding that they would not 'pledge' to do this until after the second reading 'and till we have ascertained the real feelings of friends'.[66] The vote on Forster's amendment to the second reading produced a comfortable government majority and a degree of cross-bench voting. Sixteen Tory borough members rejected the government whip but this was more than compensated for by the adherence to the bill of thirty-nine Liberal members, reflecting the strong constituency pressures evoked by the issue.[67] The government was also successful in preventing an Irish rebellion against the bill. The reason was simple. The bill offered Irish livestock farmers equal treatment and 'home' status. This was of vital importance in the southern counties, which comprised the single most important source of livestock supplied by sea to English markets.[68] Richmond had gone out of his way to allay Irish fears on this point, informing a deputation from the Irish cattle trade that tougher restrictions would not be imposed on Irish livestock than were to be introduced elsewhere in Britain.[69] But the government had another card to play. Northcote informed Beaconsfield on 29 June that although it was 'possible the Irish may give trouble', he had established 'good relations with some of them, and they are so delighted with the Intermediate Education Bill that a great deal may be done by making its progress contingent upon their being civil in other matters'.[70] There was, therefore, an absence of Irish support for Liberal attempts to derail the bill. Indeed, in subsequent divisions, most notably the compensation clauses, Irish MPs either abstained or voted against the Radicals and in favour of the transfer of compensation for slaughter from the local rate to the imperial Exchequer.[71]

Yet, notwithstanding the size of their majority at the second reading, the government was not prepared to strain the support of its borough members still further. A compromise was worked out at a gathering of the

---

[66] Northcote to Beaconsfield, 29 June 1878, Hughenden Papers, BXX/N/185. *The Times* leader of 26 June 1878, p. 9, col. c noted greater hesitancy by Northcote about the bill as a result of the sharp division of opinion.

[67] A detailed breakdown of the voting is provided by the *Daily News*, 2 July 1878, p. 2. Twenty-six of the Liberal supporters of the bill sat for county seats.

[68] Perren, 'The North American Beef and Cattle Trade', p. 436.

[69] *The Times*, 26 June 1878, p. 11, col. b. Richmond was prepared to go further, announcing his intention to reduce the 'harrassing' system of stock movements from Ireland by the system of dual inspection, by establishing a sufficient system of inspection solely in Ireland.

[70] Northcote to Beaconsfield, 29 June 1878, Hughenden Papers, BXX/N/185.

[71] See Chamberlain's amendment of 18 July 1878, House of Commons Voting Lists, 1878, no. 224.

party on 8 July.[72] The venue for this meeting was the Foreign Office, which had shown a coolness towards the bill since January. Selwin Ibbetson informed the Commons that the government was prepared to grant the Privy Council a discretionary power to allow livestock from Scandinavia and the Iberian peninsula into the interior unrestricted, 'whilst maintaining slaughter as the general rule'. Further amendments concerning store and dairy cattle were also announced, meeting the argument that such exemptions not only constituted a continuing threat of foreign contamination but unfairly favoured domestic graziers, who imported lean stock for fattening prior to sale at higher prices.[73]

The Times regarded these concessions as the wise surrender of 'an untenable position'.[74] The opposition continued to press on with the attack. This was encapsulated by J. G. Shaw-Lefevre: 'he did not object to the Privy Council having full powers, but he did contend that free trade should be the rule and compulsory slaughter the exception, which only applied when it was shown to be necessary'.[75] A blocking motion put forward by Torrens, the advanced Liberal member for Finsbury, was withdrawn at the behest of Hartington, the party leader, to allow the proposed changes to be brought forward.[76] Mundella wrote: 'We have made a wide rent in the bill and we shall open it wider in committee'.[77]

Henry Fawcett organised a meeting of advanced Liberal members to consider ways and means of preventing further progress.[78] Radical 'obstruction' was in evidence when the order for committee was read on 16 July. A series of divisions were taken on the compensation clauses relating to cattle plague, which transfered payment from the local rate to the Exchequer. This was a traditional *bête noire* for the Radicals who objected to taxpayers 'being compelled to pay twice over – by an advance in the price of meat and next by compensation'.[79] These were merely

---

[72] For reports of this meeting see Northcote to Beaconsfield, 9 July 1878, Hughenden Papers, BXX/N187; also *The Times*, 9 July 1878, p. 9, col. b and the *Leeds Mercury*, 11 July 1878, p. 3.

[73] *Hansard*, vol. CCXLI, 8 July 1878, p. 975. The previous exemptions for store and dairy cattle were the focus of radical criticism. See 'Northumbrian', *Reynolds News*, 17 March 1878, p. 3 and Thorold Rogers, 'Landlords and Farmers v. Taxpayers and Consumers', letter to the *Daily News*, 20 July 1878, p. 3.

[74] *The Times*, 9 July 1878, p. 9, col. b. A *Leeds Mercury* editorial of 5 July 1878, p. 4 interpreted the recent Liberal by-election victory at Middlesbrough as a sign of revived Liberal fortunes on the back of the issue which 'may well drive all thoughts of a general election out of the minds of Tory wire-pullers'.

[75] *Hansard*, vol. CCXLI, 8 July 1878, p. 1003.

[76] *Ibid.*, p. 1023.

[77] Mundella to R. Leader, 10 July 1878, quoted in Armytage, *A. J. Mundella*, p. 188.

[78] See report of 'Special Correspondent', *Leeds Mercury*, 4 July 1878, p. 4, stating that the meeting was to be held the following week.

[79] Remarks by Mundella, *Hansard*, vol. CCXLI, 16 July 1878, p. 1603. See also comments by Cowen (p. 1583), Chamberlain (p. 1585) and Jacob Bright (p. 1584).

delaying tactics, for the Liberal front bench now played its trump card with dramatic effect. Henry James brought forward a new proviso for clause 2, stipulating that any order made under the Act which 'in its operation would be inconsistent with existing commercial treaty obligations would be invalid'.[80] The opposition now argued that the specific exemptions, conceded in the case of Scandinavia and the Iberian peninsula from the rule of compulsory slaughter, violated the 'most favoured nation' clause in Britain's commercial treaties with other continental nations such as France and Belgium, where imported livestock remained subject to the general rule. Selwin Ibbetson and the law officers replied that no difference was made with regard to the importation of livestock to the ports of debarkation, only the manner in which they were treated afterwards.[81] This was countered by Herschell; either they could admit all animals from all countries with a power to the Privy Council to exclude where disease existed or they could exclude animals from all countries with a power to admit in cases free from disease. Instead the government proposed to entrust the Privy Council to admit or exclude certain specified countries whilst leaving all others subject to statutory slaughter at the ports.[82]

Liberal members pressed home the advantage. Harcourt declared: 'the bill threatened very seriously the foreign trade of this country ... the moment they attacked the "most favoured nation clause" they shook the foundations upon which the foreign trade of the country relied'[83] – giving a grievance to foreign countries to embark upon a policy of protection. By a series of concessions, each in turn called for by the opposition, the government now found itself in a corner. To proceed with the bill as it now stood opened the administration to the charge of undermining the whole framework of the commercial treaty system. To accept the Liberal amendment implied further retreat from the principle of universal slaughter at the ports. Support for the government now began to slip away from its own benches. J. E. Gorst called for the government to consider 'very seriously' the question raised by James.[84] Henry Chaplin, representing the farmers, threatened to oppose the bill if universal discretion was to be conceded to the Privy Council.[85] Northcote played for time. Gladstone intervened to suggest that 'if the government were prepared to say that they would give full effect to our commercial treaties, the amendment would rapidly disappear'.[86]

---

[80] *Ibid.*, pp. 1620–3.
[81] *Ibid.*, pp. 1627 and 1643.
[82] *Ibid.*, pp. 1650–1.
[83] *Ibid.*, p. 1643. See also Mundella (p. 1632) and Dilke (p. 1630).
[84] *Ibid.*, pp. 1654–6.
[85] *Ibid.*, p. 1657.
[86] *Ibid.*, p. 1668.

When the House reconvened the following day, 17 July, the ministry was rescued from its predicament by Pell and Ritchie, who proposed to streamline the schedule under clause 33, establishing a general rule of slaughter at the ports whilst granting the Privy Council a discretionary power to exempt particular countries, subject to parliamentary approval.[87] This additional security ensured the grudging support of Chaplin and other farming representatives. Northcote accepted the broad principle of the amendment and James's motion was withdrawn.[88] Forster, Chamberlain and Mundella all welcomed the principle of equal treatment whilst urging the government to reverse the *presumption*.[89] This was to be the focus of Liberal opposition during the committee stages of the bill. Nevertheless the principle of universal statutory slaughter at the ports had been defeated. The *Examiner*, under the heading 'Wholesome Obstruction' applauded Forster and Hartington for their 'pluck' in persisting with opposition to the bill. The government's intentions had been frustrated at every turn, 'and for this reason – the Opposition for once actually did oppose them. Hence ministers have, as regards the conduct of the cattle bill, had to posture before the House in a perpetual "blaze of apology" and an ever thickening "fog of surrender"'.[90]

The Cattle Diseases Bill now proceeded clause by clause through the committee stage. Progress was slow. Forster and the advanced Liberals kept up pressure to go one stage further and reverse the *presumption* in favour of slaughter at the ports. A series of amendments was tabled to strengthen the domestic clauses, with some success, but the main purpose of the amendments was to highlight disparities in the treatment of domestic and foreign cattle.[91] This continuing opposition culminated in the vote on the refashioned clause 33 on 26 July. The debate and subsequent division were used to gain further political advantage from free-trade arguments. 'Everybody knew', asserted Mundella, 'that in modern times free trade had been the greatest source of the increase in our national wealth and all classes in the community had benefited equally thereby'.[92] Mundella argued that the commercial treaty system, which underpinned Britain's foreign trade with the Continent, was put at risk by the bill. European countries would only continue to accept British

[87] *Ibid.*, 17 July 1878, pp. 1698–1703.
[88] *Ibid.*, pp. 1710–12.
[89] *Ibid.*, pp. 1709, 1718 and 1720.
[90] The *Examiner*, 20 July 1878, p. 902.
[91] For example, Chamberlain's amendment extending the period of isolation for herds infected with pleuro-pneumonia to fifty-six days was accepted without a division: *Hansard*, vol. CCXLI, 18 July 1878, pp. 1854–1927. See also Forster's comments relating to further restrictions on markets and fairs, *Hansard*, vol. CCXLI, 19 July 1878, pp. 1978–9.
[92] *Hansard*, vol. CCXLII, 26 July 1878, pp. 416–17.

manufactures if they could sell their agricultural produce in British markets. Further restrictions on continental livestock, it was argued, threatened to upset the whole pattern of trade with the continent. Mundella was supported by Henry Fawcett, who argued that the recent onset of bad trade was largely due to a fall-off in exports arising from hostile tariffs. The bill offered foreign protectionists every justification to continue their policy.[93] Such arguments formed part of a wider concern in Liberal circles in the late 1870s of a perceived threat to the free-trade orthodoxy posed both by rising foreign tariffs and the emerging domestic campaign for 'fair trade' and 'reciprocity'.[94] As such, Mundella's and Fawcett's speeches were largely directed to the wider political audience in the boroughs. In the Commons, when the new schedule concerning slaughter of foreign livestock was brought forward along the strict lines of the Pell/Ritchie amendment on 31 July, Mundella declared that 'all the substantial points for which the Opposition had contended had been obtained'.[95] This mood was echoed by Joseph Chamberlain: 'For his part ... he accepted the concession as a very liberal one on the part of the government'.[96]

Farming representatives took a dim view. J. W. Barclay, a Liberal supporter of the original bill, protested 'against the surrender by the government of everything he considered valuable in the bill as introduced'.[97] There was a clear sense of betrayal amongst the farming community. The September issue of the *Farmer's Magazine* noted: 'the government may pass a half measure to quiet Mr Forster and his party, but whether the Farmers may submit to it remains to be proved'.[98] *The Times* opined that Selwin Ibbetson's conduct had been marked 'by a succession of surrenders each intended to neutralize some particular morsel of opposition, and amounting in the aggregate to a change in the whole shape and substance of the measure'. Yet, Selwin Ibbetson was merely 'the instrument of a ministerial policy of concession which the compulsion of facts rendered inevitable'.[99]

The pragmatism of the government was illustrated by the Tory peer, Lord Winnmarleigh, at the annual meeting of the Royal North Lancashire Agricultural Association. Winnmarleigh voted for the original bill, but he added: 'I do not hesitate to say that her Majesty's Government and Parliament were perfectly justified in coming to the

[93] *Ibid.*, pp. 410–14.
[94] See Henry Fawcett, *Free Trade and Protection*, London, May 1878.
[95] *Hansard*, vol. CCXLII, pp. 809–10.
[96] *Ibid.*, p. 810.
[97] *Ibid.*, p. 811.
[98] *Farmer's Magazine*, September 1878, p. 811.
[99] *The Times*, 19 July 1878, p. 10, col. d.

conclusion they arrived at – that if the town population believed the price of meat would be increased ... no government would be justified in refusing to pay attention to that consideration'.[100] The bill was infused with a dangerous political symbolism; the first majority Conservative government since the repeal of the corn laws could not be seen to support legislation which was widely interpreted as a threat to the food supply and a return to protectionism via the back door.

IV

The government had backed down from an attempt to introduce universal slaughter at the ports; discretionary powers remained, although the *presumption* had now been reversed in favour of slaughter. This was a notable achievement for the Liberal front bench, clearly animated by the administrative detail surrounding the issue, and for the advanced Liberals, swinging popular opinion in the boroughs against the measure. In its final outcome, the bill testified to the political predominance of the boroughs and the central position of free trade and the politics of 'cheap food'. The effectiveness of the Liberal opposition on this issue contrasted sharply with the internal divisions manifested over the Eastern Question and related foreign policy matters between 1876 and early 1878. The parliamentary Liberal Party had been in disarray, the Whig leadership of Hartington and Granville openly undermined by Gladstone's interventions and isolated from opinion on the advanced wing of the party. The Cattle Diseases Bill illustrated the central importance of free trade as an issue which could unite the administrative Whigs and the parliamentary Radicals.

The most vehement opposition to the bill was voiced by the parliamentary Radicals (or 'advanced Liberals'), most prominently Jacob Bright, Joseph Chamberlain, Joseph Cowen, Henry Fawcett and A. I. Mundella. The campaign in the boroughs was dominated by the organs of popular liberalism. The *language*, the political tone and style of the campaign illustrated the posthumous influence of Richard Cobden[101] and the radicalism of the Anti-Corn Law League upon late-Victorian popular liberalism. This can be seen at a number of levels: the self-consciously drawn analogy between opposition to the Cattle Diseases Bill

---

[100] *Farmer's Magazine*, October 1878, p. 255.
[101] This theme is discussed by Anthony Howe in chapter 8, in particular section I. The late 1870s saw a revived interest in Cobden. Morley's *Life* was published in two volumes by Chapman & Hall in 1879. The Cobden Club brought out a second edition of Cobden's *Political Writings* in 1878. A plethora of popular biographies followed, for example, L. Apjohn, *Memorable Men of the 19th Century: Richard Cobden and the Free Traders*, London, 1881.

and the campaign for the repeal of the corn laws;[102] the willingness to interpret the measure as a protectionist conspiracy for the narrow benefit of the landed interest;[103] the acceptance as 'received wisdom' of the equation of free trade with lower prices and universally shared prosperity – the 'moral economy' of free trade espoused by Cobden.[104] These themes were commonplace in the speeches of radical politicians, the editorials of the radical press and the opinions of the organs of popular liberalism. Perhaps the most articulate expression of this posthumous 'Cobdenism' comes from Joseph Cowen's *Newcastle Daily Chronicle*, under the heading 'Protectionist Legislation':

The Cattle trade with Continental countries and with America is still in its infancy. Were it left to mercantile ingenuity, it would doubtless quickly reach gigantic proportions and its importance to the people of England could then scarcely be overrated. To a foreign supply, and a foreign supply alone the country looks to an abatement in the price of butcher meat. The interposition of parliament, however, bids fair to crush this trade. The British stock farmer will thus be left with a virtual monopoly of the meat market. This may be advantageous to the 'Agricultural interest'. The Landlords of England are the 'Agricultural interest'. RICHARD COBDEN, however, in his own terse and felicitous way reminded the Lords of the soil that they were mere receivers of rents ... Whatever artificial price legislation may place upon butcher meat must ultimately enhance the rent of the squires.

There is something pre-eminently heartless in the introduction of a measure that cannot fail still further to enhance the cost of an essential portion of the nation's food. It was, however, not surprising that men who acquired political notoriety by defending the BREAD TAX, when the masses were starving, should in this day of severe commercial depression, attempt to do for cattle what was done for corn.[105]

The radical campaign did not only look to Cobden for a language of opposition to the Cattle Diseases Bill; his programme of land reform

---

[102] For example, *Reynolds News*, editorial, 7 July 1878, p. 4; *Bee-Hive*, 6 July 1878, p. 11: 'The trade in meat will be made what the trade in corn was'.

[103] Report of meeting of delegates of working mens' clubs in Hackney: 'The Meat Question', *Bee-Hive*, 13 July 1878, p. 9, 'The Essex Labourers and Mr Gladstone', *The Daily News*, 22 July 1878, p. 2. Also Ajax, 'Monopoly and Mischief', *English Labourers' Chronicle*, 27 July 1878, p. 7.

[104] *English Labourers' Chronicle*, 27 July 1878, p. 7. See also resolution against the Cattle Diseases Bill carried by the Labour Representation League, reported in the *Leeds Mercury*, 1 July 1878 – 'all restrictions on commerce tend to the impoverishment of the Nation'. In 1879 Joseph Arch, speaking against 'Reciprocity', stated: 'This foreign competition has been an awful bugbear to the farmers, but it was a great blessing to the workmen during the past winter. Let us thank God for Cobden and Bright. The fruit of their labours has been seen in thousands of homes which have been blessed with the cheap loaf', quoted in Joseph Arch, *From Ploughtail to Parliament: An Autobiography*, 2nd edn, London, 1986, p. 313.

[105] *Newcastle Daily Chronicle*, 14 February 1878, p. 2, most probably written by Joseph Cowen.

provided an alternative policy for the expansion in domestic meat supply. Thus, the Liberal intellectual, Thorold Rogers, in a published letter under the heading 'The Meat Supply' argued that amongst the most important causes accounting for the declining productiveness of domestic stock farmers was the insufficient security afforded to farmers' capital – the root cause of which, he continued, lay in the landlord–tenant relationship and the present system of landownership. Rogers added, 'Cobden used to say that the advantage which accrued to the country from the abolition of the corn laws was nothing compared to that which would ensue if what he called Free Trade in Land were accorded'.[106]

By the late 1870s a posthumous and updated Cobdenite programme of land reform, which encompassed the removal of restrictions on the sale and transfer of land to promote wider ownership via the 'free' market, and ancillary reforms such as compensation for tenants' improvements and reform of the game laws, was no longer the sole preserve of the advanced wing of the Liberal Party but was endorsed by the party leadership, as an element in the Liberal programme of domestic reform. By 1979–80 Hartington had moved so far as to accept the removal of 'artificial and obsolete restrictions on the sale and transfer of land.[107] This led on in the parliament of 1880 to cross-bench support for Lord Cairns' Settled Lands Act (allowing partial sale of settled estates for improvements) and the Solicitors Remuneration Bill (simplifying conveyance). By the late 1870s the Liberal front bench had also made significant movement towards compulsory compensation for improvements for English tenant farmers,[108] which resulted in the 1883 Agricultural Holdings Act. In the short session following the 1880 Liberal landslide, Gladstone signalled the priority given to farmers' grievances by repealing the malt tax and passing a ground game bill. County franchise and local government reform waited in the wings. English land reform was thereafter subsumed by the re-emergence of the Irish land question and demoted in the order of priorities. The adoption of a modified programme of Cobdenite land reform for the English counties by the

---

[106] Thorold Rogers, letter to the *Daily News*, reprinted in *English Labourers' Chronicle*, 20 October 1878, p. 5. See also 'Cattle Diseases Bill', *Bee-Hive*, 15 June 1878, p. 3, which reiterated this point. *Farmer's Magazine*, April 1878, p. 266 carried a letter, 'The Land and the People' by a 'Free Farmer' which quoted Cobden's speech at Rochdale in November 1864 calling for a League for Free Trade in Land. See also J. R. Fisher, 'The Farmers' Alliance. An Agricultural Protest Movement of the 1880s', *Agricultural History Review*, 26, 1 (1978), pp. 15–25.

[107] Speeches at Newcastle, 19 September 1879 and Blackburn, 27 March 1880, in *The Marquis of Hartington's Election Speeches*, edited by U. Kay-Shuttleworth, London, 1880, pp. 21 and 148.

[108] See Fisher 'The Farmers' Alliance', and R. McQuiston, 'Tenant Right. Farmer v. Landlord in Victorian Britain', *Agricultural History Review*, 2 (April 1973), pp. 85–114.

Liberal leadership in 1879–80 thereafter held its place, nothwithstanding the stagnant market in land resulting from the onset of agricultural recession, largely to counter the more extreme demands regarding land nationalisation which emerged in the mid-1880s. The once 'radical' Cobdenite policy now became the new Liberal orthodoxy on the land question until it was in turn subsumed by land taxation and 'the unearned increment' during the Lloyd George era.

And what of the foreign livestock trade? Hindsight reveals 1878 to have been a high point for free-trade arguments. In 1879, following reports of disease, livestock from the United States were subjected to compulsory slaughter at the ports. Gladstone's second ministry came under repeated pressure to impose further restrictions, suffering a defeat in 1882 over foreign livestock with foot and mouth disease.[109] Paradoxically the landslide election victory of 1880 placed the Liberal leadership in a weaker position to defend its policy of 1878, because of the increased number of Liberal representatives in the counties who were prepared to vote against the party whip. If the issue showed how free trade might unite the Liberal front bench and the parliamentary Radicals, Liberal county MPs were pulled by stronger constituency pressures. During the closing decades of the nineteenth century further legislation gradually squeezed out the foreign livestock trade, which, in any case, was being replaced by imported frozen meat.[110] With an adequate alternative source of foreign supply, free-trade arguments against restrictions on foreign livestock lost their relevance. Nevertheless, the events of 1878 illustrate the importance of the free-trade lobby and the issue of 'cheap food' as a mover of popular, parliamentary and governmental opinion in late-Victorian Britain.

[109] See A. H. H. Matthews, *Fifty Years of Agricultural Politics. A History of the Chambers of Agriculture*, London, 1915, pp. 26–7. Also T. Jenkins, *Gladstone, Whiggery and the Liberal Party 1874–1886*, Oxford, 1888, pp. 172–3.

[110] See J. T. Mitchell and J. Raymond, *History of the Frozen Meat Trade*. Appendix 1, pp. 404–5 provides a summary of subsequent legislation. Livestock from the continent was prohibited entirely in 1892. Consolidating legislation in 1896 subjected all remaining livestock imports (mainly from North and South America) to slaughter at the ports. See also Perren, 'The North American Beef and Cattle Trade'.

8   Towards the 'hungry forties': free trade in Britain, c. 1880–1906

Anthony Howe

It has been commonplace to see in the part played by free trade in the making of the Liberal government of 1905 and its electoral victory in 1906 a return to the past, to the cardinal tenet of the Peelite–Gladstonian fiscal consensus which had dominated nineteenth-century politics and policy. Such an interpretation is invited both by the Liberal rhetoric of the 'hungry forties' and by the prominence of such self-conscious Cobdenites as F. W. Hirst and G. J. Shaw-Lefevre in the campaign against tariff reform. Such a view of the revival of ancestral gods made clear both the limitations of the 'old' liberalism of Campbell-Bannerman and emphasised the importance of the breakthrough to the 'new' liberalism of Asquith after 1908, when the 'old' prescriptions of peace, retrenchment and reform were finally abandoned in favour of social reform and progressive taxation.[1]

Nevertheless, this interpretation is unsatisfactory at a number of levels, for it implies strongly that free trade's attractiveness lay in its ancestry, both in its ability to act as a unifying device within the Liberal Party after the damaging post-Gladstonian splits, and as an electoral issue, able to counter the 'modernity' of tariff reform by an appeal to Pareto-type residues in the new democratic electorate.[2] This interpretation fails therefore to allow both for the extent to which the political language of free trade had developed since the 1840s, and fails to integrate it adequately into the making of new liberalism, of which it formed an essential, not an expediential, ingredient. This essay therefore sets out firstly to outline the reshaping of Cobdenism in the 1880s, suggesting that by 1886 both the content and the audience for 'Cobdenite' ideas had been significantly altered since the 1840s. Secondly, it will argue that

---

[1] For this view, P. F. Clarke, *Lancashire and the New Liberalism*, Cambridge, 1972; J. Harris, *Unemployment and Politics*, Oxford, 1972, p. 226; M. Bentley, *The Climax of Liberal Politics*, 1986. London.

[2] Interestingly, Pareto was an honorary member of the Cobden Club but it drew on his economic ideas, rather than his psychological or elite theories, in its propaganda. West Sussex Record Office, Cobden Papers 1185, 1186, Cobden Club minutes (hereafter CCM), 30 May 1891.

during the Unionist hegemony of 1886–1905 free trade was defended in ways which made its currency not simply that of history or dogma but that of a necessary element in Britain's economic prosperity in an age of empire and tariff wars as well as the indispensable element in the fiscal basis of new liberalism. Finally, it examines the way in which free trade between 1903 and 1906 was shaped not only as an appeal to the past but as part of a forward-looking element in the Lib–Lab revival on which New Liberal policies would be promoted.

1

There is no doubt that in the 1840s free trade, especially in its secular, Ricardian version, was a creed whose main audience was found among the middle classes of urban Britain.[3] The working-class tradition of free trade survived but chartism produced an unresolved ambiguity for working men, not all of whom were content to work for the free-trade cause as readily as the journalist Thomas Hodgskin.[4] Nevertheless, after 1848 the adoption of free trade as a working-class cause was an essential part of the *rapprochement* between Liberals and working men, fostered by both Bright and Gladstone. By the 1870s, it is also noticeable that many memoir-writing Chartists readily proclaimed their support for free trade.[5] But perhaps the clearest evidence for the growing working-class appropriation of the free-trade cause was the emergence of Cobden as a 'popular' hero celebrated in print and stone. For example, statues unveiled at Bradford in 1877 and Stockport in 1886 were occasions on which the Cobdenite message was reaffirmed against the stirrings of fair trade, with Cobden celebrated as the benefactor of the people, both materially and in terms of a peace-loving Europe which he had encouraged.[6]

This thriving 'cult' of Cobden was more widely expressed in a sizeable devotional literature, of the type which Collini has suggested helped impart the Victorian message of individualism.[7] But more direct political

---

[3] See, *inter alia*, A. J. B. Hilton, *The Age of Atonement: The Influence of Evangelicalism on Social and Economic Thought, 1785–1865*, Oxford, 1988; A. C. Howe, 'Free Trade and the City of London, *c*. 1820–1870', *History*, 77 (1992), pp. 391–414.

[4] For Hodgskin, C. S. Nicholls (ed.), *DNB: Missing Persons*, Oxford, 1993; N. W. Thompson, *The People's Science: The Popular Political Economy of Exploitation and Crisis, 1816–1834*, Cambridge, 1984; L. Brown, 'Chartism and the Anti-Corn Law League', in A. Briggs (ed.), *Chartist Studies*, London 1959, pp. 350–1.

[5] C. Godfrey, *Chartist Lives*, New York, 1987, pp. 329–31.

[6] *Speeches of the Rt. Hon. John Bright on the Occasion of the Inauguration of the Cobden Memorial*, 1877; *The Times*, London, 23 July 1886.

[7] S. Collini, 'Manly Fellows', in L. Goldmann (ed.), *The Blind Victorian. Henry Fawcett and British Liberalism*, Cambridge, 1989, p. 59.

messages were also conveyed in the successive biographies which appeared after Cobden's death in 1865. For example, John McGilchrist enrolled Cobden in the army of political progress, an example to encourage rejection of Palmerstonian stagnation and adoption of a high ideal of citizenship.[8] McGilchrist, an old League hand, saw in Cobden's ideas a creed as radical as that of the Chartists, which therefore constituted a suitable link between the 1840s and the parliamentary reform movement of the 1860s. Several other early biographies similarly saw in Cobden the 'man of the people' or 'the champion of the working men'.[9] Much of this literature was aimed specifically at the young, and much of it was written by former employees of the League who now devoted themselves to the literature of moral improvement for publishers such as Cassell's, and who found in the life of Cobden the most suitable vehicle to discharge 'their duty of political and economic instruction'.[10] This message also percolated strongly into the popular history textbooks of the 1860s and 1870s written by admirers of Cobden such as Thomas Bullock or later Arthur Acland, in which the free-trade battles of the 1840s were always given prominence.[11] Through this devotional and educational literature Cobden was placed at the centre of a radical tradition of continuing pertinence for the working man which was ripe for revival at particular moments in Liberal politics, whether in the 1870s against the background of Disraelian foreign policy or in the 1900s against Chamberlainite tariff reform.

Popular representations of Cobden were, of course, only one means by which the 'Cobdenite' message was transmitted into late-Victorian political culture. Other parts of that legacy remained central to high political debate and its popular reflections, as Biagini has shown in his studies of Gladstonian taxation and working-class political economy.[12] Nevertheless, Gladstonian policy was never single-mindedly 'Cobdenite', however much Gladstone himself liked in old age to see himself as 'fundamentally a Peel–Cobden man'.[13] For the transmission of the

---

[8] J. McGilchrist, *Richard Cobden: Apostle of Free Trade, his Political Career, and Public Services. A Biography*, London, 1865, esp. pp. vi, 135, 153.

[9] E.g. A. T. Scott, *In Memoriam: the Life and Labours of Richard Cobden*, London, 1865.

[10] McGilchrist, *Richard Cobden*, p. 274; see also J. E. Ritchie, *In Memory of Richard Cobden. A Biography*, London, 1865; and J. E. Ritchie, *Christopher Crayon's Recollections*, London, 1898.

[11] T. Bullock, *Richard Cobden: A Study for Young Men*, London, 1865; Bullock, *Illustrated School History of England*, London, 1877, pp. 240–51; Bullock, *Modern Europe*, London, 1863, pp. 315–16. The notion of the 'hungry forties' seems absent from this literature which emphasises the political struggle for free trade.

[12] E. Biagini, 'The Debate on Taxation, 1860–74' in E. Biagini and A. Reid (eds.), *Currents of Radicalism*, Cambridge, 1991, pp. 134–62; Biagini, *Liberty, Retrenchment and Reform*, Cambridge, 1992, pp. 93–138.

[13] Cited by H. C. G. Matthew, *The Liberal Imperialists*, Oxford, 1973, p. vii.

Cobdenite creed, we need therefore to look more widely than Liberal policy itself and, in this context, the outstanding but neglected standard-bearers of Cobdenism were the members of the Cobden Club set up in 1866. To some extent, of course, the Club was not seen as a propagandist institution, and one of its founders, Sir Louis Mallet, preferred to see in it 'a private Foreign Office for commercial questions'.[14] For others, it was primarily a Liberal Party organisation, for the education and training of aspiring politicians, and for the articulation of future Liberal policy. Its value to Liberal politics was, however, enhanced when the Liberals were in opposition. In particular between 1874 and 1880, the Club became the base for a group of advanced Liberals anxious not only to promote social reforms but also, as Jonathan Spain has shown, avid and alert in the defence of free trade and the 'food of the people' against potential protectionist measures.[15] The Club's activities extended well beyond the parliamentary sphere in the late 1870s, as it took upon itself the task of the propagation of free-trade ideas to popular audiences in order to counter the growing support for fair trade. By 1877 the Club was already considering the need for a new league-style campaign against protection at home and abroad, resulting in a flood of propaganda directed at working men, and in new links with the Agricultural Labourers' Union in 1878.[16] This campaign drew together club activists such as Mallet and A. J. Mundella with academic Liberals such as G. C. Brodrick and Arnold Toynbee. Toynbee, for example, in January 1880, enthusiastically defended free trade against the Bradford fair traders, upholding the rights of the community against those of uncompetitive industries. He also joined his pupils like E. T. Cook in campaigning in the Oxfordshire countryside on this issue in the election of 1880.[17] The impact of this free-trade crusade on the election result of 1880 should not be exaggerated, but the task of educating the new democracy in the lessons of free trade had been enjoined in earnest.[18]

This popular defence of free trade became even more urgent with the formation of the National Fair Trade League in 1881 and the election of its leader W. F. Ecroyd as MP for Preston in May 1881, a result which the combined efforts of the Cobden Club and the Manchester-based National Reform Union (NRU) failed to avert. Significantly, at this

---

[14] Balliol College, Oxford, Morier Papers, Box 44, Louis Mallet to Sir Robert Morier, 23 June 1878.

[15] J. Spain, chapter 7 above.

[16] CCM, 2 March 1878.

[17] A. Kadish, *Apostle Arnold: The Life and Death of Arnold Toynbee*, Durham (N.C.), 1986, pp. 73–7, 96.

[18] Nevertheless the most recent account of the 1880 election does highlight the economic issue, R. Shannon, *The Age of Disraeli*, London, 1992, pp. 378ff.

point, the club's leading light, Thomas Bayley Potter, began to cultivate links with the TUC through Burt, Broadhurst and Howell in order to counter the fallacies of protection among working men.[19] A special publication fund was set up, drawing on the lordly purses of the Dukes of Devonshire and Westminster as well as those of New Model employers, including Brassey and Salt. This fund supported publications such as George Potter's *The Working Man's View of Free Trade* as well as Medley's *Reciprocity Craze*, pamphlets which were now issued in hundreds, not tens, of thousands, as the Club focused its efforts on attaching working men to free trade.

This task became even more vital for the future of liberalism with the Third Reform Act's enfranchisement of the agricultural labourer, which raised the spectre of the rural masses emerging as protectionist battalions. This was particularly worrying in late 1884 as low corn prices were accompanied by a renewed landlord demand for duties on foreign corn, and with the defeat of the free trader Lord William Compton by the fair trader S. S. Lloyd in the South Warwickshire by-election of 1884. Liberal fears of a widespread protectionist backlash were now intense, with Schnadhorst, secretary of the National Liberal Federation (NLF), writing to Potter in November, that 'it looks as if we shall have to fight the battle of free trade over again. I view with considerable apprehension the ignorance on this question of the labourers who will soon have the vote'.[20] Against this background, the Cobden Club unleashed a propaganda drive of enormous proportions. In particular, it recruited Joseph Arch to the cause as author of a pamphlet which the Club distributed widely, educating the labouring population into the benefits of free trade.[21] The Club's efforts were of course redoubled with the general election of 1885, with a new publication fund, with experts on hand to translate tracts into Welsh, and with the presses at Cassell's kept hot by the production of the Club's literature.[22]

In this campaign the Club produced over ten million leaflets and tracts, which undoubtedly rivalled the better-known League campaign of the 1840s.[23] That campaign had been aimed at the £10 'selectorate' of 1832, a well-defined body easily reached by postal propaganda. This was less readily achieved in the 1880s with a household electorate, where the

---

[19] For the Club's earlier links with Howell, see Biagini, *Liberty*, p. 109n.

[20] CCM, 22 November 1884.

[21] Joseph Arch, *Free Trade vs Protection*, London, 1884 and Cobden Club leaflet no. xviii; CCM, 15 and 29 November 1884. See Nigel Scotland, chapter 6 above, for the pertinence of the Cobdenite legacy to the agricultural labourers in the 1880s.

[22] CCM, 6 February 1886. On occasions 'the entire power of the great house of Cassell & Co. had been devoted ... to the services of the Cobden Club'.

[23] Cobden Club, Annual Reports, 1885, 1886 (6.5 million by June 1885).

club's success depended upon the use of existing political organisations at the local level.[24] It therefore fostered strong links with both the NLF and NRU, and with thousands of local activists, upon whom the Club could rely for the distribution of its literature. In this work, too, valuable help was given by Bradlaugh's National Secular Society whose agents were particularly active in the free-trade cause in the 1880s.[25] There is therefore strong evidence that Club propaganda had become a staple part of the masses' political diet in the 1885 election.[26] In form the Club's literature consisted mostly of single-sheet leaflets with easily assimilable, but not simple-minded, explanations of the free-trade case by a range of authors including Sydney Buxton, George Medley, W. E. Baxter, G. J. Holyoake, John Noble and Alfred Simmons of the Kent and Sussex Labourers. Here, it may be claimed, the Club helped supply the widely felt need for political education in the countryside, and did so at a time when the printed word became perhaps the primary means of political communication as the age of Gladstonian rhetoric receded into the privatised politics of the hearth.[27] Certainly, the Liberal victory in the election of 1885 owed much to what appeared to the Gladstonians as the dispassionate political virtues of the rural electorate, disdaining the pleas of self-interested landed protectionists and upholding the keystone of the Gladstonian settlement.

Yet what message did the urban and rural working man take from the Cobdenites of the 1880s? How far was support for free trade the act of a rational democracy before the onset of jingoism and the yellow press? How far did the rhetoric of free trade offer boons to the working man in the 1880s which had been primarily open to the export manufacturers and merchants of the 1840s? At the root of the Cobdenite faith was the simple belief that free trade meant prosperity, and so embodied the essential political guarantee of working-class material welfare. The view that 'the working classes have more steadily benefited from free trade than any other class', was now underpinned by the statistics of forty years, expertly interpreted by Giffen and others.[28] The academic case for free trade made by Fawcett and Farrer was turned into a popular rhetoric

[24] For the problems of reaching voters in 1885, see A. Simmons, 'The Ideas of the New Voters', *Fortnightly Review*, 37 (1885), pp. 160–7.

[25] For Annie Besant's writings on free trade, see Biagini, *Liberty*, p. 133; CCM, 31 January and 28 February 1891.

[26] One labourer in Gloucestershire was dismissed for his part in distributing the Club's tracts. CCM, 23 January 1886.

[27] Simmons, 'The Ideas of the New Voters', on the need for publications with a 'high level of political thought'. For 'fireside' reading of the Club's literature, G. Whitelaw, *Co-operative Voting, the Only Means to Proportional Representation*, London, 1885, p. 12.

[28] G. M. Koot, *English Historical Economics, 1870–1926. The Rise of Economic History and Neomercantilism*, Cambridge, 1987, pp. 73–9.

of affluence by Medley and Mongredien, and even the onset of depression in the late 1870s was seen as a merely temporary interruption of prosperity. The popularisers drove home the contrasts between the immiseration of the 1840s and the 'progress of the working classes' since, a progress far more marked in Britain than in Germany or the United States. Working-class prosperity under free trade could, it was argued, only be jeopardised by protection and retaliation, policies which promoted the self-interest of particular groups in society, not the welfare of all. Here the moral case for a polity free from the power of vested interest groups met the economic one for free imports as the basis of the working-class 'contract' with the Victorian state, a contract which advertised the primacy of the citizen–consumer.[29]

Nevertheless, that the case for free trade was not, by the 1880s, one simply for *laissez-faire*, and the dissociation of free trade from simple notions of 'Manchesterism' is already clear by the early 1880s. Arguably, 'Manchesterism', a term first used in 1883, was only identifiable when it had already disappeared. Sir Louis Mallet, the high priest of Victorian Cobdenism, was, for example, already worried in the early 1880s about the Cobden Club's abandonment of the doctrine of non-intervention in domestic affairs, and sought desperately to disavow the Millian doctrine of socialism. As he wrote to T. B. Potter, the distinctive character of Cobden's economic policy 'was the belief that the social problem (by which I mean the reconciliation of the interests of property with those of the proletariat) was to be solved by Peace and Free Trade in the largest sense, of Free Exchange, between all Nations ... and the steady adoption of the principles of personal liberty and personal responsibility'. Yet he now saw the Club gravitating to the Chamberlainite doctrine, of 'the power of the state to right the balance between property and poverty'.[30] Certainly, a number of stalwart members of the Club, like W. C. Cartwright, Goschen, Clarendon, and Odo Russell, resigned in a rash in 1882–3, fearing the new radical direction of the Club.

How well grounded were their fears that Cobdenism was about to embrace 'socialism'? Here the nearest the Cobdenites approached to radicalism was in the pursuit of land reform, seen as the peculiar legacy of Cobden to the next generation. Early on, the Club had compiled interesting sets of essays on land tenure abroad, which had some influence on Liberal thinking, particularly with their eulogies of the peasant proprietors.[31] By 1876, the Club was ready, to the abhorrence of the Duke of

[29] For the notion of 'contract', see R. I. McKibbin, 'Why There was No Marxism in Britain', *English Historical Review*, 99 (1984) pp. 297–331; Biagini, *Liberty*, ch. ii.
[30] PRO FO 918/54 Ampthill Papers, Mallet to Potter, 10 June 1883 (copy), enclosed in Mallet to Lord Odo Russell.
[31] J. W. Probyn (ed.), *Systems of Land Tenure in Various Countries*, London, 1871; reprinted on the suggestion of Gladstone, 1881.

Argyll, to advocate the rights of tenants against those of landlords and, by 1878, as we have seen, was seeking also to cultivate its alliance with the rural labourers.[32] The Club's members, for example W. E. Baxter, remained active in the land reform movement, and in the face of agricultural depression continued to advocate tenurial reform, economic efficiency and proper cultivation of the soil as the real alternatives to reciprocity and protection. This programme fell far short of Georgeite land nationalisation but the model of efficient peasant farming opposed to the aristocratic order was one which was made effectively, alongside the better-known Radical message of Chamberlain. Certainly, in rural areas the issue of small holdings appeared as the inevitable twin of free trade in the election of 1885, for example in East Gloucestershire, where A. B. Winterbotham, an active member of the Cobden Club, ended forty-three years of unbroken Tory rule.[33] But the land was an issue in which Radical language often clothed social conservatism, as Ireland well demonstrated. Nevertheless, this Cobdenite interest in land reform was well established in the 1880s, was supported electorally as we have seen, and set up a continuing link between free trade and land reform which MPs like Shaw-Lefevre and Francis Channing would continue into the Edwardian period.[34]

Beyond land law reform, positive Cobdenite prescriptions still looked primarily to fiscal policy. Here not only did the goal of the free breakfast table remain, but cheap wine for the working man, not achieved by Gladstone's budget of 1860, was still held out as a means of reinvigorating the cause of free trade in Europe, above all by adjustments on Spanish wines, which it was believed would generate a significant expansion of British exports to Iberia. Less traditionally, free traders by the 1880s were also advocating the adjustment of railway rates, which it was held benefited the railway companies and the foreign producer at the expense of the consumer. Finally, too, in the mid-1880s the case was made for increased direct taxation on the landed interest in the form of death duties, a cause which Harcourt would acknowledge in his 1894 budget.[35] The Cobdenites therefore maintained the case for the centrality

---

[32] For Argyll in the Scottish context, see below, J. Shaw, chapter 12. Argyll's daughter, Lady Frances Balfour, became a leading member of the Women's Free Trade Union, see below, p. 216.

[33] N. Scotland, 'The Decline and Collapse of the National Agricultural Labourers' Union in Gloucestershire, 1887–96. Pt 2', *Gloucestershire History* (1988), pp. 16ff, citing *Cheltenham Free Press*, 28 November 1885; cf. Scotland's contribution to the present volume, chapter 6 above.

[34] There was also a strong Cobdenite involvement in the urban defence of the commons through the Commons Preservation Society.

[35] Cobden Club leaflet no. 38 c. 1885, 'Death Duties'. Harcourt's budget was greeted by the Club as testimony to its mentor's indirect influence, and as opening up a 'new field of taxation' as an alternative to tariffs. CCM, 14 July 1894.

of the consumer within fiscal policy, while foreshadowing the case for greater direct taxation. They therefore supply one of the missing links in the fiscal chain linking Gladstone and Lloyd George. Here were elements of a radical programme which avoided both the sharpened individualism of the message of free exchange in the 1880s (that way the Liberty and Property Defence League lay) and the collectivism of state intervention which the Cobdenites, like many Radicals, still believed was far more likely to benefit the classes than the masses.[36]

It was clear too that the international message of the Cobdenites also held an increasing appeal for the working man, for if anything the history of Europe since 1870 had emphasised the continental model of militarism, tariffs and state power in opposition to the Cobdenite message of free trade and peace. Cobdenites continued to press for commercial treaties as 'peace bonds', and to advocate schemes like the Channel Tunnel as part of their cosmopolitan vision, while pressure groups such as the International Peace and Arbitration Association drew in personnel and argument from the Cobdenites.[37] Nevertheless, the Cobdenites of the 1880s were also far more ready than their mentor in the 1830s and 1840s to countenance support for the Concert of Europe as a fulcrum of British foreign policy, although under Gladstone's direction there was, of course, a greater sense of the 'European general will' than Palmerston ever exuded. Neither the occupation of Egypt nor Home Rule seriously undermined faith in Gladstone, and there was some truth in the criticism that by 1886 the Club devoted to Cobden had become a 'Gladstone, not a Cobden Club'.[38] Certainly, Gladstone himself found in Cobdenism an ideological current more palatable and arguably more popular than that of Chamberlain's radicalism and imperialism.

II

The electoral success of the Liberals in November 1885 confirmed the centrality of free trade within popular politics, and ended the possibility of a democratic basis for protectionism such as had emerged both in the colonies and Europe. A battle fought on the high ground of principle in 1885 receded thereafter into a hole-and-corner defence of free trade, as economic debate turned to more recondite but not less important issues. This rechannelling was signalled in July 1885 when economic orthodoxy faced its first serious challenge from within the political elite with the

---

[36] For free exchange and individualism, see M. W. Taylor, *Men vs the State. Herbert Spencer and Late Victorian Individualism*, Oxford, 1992, pp. 22ff.

[37] See, for example, the work of Hodgson Pratt as a 'go-between' within these groups.

[38] Sir Edward Watkin, CCM, 10 July 1886.

appointment, by Lord Salisbury's minority government, of the Royal Commission on the Depression in Trade and Industry (RCDTI).[39] For although the reports of this commission ostensibly reinforced orthodoxy, its very existence, as the Liberals feared, sowed economic doubt, and rather like the Select Committee on Import Duties in 1840, it acted as a point of departure for policies often distasteful to policy-makers. Three main foci of discontent emerged among economic heretics: the gold standard, sugar bounties, and the empire. These issues were not for the most part the stuff of popular political debate but they generated an immense discussion among bureaucrats, politicians, and sectional interests, whether those of working men, industrialists, or City financiers. This, in turn, precipitated a rethinking of free trade arguments in ways which vitally affected the re-emergence of free trade at the electoral level in Edwardian Britain.

Firstly, the royal commission directed much attention to the fall in prices since 1873, although delegating consideration of monetary causes of depression to a separate Commission into Gold and Silver. The most obvious remedy for falling prices seemed to some an increase in money supply, which a bimetallic standard would achieve. The idea of a double standard therefore became attractive to a variety of interest groups in industry, the City, and on the land. Yet the double standard did not challenge orthodoxy to quite the extent some historians have imagined, and was fully compatible with free trade in the eyes of some of its most stalwart adherents, for example Mallet, with his strong belief in an international order which would ensure both free exchange and monetary stability. Yet by the later 1880s most free traders had accepted that this vision was scarcely realisable in the existing international climate, and were in any case unwilling to threaten the working-class standard of living through rising prices. For however distasteful to 'producers', the fall in prices and profits after 1873 had been the essential basis of the increase in working-class real wages, as most free traders were keen to point out, backed by the majority of Liberal politicians.[40]

'Fair traders' were in fact no more keen than free traders to stress monetary causes of depression, but attributed it to the very breakdown of the institutional structure of international commerce, in which

---

[39] *Parliamentary Papers, 1884–5* vol. LXXI (348); *1886*, vol. XXI, c. 4621, c. 4715; vol. XXII, c. 4715–i; vol. XXIII, c. 4797, c. 4893.

[40] See E. H. H. Green, 'Rentiers versus Producers? The Political Economy of the Bimetallic Controversy c. 1880–1898' and A. C. Howe, 'Bimetallism, *c.* 1880–1898: A Controversy Re-opened?', *English Historical Review*, 103 (1988), pp. 588–612, and 105 (1990), pp. 377–91. The issues for which Green puts the case in 'The Bimetallic Controversy: Empiricism Belimed or the Case for the Issues', *ibid.*, 105 (1990), pp. 673–83, are only tangentially those of the original debate.

bimetallists necessarily put their faith. Thus the minority report of the RCDTI concluded: 'the greatest and most permanent cause of depression [lay in] the action of foreign bounties and tariffs and the growing effect of directly or indirectly subsidized foreign competition'.[41] Economic revival depended therefore not on international negotiations, as the bimetallists favoured, but on the evolution of a 'national policy' whose central props would be retaliation and imperial preference. In particular the fiscal policy of free imports would be replaced by one of countervailing duties imposed against foreign bounties, above all on sugar, and retaliatory duties against high or prohibitory foreign tariffs. At the same time, such a fiscal policy would allow concessions to the empire which would help strengthen it in both defence and commerce. Here, then, lay a challenge to the central dogmas of free trade by critics whose analysis and policies appeared more so than those of the free traders to recognise the peculiar tendencies of the British economy in the 1880s, and whose prescriptions have seemed to historians in some ways more 'modern' than the 'complacent' defence of free trade to which the majority of commissioners in 1886 are thought to have adhered. It is therefore worth considering the somewhat recondite issues of both the sugar bounties and imperial preference in order to assess how far the free-trade case against them was based on outmoded economic logic unthinkingly inherited from the rhetoric of the 1840s.

The campaign against sugar bounties went back to the 1860s, for not only were they objectionable in theory but Liberal politicians had sought practical steps to remove them, before the 'fair traders' had taken over the cause, with some working-class support.[42] By 1886 the Liberals had foresworn further action on bounties, but the Conservatives were anxious to discourage bounties, whether unilaterally or collectively with other powers by either imposing countervailing duties on bounty-fed sugar or prohibiting the import of such sugar entirely. For men like Baron de Worms, the benefit of cheap sugar – so long as it lasted – needed to be set against the costs in terms of jobs and of damage which the competition of bounty-fed sugar beet inflicted upon the cane-produced sugar of the West Indies. Conservative governments after 1886 flirted with both these remedies but it was only with the Brussels Sugar Convention of 1902 that they reached a practical conclusion, whereby Britain agreed to prohibit the import of bounty-fed sugar and agreed to international machinery for the enforcement of this agreement. This whole campaign was, however, resisted energetically by 'cheap imports' free traders, however much

---

[41] *Parliamentary Papers, 1886*, vol. XXIII, c. 4893; Final Report, p. lxiv, para. 122.
[42] B. H. Brown, *The Tariff Reform Movement in Britain, 1881–1895*, New York, 1943, *passim.*

theorists of 'free exchange', such as Mallet, had favoured international action on sugar as on money.

How complacent was this defence of free trade, how 'modern' the case for prohibition? The main strengths of the latter were twofold. Firstly, the defence of international machinery for commercial regulation was genuinely enlightened in form, if not motives – a form of economic internationalism which attracted some Cobdenites, and in the light of which attachment to cheap imports seemed merely an argument of national expediency.[43] Secondly, the anti-bounty school was alive to the longer-term dangers that the elimination of cane sugar would complete the monopoly of Europe's 'insidious' sugar cartels. Both these arguments were ones which free traders could in theory sanction, but whose weight failed to tell against the even stronger political and economic case for the rejection of anti-bounty policies. Undoubtedly, at the heart of this opposition was the belief that sugar prices must inevitably rise, if bounty-fed imports were prohibited. By 1903 the British people were by far the greatest sugar consumers in the world, with an average consumption estimated at *c.* 90 lb per capita, and some free traders were ready to argue that sugar now occupied a place in working-class diets and living standards comparable with that of bread in the 1840s. Certainly the sugar-eating voters of Britain were a most obvious group of consumers whom politicians would alienate at their peril. Secondly, however, sugar was increasingly used as a raw material in 'new' industries, those of the confectionery trades, which were one of the most successful forms of economic diversification upon which the long-term adjustment of the economy depended. Many progressive Liberal capitalists were therefore ready as 'producers' to join the operatives as consumers in the defence of 'cheap sugar'. This argument also swayed orthodox Conservative financiers like Hicks Beach, who, as an MP for Bristol in the 1880s, was only too well aware that cocoa factories like Fry's were more important to the local economy than the old declining West Indian sugar refineries.[44]

Thirdly, beneath the enlightened international machinery of conventions, there lurked the suspicion that the major beneficiary of their action would be the West Indian sugar interest, for whose inefficiency they would continue to provide a shield; how far should the community as a whole be held to ransom for the sake of the obsolete and inefficient? More

[43] F. S. L. Lyons, *Internationalism in Europe, 1815–1914*, London, pp. 103–10 usefully traces the rise and fall of the Sugar Convention. This approach therefore had much in common with that of the 'New Internationalists' of the First World War, discussed by Trentmann, chapter 9, below.

[44] PRO CAB 37/45/52 Hicks Beach to Chamberlain, 3 December 1897.

worryingly still, how healthy was it for any democracy that policy-making should be subject to the machinations of 'log-rollers' or even particular 'overmighty' departments of state. For, as the young Winston Churchill argued, 'every country [ought] to be governed from some central point of view, where all classes and all interests are proportionately represented'. Equally alarming of course was the novel threat of the alienation of democratic powers to Brussels, the first time as Conservatives like Gorst and constitutional lawyers like Bryce, argued, 'we have ever subjected our legislation to foreign control'. Finally, sugar bounties were seen merely as a harbinger of worse to come, that is the first step towards dear food, and protection, 'a working model for future policy' in which the many would be sacrificed to the 'favour and privilege of the few'.[45] In the rejection of the anti-bounty policy it is therefore difficult to see simply a reversion to the rhetoric of the League, as its proponents claimed. On the contrary, the case for free trade was defended on the pertinent grounds of working-class welfare, economic change and political democracy. These were indeed arguments upon which many on the European left of the 1890s and 1900s were equally to advocate free trade, for the most part unsuccessfully.[46] They offered benefits sufficient to make free trade a rational, moral, economic and political choice for working men and women in Edwardian Britain, and reaffirmed the primacy of the Cobdenite current within radicalism.

Free-trade opposition to sugar bounties may be paralleled by the strong resistance to the evolving schemes for imperial federation and preference after 1885. Firstly, free-trade Liberals anxiously and successfully prevented empire becoming a monopoly of the fair traders and preferentialists by stalwartly upholding the notion of a 'fair trade empire', both from outside and within organisations such as the Imperial Federation League, the British Empire League, and the Congresses of Imperial Chambers of Commerce. Leading 'Cobdenites' like Playfair found it quite possible to become imperialists, and the rhetoric of the empire of sentiment was one which free traders readily pronounced. Not only was the notion of an imperial *Zollverein*, with tariffs raised against foreign nations, strongly resisted but there was no enthusiasm for imitating the 'progressive' colonial models of protectionism. For example, the Australian 'paradise for the workers' offered in protectionist Victoria a brand of radical and democratic politics practised by Alfred Deakin.[47] Yet this evoked little enthusiasm among either trade unionists

---

[45] *Hansard*, fourth series, vol. CXXVI, 28 July 1903, p. 713 *et seq.*; pp. 641, 644.

[46] J. Sheehan, *The Career of Lujo Brentano: A Study of Liberalism and Social Reform in Germany*, Chicago, 1966; T. Barth in *The Jubilee of Free Trade*, London, 1896.

[47] J. A. La Nauze, *Alfred Deakin*, London, 1965; S. MacIntyre, *A Colonial Liberalism*, London, 1991.

abreast of antipodean politics, let alone Liberal and Fabian commentators. Australian free traders, like Max Hirsch, had therefore no difficulty getting up impressive statements from the English labour movement affirming the dependence of working-class welfare upon free trade.[48] Nor did the Canadian policy of imperial preference adopted in 1897 evoke any significant support in Britain, but became another opportunity to reaffirm the empire of sentiment, rather than an aversion to empire *per se*. As within the Liberal Party as a whole, there grew a recognition of the necessity of empire, combined with an insistence that it should be based on trade without tariffs, on sentiment, not upon armies. 'We are all imperialists now' was true, even within the Cobdenite camp.[49]

Yet, in the late 1890s, the debates over China and the Boer War did increasingly expose the Cobdenite ambiguity over empire. For by 1897 under the pressure of growing confrontation abroad, even the Cobden Club itself had to reassess its studied indifference to foreign affairs. Hence, in the debate over the 'open door' in China, while Hobson was to assail the logical, if not practical, absurdity of defending free trade by force, the Cobden Club's *Memorandum ... on Future Policy* more equivocally upheld the duty of Britain to maintain trading rights in countries annexed by others while showing that its own interests in 'derelict' (*sic*) countries were simply commercial. 'Vigilant observation of foreign policy' was enjoined upon the Club's members, yet such vigilance after 1897 seemed to many of the Club's members strongly to vindicate its eponymous hero. Above all, the Boer War and rising military expenditure had by 1899 evoked the memory of Palmerstonian panics and the *Shade of Cobden* against them. In this latter work, Shaw-Lefevre re-emerged as an advocate of arbitration and public economy in the Cobden–Gladstone tradition.[50] The Cobden Club itself, forced on to the defensive by war, emphasised the paramount need to defend fiscal orthodoxy, thereby pre-empting a divisive stance on opposition to the war.[51] This, of course, did not prevent the pro-Boer stance of many free traders, including Jane

---

[48] M. Hirsch, *Social Conditions: Material for Comparison between New South Wales and Victoria, Great Britain, the United States*, and *Foreign Countries*, Melbourne, 1901. For earlier use of Australia in Britain, Cobden Club leaflet 46, 'Protection in New Countries', *c.* 1886.

[49] For the need for a free-trade imperial alternative to Chamberlain see, for example, J. Harter at the Cooperative Congress of 1903.

[50] Shaw-Lefevre, *The Shade of Cobden*, London, 1899, originally entitled 'Cobden and After'. See Shaw-Lefevre to T. Fisher-Unwin, 28 March 1899, in Cobden Papers 981, West Sussex Record Office. Lefevre's Cobdenite traits are naturally well brought out by Hirst's entry in *The Dictionary of National Biography*.

[51] This seems to have been the official line under the new chairman, Welby. See Welby to Jane Cobden-Unwin, 26 June 1902, Cobden Papers 1162. Cobden Club leaflets ignored the war.

Cobden-Unwin, the suffragist daughter of Cobden, while Cobdenite ideas were the stock-in-trade of groups like the Increased Armaments Protest Committee, whose secretary, G. H. Perris, was later to become the Club's secretary, and of the League against Aggression and Militarism.[52] The war therefore did much to revivify Cobdenite ideas as a critique of public extravagance, military power and irresponsible governance, but far from encouraging a reversion to the dogmas of the 1840s, this 'revival' precipitated and decisively shaped the 'New Liberal' synthesis.

As a number of historians have urged, the Boer War extended the Cobdenite critique of empire into a new analysis of the dynamics of empire.[53] Most influentially, J. A. Hobson combined his own analysis of the economics of empire with a Cobdenite appraisal of foreign policy-making. Hobson had already built up his view of the irrationality of empire for the nation as a whole but, as Clarke and others have shown, he substituted for Cobden's analysis of the court, the cabinet, the army and the aristocracy as the forces behind Palmerstonian expansionism, a new set of parasites, the financiers, a small oligarchy of mineowners and speculators, using the power of the state to further its own ends to the detriment of the nation, whose 'true' interest in domestic reform was hidden by a 'kept press' and the jingoism of the crowds. By 1902 Hobson held that free trade itself was threatened by a similar combination. For he believed that the 'trading classes' were effectively organised both to open new markets, and to ensure that annexation would be accompanied by preference. As free trade lost its hold on the traders and financiers, so too would it be abandoned by the nation, for 'the political force of the commercial interests ... must dominate her politics'.[54] The welfare of the nation, and the very existence of democracy itself could therefore only be achieved if 'a new and unexpected rally [be made] for "Manchesterism"'.[55]

The Hobsonian analysis of the Boer War and free trade, of economic interest and the state, was one to which both 'individualists' like Hirst and progressives of the Rainbow Circle could subscribe. As Clarke has shown, Hirst's own writings on the war, especially his essay in *Liberalism*

---

[52] F. W. Hirst, *In the Golden Days*, London, 1947, pp. 199ff.

[53] B. Porter, *Critics of Empire: British Radical Attitudes to Colonialism in Africa, 1895–1914*, London, 1968, esp. pp. 196ff; P. F. Clarke, *Liberals and Social Democrats*, Cambridge, 1978, ch. 3; C. Matthew, 'Hobson, Ruskin and Cobden', in M. Freeden (ed.), *Reappraising J. A. Hobson*, London, 1990, pp. 11–30; M. Taylor, 'Imperium and Libertas? Rethinking the Radical Critique of Imperialism during the Nineteenth Century', *Journal of Imperial and Commonwealth History*, 14 (1991), pp. 1–23.

[54] 'The Approaching Abandonment of Free Trade', *Fortnightly Review*, 71 (1902), p. 438.

[55] *Ibid.*, p. 444.

and Empire (1900), share Hobson's view's on financial imperialism, and were far less anti-collectivist than his views three years earlier.[56] But if the 'individualists' moved towards collectivism, the progressives moved backwards to the Manchesterism they initially aspired to transcend.[57] Ironically, progressives whose stance and creed had emerged from an analysis of the deficiencies of the Manchester School had by 1902 reaffirmed its central tenet.[58] Not only did intellectuals like Wallas abandon the Fabians on this issue, but 'New Liberals' like L. T. Hobhouse and ILPers like MacDonald rediscovered the necessity of the link between free trade and democracy, which continental socialists had long appreciated.[59]

While the Boer War had therefore re-emphasised the political necessity of free trade, it had also brought to the fore its fiscal limitations. For the war made evident the extent to which government expenditure in the late-Victorian period was running up against the limits of taxation resources, posing a short-term problem of war finance and a long-term one of discovering new engines of taxation.[60] To deal with the former the war spawned a series of fiscal expedients which posed a vital cumulative threat to fiscal orthodoxy, and in turn to the political morality of free trade. Firstly, in 1899 there was an attempt to use the increase in wine duties as the basis for reciprocity with the Australian colonies, a device strongly resisted by the Board of Trade as threatening 'the most important change in our trade policy since Sir Robert Peel'.[61] Secondly, the budget of 1901 saw the return of sugar duties for the first time since 1874. As a threat to cheap food, they incurred the same opposition as the anti-bounty policy considered above, while their regressive character, and challenge to the 'free breakfast table', were ideally poised to bring together not only the old forces of liberalism but the new ones of the Independent Labour Party (ILP).[62] The second unorthodox ingredient in Hicks Beach's finance in

---

[56] Clarke, *Liberals*, p. 78.

[57] M. Freeden, (ed.), *Minutes of the Rainbow Circle, 1894–1924*, Camden Society, fourth series 38 (1990).

[58] Clarke, *Liberals*, well brings out this revaluation of old liberalism, oddly without discussing the centrality of free trade to the old radicalism which was now newly appreciated by the 'collectivists'. See too Freeden, (ed.), *Rainbow Circle, passim*.

[59] See T. Barth in *Jubilee of the Repeal of the Corn Laws*, London, 1896. For Cobdenism in the thought of E. Bernstein, see R. A. Fletcher, 'British Radicalism and German Revisionism: The Case of Bernstein', *International History Review*, 4 (1982), pp. 339–70, esp. 353 n., p. 83.

[60] A. Friedberg, *The Weary Titan: Britain and the Experience of Relative Decline, 1895–1905*, Princeton, 1988, esp. ch. 3.

[61] PRO CAB 37/49/27 A. E. Bateman, 29 April 1899.

[62] See Cobden Club leaflets, seriatim; K. Hardie, *Hansard*, fourth series, vol. XCII, c. 734, 18 April 1901. Nevertheless, the political and patriotic context of war taxation made public opposition difficult. Thus Welby reported: 'the Government are gratified with the

1901 was the reintroduction of the coal export duty, abolished by Peel in 1845. At a time of growing industrial discontent in the coalfields, this was probably the single most effective means of reinvigorating the alliance between aristocratic landlords, mineowners and the working class who now joined forces to oppose the departure of the state from its position of neutrality with regard to the operation of the economy.[63]

Thirdly, and most controversially, it was as part of emergency taxation, that the corn duty, abolished in 1869, was now reimposed as the most profitable expedient left in the government's armoury.[64] Not only did this measure reintroduce the rhetoric of the 'dear loaf' and 'bread taxes' into political debate but, far from being a war tax, it was taken to indicate the future direction of Tory finance, above all the reliance upon taxation of working-class consumers rather than resorting to income tax.[65] This theme, for example, was forcefully argued by Harold Cox, secretary of the Cobden Club, a Radical associate of Webb in the 1890s and yet to begin his odyssey to the political right, a stalwart by 1906 of individualism and later of conservatism. But the 'bread tax' also brought home to the Liberal Party the opportunities for unity which Tory finance offered, and which Tory party managers most feared. Quickly and emphatically, leading Liberals rediscovered their links with Lancashire, and their acquaintance with the Manchester School, with a carefully orchestrated anti-corn law demonstration in 1902, complete with the endorsement of Cobden's daughter Jane.[66] Here the catchwords of the 1840s were rediscovered, but were suitably readjusted to meet the needs of a radically transformed electorate. Cobdenites and Liberals aimed above all to put free trade at the heart of popular political argument, taking up the campaign against fair trade in the 1880s. This direction was vindicated when the corn tax acquired a preferential twist, with the demand that Canada and other colonies should be exempt from this duty, giving at last a practical cast to decades of discussion of an imperial *Zollverein*. As the free traders had persistently warned during the budget debates, fiscal heterodoxy would end in a vital challenge to Britain's sixty years of free-trade policy.

---

acquiescence of the working man in the Sugar Tax. Are they or we in a fool's paradise? I doubt our being able to get up an effective mass meeting.' Welby to Fisher Unwin, 5 May 1901, Cobden Papers 1124.

[63] The Liberal George Harwood atypically supported this duty, but there seems much evidence against Friedberg's contention that both sugar and coal duties 'faced little serious challenge'. This was true within parliament during wartime but not outside the chamber. Friedberg, *Weary Titan*, p. 109.

[64] British Library, Add. Ms. 48679, Hamilton Diary, 5 and 13 February; Friedberg, *Weary Titan*, p. 116.

[65] See, for example, *Cooperative Yearbook 1902* for criticism of the budget on these lines.

[66] Cobden Papers 1127, press cuttings, 16 May 1902.

Such a challenge required not only the defence of a revenue tariff but new sources of taxation. For free traders, these were readily available in both direct taxes on income, and on land values. Both of these received renewed attention in the Boer War and its fiscal aftermath, as 'Cobdenites' like Hirst and progressives like J. M. Robertson were prepared to advocate increased taxation for welfare, while being of course far more equivocal about taxation for war.[67] Free trade now lay at the heart of the progressive vision, for it alone presaged the raising of revenue for social reform from direct taxation, a premiss which even individualists like Hirst and Cox shared.[68] This in turn guaranteed the autonomy of the state from the power of organised capital, and made possible a foreign policy in which truly national or even international considerations would be brought to bear. This was the moral case for free trade which attracted déclassé intellectuals like Bertrand Russell as well as the democratic masses to whom Hobson rather pessimistically looked in 1902 for its effective defence against the 'possessing classes'.[69]

Hobson's pessimism in 1902 was in part based on his belief that the Liberals themselves would renege on free trade. He feared that alliance of imperialists of both parties to which other staunch free traders, like Sir Edward Hamilton at the Treasury, looked for the dynamic reconstruction of English politics. Here Hobson misjudged the Liberal imperialists, for, however much they seemed at times to question free trade, their unorthodoxy rarely extended as far as tariff reform.[70] On the contrary, the concern of the 'Limps' with efficiency actually provided new tools with which to defend free trade.[71] For the Liberal imperialists had addressed the same problems of economic development and industrial decline, for which the tariff reformers have acquired the questionable reputation as 'modernisers'.[72] The Liberal League pamphlets of 1902 had in particular considered the issues of efficiency and education which now became crucial elements in the Liberal case for free trade. Haldane, for example, by 1902 concluded that the German model of the *Zollverein* was inapplicable to the British empire but that the German concern with education was not. Haldane thus recalled: 'what was threatening our industrial position was want of science among our manufacturers ... the campaign

[67] See M. Freeden, *The New Liberalism: An Ideology of Social Reform*, Oxford, 1978, pp. 134–45.

[68] For a typical view of the necessity of free trade to the redistribution of wealth, *The Scottish Cooperator*, 18 December 1903, p. 1012.

[69] 'Abandonment of Free Trade', *passim*, esp. p. 444.

[70] Matthew, *The Liberal Imperialists*, pp. 164–8.

[71] Matthew, *The Liberal Imperialists*, esp. pp. 224ff.

[72] See esp. S. Newton and D. Porter, *Modernization Frustrated: The Politics of Industrial Decline since 1900*, London, 1988.

in which we were engaged against the policy of Protection ... was our opportunity for pressing the countercase for science and organisation'.[73] This case was of course by no means new, having been well made by Liberal imperialists like Playfair in the 1880s, but in the early twentieth century it bore restatement and demonstration. It led, for example, to the strong Liberal interest in the foundation of Imperial College in 1903.[74] Here was no complete recipe for economic revival but at least some sign that the problem needed still to be addressed within a free-trade framework, that the state, even for the free trader might have a part to play, and that tariff reform was as likely to frustrate economic modernisation as it was to undermine a healthy democracy.[75]

By 1903, therefore, it is clear that one part of the tariff reform case against free trade, its adherence to a philosophy of individualism and *laissez-faire*, was fundamentally adrift. For, as Hobson noted, 'the former intellectual apprehension of Free Trade as an integral portion of the *laissez-faire* principle of government now remains little more than a discredited gospel of a doctrinaire remnant'.[76] Far readier was the identification of free trade with social reform which the historians of 'new' liberalism have noted in office after 1906, but which belongs as much to the years of opposition to Conservative government and its perceived economic heterodoxy. Free trade by 1903 had been reassessed as part of a new intellectual synthesis attractive to both pro-Boers and Liberal imperialists. It did not commend a return to the 1840s but was re-evaluated as central to economic progress, political democracy and social welfare. The rallying of the Liberal Party to free trade after 1903 may therefore appear as the pragmatic rejoining of divided factions around a threatened Gladstonian tribal god, but it rested fundamentally upon different ideological premises from the outmoded Ricardian and evangelical arguments on which the nation had been first drawn to the free-trade cause. Whether this new synthesis would successfully combat the forces of protectionism, jingoism and the press seemed doubtful to Hobson in 1902, yet the free-trade response to the tariff reform campaign, launched officially by Chamberlain in May 1903, revealed the needlessness of his fears.

---

[73] E. Haldane (ed.), *Richard Burdon Haldane: An Autobiography*, London, 1928, pp. 151–2.

[74] W. Page, *Commerce and Industry: A Historical Review*, London, 1919, p. 337.

[75] See, e.g., J. A. Spender, 'Free Trade and its Fruits', *Fortnightly Review* (September 1903), pp. 410–11.

[76] 'Abandonment', p. 434. This remnant was perhaps strongest among the Unionist free traders after 1903.

III

As will be clear from the above, the ideological groundwork of the opposition to tariff reform had been effectively laid in the years before 1903. What was required in 1903 was not the rediscovery of the pamphlet literature of the 1840s but an effective political campaign in order to harness free trade to the Liberal Party and to pre-empt the electoral appeal of tariff reform, as a ploy to attract the working-class vote.[77] Hobson's 'scattered unorganised consumers whose policy is Free Trade' were, between 1903 and 1906, to be mobilised into the effective electoral battalions which swept aside the challenge of tariff reform in 1906, and made difficult its recrudescence thereafter. This final section will briefly indicate the lines on which such a campaign developed without tracing in detail the evolution of the free-trade platform between 1903 and 1906.

In such a campaign it was wholly natural that the model of the Anti-Corn Law League should be taken up, for no other nineteenth-century pressure group had rivalled its perceived effectiveness, deriving in part from its non-party basis, and its concentration upon economic rather than political arguments. Its history therefore necessarily recurred to the minds of politicians. The Marquess of Ripon, a former Hughesian Christian socialist, not an old Cobdenite, thus recommended to Herbert Gladstone:

I should suggest that a *non-party* League or Association should be formed at once which might embrace Free Traders and Economists of all kinds. There is, of course, the old Cobden Club but it has been of late years rather ridiculous and I would not base my new Association upon it. What is, of course, needed above all things is a new Cobden, but that is an article not easy to find. The truth is that economical questions have been very little thought of for some time; our free trade policy was supposed to be unassailable and people have troubled themselves very little about the arguments by which it can be defended. The work of the forties has to be done over again.

Not surprisingly, too, Ripon expected that there must be plenty of men in the manufacturing districts ready to take up their fathers' work.[78] Such men had in fact already been in short supply by the 1860s as Cobden had himself discovered[79] and Ripon perhaps exaggerated the economical ignorance of the public; but Gladstone responded enthusiastically to his suggestion, sharing his view of the need for a strong agitating body, with

---

[77] E. H. H. Green, 'Radical Conservatism: The Electoral Genesis of Tariff Reform', *Historical Journal*, 28 (1985), pp. 667–92.
[78] British Library, Herbert Gladstone Papers (hereafter HGP) Add. Ms. 46018, ff. 24–6, Ripon to Gladstone, 29 May 1903.
[79] A. Howe, *The Cotton Masters 1830–1860*, Oxford, 1984, pp. 245, 248.

a countrywide organisation.[80] With the support of the ex-cabinet, he therefore set about the organisation of the Free Trade Union (FTU), securing a committee headed by the wealthy Arnold Morley and, as secretary, the progressive intellectual L. T. Hobhouse.[81] The FTU was to be a central organisation devoted to combat the fiscal policy of Chamberlain and Balfour, largely 'by argument and concrete illustration'.[82] Funds were raised with some success, with appeals to scions of old Leaguers, such as William Agnew, alongside more novel and more questionable capitalist breeds with, for example, £2,000 from the Randlord J. B. Robinson via Lou Lou Harcourt.[83] Soon the FTU had promises amounting to £20,000, but with expenditure running at £2,000 per month they feared the greater resources of the Tariff Reform League (TRL), itself seeking to raise £50,000 over four years, and 'in addition they must have much larger private funds'.[84] Still the FTU's resources, although small by comparison with those of the Anti-Corn Law League in the 1840s, were ample for a successful educational body. By July 1903, the first number of the *Free Trader* had appeared, the work of Hobhouse aided by the New Liberal, Chiozza-Money. Hobhouse had also begun the energetic production of free-trade leaflets, of which twenty-five million had been distributed by January 1904. The *Free Trader*, by contrast, was aimed at a select audience: 'nine tenths of its value lies in one tenth of its circulation', keeping 'serious students' and MPs informed of events, arguments and fallacies. The FTU also imitated the League's strategy of free-trade missionaries, going among the people, countering the efforts of the TRL and active in by-elections.[85]

However, two controversial issues initially hampered the FTU: the degree to which it was to be a party organ, and the extent of its national organisation. The first was decided relatively quickly, with the FTU welcoming all free traders – an umbrella organisation, the handle firmly held by Gladstone but with Unionists and Labour men welcome under its shelter. The second continued to bedevil the union, for Hobhouse felt himself at variance with the committee in his desire for a network of branches, on the lines of the Anti-Corn Law League, to create some

---

[80] British Library, Campbell-Bannerman Papers (hereafter CBP), Add. Ms. 41216, Gladstone to Campbell-Bannerman, 1 June 1903.
[81] Vaughan Nash, future secretary of the post-war reconstruction committee and W. H. Perkin, clerk to George Peel at the Gold Standard Association had also been possibles, but the latter, 'hardly the *class* of man we want'.
[82] HGP, Add. Ms. 46060, ff. 224–9 Draft manifesto, n.d. [June 1903].
[83] CBP, Add. Ms. 41216, ff. 312–17, Gladstone to Campbell-Bannerman, 24 July 1903.
[84] HGP, Add. Ms. 46106, ff. 127–9, memo on the position and prospects of the FTU, 13 January 1904. See F. Coetzee, *For Party or Country?*, Oxford, 1990, pp. 64–70 for the funds of the Tariff Reform League.
[85] HGP, Add. Ms. 46061, McKenna to Gladstone, 14 January 1904, 6 and 13 January 1905.

organisational tie between the country and the council.[86] This division centred upon timing; was the FTU's work to be merely educational, with a view to an early election, say in April 1904, or was it to look to the longer term, in which case a radical rethink was necessary, creating a system of branches, and individual membership, so that 'a more national and democratic or at least popular character should be given to our organisation'.[87] Since this question was itself unanswerable, and the Liberals were to spend three years expecting an imminent dissolution, a *via media* inevitably emerged, with no fully-fledged national organisation but the encouragement of spontaneous free-trade organs for local purposes, avoiding close identification with the Liberal Party and attracting Unionists as well. This would also relieve the FTU of financial support for local branches. In this rather unsatisfactory way, there emerged some cooperation with local Free Trade Leagues in Oxford, Cardiff, Halifax, Manchester, Hampstead and Surrey, but federation among free traders remained intellectual, not organisational. Yet local work was effectively initiated and became a vital part of the overall response to tariff reform.[88] There did also emerge a coordinating committee headed by the Duke of Devonshire, linking the Cobden Club, FTU and the Unionist Free Trade Club (UFTC), and publishing a circular letter, edited by E. G. Brunker.[89] Here then the model of the League was effectively readopted, in both propaganda and electoral work. But of course, in the age of mass parties, this work was necessarily done in harness with the Liberal Party, and was not that of an autonomous extra-parliamentary body.

The lessons of the 1840s were developed in other ways, for if Edwardian Britain could not spawn a new Cobden, the family connection was kept vigorously alive, especially by Jane Cobden and her spouse, Thomas Fisher Unwin.[90] This couple self-consciously guarded the Cobdenite legacy after their marriage in 1892. Unwin had joined the committee of the Cobden Club and Cobden's home in Sussex, Dunford House, had become an active free-trade shrine, visited by distinguished foreign visitors, as well as native admirers. As an avant-garde publisher, Unwin was not only identified with progressive causes, but was also in a position to replicate the services Cassells provided in the 1870s and 1880s, producing a tremendous outpouring of free-trade literature.[91] Jane Cobden, already well known for her part in London progressivism and

[86] HGP, Add. Ms. 46061, ff. 52–3, Hobhouse to Gladstone, 30 October 1903.
[87] HGP, Add. Ms. 46061, ff. 65–6, Hobhouse to Gladstone, 11 December 1903.
[88] On these points, see esp. HGP, Add. Ms. 46106, pp. 127ff, 13 January 1904; p. 140, 9 May 1904.
[89] *A History of the Cobden Club*, London, 1939, p. 51.
[90] For Jane Cobden's activities in local government, see M. Pugh, chapter 2 above, pp. 62–3.
[91] S. Unwin, *The Truth about Publishing*, London, 1960, ch. 7, 'T. F. Unwin, 1848–1935'.

opposition to the Boer War, now became fully committed to the free-trade cause. Above all, she invented the 'hungry forties', a term rapidly popularised with her publication of *The Hungry Forties: Life under the Bread Tax* in 1904. This evocation through the collective memory of poverty and oppression became thereafter a leading propagandist device. The historicist appeal of the corn law issue took on an altogether new importance and added powerfully the popular verdict of history to the rational arguments of the New Liberal free traders. Active as a writer and speaker, Jane Cobden also took up the unfinished Cobdenite business of land reform, cooperating with F. J. Shaw (Brougham Villiers) in *The Land Hunger* in 1913.[92] The Unwins, as partners and publishers, thus rejuvenated and immensely enriched the literature of Cobdenism in Edwardian Britain.[93]

The former standard-bearer of Cobdenism, the Cobden Club itself had, however, by the early twentieth century, relapsed from its high activism of the 1880s, with the Boer War an immobilising force against which it struggled to find an effective voice. In particular, the austere and aloof chairman Welby restrained the populist endeavours of the Club's secretary, Harold Cox. The Club continued its outflow of propaganda but its leaflets were now easily outnumbered by those of other free-trade bodies, and its main contribution lay in its weightier brochures. For example, in 1903 its *Fact versus Fiction* provided one of the most comprehensive refutations of Chamberlain's arguments in favour of tariff reform. Nevertheless, the Club did not retreat entirely into intellectual activity, and with its membership enormously boosted in 1903, it sought above all to reinvigorate the popular links it had forged in the 1880s. It appointed the leading Lib–Lab politician, Fred Maddison, as its organising secretary, with the task of defending free trade among the working classes, and the Club exploited its relative independence from party politics as an asset in appealing to Labour.[94] In particular, Cox had maintained close links with cooperative bodies, valued allies in the defence of working-class consumption, and had organised numerous expressions of working-class opinion in favour of free trade, with an impressive endorsement of the Club's policy by 940 labour leaders in September 1903. However, by December 1903, Cox had clashed with Welby over the Club's role and his part within it, with Cox seeking a 'fighting campaign', led by himself, and with Welby critical of his independence, lack of tact

---

[92] Interestingly, her sister Anne Cobden-Sanderson adapted Cobden's ideas on land reform for the benefit of the ILP, in *Richard Cobden and the Land of the People*, preface by Keir Hardie, London, 1910.

[93] One might also note the dynastic tie in the case of F. W. Hirst, husband of Helena Cobden, a great-niece of Richard.

[94] HGP, Add. Ms. 46061, Welby to Gladstone, 10 January 1904.

and fondness for power.[95] After Cox's eventual departure, the Club
played a subordinate part in the free-trade campaign, which was in any
case dictated by its relative poverty, although in 1904 it joined the enthusiastic and polemical celebration of the centenary of Cobden's birth, with
an effusion of publications and a great Alexandra Palace demonstration.
But under its new secretary Perris, a notable pacifist, the club returned
more characteristically to an attention to government expenditure, above
all to the arms race with Germany, and the war scares – themes more
palatable to its leading members like Lefevre, Welby and Hirst.[96]

There was, therefore, much in the campaign against tariff reform
which took up the League model of the 1840s – ostensible evidence to
support Chamberlain's and Balfour's polemical claim that free trade had
not moved beyond the 1840s. But even organisationally there were novel
elements which helped realign free trade as a popular and democratic
cause. This was above all seen with respect to women and the working
classes. For example, the FTU set up a women's branch, which recruited
the wives of Liberal (and some Unionist) politicians, led by Mary
Harcourt, and which provided an active defence of free trade by women
speakers in the constituencies. Free trade, almost uniquely, appealed to
women as citizen–consumers, and not least among its strengths was its
ability to bring together not only Liberals and Unionists but suffragists
and anti-suffragists.[97] The Women's Co-operative Guild under Margaret
Llewelyn Davies, stalwart opponents of dearer bread allied with the
moral benefits of free trade, also campaigned strongly.[98] For Labour, the
attraction of free trade was not only emphasised by the Cobden Club's
activities, but progressive publications like Massingham's *Labour and
Protection* (1903) reiterated the political and material benefits of free
trade. Trade unions also rejected clearly tariffs and in doing so most were
prepared to endorse free trade, which became the ideological coating of
the Lib–Lab pact formed in 1903. Similarly, however much the
Independent Labour Party wished to assert its ideological independence

---

[95] They had earlier clashed over whether Cox should fight a by-election in Sheffield, Welby
fearing the damage the defeat of the secretary of the Cobden Club in a stronghold of
protectionism would do. HGP, Add. Ms. 46060, f. 213. Welby to HG, 20 June 1903. On
Cox's resignation, Cox to Gladstone, 14 December 1903 and Welby to Gladstone, 15
December 1903 and 10 January 1904; 21 February 1904, Welby looking forward to a
quieter life with Cox's departure; 'Poor dear Cox was able and active but a great trial. I
never came across such a vain man'.

[96] Perris had been secretary of the Increased Armaments Protest Committee in 1896.
Typical of the Club's direction was *The Burden of Armaments*, London, 1905.

[97] Millicent Fawcett (on whom see Pugh above, pp. 59–60, 62) thus successfully married
her political economy and her suffragism. Her *Political Economy for Beginners*, 9th edn,
London, 1904, took account of the Sugar Convention and fiscal reform.

[98] 'What Co-operative Women Think', *Free Trader*, 23 October 1903.

from Liberal thinking, there can be little doubt that free trade restrained this tendency. For example, its tracts in 1903 shared nine-tenths of their ideas in common with the FTU, a version of popular Cobdenism with the postscript of nationalisation.[99]

The ILP was, of course, eager to dissociate its working man's version of free trade from the Liberal capitalist version, but the latter, as we have seen in this chapter, was not the crude cover for the defence of the capitalist and rentier which their polemics suggested. Both of these latter groups remained loyal in substantial numbers to free trade, despite Chamberlain's hopes. But many industrialists hastened to endorse free trade, not only as antediluvian Leaguers, nor simply as exporters fearing retaliation against Britain, nor as 'cheap fooders', but also as Liberals and progressives. In several cases, they aimed to provide a new positive content to free trade, as a recipe for economic change. This is, for example, clearly seen in the Brunner-Holland initiatives for public works in 1903–4, asserting the duty of the state to invest in the infrastructure.[100] It is also clear that although it was not the City of London which ensured free trade's survival, as some believe, the City of London did in part mobilise behind free trade, although it did so with little electoral effect. For in the City of London, Sir Edward Clarke, an erstwhile fair trader, was driven from the field as a free trader in 1906, and in 1910, Sir Hugh Bell, a northern ironmaster, was soundly defeated. There was nothing novel in the City free traders' arguments, but their articulation provided a reminder that, on some issues, the interests of industry and the City were as likely to be complementary as conflictual and that the interests of the City were by no means necessarily at variance with those of the working man.

The free-trade debate enjoined in 1903–4 therefore was no stale rerun of evangelical and Ricardian arguments between landlords and cotton lords, but a debate central to the nature and understanding of welfare and democracy, of the modernisation of the economy and the working of the liberal international order. Free trade was no mere accidental or expediential survival within Edwardian 'new' liberalism but in many ways its central core, the strand of continuity which doctrinally and politically held together Liberal opposition to aggressive imperialism abroad, and to

---

[99] E.g. P. Snowden, *The Chamberlain Bubble*, London, 1903; ILP, *Tracts for the Times. Facts for the Workers about Protection, Free Trade and Monopoly*, London, 1903. Frank Trentmann, chapter 9 below, puts more strongly the case for the ILP's ideological autonomy.

[100] CBP, Add. Ms 41237, ff. 203–4, Brunner to Campbell-Bannerman, 15 and 16 November 1903. In this context, see also H. Thompson, *The Canals of Britain*, Cobden Club, 1902. For a discussion of this episode, J. Harris, *Unemployment and Politics*, pp. 215ff.

a protectionist state at home. Its ability to provide this continuity lay not only in its constancy of principle but its malleability of instruments, whereby a doctrine of wages and welfare, of taxation and expenditure, of free exchange and peace, peculiarly appropriate for the cotton masters of the 1840s, could seamlessly transpose itself into the essential basis of Edwardian social democracy.

9　The strange death of free trade: the erosion of 'liberal consensus' in Great Britain, c. 1903–1932

Frank Trentmann

I

To a Victorian observer contemporary politics would have looked strangely familiar. The political landscape is haunted by the sudden reappearance of mid-Victorian ghosts: a united Germany, angry French peasants and free trade. The British government has not missed the golden opportunity created by the revival of nationalism to appoint itself once more the 'true' guardian of internationalism. Naturally, this is legitimised by reference to Britain's historical record; typically, it is supported by references to the alleged lessons of the past. Just as Edwardian free traders were fond of citing the 'hungry forties', the present Foreign Secretary has chosen the misery of the 'thirties' as an example of the 'ruinous effects of "beggar-my-neighbour" protection'.[1]

Yet here the similarities end. The excitement generated by fiscal controversies has been marginal since Britain abandoned free trade in 1931. To question the virtues of free trade does not ruin governments, split parties or dominate general elections. Nor did GATT aim at universal free trade: it aimed at *freer* international trade. No political party in the west any longer holds the pure vision of economic liberalism. Cobdenites would feel little sympathy with the accepted level of subsidies, regulation, or 'hidden' protectionism. This loss of purity has been accompanied by a fundamental realignment of the political forces of liberal internationalism. Not only has the traditional champion of protectionism, the Conservative Party, become the stronghold of liberal

For comments I should like to thank Professors Peter Clarke and Andrew Porter. This chapter is part of my larger forthcoming study 'The Survival and Decline of Free Trade: The Transformation of Liberal Political Economy and Political Culture, Britain c. 1897–1932.' I am grateful for assistance from the Leverhulme Trust.
[1] Douglas Hurd, *Sunday Telegraph*, 23 February 1992, p. 22, but see also the critical letters in *ibid.*, 1 March 1992, p. 24. For a more favourable verdict see M. Kitson, S. Solomou and M. Weale, 'Effective Protection and Economic Recovery in the United Kingdom during the 1930's', *Economic History Review*, 44, 2 (1991), pp. 328–38.

economics, the recent debate about GATT has also exposed just how much free trade today is greeted with cynicism in its traditional radical home. The former mouthpiece of the Manchester School, the *Guardian*, has turned to attack the 'hollow gods of free-trade' and, looking back nostalgically to an era of domestic economic engineering, now looks forward to President Clinton to 'follow in the fine tradition of ... Hamilton'.[2] In short, free trade has lost its status as a secular religion: it is a tendency, at best, to be encouraged within limits, not a scientific law to be blindly obeyed.

The aim of this chapter is to trace the historical roots of this demystification of free trade and to analyse the qualifications, revisions and limits to which free trade – as Cobden and Gladstone had known it – had become subjected by the time of the world depression. In focusing on continuities in British radicalism, recent scholarship has re-emphasised the making of a 'liberal consensus' around free trade in the mid-Victorian years, its importance to the political strength of the Liberal Party, and its influence in shaping the outlook of the Labour Party.[3] The triumphant defence of free trade in the elections of 1906, January 1910, and 1923 has generally been held to prove the persistence of this 'liberal consensus'.[4] Liberal and Labour opposition to tariff reform in these years is overwhelming, indeed nearly universal, and does not need repeating. What is lacking, however, is an analysis of the ideological sources of that opposition.

Arguments about the continuity of radicalism presume the existence of a shared, identifiable body of ideas that is passed down from one generation to the next. To what degree is it possible to speak of such ideological continuity or consensus in the meaning of free trade for two generations of Liberals and Labourites? Many roads lead to Rome: a shared enemy (Conservative protection) does not necessarily imply shared beliefs. The electoral defeats of protection have disguised a more fundamental process in the history of twentieth-century political economy: the erosion of free trade culture. The political fall from power marked by the general tariff in 1932 was preceded by decades of ideological decomposition. A key aspect in this process was the changing meaning of free trade to those new movements which displaced radicals at the centre of progressive politics: 'new' Liberals, Labour, socialists and 'new internationalists'. Radical free trade had been built around three

---

[2] *Guardian*, 28 November 1992, p. 36.
[3] Eugenio F. Biagini and Alastair J. Reid (eds.), *Currents of Radicalism: Popular Radicalism, Organised Labour and Party Politics in Britain, 1850–1914*, Cambridge, 1991. See also the chapters by Spain and Howe in this volume.
[4] P. F. Clarke, *Lancashire and the New Liberalism*, Cambridge, 1971; Chris Cook, *The Age of Alignment, 1922–9*, Toronto and Buffalo, 1975.

interlocking assumptions about consumption, exchange and the invisible hand of the market price mechanism. The discourse of 'the consumer' was the political expression of this ideological integrity. As a radical language it suited Victorian England with its limited foreign competition and limited political participation. The theme of this chapter is to trace progressives' disillusionment with this consumerist ideology under the challenge of foreign competition, total war, unemployment and corporate capitalism. By exploring points of contact and tension between radical and progressive ideologies, then, this analysis will not only bring out the reformulation of 'radical' ideas on international trade, but also relate the performance of these ideologies to the changing nature of political economy. In this sense it is designed to test the principal methodological assumptions underlying the approach of radical continuity and, arguably, much of modern British historiography[5] – that is, interpretations stressing the autonomy of politics as against social, cultural or economic dynamics in the making of modern politics.

II

Like any sacred idea, free trade was not spared the competition over meanings that inevitably follows the competition for exclusive legitimacy in modern politics. Many protectionists, keen on ridiculing it as an unattainable, abstract conception, defined it as full reciprocity in the conditions of exchange; others, like Balfour, insisted on being free traders when advocating retaliation as the only effective way towards greater international free trade.[6] To free traders by conscience such a rationale was a dangerous version of the 'fair trade' heresy – protectionism in disguise, bound to end in naked protectionism and international friction. Free trade in its ruling orthodox version was still equated with freedom of commerce as a practice as much as a vision: it 'demands simply that trade shall be free'.[7] It was opposed not only to tariffs but to trade restrictions in general. And it was unilateral. It is this liberal, historical meaning

[5] Clarke, New Liberalism; Stefan Collini, Liberalism and Sociology: L. T. Hobhouse and Political Argument in England, 1880–1914, Cambridge, 1979; Michael Freeden, The New Liberalism: An Ideology of Social Reform, Oxford, 1978; for a social-history critique, see Michael Savage, The Dynamics of Working-Class Politics: The Labour Movement in Preston, 1880–1940, Cambridge, 1987; a conservative example is J. C. D. Clarke, English Society 1688–1832: Ideology, Social Structure and Political Practice during the Ancient Régime, Cambridge, 1985.
[6] J. L. Garvin in Compatriots' Club Lectures, London, 1905; cf. A. J. Balfour, Economic Notes on Insular Free Trade, London, 1903.
[7] Thomas Lough in H. W. Massingham (ed.), Labour and Protection. A Series of Studies, London, 1903, p. 146.

of free trade that is used here and against which rival meanings and arguments must be measured.

Free trade stood for a politico-economic programme that looked towards an open world economy as the engine of national wealth. This programme was built around a triad of liberal axioms: exchange, price and consumption. Exchange is postulated as a mutually beneficial satisfaction of desires. The invisible hand of the market – the price mechanism – promotes the most efficient division of labour. Finally, consumption is considered the sole end of all production. The integrity of free trade as a wider belief system rested ultimately on the strength of these three pillars. To question the efficacy or desirability of one was to disturb the harmony and verisimilitude of the *Weltanschauung* as a whole.[8]

The assumption of a natural pre-existing harmony between human interests found its most forceful expression in the politics of 'the consumer'. Against the protectionist 'dear loaf', free traders extolled the wholesome effects of 'cheapness'. Against the rule of aristocracy, monopoly, and 'vested interest' they preached the liberal gospel of a united nation of consumers. The language of consumption extended beyond the political marketplace. It included the disenfranchised. It included the poor and the unemployed. It included women.[9] The consumer was a democratic citizen. '[It is] the British consumer, who is after all the most important person', the Radical industrialist Alfred Mond emphasised in 1904.[10] It was this consumerist bias that underlay the first

---

[8] The primacy of the consumer was a 'self-evident maxim' to Adam Smith, *The Wealth of Nations*, book IV, ch. viii, book V, ch. i. For an Edwardian restatement of the classical case for free trade, see A. C. Pigou, *The Riddle of the Tariff*, London, 1903; also W. H. Beveridge (ed.), *Tariffs: The Case Examined*, London, 1931, which is showing signs of such tension after years of persistent and vigorous assaults on its axioms, not least by the formidable pen of a former 'believer', Keynes.

[9] In the early-Victorian campaign against the corn laws, women figure as embodiments of moral purity, cf. A. Tyrrell, '"Woman's Mission" and Pressure Group Politics in Britain (1825–60)', *Bulletin of the John Rylands University Library*, 63 (1980–1). It might be noted that early twentieth-century Liberals found it easier to appeal to the plight of the poor than to rally women as housekeepers behind the Cobdenite cause. The role of Women's Free Trade Union was limited and marginal compared to that of the cooperative Societies. In general, Liberal references to the interests of women were relatively rare in the Edwardian period, e.g. 'Ask your Wife what She Thinks of Mr Chamberlain's Proposal to Tax Food', *Set of Leaflets on Preferential Tariffs and Current Political Questions*, October 1903, no. 1939. This acted as a liability in the post-war world of female suffrage and prevented Liberals from making the most of the safeguarding duties. For an attempt to capitalise on the duty on fabric gloves for the 1929 elections, see the Free Trade Union's *A Word to the Young Woman Voter, An Afternoon with the Tax Collector* (1929) and 'Women Should Vote Liberal' in *The Liberal Candidate's Handbook*, April 1929, pp. 38.

[10] H. Cox (ed.), *British Industries and Free Trade: Essays by Experts*, London, 1904, p. 222.

commandment of orthodox finance: to defend the interests of the greatest number.[11] Within the primacy of consumption there was no room for protectionist proposals. Significantly, even proposals to counteract dumping were ruthlessly opposed by the Treasury on the ground that dumping benefited 'the consumer, who is the whole nation'.[12] This free-trade definition of the national interest found its symbolic embodiment in Liberal campaign posters attacking sugar duties: Asquith appeared as John Bull, handing out cheap sugar to poor children.[13]

This view of the state as a society of consumers lay at the heart of liberal political economy. Trade took place between individuals not states. The state's function was to allow for the unrestricted pursuit of cheapness natural to the individual that guaranteed maximum wealth for all. The equation of 'the consumer' with the national interest found its constitutional location in parliament. Parliament represented the nation as taxpaying consumers. It was this notion that produced the other commandment of fiscal orthodoxy: taxation for revenue only, lest the taxpayer be mulcted for the benefit of vested interests. Historians specialising in the eighteenth century will easily detect here resonances of the radical fight against 'court and corruption'. When protectionism raised its head afresh in the twentieth century, Liberals were quick to fire this traditional radical ammunition. Only the target had moved. Tariffs were now feared to erect 'the Temple of British Trusts'[14] as well as strengthening landed monopoly. Popular liberalism did not fail to capitalise on the anxieties created by modern industrial organisations. In 'A Voice from America' the Free Trade Union warned the electorate in 1910:

In Great Britain to-day we have *one trade* in politics, that is more than enough for most of us. But *under Tariff Reform every trade would be in politics for what it could make by taxing the people.* STICK TO FREE TRADE, *Free Trade Means Freedom from Trusts.*[15]

---

[11] For the most comprehensive restatement of the principles of Gladstonian finance, see Edward Hamilton's papers at the Public Record Office (PRO), especially, T 168/52 which contains his confidential ms., 'The Question of New Taxation Discussed', 13 December 1901. Hamilton had been Gladstone's private secretary in 1880–5 and proved a faithful disciple in 1903 when organising the Treasury defence of free trade as Permanent Financial Secretary.

[12] PRO T 168/54, 'The Conditions and Effects of "Dumping"', 7 July 1903, p. 6.

[13] 'Bad for the Quack Doctors', British Library of Political and Economic Sciences (BLPES), Coll. Misc. 519, no. 25.

[14] J. M. Robertson, *The Battle for Free Trade*, London, 1923, p. 30. The dogmatic state of popular liberal political economy at the time was reflected in the consensus that tariffs were the mother of trusts, most forcefully and persistently upheld by that last Cobdenite, F. W. Hirst, e.g. *Monopolies, Trusts and Kartells*, London, 1905, a study which grew out of a prize-winning essay for the Cobden Club during his Oxford days. For a Liberal minority view appreciating the non-fiscal origins of trusts, see J. A. Hobson in the *Report of the Proceedings of the International Free Trade Congress*, London, 1908, pp. 401–5.

[15] Free Trade Union, *General Leaflets*, London, 1910, no. 124, emphases in the original.

Internationalism, next to 'the purity of politics' and a natural harmony of interests, completed the trinity of free-trade ideals. Consumption, again, was central and provided the cement between free trade and good-will among nations. 'It is through consumption', Hobson restated the Cobdenite gospel, 'that the co-operative nature and value of commerce is realized. Production divides, consumption unites.'[16]

III

To its faithful disciples free trade was never just a theory or policy: it was a prophecy. Cobden believed its establishment had ushered in the dawn of international peace. By the 1880s the continent had turned back to protection and spoiled Cobden's anticipation of universal free trade. A decade later imperialist powers were at each other's throats. British Liberals were disturbed to discover that jingoism and imperialism had taken root in the mother country of free trade. Their complex reaction to this uncomfortable news must be beyond the confines of this chapter. Of interest here is the ambiguous relationship of the 'new' liberalism to the 'old' in the opposition to the 'new mercantilism'. Historians of social thought have portrayed the 'new' liberalism as a fountain of youth instilling fresh intellectual energy and purpose into the moribund body of Gladstonian liberalism.[17] To what degree can this argument about social reform be extended to political economy? Did 'new' Liberals revitalise free trade?

At the level of political action, imperialism provided radicals and social democrats with a common enemy and a common platform. The individualist Courtney and the collectivist Hobson were brothers-in-arms in fighting imperialism as a repudiation of free trade. Like militarism in the days of Paine and Cobden, imperialism resulted in armaments, swollen expenditures, and, hence, in fiscal reform. It also shared the mentality of protectionism. Sooner or later, Hobson warned, '[i]mperialism ... will openly adopt the Protectionism required to round off this policy'.[18] The experience of imperialism, the Boer War's fiscal legacy in the form of coal and corn duties, and the depression, had prepared Liberals for the protectionist assault to be unleashed in 1903.

[16] J. A. Hobson, *The New Protectionism*, London, 1916, pp. 6f.

[17] See the references in footnote 6. For different assessments of Hobson, see now John Pheby (ed.), *J. A. Hobson after Fifty Years: Freethinker of the Social Sciences*, London, 1994.

[18] J. A. Hobson, *Imperialism: A Study*, London, 1902, pp. 72f; BLPES, Courtney Papers, LSE Coll. O./9, Courtney to [G. R.] Bethell, 1 January 1903: '[t]he Boer war leaves us that heritage of swollen expenditure & bad taxation on which you comment & I am afraid we shall have a good deal of trouble before things get better'. Courtney, *The Competition of Nations*, Edinburgh, 1902.

At the level of ideology, however, Hobson's 'new' liberalism introduced considerable tension into the canon of liberal internationalism,
and this ultimately affected priorities for action. This tension was itself
inherent in Hobson's attempt to reconcile the 'old' moral outlook with
the 'new' intellectual apparatus of underconsumption in *Imperialism*; it
was never satisfactorily resolved thereafter.[19] The need to close ranks
against the forces of protectionism rendered Edwardian Liberals naturally indisposed to internal debate, but old radicals, like Courtney, were
fully aware of the dangerous implications that Hobson's revisionism had
in store for Cobdenism.[20] For Hobson not only reasserted the radical
conclusion that, for the nation, imperialism did not pay. He also shifted
the focus of analysis from atavistic 'corruption' to financiers as the
modern agents of militarism. Unregulated international trade and
finance appeared a Janus-faced phenomenon that looked as much
towards war as towards peace – a notion that became the orthodox
picture with the outbreak of war in 1914. Hobson evaded the dilemma by
distinguishing between 'ordinary commerce' and 'illegitimate and speculators' imperialistic commerce'[21] – precisely where the first ended and the
latter began remained unclear.

Hobson located the 'taproot of Imperialism'[22] in the maldistribution of
national income. This turned the internationalist programme into a
domestic one. Already, in 1895, he had lashed out at 'the older economists' for their belief in free competition and free trade as the guarantors
of economic progress and social welfare. Modern capitalism was pushing
up the share of fixed capital. A competitive environment no longer auto-
matically secured a rate of profit sufficient for future investment and
growth. Combination and public monopolies, not competition and
laissez-faire, would be the answer to this crisis. In Hobson's view the
modern machine age moved towards wasteful overproduction, ever more
violent cyclical depressions, and a growing disparity between social
welfare and productive capacities. On the new stage of 'modern
capitalism' there was little room for free trade's traditional part as a
radical panacea:

[19] A different interpretation, stressing successive shifts rather than inherent tension, is P. J.
Cain, 'Variations on a Famous Theme: Hobson, International Trade and Imperialism,
1902–1938' in Michael Freeden (ed.), *Reappraising J. A. Hobson: Humanism and Welfare*,
London, 1990, pp. 31–53. My criticism of this view is not limited to the sphere of tariffs;
for instance, *Imperialism*, ch. 10, already carries within it a strong argument for joint international economic intervention in 'backward' areas, *versus* Cain, p. 32. See also below
n. 25, n. 32; I shall discuss this at greater length elsewhere.
[20] Leonard Courtney, 'What is the Advantage of Foreign Trade?', *Nineteenth Century*, 53
(May 1903), pp. 806–12.
[21] Hobson, *Imperialism*, p. 337.
[22] The famous title of ch. vi of *Imperialism*.

[f]ull free trade would supply, quicken, and facilitate the operation of those large economic forces ... the tendency of capital to gravitate into larger and fewer masses, localised where labour can be maintained upon the most economical terms: a correspondent but lower and less complete organisation of labour in large masses: the flow of labouring population into towns, together with a larger utilisation of women and (where permitted) children for industrial work: a growing keenness on antagonism as the mass of the business-unit is larger, and an increased expenditure of productive power upon aggressive commercial warfare: the growth of monopolies springing from natural, social, or economic sources, conferring upon individuals or classes the power to consume without producing, and by their consumption to direct the quantity and character of large masses of labour.

The complete realisation of full free trade in all directions has no power whatever to abate the activity of these forces, and would only serve to bring their operation into more signal and startling prominence.[23]

Whereas old radicals like Morley and Courtney continued to see in free trade 'the propagation of the good faith that ... the prosperity of one people gives the *best* promise for the prosperity of the other',[24] Hobson progressed on a domestic road to prosperity, towards a golden age of social democracy via the re-distribution of *domestic* wealth.[25]

The fresh emphasis on redistribution of wealth and domestic welfare was not limited to Hobson. Although few could rival the heretical elegance of his model, many social democrats came to a similarly critical reassessment of radicalism. Cobden was charted with shirking the central issue of land monopoly, with being indifferent to securing domestic production and employment, and with denying that home supply could be cheap supply,[26] all central issues for social democrats, and all positions that justified inroads into fiscal orthodoxy. From an economic perspec-

---

[23] J. A. Hobson, *The Evolution of Modern Capitalism: A Study of Machine Production*, London, 1894, p. 354.

[24] *Peace and Justice*, being four speeches delivered at the seventeenth Universal Peace Congress, 1908, by the president, the Rt. Hon. Lord Courtney of Penwith, p. 16, my emphasis. For Morley, see his speech at Newcastle, 18 April 1903.

[25] Hobson, *Imperialism*, Part I. This does not, however, mean, as Cain suggests, that to Hobson 'imperialism could only be eliminated by a prior transformation in the nature of advanced capitalism', Cain, 'Variations on a Famous Theme', p. 31. Not an insignificant problem in interpreting Hobson is the overdetermined nature of his arguments: in Hobson causation is always a nexus of multiple conditions. Part II focuses on the political power of rentiers, the press and the absence of true democracy. Ultimately, imperialism was not the product of unreformed capitalism but of unfulfilled democracy. It would, he claimed, disappear in 'an intelligent' *laissez-faire* democracy which gave duly proportionate weight in its policy to all interests alike', p. 53. Note the emphasis on cultural sources of reaction and imperialism, especially in his analysis of leisure, indebted to Veblen.

[26] Bodleian Library, Zimmern Papers, Ms. 11, Ensor to Zimmern, 2 January 1903, singled out Cobden's blindness to the land question as 'an error so fatal as to fairly swamp all the good that can be credited to him'.

tive, twentieth-century radicalism was introverted, nineteenth-century radicalism extroverted. Not only was free trade no longer held sufficient in the fight against imperialism, it was reduced to a subordinate precondition of social reform.

Together, the 'new' liberal emphases on domestic oversaving, the cost of imperialism, and the existence of illegitimate trade, inevitably put a fundamental question mark behind the Cobdenite belief in the benefits of international exchange. To argue that a *particular* form of trade – 'illegitimate trade' – diverted domestic capital into unremunerative channels posed the logical question about the relative benefits of trade in *general*. It was a slippery slope. It led Hobson to the conclusion that the

pressure to find external markets ... is not based on any natural economic necessity. There is no natural limit to the quantity of wealth which can be produced, exchanged, and consumed within Great Britain.[27]

Hobson, it must be stressed, did not doubt the utility of trade in principle, nor the benefits to be derived from exchange or the division of labour. Rather he minimised the international relative to the domestic contribution in the creation of wealth.

The outbreak of the fiscal controversy in 1903, a year after the publication of *Imperialism* demonstrated to Hobson the 'need for more rigorous thought' on the subject and led him to a more theoretical analysis of the nature of free exchange.[28] Though a comprehensive rejection of protection, *International Trade* can be seen as a failure to resolve the tension between domestic and international imperatives. Indeed Hobson's adherence to free trade now acknowledged three important qualifications: foreign monopoly, unemployment, and 'aggressive dumping'. If nations acted as 'non-competing' groups extorting monopoly prices it was theoretically possible to 'tax the foreigner'.[29] Unlike fellow Liberals, Hobson was also aware of the dislocation caused by aggressive dumping, as distinct from the casual unorganised dumping of surplus stock. Indeed, an anti-dumping tariff, he felt, offended 'no sane principle of free exchange'.[30] He rejected it on grounds of expediency not principle. A tariff would have to be created promptly and required prior commercial intelligence of foreign corporate strategies difficult to come by. Above all, Hobson had little confidence in putting 'the clumsy and ineffectual weapons of import duties into the hands of imperfectly wise officials'.[31] Such reasoning combined the long tradition of radicals' belief

[27] Hobson continued 'except the limits imposed by restricted natural resources and the actual condition of the arts of industry', *Imperialism*, p. 32.
[28] Hobson, *International Trade: An Application of Economic Theory*, London, 1904, p. v.
[29] *Ibid.*, pp. 49f, 144.
[30] *Ibid.*, p. 139.
[31] *Ibid.*, pp. 140f.

in the inherent corruptibility of government with the administrative pessimism of liberal political economy.

The discussion of the relation between protection and unemployment showed how much progressive liberalism had to lean on this political crutch as the economic support of liberal economics was giving way. The classical case for free trade rested on the assumption of full employment and elastic labour markets. Once that assumption was suspended, the case for free trade became a political not an economic one. Anticipating Keynes by a generation, Hobson admitted as early as 1904 that protection might increase national wealth by bringing unemployed labour and capital back into production.[32] Unlike Keynes, however, Hobson did not find his way to a pragmatic advocacy of tariffs. His resistance was fuelled by three reservations.[33] First, he failed to see how a scientific tariff could be devised to utilise unemployed resources without displacing profitably employed capital and labour. Second, Hobson had an alternative growth programme in social reform. Maldistribution of wealth caused by over-saving was the 'taproot' of economic decline and would be exacerbated by duties. Last but not least important, he failed to break out of the liberal mindset in which there was no room for a detached (let alone sympathetic) consideration of tariffs as a mere technical tool say, for structural reform. It was still impossible to disentangle the politics from the economics of regulated trade. Tariffs were inseparable from class rule; once established their growth was feared to be unstoppable as parliamentary government would be taken over by vested interests.

The rise of 'social liberalism' was a wider European movement. The British development was peculiar, significantly, in combining new social reforms with an older political programme, headed by free trade. Progressive liberals in Germany,[34] like Friedrich Naumann, embraced imperialist *Weltpolitik* and a modernist vision of the corporate firm (*Grossbetrieb*); in Britain they defended internationalism and the pubic interest of the consumer, a central aspect of liberal culture, as noted

---

[32] *Ibid.*, ch xi, esp. p. 155 versus Cain's view that he did not reach this conclusion until 1922, in 'Variations on a Famous Theme', p. 43; on Keynes's pragmatic acceptance of tariffs now, Peter Clarke, *The Keynesian Revolution in the Making, 1924–1936*, Oxford, 1988, ch. 9.

[33] Hobson, *Imperialism*, esp. pp. 158–81.

[34] Gangolf Hübinger, 'Hochindustrialiserung und die Kulturwerte des deutschen Liberalismus', in Dieter Langewiesche (ed.), *Liberalismus im 19. Jahrhundert*, Göttingen, 1988, pp. 193–208; Stefan-Georg Schnorr, *Liberalismus zwischen 19. und 20. Jahrhundert: Reformulierung liberaler politischer Theorie in Deutschland und England am Beispiel von Friedrich Naumann und Leonard T. Hobhouse*, Baden-Baden, 1990, Dieter Langewiesche, *Liberalismus in Deutschland*, Frankfurt a.M., 1988, pp. 187–227. Max Weber's attitudes were more ambiguous than often thought: see Detlev Peukert, *Max Webers Diagnose der Moderne*, Göttingen, 1989; Wolfgang Mommsen, *Max Weber. Gesellschaft, Politik und Geschichte*, Frankfurt a.M., 1974

earlier. This defence, however, was no simple sign of a continuity. It revised, even transcended, orthodox positions, an achievement that can be seen to have prevented the dissociation between a belief in cultural and economic progress, so typical (and troubling) for German liberalism at the time. In Britain, the new liberal language of politics placed a fresh emphasis on the consumer rather than the productive firm.

At the same time as Hobson's 'social economics' shattered free trade as an economic panacea, it updated its moral and social significance. It detached from its meaning the freedom to produce but defended the freedom to exchange and consume. If distribution was the tightrope between 'old' and 'new' liberalism, consumption was the balancing rod. The combination between organic notions of social evolution and the reaction against liberal economics as the ideological mouthpiece of selfish producers did not favour mechanistic, productivist languages. The idea of the 'unproductive surplus' identified 'underconsumption', not productive capacity, as the key problem: redistribution of 'social income' not industrial policy was the answer. This analysis, which identified inequalities ('forced gain') in any market (labour and capital as well as land), went beyond the traditional focus of radicalism and its favourite remedies, land taxation and cooperation.[35]

The broad notion of social surplus was reinforced by a deep concern for the *cultural* implications of modern capitalism. Hobson found in it a 'dangerous paradox' exposing 'man ... to two opposed forces, tending on the one hand to greater narrowness of production, on the other, to greater width and complexity of consumption'.[36] Accompanying specialisation, mass production and bureaucracy threatened to erode the social and political capital of liberal communities. It promoted an individualist, acquisitive materialism at the expense of the 'social meaning' of work and community – a view that biased British new liberals against technocratic programmes. How was this modern dilemma to be overcome? Consumer cooperatives, a 'single tax' on landed monopoly, or higher wages were no longer effective answers. Economics needed to be subordinated to a new set of ethics. The first step was now redistribution of income and socialisation of large combinations. The enormous faith in the evolution of a corporate spirit suggested, secondly, that progress lay with harmonising (not differentiating) consumption and production. High wages were not enough to counter the 'cheap conformity' of industrial society. 'It is to the improved quality and character of consumption that we can alone

---

[35] J. A. Hobson, *The Economics of Distribution*, London, 1900. For an organic presentation of the unproductive surplus, see his *Industrial System: an Inquiry into Earned and Unearned Income*, London, 1909.

[36] Hobson, *Work and Wealth: A Human Valuation*, London, 1914, p. 237.

look for a guarantee of social progress'.[37] Significantly, Hobson believed, this would leave only a few standardised industries. The competitive, materialist consumer was turned into what he liked to call 'the citizen-consumer', a cooperative, creative individual with a sense of 'social service ... [and] fuller participation in the active foundations of citizenship ... local and national politics ... and in the numerous forms of voluntary association'.[38] Here the centrality of the consumer and free trade manifested not simply a long-standing concern for social harmony, let alone for commercial interests, but a progressive commitment to strengthening the civic sphere and democratic government against sectional producers (capital and labour), ideally by giving the consuming public a direct voice in state and industry.

The domestic logic of 'new' liberal thought, then, fits uneasily into the inherited body of radicalism. Paradoxically, Hobson was a dogmatic internationalist in spite of himself. He was an internationalist by moral persuasion rather than by economic reasoning. This moral internationalism was sustained by a belief in the virtues of exchange. Free trade was the international dimension of the communitarian side of consumption. In the final analysis, it rested on the assumption of a pre-existing natural harmony of interests of mankind which had informed radicalism since the Enlightenment but, by the late-Victorian period, was giving way in the domestic sphere. How would this tension between international morals and social democracy be resolved in an age of mass unemployment, 'sweated' competition, and international cartels?

IV

The defeat of protection was never simply the triumph of the Liberal middle class or 'Manchesterism'. After the Reform Bill of 1884 fiscal orthodoxy was at the mercy of a predominantly working-class electorate, which, by the turn of the century, was being wooed by a new player in progressive politics: the Labour Party. How did 'free trade' adjust to this challenge? As the pinch of protection retreated into distant memory, Cobdenites began to fear electoral reaction in times of depres-

---

[37] Hobson, *Evolution of Modern Capitalism*, London, 1897 edn, p. 368. 'As producer, a man performs one single economic function; as consumer, he brings into personal unity and harmony the ends of all the economic functions. That is why in the new Social Order a consumers' State is entitled to direct the flow of new productive power into several industrial channels, and to form a final court of appeal for the settlement of such conflicting claims and interests of the several industries or professions as cannot be adjusted by the unprincipled compromise or give and take of a purely functional assembly', *Incentives in the New Industrial Order*, London, 1922, pp. 151f.

[38] Hobson, *Work and Wealth*, p. 248.

sion.[39] Their remedy was a consumerist syllabus. Throughout the Edwardian fiscal controversy, Liberals adopted a self-conscious campaign to educate the worker as a consumer, by preaching Liberal axioms of trade, by highlighting the poor living conditions in select protectionist countries, and by constructing a collective memory of the 'hungry forties'.[40]

In the end, Liberal fears about working-class defection proved groundless. The labour movement did not need to be drummed into opposition to tariff reform. Already in the summer of 1903 the Labour Party and trade unions declared against protection.[41] An equally important stronghold was the Cooperative movement. Free trade and cooperation had grown in strength arm in arm in the mid-Victorian period. The organisational overlap remained striking, both in personnel and agitational work, such as lantern lectures, educational classes, and other forms of popular propaganda. In July 1903 the Parliamentary Committee of the Cooperative Congress committed the machinery of the Cooperative Union to support the Cobden Club's campaign. With a popular membership of two million consumers, it came only second to nonconformity in importance to pre-war liberalism.[42]

To the young Labour Party, as to 'new' Liberals, the fiscal controversy provided a welcome opportunity to state their own case. Led by Hardie, Snowden and MacDonald, the Independent Labour Party (ILP) was the first in the field in printing literature and organising rallies in the summer and winter of 1903.[43] Since it has become fashionable to emphasise the

[39] See, for instance, *Cobden Club, Report 1899*, London, 1900, pp. 14f.

[40] *The Hungry Forties*, introduced by J. Cobden Unwin, London, 1904; Free Trade Union, *General Leaflets*, London, 1910, nos. 80, 88, 101, 145, 150–3, 159, 184. Cf. chapter 8, above, pp. 193–218.

[41] Labour Representation Committee (LRC) Minutes, 18 June 1903, 30 October, 1903, BLPES, LSE Coll. Misc. 196; and see the leaflet *To the Trade Unionists of Great Britain and Ireland, A United Labour Manifesto* signed by eleven Labour MPs, the members of the parliamentary committee of the TUC, the management committee of the General Federation of Trade Unions, and the LRC; also *We are more than Free Traders*, LRC Leaflet no. 10, 12 December 1903.

[42] Cooperative Union Archives, Manchester, Parliamentary Committee of the Cooperative Congress minutes, 4 July 1903, also 25 July, 1 August, 7 and 9 November 1903 and 11 January 1904. J. C. Gray, the general secretary of the Cooperative Union in 1906, for instance, was also a vice president of the Free Trade League, see the short biography in *Birmingham: A Handbook to the Thirty-Eighth Annual Co-operative Congress*, Whitsuntide 1906, etc., Manchester, 1906, pp. 11–14. Free trade formed a central part in the Cooperative Educational Programme, which by 1905 had expanded to attract a total of over 9,000 pupils per year, see The Cooperative Union Limited, *Co-operative Educational Programme*, Session 1915–16 (1916), Appendix I, and pp. 7, 11, 18, 23, 69. The Women's Cooperative Guild was active in sending free trade resolutions to local MPs, see *Souvenir of Cooperative Congress at Stratford, 1904*, Manchester, 1904, p. 69.

[43] *Report of the Twelfth Annual Conference of the Independent Labour Party*, Cardiff, 4 and 5 April 1904, pp. 10–14 (Conference report hereafter cited as *ILP Report*). For Labour

continuity of liberal radical ideas in the early Labour Party it may be useful briefly to examine Labour's attitude to free trade. To what degree is it possible to speak of a convergence of ideas on 'the left'?[44]

Consistent with Liberal arguments Labour denied that protection would improve wages, lower unemployment or return the people to the land. Tariffs were denounced as the instruments of monopolistic producers and imperialists. Free trade, in its limited fiscal sense of 'free food', was a central aspect of distributive justice. From its birth, the abolition of indirect taxation was a constitutional principle for Labour. Here was a platform of joint action with 'new' Liberals. MacDonald, in particular, played the progressive ticket. Addressing a 'new' Liberal audience, shared ideas were stressed; naturally they ought to be read with an awareness of the context.[45] An examination of Labour's arguments in its home constituency, by contrast, reveals the limits of agreement.

To Labour, free trade was never a fetish. Working men were reminded that they had remained oppressed and impoverished under the free-trade regime. 'A great deal of non-sense is being talked about the blessings of Free Trade, and the prosperity of the Free Trade era', Snowden insisted. Was progress not the achievement of trade unionism and state regulation of industry? In contrast to Liberal claims, the contribution of free trade to wealth was reduced to that of 'a useful condition but not an active force'.[46]

Labourism was a denial of consumerism. Along with the rejection of tariffs went a rejection of the liberal principle of cheapness. The collective standard of living took precendence over the individual freedom to buy in the cheapest market. This shifted the yardstick of trade from wealth to that of working conditions – from consumption to production – a shift reflected in resolutions favouring the prohibition of 'sweated' imports.[47]

---

literature see LRC minutes, cited in footnote 41. The Liberal Publication Department made free and unauthorised use of some leaflets under its own name, BLPES, LSE Coll. Misc. 196, Ramsay MacDonald to anon, 22 January 1904.

[44] For a fuller discussion, see Frank Trentmann, 'Wealth versus Welfare: The British Left between Free Trade and National Political Economy before World War I', *Historical Research*, forthcoming.

[45] *ILP Report*, 1893, pp. 10–12. See also the official *The Zollverein and British Industry*, London, 1903, by MacDonald and his appeal for a progressive alliance in 'The Electorate and the Tariff Temptation' in *New Liberal Review*, 6, 34 (November 1903) pp. 436–48.

[46] [Snowden] *Facts for the Workers about Protection, Free Trade, and Monopoly*, Tracts for the Times, no. 3, London, n.d. [1904], p. 10.

[47] *ILP Report*, 1904, pp. 27f. The resolution was proposed by Councillor Parker (Halifax) and had only two dissentients criticising the practicability of the proposal; also MacDonald, *The Zollverein and British Industry*, esp. pp. 20, 113, 163. For an earlier statement by the Social Democratic Federation [H. H. Champion], *The Facts about the Unemployed, An Appeal and a Warning, by one of the Middle-Class*, London, 1886. The important issue of which imports would not fall under the category 'sweated' in a high wage country like Britain was, interestingly, not considered.

The fiscal voice of the party was Philip Snowden. Labour's chief protagonist in the debate is typically portrayed as a miniature version of the Grand Old Man. However appropriate this picture may be for his orthodox record as Chancellor of the Exchequer in the first two Labour governments (1923–4, 1929–31), references to Gladstone's memory carry less historical weight for his Edwardian apprenticeship.[48] Snowden's case (and Labour's) against protection, it must be stressed, emerged from a socialist not a liberal analysis. Poverty was the product of monopoly. In Labour's hands the liberal icon of the 'dear loaf' was used to illustrate a socialist message: labour (not capital) created 'the big loaf of wealth' but received only a crust while the 'idle and leisured class' appropriated the bulk in rent and profit.[49] This had a certain radical ring, centred on the dichotomy of productive people and unproductive elite, which allowed for pragmatic alliances with Liberals in joint attacks on rentiers and the 'unearned increment'. Yet here the convergence ends. If 'radical' means going to the roots of a problem, as Marx had put it, to Labour the root of poverty was the capitalist process as such. Industrial anarchy was inherent in capitalism. To Labour, protection was not a political challenge but a political reality – in the form of monopoly, trusts, and rent. In contrast to Liberals, unemployment, poverty and imperialism were understood in a basic socialist sense as the inevitable outcome of the profit motive, overproduction and immiseration.[50]

From this diagnosis socialists would arrive at different prescriptions. Yet beyond the manifold political tensions between dogmatism and revisionism[51] it is possible to discern ideological affinities. 'Monopoly' was at the heart of that shared outlook, and is crucial to an understanding of socialists' ambiguous relationship with free trade. At one level, monopoly was pictured as a brake on the Liberal wheels of free trade, preventing the most efficient division of labour. Fabians, in particular, used this argument to advertise to Liberals the imperative need for social reform.[52] The

---

[48] Keith Laybourn, *Philip Snowden: A Biography, 1864–1937*, Aldershot, 1988, is typical in the failure to make use of Snowden's fiscal writings.

[49] The image and citation is taken from the ILP's weekly *The Platform*, 137, 13 February 1904, 'The Real Loaf Question'.

[50] *The Platform*, 134, 23 January 1904, 'The Essentials of Life' is a typical, popular version.

[51] See the recent discussion by Duncan Tanner, 'Ideological Debate in Edwardian Labour Politics: Radicalism, Revisionism and Socialism' in Biagini and Reid (eds.), *Currents of Radicalism*, pp. 271–93.

[52] Sidney and Beatrice Webb, *Industrial Democracy*, second edn, London, NY, Bombay, 1902, Appendix II: the Fabian Society, *Fabianism and the Fiscal Question: an Alternative Policy*, drafted by Bernard Shaw, London, 1904, esp. pp. 21f. This insight was yet far removed from a positive notion of 'picking winners' or development economics. The Webbs' analysis strongly impressed Ensor (in Manchester of all places), who passed it on to Zimmern as a 'good fiscal tip', noting that '[t]he unsatisfactory feature in our trade-balance is not growth of imports, but growth of certain exports (sweated manufacturers,

enemy of British wealth, the Webbs argued, was not cheap foreign but cheap domestic labour. 'Sweating' conditions operated as hidden subsidies pulling resources away from more efficient employment. Liberal thinkers had only learnt half the lesson, the Webbs concluded: free competition did not produce the most favourable division of labour but 'industrial parasitism'. Free trade was an imperfect mechanism. As long as social inequality and rent persisted, the forces of free trade were distorted.

At a more popular level, Cobdenism was rejected as a misguided vision. Cobden's dream of fostering commercial exchange and interdependence between nations was denounced as a dangerous delusion. To Labour, free trade had fulfilled its historical function: it had killed feudalism. At the same time it had set economic development on to a dangerous track: Britain was over-industrialised, at the mercy of foreign foodstuffs and raw materials, and foolishly squandering her natural resources by exporting coal and iron. In the short run, socialists grudgingly accepted free trade as a necessity for an export-oriented economy. In the long run, they rejected it as inimical to preserving and controlling Britain's natural wealth. The Cobdenite ideal of international exchange and specialisation now met its rival in the socialist project of national control and development. This ideal was not simply a 'lost' marginal tradition[53] but informed a broad spectrum of opinion stretching from Blatchford to Snowden. It must be understood in the context of anxieties about the rise of new industrial powers and neo-mercantilism. As Snowden preached the official gospel:

The idea of the Manchester School that we should devote ourselves to building up a foreign trade, that England should be the workshop of the world, was a mistake. *The tendency all over the world is for manufactures to settle down where the raw material is grown. Each country must devote itself to developing its natural resources.* This is the new policy we must adopt. We want Protection against landlordism, capitalism, and the giant monopolies which are draining the life's blood of the nation. We want to turn our attention to the land, to make that the basis of our national industry.[54]

Here was a glimpse of the transition from the Cobdenite belief in international competition as a pre-ordained divine plan to the twentieth-

&, possibly, coal). This the Libs. don't recognise'. Bodleian Library, Zimmern Papers, Ms. 11, 15 December 1903.

[53] Cf. David Howell, *A Lost Left, Three Studies in Socialism and Nationalism*, Manchester, 1986, esp. Part III; See also J. O. Stubbs, 'Lord Milner and Patriotic Labour, 1914–1918', *English Historical Review*, 87 (1972), pp. 717–54.

[54] 'An Imperial Zollverein', *The Platform*, 103, 20 June 1903, reprinted from *ILP News*, my emphasis; see also Snowden, *The Chamberlain Bubble: Facts about the Zollverein, with an Alternative Policy*, Tracts for the Times, no. 1, London, 1903, p. 16. For Blatchford see *Clarion*, 10 June 1910.

century ideal of national planning. The mould of the liberal tradition was broken.

One new result was the combination of land reform with economic nationalism. The nationalisation of land was interestingly envisaged to usher in a golden age of rural villages absorbing the industrial population and raising food for seven million more Britons.[55] This fantasy of a more self-sufficient Britain is a telling comment on the evolution of conflicting radical ideas. The socialist response to tariff reform was to debate the respective virtues of two radical enterprises: free trade or land reform of an extreme kind (nationalisation). Whereas 'new' Liberals at the time (and historians since) have stressed the affinities between Liberals and Labour around the project of land reform, my interpretation has sought to put the conflict between radical ideologies back into the picture.[56] In the hands of Labour, the evolution of a new progressive language – socialist control of natural resources – did not reinforce but undermined the integrity of free trade.

V

The First World War marks a watershed in the history of British liberalism. While its impact on the decline of the Liberal Party has received generous attention[57] the repercussions of total war on its central pillar of strength, free trade, have been ignored. Preoccupation with electoral and 'high political' history has created a picture of continuity, in which the Edwardian dichotomy between free trade and protection is comfortably extended to the war and post-war years.[58] Nothing could be further from the truth. The pressures of war led to a fundamental revision of the central tenets of liberal political economy and culture. This revision, I would like to argue, occurred at three points. At the political level, nineteenth-century internationalism was displaced by a 'new internationalism'. At the economic level, the place of free imports and free competition was taken by a belief in the virtues of regulated trade. At the industrial level, free trade consumerism was challenged by the rise of productivism.

[55] 'Protection or Socialism', *The Platform*, 7 November 1903.
[56] L. T. Hobhouse, *Democracy and Reaction*, London, 1904, ch. ix. On land reform in general, Avner Offer, *Property and Politics 1870–1914: Landownership, Law, Ideology and Urban Development in England*, Cambridge, 1981.
[57] The most recent account is John Turner, *British Politics and the Great War: Coalition and Conflict 1915–1918*, New Haven, 1992.
[58] Robert E. Bunselmeyer, *The Cost of War 1915–1919, British Economic War Aims and The Origins of Reparation*, (Ct), Hamden, 1975; Robert C. Self, *Tories and Tariffs, The Conservative Party and the Politics of Tariff Reform, 1922–1932*, London, 1986.

To avoid misunderstanding, this is not an argument about the whole-sale disenchantment of the liberal community with free trade. Some remained reverent disciples of the old faith; leading members of the Cobden Club, like Hugh Bell, George Paísh, and F. W. Hirst come easily to mind.[59] All ideologies are survived by a band of stubborn faithful. Rather the rest of this chapter is concerned with the disintegration of free trade as a hegemonic *Weltanschauung*, and what this can tell us about the nature of political and ideological change in modern Britain.

Cobdenism was internationalism without a theory of international relations. Foreign policy was explained as a function of domestic politics. International antagonism and war were presented as the workings of aris-tocratic corruption and selfish profiteers. In the Enlightenment tradition, limiting governmental interference with trade was hoped to remove this source of friction and to allow commerce and consumption to weave together the world in its 'natural' unity and peace.[60] It was not so much a cosmopolitan but an internationalist creed, one that was closely linked to the emancipation of oppressed nationalities and the defence of national sovereignty. None of these principal assumptions survived the war unscathed.

The war proved the aggressive, expansionist potential of nationalism. It prompted a wide-ranging discussion about the need of future interna-tional government, which, in turn, prompted a reassessment of national sovereignty. From this debate liberals arrived at three different positions. Each marked a break with radical internationalism.

First, the need to de-politicise nationalism was emphasised. Some, like Hobson, proposed to substitute self-government for the idea of nation-ality. Another group, led by Zimmern, sought to divide the nation-state into separate cultural and political components and insisted on 'inter-statism'; significantly, he attacked Mill's influential ideas on the

---

[59] F. W. Hirst, *Safeguarding and Protection*, London, 1926, with a characteristic preface by Bell. Just how faithful these guardians of Cobden's memory were can be seen from their unwillingness to modify their master's teachings at all – not even at the height of the world depression, as continental champions of freer trade in a *union douanière européenne* were to find out in a joint conference, *United States of Europe*, report of a conference held in May 1930, Cobden Memorial Association, 1930. Cobdenites enjoyed home advan-tage: the conference took place at Cobden's birthplace, Dunford House, Sussex.

[60] For Cobden free trade was the 'International Law of the Almighty', cited Mallet (ed.), *Political Writings of Richard Cobden*, London, 1903, vol. I, p. vi. John Morley, *The Life of Richard Cobden*, second edn, London, 1896. Cf. *The European Diaries of Richard Cobden, 1846–1849*, ed. Miles Taylor, Aldershot, 1994. See also John W. Derry, *The Radical Tradition: Tom Paine to Lloyd George*, London, 1967.

[61] J. A. Hobson, *Towards International Government*, London, 1915; Alfred E. Zimmern, 'Nationality and Government', read before the Sociological Society on 30 November 1915, reprinted in *Nationality and Government with Other War-Time Essays*, London, 1918, pp. 32–60.

subject.[61] At the philosophical level, sovereignty, like individual freedom, was now defined in terms of positive right. Against libertarian criticism, a league of nations was defended as an indispensable pre-condition for the free self-determination of states. In Barker's succinct words:

States may be masters of their fate in the days of a Confederation as they could not be in the days in which their freedom was unchartered libertinism of force. Force is never free; it is always limited by other forces.[62]

As in the context of individual and social rights discussed earlier, the application of collectivist thought to the international sphere inevitably provoked an impassioned debate about the space between international right and national freedom that continues to this day. Inevitably, revision did not stop short at the delicate subject of fiscal sovereignty, the third place of departure from traditional internationalism.

European fiscal history after Versailles was the story of multiplying boundaries, the further erosion of the most-favoured-nation clause, and the proliferation of discriminatory trading practices. Liberal designs for economic disarmament took many forms. Surviving Cobdenites sent George Paish on a European mission in 1926 to proselytise the virtues of free trade – to little effect.[63] A growing number of liberals, however, refused to adhere to the orthodox practice of preaching free trade. The fiscal barriers (and eccentricities) of new states now struck many a liberal as a danger to world prosperity and an anomaly best abolished by international reform from above. Advocates of a Central European *Zollverein*, like Keynes, began to show little respect for national fiscal sovereignty.[64] Internationalism was caught in a dilemma. Zimmern concluded '[y]ou cannot, as English liberals often fondly imagine, have political nationalism without custom-houses'.[65] The successful establishment of confidence in international cooperation made it imperative to respect fiscal sovereignty as an indispensable condition of state autonomy, even if it involved protective duties.

'New' internationalists did not cease to work for fiscal disarmament at the international plane but the aim of political action shifted from free trade to equality of trade. Cobdenism was no longer attractive as a panacea for international relations. For 'new' internationalists the prin-

---

[62] Bodleian, Zimmern Ms. 83, E. Barker, 'The Powers of a League of Nations more Especially as Regards the Internal Affairs of its Members', n.d. [1918], a memo for the League of Nations Society; Barker was a fellow classical scholar and, in 1928, became the first professor of political science at Cambridge.

[63] BLPES, LSE Coll. Misc. 621/1, Paish Mss, 'My Memoirs', for an account of his tour to promote free trade societies, for which he had been 'requested' by Hugh Bell.

[64] Keynes, *The Economic Consequences of the Peace*, London, 1919, pp. 248ff.

[65] Zimmern, *Europe in Convalescence*, London, 1922, p. 186.

cipal target was no longer protection *per se*, but differential treatment, colonial preferences in particular. The inequality of commercial access was now identified as the chief enemy of world peace, against which 'new' internationalists were happy to advocate international institutions and retaliation as a legitimate measure to guard collective welfare against the excesses of national freedom.[66]

The advocacy of fiscal penal action shows how much liberal opinion had broken out of the Edwardian mindset, in which there had not even been room for the modest penalties under the Brussels Sugar Convention.[67] It manifested a fundamental disillusionment with traditional liberal politics. Arbitration, disarmament, publicity and parliamentary control of foreign policy, of course, continued to be preached.[68] Yet this ought not to obscure the more interesting development by which these radical causes became located in an altogether different type of internationalism: a 'new' internationalism that amounted to nothing less than a revolution in international relations. The war produced a crisis of the nation-state. This crisis affected the question of national sovereignty as well as the general relationship between politics and economics. Was it any longer advisable to rely on market forces for international harmony? Was the nation-state equipped to deal with the forces of modern capitalism in the collective interests of peace and welfare?

The answer of the 'new' internationalism to both questions was an emphatic 'No'. This was, above all, the lesson of the economic blockade. The effectiveness of economic warfare was incompatible with the optimistic reasoning that war could not pay which had informed Cobdenism and its revised version of Angellism before the war.[69] The radical project

[66] Bodleian Library, Zimmern Ms. 83, Zimmern, 'The League of Nations and Fiscal Policy', n.d. [October 1918], which is also appreciative of the potential conflict between the Wilsonian principles of equality of access and mandates. On the importance of securing equality of opportunity in an economic settlement of the League of Nations, also *ibid.*, G. Murray, 'Principles of Immediate Policy', December, 1918; G. Lowes Dickinson to the *Manchester Guardian*, 9 August 1916 advocating international commissions. Representative of the 'new' internationalists' disillusionment with pure free trade, Zimmern, 'Fiscal Policy and International Relations', a paper read to the British Institute of International Affairs on 29 January 1924, reprinted in *The Prospects of Democracy and other Essays*, London, 1929, pp. 233–56.

[67] Under the Brussels Sugar Convention of 1902 importing countries had to impose countervailing duties on the import of bounty-fed sugar. Britain resigned in 1912, under the Liberal Asquith government.

[68] This continuity, and consequently the liberals' alleged failure to learn 'the lessons of history', is the customary picture painted in many histories of the peace movement, e.g. James Hinton, *Protests and Visions, Peace Politics in Twentieth-Century Britain*, London, 1989.

[69] Norman Angell, *The Great Illusion: A Study of the Relation of Military Power in Nations to their Economic and Social Advantage*, London, 1910; Zimmern 'Fiscal Policy and International Relations', in *The Prospects of Democracy*, pp. 233–56, also his *The Economic*

of keeping politics and economics separate was exposed as the 'great illusion' once economic organisation became an integral part of national defence. The blockade also highlighted the economic forces underlying international friction, hitherto ignored in the politicised world-view of radicalism. Scarce raw materials, their uneven international distribution and control, industrialisation dictated by the needs of war – these sources of post-war nationalism did not fit easily into the traditional free-trade view of international tension as the function of domestic corruption. Democratic government was no safeguard against economic nationalism; internationlists had learned painfully.

This learning process resulted in what might be called 'the discovery of the political economy of international relations'. New internationalists abandoned the naive radical assumption that democratisation would establish the freedom of trade needed to establish peace.[70] The view from Geneva acknowledged the economic lessons of war, especially how competition for raw materials created political antagonism and an atmosphere of uncertainty highly susceptible to the forces of nationalism.[71] Free trade was ill-equipped to combat the push for industrial development behind tariffs and greater self-sufficiency reinforced by fears of future war and dependence. Instead 'new' internationalists looked towards cooperation via the League of Nations as confidence-building measures imperative for the removal of economic barriers.

Already before the end of the war unregulated commerce was recognised as a serious menace to this process. At a conference in September 1918 on inter-allied economic problems, liberal and social democratic administrators and intellectuals paid lip-service to the failure of radical internationalism.[72] The joint principles of national independence in economic policy and freedom of commerce were proclaimed dead and dangerous in a world of shortages and international cartels. Competition

---

Weapon in the War Against Germany, London, 1918, and *The Third British Empire, Being a Course of Lectures delivered at Columbia University, New York*, second revised edn, London, 1927, pp. 107ff.

[70] Hobson, it may be noted, remained an 'old' internationalist on this count well into the war, in spite of (or perhaps because of) his continuous efforts to revise Cobden's teachings. Hobson's reaction to the war is told in Peter Clarke, *Liberals and Social Democrats*, Cambridge, 1978, esp. pp. 174–86.

[71] Churchill Archives Centre, Cambridge, Noel-Baker papers 4/188, International Consultative Group (For Peace and Disarmament), Geneva, 'Some Notes and Reflections concerning the Problem of Raw Materials', 5 May 1937.

[72] PRO, Reco 1/777; Bodleian, Zimmern Ms. 80–1, see the twenty-one page long anonymous memorandum, 'A Conference was held at Balliol College, Oxford, during week end September 28–30 to consider Inter-Allied Economic Problems', n.d. [1918] hereafter cited as 'A Conference'. The author was probably M. Bryant of the Food Ministry. Amongst those present were T. Jones, R. H. Brand, E. M. H. Lloyd, E. F. Wise, Keynes and Zimmern. A second conference was held on 7 October 1918.

– between governments and corporations threatened to exacerbate not resolve scarcities and needlessly prolong dislocation and antagonism. This was not just short-term pragmatism. It reflected the growing hope amongst many Liberals as well as former Conservative free traders that some structure of international regulation might be continued after the post-war transition period, especially in crucial raw materials, such as nickel and oil, and serve as an embryonic international organisation.[73] The political costs of relying on the market in distributing scarce key resources had become unbearable.

The experience of war forced Liberals to acknowledge structural changes in the nature of capitalism which could not be incorporated into received liberal theory. In the age of international cartels and corporations the traditional policy choice between state control and market changed meaning. Confronted with international steel cartels and beef trusts the Balliol conference declared it 'worth considering whether an international control arranged by the Governments themselves was not better than syndication of international capitalists'.[74]

The 'new' internationalist programme, then, substituted cooperation for competition, at the economic as much as at the political level. It must be understood as liberalism's response to the changing nature of modern political economy. This was characterised by the declining capacity of the nation-state to offer institutional responses to the challenges of national planning and monopolistic competition that could ensure liberal democracy, national wealth and world peace. International cooperation was to relieve the over-strained liberal state of burdens it was incapable of handling on its own.

Alfred Zimmern's life is a colourful and symptomatic reflection of this stage in the transformation of liberalism. A committed Edwardian free trader in his days at Oxford, he was transformed into a leading 'new' internationalist scholar–politician by face-to-face contact with economic war in Whitehall.[75] Unlike nineteenth-century Cobdenites he took refuge

---

[73] PRO, Cab 27/44, EDDC37, Robert Cecil, 'Inter-Allied Control of Imports', 10 September 1918. An Edwardian free fooder, Cecil emerged during the war as the leading Conservative proponent of inter-allied machinery as an indispensable basis for international organisation as well as social peace after the war. A. E. Zimmern, *The Economic Weapon in the War Against Germany*, London, 1918, and 'International Organization, Its Prospects and Limitations', *Atlantic Monthly* (September 1923), reprinted in *The Prospects of Democracy and other Essays*, esp. p. 222.

[74] 'A Conference', p. 19.

[75] Bodleian Library, Zimmern Ms. 136, 'The Seven Deadly Sins of Tariff Reform', n.d. [1905]. Zimmern rose to fame with the publication of *The Greek Commonwealth* in 1911. He subsequently worked for the Board of Education as an inspector until 1915. Towards the end of the war he joined the political intelligence department of the Foreign Office. From 1925 to 1939 he was the director of the School of International Studies, Geneva, see Salter's appreciation in *Dictionary of National Biography 1951–1960*, pp. 1096–7. These themes will be developed at greater length in my forthcoming monograph.

in constructive international politics not commerce. Zimmern was amongst the first to call attention to the dilemma of British modernity: the growing mismatch between economic modernisation and antiquated political institutions.[76] The British state had been slow to re-adjust to the transformation of the world economy, not least because of the radical distrust of government. The Great War added a socio-political aspect to this dilemma. It reminded liberals that a failure to defuse this time bomb might not only bring war but revolution at home and the end of liberal democracy. To bring politics into line with economic modernisation, Zimmern looked towards two parallel reforms: industrial self-government at home and cooperation at the international level, not least through channels of intellectual exchange.[77] International cooperation was a domestic as much as an internationalist project. It tried to overcome free trade's failure to create a sense of active citizenship without resorting to statist bureaucratic models. It was designed to foster new bonds of civic duty and collective responsibility which extended idealist and Platonic notions of association, popular before the war, and appealed naturally to this classical scholar's concern for the 'good life'. This, in his view, had been exorcised by the individualist materialism of free trade and *laissez-faire*.[78] The 'new' internationalism called in the new world to remedy the defects of the old.

VI

The 'new' internationalism was not the monopoly of Liberals. Socialists and social democrats were receptive to many of its ideas. Indeed, much of their formulation had been a cooperative effort, as between Arthur Salter and E. F. Wise, who served at the heart of the economic war machinery.[79] This working relationship continued after the war. One prominent example was Hobson's contribution to the ILP's *Living Wage*

[76] Alfred E. Zimmern, 'The New International Outlook', two lectures at the Fenton Foundation of the University of Buffalo delivered in November 1926, *University of Buffalo Studies*, 5, 1 (1926).

[77] 'Nationality and Government', 'Progress in Industry' (August 1916), and 'The Labour Movement and the Future of British Industry' (June 1916) in *The Round Table*, reprinted in *Nationality and Government*, London, 1918, pp. 32–60, 172–203, 204–42 respectively.

[78] In 'Capitalism and International Relations', a paper read at a Ruskin College conference on 22 September 1917, Zimmern argued that the selfish spirit of materialism had made the war possible, reprinted in *Nationality and Government*, pp. 278–97; also his *The Prospects of Democracy*, London, 1928, an address delivered to the Royal Institute of International Affairs on 8 November 1927. Cf. José Harris, 'Political Thought and the Welfare State, 1870–1940: An Intellectual Framework for British Social Policy', *Past and Present*, 135 (1992), pp. 116–41 and chapter 14 below.

[79] J. A. Salter, *Allied Shipping Control: An Experiment in International Administration*, Oxford, 1921. Wise was chairman of the central commission on leather supplies during the war.

programme in 1926.[80] Is this evidence for a 'radical consensus'? References to Hobsonian underconsumption are difficult to miss in the text. The conclusion reached, however, was for a systematic control of trade fundamentally at odds with Hobson's and Liberal views as well as with the orthodox fiscal policy of the Labour government. An analysis of this paradox may clarify an important chapter in the evolution of Labour thought and help to identify further the points of convergence and conflict between Liberal and socialist views on international trade.

Overindustrialisation and overdependence on foreign trade were twin themes of the ILP in the 1920s as they had been before the war.[81] What had changed was not the assumption of ideas but the assumption of office by the first Labour government in 1923. The touch of political power altered the relationship between what was politically thinkable and what politically feasible. It culminated in the conflict between the ILP's programmatic 'socialism in our time' and Snowden's increasingly liberal reformism that led to his resignation from the ILP in 1927 and the final schism in the labour movement four years later.[82] Well might socialist admirers of the young Snowden be forgiven for expressing surprise at their hero's fall, which was naturally blamed on those omnipresent culprits of the time: the Governor of the Bank of England, Montagu Norman, and the Treasury knights.[83] Confronted by the failed promise of their leaders in power and 'the intractable million' unemployed in the streets, the ILP formulated its own programme.

The Living Wage proposals pushed pre-war assumptions to their logical conclusion. They reflected the impact of war, post-war depression, and mass unemployment on an inherited body of ideas. The Liberal axiom that trade consisted of reciprocal benefits was openly rejected. At the level of exchange, trade was represented as a zero-sum game. Britain's capture of foreign markets merely resulted in unemployment abroad:

[t]he common phrase 'capture foreign markets' expresses in itself ideas of capitalist commercial conquest which are entirely alien to socialist thought. Employment gained for British workers by 'capturing the foreign market' means inevitably unemployment for the workers in the dispossessed country.[84]

---

[80] H. N. Brailsford, John A. Hobson, A. Creech Jones, E. F. Wise, *The Living Wage*, a report submitted to the National Administrative Council of the Independent Labour Party, London, 1926.

[81] Representative is *Socialism and the Empire*, report of the ILP Empire Policy Committee submitted to the annual conference of the party, 1926, p. 9. See also above, pp. 230–5.

[82] *ILP Report*, 1928, pp. 24, 41f.

[83] John Paton, *Proletarian Pilgrimage: An Autobiography*, London, 1935, pp. 306ff.

[84] John Paton, then ILP secretary, *Wealth, Work, and Wages*, London, 1929, p. 6.

At a dynamic macro-economic level, trade even appeared to be a minus-sum game.[85] The classical case for free trade had rested on the beautifully simple notion of trade as mutually profitable exchange. Instead of equal profit, socialists stressed the unequal social value and the exploitative dynamic in exchange between societies at different stages of development. Far from enhancing global wealth, trade widened the gap between productive and consumptive capacity. Ultimately, this would produce a global catastrophe in distribution. It was at this point that the ILP employed Hobson's underconsumptionist ideas. Redistribution of wealth was indispensable to narrow the gap between production and consumption.[86] Hobson's contribution, then, resembled not an intellectual design but a technical tool in an indigenous 'overproductionist' tradition. Social reform, it was argued, had failed to slow the engine of overproduction and immiseration. The search for an effective brake led to the discovery of price controls.

Regulation of prices was the magic wand in the ILP's economic kit. Its intellectual discovery was crucial for the political decision in favour of trade controls. To question the utility of flexible prices struck at the very heart of the Liberal axiom underlying free trade: that the price mechanism ('the invisible hand') produces the most beneficial allocation of resources. In the post-war years of mass unemployment, violent trade fluctuations and declining old export industries this assumption became ever more questionable and led to a search for diminishing Britain's dependence on world trade. Price controls provided socialists with remedies to all these problems. To establish a 'living wage' would increase purchasing power, but required price controls lest inflation equalised wage advances. It was recognised that:

perhaps the chief instrument in our policy for maintaining the real value of the Living Wage, would lie in the opportunities for stabilisation and standardisation which the national importation of foods and raw materials would afford.[87]

State-controlled import boards promised economies of scale and the elimination of that much hated figure, the middleman. Above all, this offered a rudimentary incomes policy, one of the few instruments in a capitalist society a Labour government might control against employers' attacks on wages – made more attractive after the failure of the General Strike in 1926. To stabilise prices was also to lower the oscillations of the trade cycle. This and the control of raw materials were to provide the means of industrial control necessary to stabilise depressed trades, assist in their reorganisation and, ultimately, prepare for their nationalisation.

[85] John Wheatley, *Socialise the National Income!* ILP, 1927.
[86] *The Living Wage*, ch. 2.
[87] *Ibid.*, p. 42.

Socialists did not have to look as far as Moscow for instruments of price regulation. They found inspiration (and expertise) closer to home. Again, the war had left its mark. References to the successful working of food and raw material controls in wartime abound in the discussions of import boards.[88] Trade controls were no longer rejected simply on grounds of distributive justice. While it had still been possible in 1916 to proclaim that 'Socialism is the ally of the worker and Protection the ally of the monpolist and profiteer', the experience of industrial decline in the 1920s turned the issue into one of political control.[89] Once British industry failed to compete at world prices, import boards (not free trade) appeared imperative to defend the worker's standard of living against cheap imports and employers' demands for lower wages. The ILP's defence of its programme at the height of the depression showed the distance from fiscal orthodoxy: tariffs were rejected not because they were a departure from free trade but because they were not going far enough! Protection was not sufficiently scientific to control the forces of organised competition. It could not deal with dumping, nor with fluctuations in world prices, Fenner Brockway explained.[90] Hobson, as has been seen, had arrived at a similar diagnosis before the war, but failed to see his way to propose regulated trade as a remedy.[91] The reason why socialists were able to emerge with a prescription of import boards must be sought in the connection of their overproductionist analysis, which minimised the utility of social reform, with the experience of war, which highlighted the failure of the price mechanism and advertised institutional controls.

Had internationalism been abandoned for the pursuit of economic nationalism? It is not altogether helpful to see this debate in terms of a dichotomy between internationalism and nationalism, let alone to liken it to Chamberlain's tariff reform.[92] All it shared with advocates of protection was an insistence on the costs of freedom of trade. Unlike tariff reformers, the ILP (and not just Wheatley) identified the source of

---

[88] *Ibid.*, pp. 14, 39f, 42f, also ILP Study Courses no. 3, *Socialism at Work* by Ernest E. Hunter with notes for lectures and class leaders, ILP, 1921, esp. 'study five'. War controls also informed the ILP's 'Socialist Policy for Agriculture' which advocated a monopoly for the purchase, importation and storage of wheat, flour and meat; amongst the signatories of the report were Brailsford, Wise and Hunter, the chairman of the Agricultural Committee, see *ILP Report*, 1924, App. 10. Compare the Liberals' confidence that 'nothing which has happened during and since the War serves to diminish the overwhelming force of the Free Trade argument', in *Britain's Industrial Future*, being the report of the Liberal Industrial Inquiry, London, 1928, p. 57f.

[89] *ILP Report*, 1916, p. 19; cf. *ILP Report*, 1931, p. 43.

[90] A. Fenner Brockway, *A Socialist Plan for Employment*, London, 1931, pp. 3f, reprint of a speech on a Tory Motion of Censure, 16 April 1931.

[91] See above pp. 227–8.

[92] Howell, *A Lost Left*, Part III, esp. p. 262.

British decline not in 'unfair' competition but in the systemic dilemma of capitalist 'overproduction'. Labour remained fundamentally opposed to imperialist schemes of differential duties.[93] The ends of its policy were equally opposed to neo-mercantilism. Import boards were greeted as a first step towards establishing equality of trade and cooperative trading in a world which appeared hopelessly set on a downward spiral of cut-throat competition.[94] The contribution of foreign trade to national wealth, it is true, was minimised, but as shown earlier, this was hardly a new feature in Labour thought. Nor were restrictions on trade the preserve of hard-line socialists. They extended from Wise to Moseley. The second Labour government (1929–31) also committed itself to stabilising wheat prices, though it found it more difficult to reach agreement on whether this was to be done by import boards or quotas; members also became fond of subsidising employment in the beet-sugar trades.[95] The cooperative movement too began to stress the primacy of an expansionist policy at home. At the height of the world depression a free trader warned that not only socialists but 'even sane cooperators are unintentionally assisting it [the tide of protection], either through preoccupation with the worker or with the Empire, or because of a revolt against everything good or bad, formerly associated with the "musty shibboleths of Manchesterism"'.[96] Many socialists were at least as enthusiastic about international regulation of scarce raw materials as liberal 'new' internationalists. Some looked as far as a world economic council to regulate international trade and raise the standard of living.[97] The alternative, then, was not a simple one between nationalism and internationalism, but one about the sequence and means of politico-economic reform. Rather than trust the

---

[93] ILP Report, *Socialism and the Empire*, London, 1926.

[94] *The Living Wage*, pp. 49f.

[95] PRO, Cab 27/417: Cabinet Committee on Agricultural Policy, which included Wise; Cab23/65: Cab52(30)-1, 17 September 1930 rejecting Import Boards because of anticipated imperial difficulties. For the growing popularity of Import Boards as an alternative to tariffs and free trade, Wise in *Manchester Guardian*, 14 July 1930 and *House of Commons, Parliamentary Debates 1929–1930*, vol. CCXLI, pp. 1400ff. For a defence of the sugar subsidy against Liberal attacks, PRO 30/69, Ramsay MacDonald Mss 1174: Noel Buxton to MacDonald, encl. Buxton to Greenwood 24 April 1929. Cf. Robert Skidelsky, *Oswald Mosley*, London 1975, chapters 7–11.

[96] J. T. Davis, *Free Trade and the Consumer: A Review and a Policy for Cooperators*, Manchester, n.d. [1931], p. 3. Cf. especially, the Cooperative Union's series *Britain Reborn* with plans for Home Trade Development Councils and its emphasis on the priority of national employment in economic policy. Still adamantly opposed to tariffs as unfair, it was now prepared to consider legal action against 'unfair' competition, *Britain Reborn*, no. 4, *Buy British*, Manchester, n.d. [early 1932].

[97] *ILP Report*, 1927, App. 9; Wheatley, in 1923, envisaged the establishment of a 'super-Parliament which would see that the resources of Europe were used for the blessing of the entire European population' as a solution to economic dislocation, *ILP Report*, 1923, p. 90.

slow workings of world opinion in raising the standard of living, the ILP looked towards domestic action to replace competitive with cooperative structures, which in time, it was hoped, would become bridgeheads for international cooperation.

VII

Socialists arrived at trade controls on the road of distributivism; the price mechanism had been the carrier. It was not the only route available for critics of the market. To question the utility of the 'invisible hand' was a mere first stop on a journey which had left behind the free-trade home but was not yet bound for a particular destination. The liberal train got separated at different points. By the 1920s a party of Edwardian radicals arrived safely at the platform of productivism. Its leader was none other than the former Radical and treasurer of the Free Trade Union, the chemical industrialist, Alfred Mond.

Mond's name is generally associated with the industrial conferences between employers and trade unionists in 1928–9.[98] 'Mondism', how-ever, was only one facet of a holistic productivist creed. Mond, unlike socialists, identified production not consumption as the weak spot of the British economy. In comparison with German and American firms, Britain was left 'with the least organised system of production and markets,'[99] he lamented in 1927. The market no longer guaranteed effi-ciency in an age of organised capitalism. Instead of the price mechanism and competition, productivists looked towards the 'visible hand' of ratio-nalised corporate structures as the foundation of future growth.

Productivism had implications far beyond the sphere of the firm or industrial relations. The corporate firm served as a microcosm for the national economy. It supplied producers with a new map of political economy. The principles informing policy shifted from consumption to production and from competition to planning. This, in turn, created the new gods of industrial concentration, bigger markets, and price stability, a trinity which the individualist consumerism of free trade was unable to serve.[100] As one productivist summed it up:

---

[98] G. M. Macdonald and Howard Gospel, 'The Mond–Turner Talks, 1927–1933: A Study in Industrial Co-operation', *Historical Journal*, 16, 4 (1973), pp. 807–29.

[99] Alfred Mond, *Industry and Politics*, London, 1927, pp. 224f, in a discussion of 'interna-tional cartels', based on an address to the Royal Institute of International Affairs, 10 May 1927.

[100] See Frank Trentmann, 'The Transformation of Fiscal Reform: Reciprocity, Modernisation and the Fiscal Debate within the Business Community in the Early Twentieth Century' in *Historical Journal* (forthcoming).

[t]he best way to create wealth is to keep the producing machine revolving at its highest possible momentum ... It is production that provides employment. It is an extension of production that Safeguarding is designed to achieve.[101]

At the level of the world economy the logic of industrial concentration legitimised a new corporate imperialism. To Mond the 'logical consequences of the economic groupings of industries is the economic grouping of countries themselves'.[102] The development of imperial markets was indispensable if Britain was to avoid industrial and political isolation. At the level of domestic politics, productivism resulted in the unconsummated producers' alliance between progressive employers and trade unionists. Concern with economies of scale, employment and market development had also led the TUC, by 1930, to press for a Commonwealth economic bloc and the adoption of select tariffs to encourage rationalisation.[103]

Is it possible to say when and how Liberal industrialists, like Mond, arrived at the crossroads of productivism? The post-war challenge of industrial retardation, structural unemployment and international cartels certainly helped; the formation of (Imperial Chemical Industries) ICI in 1926 illustrated the pressures for reorganisation.[104] Its origins, however, must be sought in the experience of war. They can be traced in the papers on the Balfour of Burleigh Committee, appointed in 1916 to consider commercial and industrial policy after the war. Work on the committee quickly turned Mond from a free trader into an advocate of a post-war programme of imperial self-sufficiency in raw materials and of fostering organised industries by subsidy or tariff.[105] This transition was not primarily caused by fear of German dumping but, as in the case of 'new' internationalists, by a discovery of the economic dimension of modern war. Adam Smith, of course, had already conceded that defence was more important than opulence. What was new in the war – and fatal to

101 Alexander Ramsay, *The Economics of Safeguarding*, London, 1930, and the supportive foreword by Gilbert Vyle, president of the British Engineers' Association.
102 Alfred Mond, *Industry and Politics*, p. 9. Also his *Imperial Economic Unity*, London 1930.
103 *Commonwealth Trade: A New Policy*, London, 1930; see also, Conference on Industrial Reorganisation and Industrial Relations, *Interim Joint Report on Unemployment*, London, 1929.
104 Fusion was assisted at the time by Mond, Brunner and Co.'s financial difficulties, United Alkali's competitive problems due to antiquated processes, and the general need for concentrated strength and pooled resources in negotiations with combines abroad. Beyond centralising financial control, however, the progress of rationalisation was slow, see L. F. Haber, *The Chemical Industry 1900–1930; International Growth and Technological Change*, Oxford, 1971, pp. 291–300.
105 PRO, BT 55/8, C and I. P. 2, 'Memorandum by Sir Alfred Mond on the Committee's Terms of Reference', n.d. [*c.* August 1916]. Typical for his anxiety about future allied and neutral as much as enemy competition, *ibid.* and his questions to Wintour, BT 55/10, C and I. P. 8, Evidence No. 7 (7/12/1916), p. 21.

free trade – were two conclusions. First, it was acknowledged that, potentially, economic warfare was intrinsic in trade: the difference between encouraging pacific competition and preventing 'peaceful penetration' was a very delicate one. Free traders were forced to reconsider whether the 'open door' was beneficial if it invited 'foreign invasion' or monopolistic takeovers, as attributed to Wilhelmine Germany. The second conclusion was that the national defence interest, in peace and war, required independence in essential raw materials and 'key' industries. To many Liberals, shortages during the war were a painful reminder that market-oriented fiscal orthodoxy had encouraged the transfer to the enemy of essential trades, like dyestuffs. Free trade became associated with an excess of atomistic competition and suspicion amongst capitalists that was ill-equipped to meet the rise of organised large-scale combinations abroad, let alone defeat the Central Powers.

Consumerism broke down irreversibly. It was no longer acceptable to expose major industries, like iron and steel, to unfair competition, Mond told members of parliament during the debate over safeguarding in 1921. 'Neither should the British manufacturer or the British workman be compelled, in the interests of some so-called consumer, *in vacuo*, to see the destruction of our industries.'[106] In cabinet, he now worked also for a massive development loan of one hundred million pounds for imperial and home development, especially in transport, housing, and state subsidies to private firms. Progressive Liberals found a new compromise in balancing the call for some duties and subsidies with schemes for public agencies to prevent their selfish abuse.[107]

VIII

The world depression (1929–32) dug the grave of free trade. It did not kill it. Free trade, as a secular religion, had died a slow death in previous decades. If few Liberals or socialists had been converted to protection pure by the 1920s, few were any longer finding their intellectual home in nineteenth-century free trade. Outside an ever-diminishing group of Edwardian Liberals, the defence of fiscal orthodoxy, especially after the war, ceased to be a defence of the radical *Weltanschauung*, as Cobden and Asquith had known it. What had been a paradigm for freedom of exchange, world prosperity and peace had become to many a mere opposition to a particular type of interference with trade feared for its social

[106] House of Commons, 9 May 1921, Hansard, vol. 141, col. 1603. PRO, Cab 24/139, CP4267, 'Notes on a Further Political Programme', memorandum by the Minister of Health (Mond), 5 October 1922.

[107] PRO, Cab27/44, EDDC27, Mond, 'Trade Policy after the War', 23 July 1918.

injustice (protection). The rich meaning of free trade had been diluted to mean little else but the undesirability of import duties, not of economic regulation in general.

To cast the fiscal debate in simple terms of 'free trade versus protection' merely repeats the not very helpful contemporary Cobdenite picture of the forces of progress fighting an army of reaction. It is high time to break out of this historiographical mould. What is needed is not more high political detail but a grasp of the fundamental transformation of liberal political economy and culture. Beyond the realm of elections lay a universe of new ideas and progressive politics which former free traders gained by abandoning the narrow, idealistic outlook of nineteenth-century radicalism. Political realism is not the worst exchange for the loss of idealistic innocence.

The analysis presented here has important implications for the interpretation of British radicalism. Radical ideas have multiple contexts; free trade to a Liberal is not free trade to a social democrat or socialist. To understand the political nature and function of radical causes it is necessary to locate them in their wider ideological structure, since their ultimate meaning is derived from that very structure. The existence of different ideologies does not, of course, preclude temporary political alliances, as the history of free trade shows. But, it makes them contingent not determinate, affinities that, under pressure, can turn into tensions and develop different, even opposed meanings. In the story of free trade this was acted out in the struggle between freedom of trade and regulated trade. It reflected the tension between the rival principles of competition and cooperation at the domestic and international levels.

In the final analysis this must be understood as a conflict between individualism and versions of collectivism. Free trade as a liberal *Weltanschauung* was informed by an atomistic mechanistic individualism which presumed a pre-ordained harmony of interests and extended the underlying axiom of individual freedom to the political, commercial and international spheres. Collectivism not only questions the existence of this self-perfecting mechanism but, by denying the natural autonomy of the individual, could legitimate policies which sacrificed individual freedom for the pursuit of collective ends. Collectivism has no room for the individualist insistence that it is the birthright of the individual to buy and sell where he pleases: the market becomes a collective institution.

Politics was not immune from the tension between these rival intellectual universes. The Edwardian conflict between individualist Unionist free traders and 'new' Liberal redistributive finance, Liberal divisions over the safeguarding of 'key industries' after the war, the shift from a concern for consumption and wealth to that for production and employment – these were its unmistakeable political manifestations. Rather than seeing the history of radicalism in terms of continuities, then, the transformation of free trade brings out a crucial bifurcation: first, between competitive and cooperative traditions in the nineteenth century, then, in the twentieth century, between individualist and collectivist traditions.

The erosion of free trade cannot however be grasped solely by reference to the autonomy of political ideas. Rather, this discussion has suggested the limits of this approach by pointing to the failure of 'new' liberals to apply their organic collectivist thought to the economic sphere. 'New' social reformers, the Hobhouses and Hobsons, were conspicuous only in the limits of their contribution to politico-economic reform. This was the work of 'new' internationalists, socialists, social democrats and productivists.

This paradox cannot be explained by reference to political party or economic theory alone. The collectivist transformation was accelerated by economic war rather than economic theory; Keynes's call for a revenue tariff in 1930 – indeed Keynesianism – may profitably be seen as the end, not the beginning, in the overhaul of economic liberalism. As the discussion of the 'new' internationalism, social democracy and productivism suggests, the war was central in undermining the verisimilitude of liberalism by bringing to light the politico-economic structures of an organised capitalism fundamentally different from Victorian individualist–competitive capitalism. Modern capitalist structures did not, perhaps, determine the precise outcome of this transformation in liberal political culture, but it would be equally impossible to explain it without relation to political economy. If any, this is the lesson from the story of the strange death of free trade.

Part III

Democracy, organicism and the challenge of nationalism

10 Land, religion and community: the Liberal Party in Ulster, 1868–1885

Graham Greenlee

Throughout the nineteenth century, economic and political power in rural Ireland was concentrated in the hands of wealthy landowners and their political patrons in the Conservative and Whig parties. However, from 1868, this political status quo was effectively challenged by Liberals in Ulster and Nationalists in the rest of Ireland. The Liberals gave a political lead to tenants in rural Ulster, who sought redress of their economic grievances through grassroots involvement in politics – the core of Gladstonian liberalism. There was considerable sympathy for the plight of Irish tenants in British radical circles. They supported Irish demands for the abolition of laws which upheld religious and economic inequality, hoping this would reconcile Irish Protestants and Catholics and strengthen Ireland's place within the Union. Liberals in Ulster agreed with this analysis of Ireland's problem. They appealed to tenants as the 'ambassadors of metropolitan Gladstonianism ... [and] ... presented themselves as ... a direct channel of appeal to the most powerful of all potential allies – a metropolitan government'.[1]

In this way the party made a considerable impact in Ulster elections between 1868 and 1880. At the height of their popularity, by exploiting tenant dissatisfaction at conditions in the countryside, they represented nearly half the rural constituencies of Ulster. However the Liberals failed to sustain a populist movement when faced with political competition from Celtic nationalism and a democratising Conservative Party. This chapter will analyse how the entering of the national question into Ulster politics adversely affected the ability of the Liberal Party to sustain its political representation in rural Ulster.

I would like to thank Dr Anthony Malcomson, Deputy Keeper of the Records, the Public Record Office of Northern Ireland, for permission to quote from the O'Hagan papers. Moreover I would like to include the following acknowledgements: D. 1905/2/17A/5 (Sir Charles Brett); D. 2777/9/50/4 (The National Library of Ireland); D. 236/488/2 (the late T. G. F. Paterson).

[1] P. Gibbon, *The Origins of Ulster Unionism: The Formation of Popular Protestant Politics and Ideology in Nineteenth Century Ireland*, Manchester, 1975, p. 109.

I

In 1868 political discontent within the northern Presbyterian community centred on the question of the religious establishment of the Church of Ireland, the small number of Presbyterians appointed to government posts and the lack of Ulster MPs of this denomination. The Liberals in Ulster opposed this aspect of the Episcopalian political ascendancy and, not surprisingly, Presbyterians dominated the party's leadership. However, whilst presbyterianism and liberalism have often been regarded as synonymous in Ireland, throughout the nineteenth century election returns indicate that a majority of Presbyterians consistently supported Conservative candidates in Ulster constituencies. Indeed 'despite all boasts to the contrary [liberalism] was identified with Presbyterianism only in Down and Antrim. Elsewhere Liberals were a minority of Presbyterians'.[2] By contrast to Nationalists in the rest of Ireland, Ulster Liberals supported religious and land reform because they thought this would reconcile Ireland to the Union. Local Liberals looked with satisfaction and pride at the economic prosperity Ulster had enjoyed since the Act of Union. Consequently they regarded the continuance of the existing constitutional arrangement as vital to the long-term prosperity of Ireland.

Throughout the 1860s and 1870s Liberals faced considerable problems in building up support in both rural and urban Ulster. Sectarian tensions were traditionally strong and periodically boiled over into serious intercommunal conflict. Conservative political and religious leaders had in the past roused the latent anti-Catholic sentiment in the Protestant community for party advantage.[3] It was in such a hostile political environment that the Liberal Party had to operate. The lack of a secret ballot before 1872 had hindered the party's fortunes in rural areas as tenants who publicly opposed the landlord's candidate could face harassment or even eviction.[4] Nevertheless, land agitation had been strong in Ulster during the 1850s especially amongst Presbyterians who, although constituting the majority of the population in Antrim and being significant in other counties, were not major landowners. Some Presbyterian ministers were enthusiastic in their support for the cause of land reform; one such minister, Revd N. M. Brown of Limavady was the originator of the '3Fs' – free sale, fair rent and fixity of tenure – which were to constitute the

---

[2] *Ibid.*, p. 108.
[3] The Reverend Henry Cooke, the champion of Presbyterian orthodoxy, forged a new Conservative alliance between the majority of Ulster Presbyterians and Episcopalians to oppose Catholic emancipation in the 1830s. See R. F. Foster, *Modern Ireland 1600–1972*, London, 1988, p. 303, footnote viii.
[4] See J. Bardon, *A History of Ulster*, Belfast, 1992, p. 356.

basis of the demands of land campaigns in the 1870s and 1880s.[5]

The traditional interpretation of nineteenth-century Irish economic history that tenants were the victims of exploitative landlords has undergone considerable revision in recent years.[6] Rents in post-famine Ireland did not keep pace with rises in agricultural prices 'with the result that tenants as a group found themselves in the happy position of enjoying a substantial rise in gross farming profits between the early 1850s and the mid-1870s'.[7] Tenants were actually the chief beneficiaries of post-famine agricultural growth. Vaughan comments: 'evictions were infrequent, rents were neither high nor often raised ... most tenants were not impoverished but enjoyed growing prosperity'.[8] In the north, rising prosperity was related to the Ulster custom. This was the principle that no eviction of a tenant should take place providing rent was promptly paid. Also, a tenant, on giving up his holding, could demand the payment of a lump sum from the incoming tenant to cover improvements he had made to the land. The good relations between landlords and tenants in Ulster, when compared to the rest of Ireland, was commonly put down to the existence of the custom. However, the Ulster custom had no formal recognition in law, and insecurity amongst tenants was rising by the early 1870s: they feared landlords would impose higher rents because of visible signs of growing tenant prosperity. Newly emerging tenant groups were already demanding that the custom be put on a firm legal footing.

The election of Gladstone as leader of the British Liberals was to be of great significance for liberalism in Ulster. He had a vision of how to pacify Ireland, it being to bring 'Irish laws and Irish institutions into harmony with the interests and feelings of the great bulk of the Irish people and by ruling Ireland no longer through or in the interests of a small class of people but in the interests of the people as a whole'.[9] Local Liberals were delighted with the new direction of Irish policy and were to warmly welcome the disestablishment of the Church of Ireland in 1869. This 'showed that the influence of the old Protestant ascendancy, which had hitherto played such a large part in moulding government policy towards Ireland, was now in decline'.[10] Stirrings of a revival of support were

[5] See B. M. Walker, *Ulster Politics – The Formative Years, 1868–1886*, Belfast, 1989, p. 20.

[6] See W. E. Vaughan, 'Landlord and Tenant Relations in Ireland between the Famine and the Land War 1850–1870', in L. M. Cullen and T. C. Smout (eds.), *Comparative Aspects of Scottish and Irish Economic and Social History, 1600–1900*, Edinburgh, 1977, pp. 216–26. Also B. L. Solow, *The Land Question and the Irish Economy 1870–1903*, Cambridge (Mass.), 1971.

[7] K. T. Hoppen, *Ireland since 1800: Conflict and Conformity*, London, 1989, p. 84.

[8] Walker, *Ulster Politics*, p. 4.

[9] J. J. Shaw, *Mr Gladstone's Two Irish Policies – 1868 and 1886*, Belfast, 1888, p. 5.

[10] P. McKeown, *The Land Question and Elections in South Antrim 1870–1910*, Queen's University Belfast unpublished M.SSc. thesis, 1983, p. 14.

evident at the 1868 general election. Increasing efforts were made amongst the newly enfranchised urban electorate, especially in Londonderry, where with the aid of Catholic and Presbyterian clergy a seat was taken by the Liberals. In Belfast, the heartland of conservatism, a split in local Tory ranks allowed an independent candidate and a Presbyterian Liberal to win both seats. In total the Liberals captured four seats, mainly in urban districts. Activity in the rural areas was small-scale with only one seat being contested. This indicates that as late as 1868 the land question was not a vital issue in rural Ulster. The reasons for the Liberals' moderate success at this time were essentially negative: Liberals exploited the mistakes other parties made in selecting candidates, and also relied on intra-party rivalry to allow them to win, often on a minority of the poll.[11] The party had not yet mobilised mass popular support in the rural districts of Ulster.

Gladstone made it clear after the Disestablishment Act of 1869 that he favoured land reform in Ireland. The result of this was the 1870 Land Act, which sought to extend the Ulster custom to the rest of Ireland. By introducing this Act the Liberals were abandoning the attempt to assimilate Irish agriculture to the British model.[12] Gladstone indicated that by this measure the ancient right of the Irish people to profit from the land they worked was being restored. It was also hoped that this Act would remove the root cause of Irish poverty which was commonly believed to be the tenants' lack of security of tenure.

The Act itself legalised the Ulster custom where it had existed before and gave legal support to similar practices in places where it had not existed. Under the Act, a tenant was allowed to sell his interest in his holding and receive compensation for improvements he had made to it and compensation if evicted in places where the custom had previously existed. Where it had not previously existed, tenants would receive compensation for improvements on giving up the farm and compensation if evicted. Land courts were set up to settle disputes between landlords and tenants over the terms of the Act. Very soon, however, the benefits of the Act were brought into question and a number of serious weaknesses were identified which were hampering the effectiveness of the legislation. The burden of proof lay with the tenant to prove tenancy was

[11] The Conservatives in Belfast were split over whether to field a working-class candidate, and neither of their official candidates was a Presbyterian. This allowed the Liberal Thomas McClure to gain one of the seats, despite attracting only 27 per cent of the total poll. See *Northern Whig*, 14 October 1868, 2 December 1868; also Walker, *Ulster Politics*, p. 60.

[12] See C. Dewey, 'Celtic Agrarian Legislation and the Celtic Revival: Historicist Implications of Gladstone's Irish and Scottish Land Acts 1870–1886', *Past and Present*, 64 (1974), pp. 30–70.

subject to the custom. This was an expensive and lengthly process, and one which a landlord would find easier to pay for than a tenant. The lack of pre-existing legal definition of the custom caused great confusion in the land courts.[13] Furthermore the compensation procedures were long and cumbersome and served to discourage the continuance of legal proceedings, the financial costs of defeat being an added anxiety. Disappointment with the feeble provisions of the Act was universal. In the wake of the passing of this measure some landlords began to raise rents, thus devaluing the Ulster custom.[14] This meant that life was even harder for tenants in some places, as the legal security afforded by the Act was not an effective substitute for traditionally low rents. However, in response to the landlords, a large number of tenant-right associations sprung up across rural Ulster and began agitating for further changes in the landowning system. This was to have far-reaching consequences for the political system as 'farmers who had begun to question the landlord's economic rights over them would be more likely than ever to resist his political influence'.[15]

II

The growth of tenant-right associations across rural Ulster was by no means uniform and could vary considerably from estate to estate. For example, enthusiastic tenant associations were formed in north Antrim at this time while tenants on a neighbouring estate to the south showed minimal activity.[16] However, the 1872 Ballot Act had generally increased the power of the tenant-right movement. In providing tenants with protection from intimidation at the poll, the Act 'enabled Irish electors to vote free from the influence of their landlords'[17] for the first time. However, at this time the measure was to have a more dramatic impact in the rest of Ireland than in Ulster. Northern Protestant farmers still recognised the right of landlords to own the land and profit from it. Nevertheless, even these tenants were beginning to take a more independent political line. The Liberals often used the new tenant-right associations to select candidates and it was through such organisations that the

---

[13] See P. Bew and F. Wright, 'The Agrarian Opposition in Ulster Politics 1848–1887', in S. Clark and J. S. Donnelly (eds.), *Irish Peasants: Violence and Political Unrest 1780–1914*, Manchester, 1983, pp. 201–3, for a critical evaluation of the 1870 Land Act.

[14] See T. MacKnight, *Ulster As It Is, or Twenty-Eight Years Experience as an Irish Editor*, 2 vols., London, 1896, vol. I, p. 262.

[15] J. Whyte, 'Landlord Influence at Elections in Ireland', *English Historical Review*, 80 (1965), p. 756.

[16] See McKeown, 'The Land Question', pp. 13–36.

[17] Whyte, 'Landlord Influence', p. 755.

party was to seriously challenge Conservative domination of political representation in rural Ulster at the 1874 general election.[18]

However, political developments in the early 1870s were not moving solely in the Liberals' direction. Nationalism was beginning to show signs of life in the north as it had already done in the rest of Ireland, a development which had devastated liberalism there. The Irish Catholic bishops were disappointed with Gladstone's proposals for the reform of education, which did not, in their view, give the church hierarchy sufficient control over the universities. The Liberal leader found it difficult to support state endowment of a Catholic university, the principle of state support of religion in Ireland having been weakened by the Disestablishment Act of 1869. The Catholic hierarchy shifted their support to Isaac Butt's home government movement, and this was crucial in determining the outcome of the 1874 election in Ireland. Outside of Ulster the Liberals collapsed from sixty-two to four seats, whilst the Nationalists captured fifty-eight seats.[19] Northern Catholics were also dissatisfied with the local Liberals' generally unsympathetic attitude to the issue of denominational schooling. This led to some Home Rule candidates standing against them. However, the general impression was one of 'little activity or organisation on the part of the supporters of home rule in Ulster'[20] in the early 1870s except in Cavan. This county elected the only Home Rulers in Ulster in 1874.

Despite disappointment with the 1870 Land Act in rural Ulster, local Liberals were cautious about the need for further land legislation. The danger arose that 'if the Liberals' position on the land question became indistinguishable from that of other candidates, their capacity to build up a coherent following would be severely diminished'.[21] Indeed at a by-election in Tyrone in 1873 an independent Conservative, rather than a Liberal, was adopted as a tenant-right candidate, and only narrowly lost. Cross-community support for this candidate was still strong at the general election the following year. A Catholic tenant-right group urged their co-religionists not to 'stand by with folded hands and apathetic hearts when your friends and neighbours are battling against landlord ascendancy'.[22] The Liberals reacted to the threat of Catholic desertion by integrating the newly formed tenant groups more closely into the party.

[18] The Antrim, Down and Londonderry tenant associations selected Liberal candidates for the 1874 election. See *Northern Whig*, 12 September 1873, 31 January 1874 and *Londonderry Sentinel*, 29 January 1874.
[19] See Walker, *Ulster Politics*, p. 114.
[20] P. Roebuck (ed.), *Plantation to Partition: Essays in Ulster History in Honour of J. L. McCracken*, Belfast, 1981, p. 203.
[21] Clark and Donnelly, *Irish Peasants*, p. 203.
[22] *Northern Whig*, 10 February 1874.

Through these groups the Liberals kept in touch with changes in tenant demands, and they also proved to be invaluable as organisers at election time.[23] Whether tenant-right associations were a reliable substitute for proper Liberal organisations is doubtful. Their support could well prove to be transitory, as events at Tyrone had suggested. Certainly the lack of strong Liberal associations, independent of tenant-right associations, was to affect the long-term survival of the party, especially in rural Ulster.

A national tenant-right conference was held in Belfast prior to the 1874 general election. The 1870 Act was condemned as inadequate and calls were made 'in favour of the ancient Ulster custom being extended to the whole of Ireland'.[24] With a view to the coming election, farmers were urged to elect representatives who supported these points.[25] Conservative candidates in general seriously underestimated the strength of feeling on the land issue and few of them pledged to support amendments to the 1870 Act. Most of the Liberal candidates supported the sentiments expressed at the conference. The Ulster Liberal Society looked to tenant-right associations for assistance in selecting candidates in Antrim, Down and Londonderry. They won one seat in Down and both Londonderry seats,[26] mainly because of the existence of sizeable Presbyterian electorates, although they were aided by the Conservatives having a poorly organised campaign. In Donegal the Liberals narrowly failed to capture a seat, despite the support of Catholic and Presbyterian clergy. Sentiment favourable to the British Liberal leader was strong; as a meeting in Letterkenny broke up, 'loud cheers for Gladstone and for prosperity for Ireland' were expressed.[27] In total, Liberals won six seats, mainly in rural Ulster, and this represented a serious breach into what had previously been a Conservative stronghold. Moreover, they held on to their solid support in the Catholic community, thanks largely to the lack of an organised Home Rule movement north of Cavan. The Ballot Act also made life easier for the Liberals, as tenants felt safer voting against their landlords' choice of MP. Disintegration of the traditional patterns of support was most evident in the rural western counties, although the party did poll well in some districts in east Ulster. The election of 1874 heralded the revival of liberalism in Ulster, being 'fuelled by ... discontent amongst tenant farmers about the limited benefits of Gladstone's land act of 1870'.[28]

---

[23] Tenant farmers were amongst the most prominent helpers of the Liberal Party Agent, C. H. Brett. See Public Record Office Northern Ireland, L'Estrange and Brett Papers, D1905/2/17A/5.

[24] *Weekly Northern Whig*, 24 January 1874.

[25] *Ibid.*

[26] Walker, *Ulster Politics*, pp. 104–5.

[27] *Northern Whig*, 31 January 1874.

[28] J. R. B. McMinn, *Against the Tide – A Calendar of the Papers of Reverend J. B. Armour, Irish Presbyterian Minister and Home Ruler 1869–1914*, Belfast, 1985, p. xxviii.

The borough elections of 1874 were fought on different issues to those of the counties, and the Liberals found it more difficult to find a platform that would unite their Presbyterian and Catholic supporters in sufficient numbers so as genuinely to threaten the Conservatives. The party did win the Dungannon seat with a Presbyterian candidate who was a major local employer and who appealed across the religious divide.[29] In constituencies where the opposition was united or where there were few Presbyterians, the Liberals made a poor showing.[30] Overall the results of this election showed that the character of Ulster liberalism had undergone an urban to rural transformation and success was built upon a much firmer electoral foundation. It was clear that 'under the new social pressures of the countryside the common political interest between landlords and tenants ... was breaking down. The Liberal Party, with its expanding organisation based on the tenant associations, now provided the political leadership for this new rising protest'.[31] After the election, the Ulster Liberal Society started work in the counties where the party had enjoyed most success in an attempt to solidify their achievements. They also formed Liberal organisations in other counties where they thought they could successfully compete in the future.[32]

Liberals continued to have a difficult relationship with their main body of supporters throughout the 1870s. Catholic politics had undergone considerable change throughout the nineteenth century: 'A cautious and even timid attitude towards government, the legacy of a long period of dependence on official toleration, gave way to an increasingly assertive defence of what were seen as Catholic interests ... the main use the Catholic church authorities made of their enhanced status was to press their claims in education matters'.[33] This had brought them into conflict with the mainly Presbyterian Liberals leaders, who were hostile to denominational schooling. Indeed the National Education League was formed by the leading Presbyterian Liberal Thomas Sinclair to promote a non-denominational educational system. The political relationship which had developed between Catholics and Presbyterians in the Liberal Party was based on a sense of common exclusion from political power. Hoppen has observed that 'many Presbyterians felt excluded by Church of Ireland toryism, while Catholics, in the absence of organised northern nationalism, had no one else to support'.[34]

---

[29] See Walker, *Ulster Politics*, p. 107.
[30] In Armagh and Enniskillen the Liberals failed to attract sufficient Protestant support and were confronted by a united Conservative Party. See *Armagh Guardian*, 30 January 1874 and *Impartial Reporter*, 19 February 1874.
[31] Walker, *Ulster Politics*, p. 116.
[32] *Ibid.*, p. 118.
[33] S. J. Connolly, *Religion and Society in Nineteenth Century Ireland*, Dundalk, 1985, p. 35.
[34] K. T. Hoppen, *Election, Politics and Society in Ireland 1832–1885*, Oxford, 1984, p. 265.

There was not only tension within the party over the education question, but also over the lack of Catholic Liberal candidates. The local party hierarchy 'had refused to accept Catholic Liberal candidates and also as a rule the Catholic clergy had accepted their wish as a price for defeating the Conservatives'.[35] To have a hope in any seat the Liberals needed to attract a significant level of nonconformist support. For example, when the Liberals contested a by-election in Newry in 1868 only 15 per cent of Presbyterians supported them, but this proved to be crucial in gaining the seat.[36] As a result the Liberals would often appeal to this portion of the electorate by selecting a Presbyterian candidate. There was considerable resentment within this community over their lack of representation within the Conservative Party, so Liberal moves in this direction were well calculated.[37] Although Presbyterian involvement in land agitation was largely driven by economic self-interest, 'the religious difference between [Anglican] landlords and many of their [Presbyterian] tenants was probably an additional element in the hostility'.[38] Therefore, in concentrating on the land question, Liberals further encouraged Presbyterian support.

III

Despite their success in rural Ulster in 1874 the party appeared to be facing several problems. Presbyterians were indicating their desire for more parliamentary representation but as yet they were not particularly concerned whether this was within the Conservative or Liberal party. At the same time Catholics, who were largely excluded from political office, were questioning whether supporting the Liberals was in their best interest. Local Liberals refused to change their hostile stance towards segregated education. As a consequence, they lost a by-election in Down in 1878, when many Catholic voters preferred to support a Conservative candidate who appeared sympathetic to their demands for Home Rule and education reform.[39] Although the rising importance of the land issue at the end of the decade was to allow the Liberals to consolidate their support at the next election, in the long term their inability to represent specifically Catholic interests was to have serious repercussions for their survival as an independent political party.

---

[35] P. A. E. Bew, *Land and the National Question in Ireland 1858–1882*, Dublin, 1979, p. 184.
[36] In this contest thirty Presbyterians supported the Liberal candidate, who won the seat by 386 votes to 373. The religion of voters was recorded in election poll books by a contemporary. See Gibbon, *Origins of Ulster Unionism*, p. 111.
[37] See Walker, *Ulster Politics*, p. 107.
[38] *Ibid.*, p. 20.
[39] *Ibid.*, pp. 124–5.

The Liberals' position on the land issue, although more conciliatory than that of the Conservatives, had remained at odds with that of tenant groups outside of Ulster. The southern land agitators' ultimate aim of removing landlordism contrasted sharply with the aims of Protestant farmers who wished to accommodate both the landlord and the tenant interest. Until the late 1870s 'there were in effect two agrarian movements in Ireland and sections of Ulster Catholics were refusing to support their northern agitation which seemed relevant neither to their condition nor to that of the island as a whole'.[40] However, by the turn of the decade, the Liberals had adopted a more radical land policy, not so much because Catholics in rural Ulster were threatening to desert them for the Nationalists but because an agricultural depression radicalised even the traditionally cautious Protestant tenants of Ulster. Local Conservatives failed to persuade their government that the political survival of the party in rural Ulster depended upon a rapid solution of the land question. With the conditions of the tenants rapidly declining, dissatisfaction in the rural community set the stage for the consolidation of changes to Ulster's electoral representation.

The difficult times which returned to rural Ireland in the late 1870s were caused by unusually severe winters, which resulted in poor crops, coupled with growing competition from foreign markets. These changes in market conditions came as a severe shock to tenant farmers who had enjoyed relative economic prosperity since the famine in the 1840s. Although all sections of the rural community were affected 'it was only the farmers who responded with large-scale collective action'.[41] Land courts had interpreted the provisions of the 1870 Act in a restrictive manner while landlords proved unwilling to offer much help to their tenants during the crisis. The depression was to radicalise tenants to such an extent that the years 1879 to 1881 marked 'the most effective undermining of landlord [political] hegemony in the north'.[42] Tenants began to combine in defence of their common interests, and by the early months of 1880 local tenant associations were calling for more fundamental reform than had previously been the case.

Although 'there was no equivalent of the land war in Ulster and agrarian crime was less evident ... distress ... was felt across the province and even large farmers had to draw upon their capital to survive'.[43] As a result of this economic downturn, by March 1880 20,000 people in

---

[40] Clark and Donnelly, *Irish Peasants*, p. 208.
[41] S. Clark, 'The Importance of Agrarian Classes: Agrarian Class Structure and Collective Action in Nineteenth Century Ireland', *British Journal of Sociology*, 29 (1978), p. 31.
[42] Clark and Donnelly, *Irish Peasants*, p. 194.
[43] D. G. Boyce, *Nineteenth Century Ireland: The Search for Stability*, Dublin, 1990, p. 194.

Ulster were receiving poor relief, an increase of 25 per cent in two years.[44] Pressure on the Liberals to move to a more advanced position on the land issue increased when the Land League began to organise in parts of the rural north. The league capitalised upon tenant dissatisfaction at levels of rent and evictions, and attracted considerable support from both Catholics and Protestants by ignoring the issue of Home Rule. Faced with this potentially serious threat to its support, the Liberals came to an understanding with the Land League which allowed the party to strengthen its support within the farming community. By then the party had 'adopted a programme more or less identical to that of certain farmers' clubs in Munster and Leinster'[45] and had 'outbidden the Conservatives by calling for the "3Fs" [and] the arbitration of rents'.[46] By abandoning their earlier caution the Liberals opened the way for large-scale political cooperation between rural Catholics and Presbyterians. This set the stage for considerable Liberal success at the forthcoming election.

IV

Levels of cross-denominational voting in by-elections, notably at Donegal in 1879[47] indicated that the Liberals' more advanced position on the issue of land was now enthusiastically endorsed by tenants of all denominations. Although this indicates that radical Presbyterian politics remained strong in nineteenth-century Ulster, this radicalism occurred within the context of support for the Union. Bew argues that liberalism gave 'the Protestant tenant farmers the means and opportunity to further their interests by independent action within the metropolitan political system of the United Kingdom'.[48] Presbyterian and Catholic cooperation on the land issue was only possible during periods when other more divisive issues, such as Home Rule, were put aside. Significantly, in drawing Catholics into participation in an all-Ireland struggle for land reform, the Land League had completed the first stage in integrating them fully into the body of Irish nationalism.

The results of the 1880 election were a considerable achievement for

---

[44] *Ibid.*

[45] Clark and Donnelly, *Irish Peasants*, p. 211.

[46] Boyce, *Nineteenth Century Ireland*, p. 195.

[47] The Donegal contest of 1879 indicated growing support for the Liberals within the Presbyterian community, while Catholic support remained solid. This enabled the party to win the seat by the considerable margin of 683 votes. See Walker, *Ulster Politics*, pp. 127–8.

[48] Clark and Donnelly, *Irish Peasants*, p. 193.

the Liberals and the basis of their success was the high level of cross-denominational voting. In Donegal and Monaghan the party campaigned almost exclusively on the issue of land. They received support from both Catholic and Presbyterian clergy and this allowed them to poll well in both these communities. Despite there being religious tension between elements of their support in Monaghan, the Liberals won both seats in both counties.[49] In Londonderry the party won both seats because of the presence of strong and effective local Liberal committees, aided by the Ulster Liberal Society.[50] The party was also helped by the local tenant-right associations and strong cooperation between Catholics and Presbyterians. With reference to the Londonderry contest, Harbinson, a local Catholic, commented that 'a considerable number of Catholics, knowing that the Presbyterians would stand by Mr McClure [himself a Presbyterian] acted so as to put Mr Law [another Liberal] foremost'.[51] The Conservatives faced problems in Armagh where the local party had split over whether or not to field a tenant-right candidate of their own. The Liberals took advantage, putting forward a Quaker tenant-right campaigner, and this allowed them to capture a seat in what was normally a strongly Tory area.[52] The Liberals' campaign here was also aided by the intervention of a local Catholic priest. At a meeting in Forkhill the local priest, 'though he seldom mixed in politics', expressed support for the Liberal candidate 'because he loved tenant-right'.[53] The party also captured a county seat in Tyrone where they were heavily dependent on Catholic support. In the same letter cited above, Harbinson commented: 'I am confident there was not a score of Catholics in Tyrone but plumped' for the Liberal candidate.[54] In Antrim and Down the Liberals were to be disappointed. They lost out by only twenty votes out of a poll of 7,000 in Down but sustained a more sizeable defeat in Antrim where the local Conservative Association ran a very efficient campaign. The high number of Belfast electors also came to the aid of the Conservatives in this constituency. Only the 'absence of a substantial Presbyterian vote in Fermanagh'[55] and a poor candidate prevented a Liberal success there. Overall it would appear that the Liberals captured almost all the support of rural Catholics, while they increased their strength considerably amongst Presbyterian tenants. On average they polled around 50 per cent of rural Presbyterians and in some areas this rose to as many as 70 per cent.[56]

---

[49] See Walker, *Ulster Politics*, p. 133.
[50] *Ibid.*, pp. 137–8.
[51] J. Harbinson to Lord O'Hagan, 25 April 1880: Public Record Office Northern Ireland, O'Hagan Papers, D2777/9/50/4.
[52] Walker, *Ulster Politics*, pp. 134–5.
[53] *Northern Whig*, 3 April 1880.
[54] Harbinson to O'Hagan, O'Hagan Papers, D2777/9/50/4.
[55] Walker, *Ulster Politics*, p. 137.
[56] *Ibid.*, pp. 143–4.

Party organisation had shown a dramatic improvement since 1874 and this contributed significantly to the high level of Liberal success in rural Ulster. An extensive canvass of the electorate took place and enthusiastic and well-attended public meetings were held to publicise the Liberal cause. However, the borough elections were a different matter. There the Conservative political machine was much superior to that of their opponents and the Belfast Liberal Association had collapsed in the aftermath of the disastrous performance in 1874. Belfast was one of the fastest-growing British cities in the nineteenth century. Its population grew from 19,000 in 1800 to 378,000 by 1911. The city's wealth and prestige 'gave [it] a newly dominant position not only in Ulster's economy but also in its politics and society'.[57] However, liberalism was only a minor political force in the city, a deeply disturbing state of affairs for the party. Although a Liberal committee was formed to help the party's candidate in Belfast, he still came bottom of the poll. The Liberals did hold on to the Dungannon seat, but only by the narrowest of margins, and after an appeal to an electoral court this too was lost. The failure of urban liberalism put a cloud over successes elsewhere. After the election an editorial in the *Northern Whig* pleaded: 'we want a new Liberal society in Belfast; we want active Liberal societies in the various boroughs'.[58] This plea was to fall on deaf ears. Far from extending its influence into the cities in the coming years, the party was to face a serious challenge to its position in rural Ulster.

The 1880 election had inaugurated a peaceful revolution in the Ulster countryside. Landlordism as a political force had been destroyed by cooperation between rural Presbyterians and Catholics. The Ulster Liberals had a strong political mandate to press Gladstone for more substantial land reform. After the election Gladstone, under pressure from local Liberals, became more sympathetic towards further land legislation. However, rising expectations of reform were 'seriously checked by the defeat of the [tenant] compensation bill in the Lords in August 1880'.[59] As a result, a new Land League campaign in Ulster received 'support not only from Catholic tenants, but also to a degree which surprised and alarmed the landlord classes, from Protestant tenants as well'.[60] While Protestants did not join the League in great numbers they 'did tolerate it and ... conceded to it a certain ambiguous sympathy'.[61]

---

[57] A. C. Hepburn (ed.), *Minorities in History*, London, 1978, p. 84.
[58] *Northern Whig*, 17 April 1880.
[59] F. Thompson, 'Attitudes to Reform: Political Parties in Ulster and the Irish Land Bill of 1881', *Irish Historical Studies*, 24 (1985), p. 330.
[60] *Ibid.*
[61] P. J. Drudy (ed.), *Ireland: Land, Politics and People*, Cambridge, 1982, p. 83.

Despite this intervention by the league, for a short time Liberals continued to be the main beneficiaries of rural unrest. However, they had to distance themselves from the Liberal government's policy of coercion to retain Catholic support. This enabled the party to win a by-election in Tyrone in 1881 despite the late intervention of the Home Rule candidate. There was joy in the non-Nationalist press which perceived this result as a political setback for Parnellism in the north. The return of a Liberal MP in this county in a by-election was further evidence of the decline of the appeal of conservatism in rural Ulster. One such Tory, on observing the level of inter-denominational voting, lamented: 'it is too bad that what was once called Protestant Tyrone could not return a Conservative member ... I believe numbers of Orangemen voted against their grand-master. The fact is the Protestants as well as Roman Catholics do not want an Orangeman or even a Fenian if he is a gentleman or a landlord.'[62]

V

Despite coming under pressure from some colleagues, most notably Bright, to resolve the Irish land question by way of state-aided land purchase, Gladstone decided to introduce the concept of dual ownership of land as well as dealing with levels of rent and eviction. The 1881 Act set up an 'independent commission ... to determine equitable rents in disputed cases; tenants paying such rents would be secure from eviction; and the tenant was given the right to sell his interest in his holding with only a minimum of reference to his landlord'.[63] British Tories bitterly opposed the 1881 Land Act as they regarded its provisions as confiscatory. By contrast, Conservatives in Ulster took a markedly different attitude. While they opposed those parts of the bill they felt impinged on their interests, they were careful not to oppose the measure in principle. Indeed thirteen out of eighteen Ulster Conservative MPs supported the bill at second reading in parliament. Their actions kept open a possible *rapprochement* with northern Protestant tenants which would allow them to reassert their political dominance in rural Ulster. The 1881 Land Act was extremely popular amongst northern Protestant tenants and many of them flocked to the land courts as soon as they were set up to have their rents reduced.[64] The Chief Secretary for Ireland saw the Act as a counterbalance to the coercion which had been introduced the previous

---

[62] James Crossle to Sir William Verner, 8 September 1881: Public Record Office Northern Ireland, Verner Papers, D236/488/2/p. 232.
[63] Boyce, *Nineteenth Century Ireland*, p. 170.
[64] H. C. G. Matthew, Introduction, *The Gladstone Diaries*, vol. x, *1881–1885*, Oxford, 1990, p. cxviii.

summer. In response to agrarian crimes committed by the Land League the government banned this organisation and gave the police the power to detain without trial those suspected of using violence or intimidation for political ends. Included in the round-up was Parnell, the leader of the Irish parliamentary party, who was put in Kilmainham jail. This set off a wave of unrest across the south and west of Ireland which helped to poison the political atmosphere in the island.

Parnell complained that the Ulster Liberals had played little part in agitating for the Act, yet had been the first to take advantage of it. However, the party had consistently pressed Gladstone for land reform. Indeed the Act 'implemented almost exactly the same programme on which they [the Ulster Liberals] had been campaigning for much of the last decade',[65] and consequently it was a source of justifiable pride for the party. Once the Act took effect, in Ulster there was a diminution of serious conflict between landlords and tenants. Better harvests in the following years also helped take the edge off agrarian radicalism. In removing the worst grievances suffered by northern farmers, the Act removed the need for Protestant tenants to cooperate with their southern counterparts. Indeed, Bew argues that the Act was 'a concession to the tenants so as to detach them from the league'.[66] Northern Protestants were to part company with the league when more extreme land policies were introduced. Catholic tenants believed the final solution to the land problem should see the removal of landlords from the countryside, whereas Protestant tenants continued to support the system of dual ownership of land by both landlord and tenant which was the central principle of the 1881 Act.

VI

The gap between Protestant and Catholic tenants was widened by the closer identification of the land movement with the cause of Home Rule. As the land campaign now appeared to have run out of steam, Parnell began pressing for Irish self-government. A contemporary noted: 'in the north there has been a considerable change in the feelings of the better class of Liberal Presbyterians since the Kilmainham treaty and the Dublin assassinations ... there seems to be a growing feeling that the policy of the Nationalist Party is to stamp out the English garrison and make Ireland a purely Roman Catholic country'.[67] Many Protestants feared that under Home Rule the Nationalists would force them to leave

---

[65] Thompson, 'Attitudes to Reform', p. 327.
[66] Bew, *Land and the National Question*, p. 157.
[67] Sir Thomas Bateson to Lord Salisbury, June 1882. Quoted in Bardon, *A History of Ulster*, p. 371.

Ireland. The Conservatives now focused attention on the threat posed to the Union by the newly formed and more militant Irish National League. The Orange Order was used to confront the league's advance across the north and 'a landlord defence association ... drew together both Protestant landlords and tenants and began to undo the work of the [Liberals] in maintaining a multi-denominational organisation'.[68]

The emergence of the Irish National League, which replaced the banned Land League, was to integrate northern Catholic tenants more closely into the Home Rule movement. By-elections from the mid-1880s on show a marked decline in levels of cross-denominational voting. The potential for a new political realignment now existed, with a Conservative Party appealing to Protestant fears about the future of the Union squaring up to a Nationalist Party which was extending its interests northwards. At the same time 'the Liberal Party's concentration upon tenant-right had suddenly lost its momentum, as Protestant tenants decided they had gained all they were likely to win from Gladstone'.[69] Consequently the Liberals were gradually squeezed to the margins of the political scene. In this respect the Monaghan by-election of 1883 was a significant turning-point in Ulster political history. It marked the beginning of the end of the Liberals as a political force in rural Ulster, and the beginning of the Nationalist invasion of the north. The inspiration behind the invasion was the circumstances surrounding the Nationalist defeat in Tyrone in 1881. Loughlin argues: 'the exultant coverage it received in the English press led [Parnell] to favour the wild demonstrations that took place during the invasion of Ulster in winter of 1883–4'.[70] Such demonstrations of Irish Nationalist fervour served to increase Protestant concern that their British citizenship was under grave threat.

Irish nationalism had developed very slowly in Monaghan with only one branch of the Land League being active by late 1882. Nevertheless, when the by-election was called, Parnell urged local Catholics to desist from pledging support to any candidate until a suitable one had been selected. Eventually one of the best-known Nationalists, Tim Healy, was chosen by local Catholics to contest the seat. During the campaign the Nationalists stressed Healy's credentials as a land reformer, and he was favourably associated with the progressive clauses of the 1881 Act. This allowed him to attract considerable support from local Presbyterians. Relations between the Liberals and local Catholics were at an all-time

[68] J. Loughlin, *Gladstone, Home Rule and the Ulster Question 1882–1893*, Dublin, 1986, p. 124.
[69] S. Gribbon, 'The Social Origins of Ulster Unionism', *Irish Economic and Social History*, 4 (1977), p. 67.
[70] Loughlin, *Gladstone*, p. 124.

low because of the government's policy of coercion in Ireland. This combination of an unpopular Liberal Party facing a Nationalist candidate who had widespread appeal across the community was to result in one of the most stunning by-election reversals for a government candidate in Irish political history. The Liberals slumped to just 6 per cent of the poll in a seat they had captured three years before. Parnell was exultant at the size of his victory while the Liberals were demoralised by the crushing nature of their defeat. With 'Home Rulers raising the hopes of Catholics … the future of the Liberals was bleak indeed'.[71]

To cope at the next general election, which was to be contested with a greatly expanded electorate, all the parties needed to update their party structure. Active local associations were needed, as were experienced agents who would carry on with the vital work of revising the election register. The National League moved into Catholic areas of the north and established constituency organisations. Nationalist election agents also began to appear. Some of these had been agents for the Liberals, notably in Monaghan and Dungannon. Magee indicates that 'branches of the Irish National League were established in Catholic areas of Fermanagh, Tyrone, Derry, south Armagh, south Down; enthusiasm was generated by the visits of charismatic figures … [and] greater attention was given to the registration of voters'.[72] During 1885 Parnell was to turn the Irish Parliamentary party into a tightly disciplined political force. The National League was used to control the selection of candidates, and in October 1885 Parnell announced that Home Rule would be the sole issue during the election. This demand appealed across all classes and enabled the party to appeal to large and small farmers as well as labourers. In this way agrarian radicals within the movement were marginalised. Parnell moved to nullify another possible source of division within the Catholic community. In the summer of 1885 he adopted the church hierarchy's views on higher education in return for their support for Home Rule. He also gave the clergy the right to attend conventions which selected Nationalist candidates. These developments were to increase Protestant concern about the influence of the Catholic church in Ireland under any Home Rule settlement.

The development of nationalist politics in the north did not go unnoticed in the Protestant community. The Orange Order strongly resisted the invasion of Ulster. The result 'was a series of demonstrations, counter-demonstrations, riots and disturbances so that over the next three years attitudes hardened [and] politics polarised'[73] especially in

---

[71] J. Magee, 'The Monaghan Election of 1883 and the Invasion of Ulster', *Clogher Record*, 22 (1974), p. 157.
[72] *Ibid.*, p. 165.
[73] F. Thompson, 'The Armagh Elections of 1885–6', *Seanchas Ard Mhacha* (the journal of the Armagh diocesan historical society), 9 (1977), p. 360.

rural areas of Ulster. The landlord element within the northern Protestant community now 'saw the sense of the [Orange] Order's advice to meet tenant demands as far as possible and thus prepare the way for a united Protestant ... front against the assault of Irish nationalism of which they believed the Land League was the vanguard'.[74] With the growth of Irish nationalism presenting a serious threat to the Union, Protestant tenants increasingly favoured the robustly unionist Conservatives over the more restrained Liberals. In remote rural areas, the very places where the Liberals were strongest in 1880, support for the party rapidly disintegrated as Catholic tenants and some leading officials switched allegiance to the Nationalists. Also with local 'conservatives and liberals ... approaching agreement on the principle on which the land problem could be resolved',[75] land ceased to be an issue on which the Liberals could exploit differences between themselves and the Conservatives.

By contrast, support for the Liberals held up in parts of east Ulster for a period. The party polled well in a by-election in Down in 1884 and the following year won a seat in Antrim for the first time with a Presbyterian candidate whose opposition to coercion retained his appeal to Catholic tenants. It appeared that 'Presbyterians in west and south Ulster abandoned the [Liberals] at an early stage, as the agrarian campaign became increasingly bound up with Nationalist political advance. The Presbyterian tenant farmers of the securely Protestant north east ... remained loyal much longer to the Liberal cause'.[76]

However, even this support would be adversely affected by the Conservatives exploiting class tension between the newly enfranchised agricultural labourers and their tenant-farmer employers. Agricultural labourers had traditionally regarded the larger farmer with hostility. They were critical of the large farmer who 'claimed fair rent and fixity of tenure for his farm ... [but] refused to share any benefits or allow equal privileges to his [labourer] employee'.[77] For example, the Liberal MP for Londonderry was criticised by labourers for not supporting a bill which would have extended the benefits of the 1881 Land Act to leasehold and townpark tenants.[78] In fact, the labourer 'had no interest in tenant-right and often got better wages and conditions when employed directly by landlords'.[79] Attempts by the Orange Order to 'integrate labourers'

[74] Boyce, *Nineteenth Century Ireland*, pp. 196–7.
[75] Thompson, 'Armagh Elections', p. 370.
[76] Connolly, *Religion and Society*, p. 34.
[77] Gibbon, *Origins of Ulster Unionism*, p. 117.
[78] *Londonderry Standard*, 1 October 1885.
[79] Bardon, *A History of Ulster*, p. 375.

resentment against farmers with opposition to the league'[80] worked successfully for the Conservatives. One of the local Conservative leaders commented that in the aftermath of the franchise reforms the Protestant labourers controlled 'the representation of all the non-nationalist seats in Ulster. The farmers are really nowhere'.[81] Although tension between landlords and tenants in rural Ulster was to survive the political developments of the early 1880s, a more fundamental political cleavage around the question of the Union was emerging.

The Liberals remained organisationally weak up to the next election and were able to fight the Conservatives effectively in only a few constituencies. Urban liberalism remained particularly weak, despite the new hope engendered by the opening of the Ulster Reform Club in Belfast in 1885.[82] Structural changes in the electorate had presented a serious challenge to an already lethargic Liberal Party. The 1883 Corrupt Practices Act restricted the amount of money a candidate could spend. This made any potential candidate reliant upon a strong party machine. The 1884 Franchise Act introduced a general adult male household suffrage. Many agricultural labourers and small farmers were enfranchised and now formed a significant part of an electorate which had expanded by between three and fourfold. The Liberals' reaction to these changes reflected a surprising lack of faith in the electorate, and pessimism about their political prospects: 'The Bill, of course, when passed will take power from the more respectable tenant farmers and give it to the agricultural labourers, who for the most part in the Ulster counties are either Nationalists or Orangemen ... the old Ulster Liberals will suffer most.'[83] Further changes were brought by the 1885 Redistribution Act which redrew Ulster's constituency boundaries. Most of the small boroughs were to disappear and the counties were divided up into more even electoral units. Due to such changes, the Liberals were projected to lose six of the nine seats they currently held.

The Conservatives reorganised their local associations and brought both rural and urban Protestant labourers into the party through the Orange Order. Liberals in Belfast did make some attempt to incorporate the newly enfranchised into their organisation. The Belfast Liberal Association attempted to organise at ward level and to create an infra-

---

[80] Clark and Donnelly, *Irish Peasants*, p. 223.
[81] Lord Deramore to the Marquis of Salisbury, 29 April 1887. Cited in Walker, *Ulster Politics*, p. 222.
[82] The Liberal candidates polled less than 13 per cent of the poll in East Belfast and only 18 per cent in South Belfast at the 1885 general election. See *Weekly Northern Whig*, 5 December 1885.
[83] MacKnight, *Ulster As It Is*, vol. II, p. 56.

structure of registration and electoral societies in the main districts. They also formed a working men's association. However, at the first meeting of this body in October 1885, 'the platform was dominated by the Liberal bourgeois; the speakers were all employers, and the speeches concentrated on general Liberal principles with no reference to specifically working-class economic or social grievances'.[84] Liberal 'radicalism' was confined to references to the proud Liberal record on the land question, hardly the most relevant issue in an urban constituency.

VII

The 1885 election was to be the nadir of Liberal performance in Ulster politics, the party losing all the seats it held prior to dissolution. The most important issue of the election was undoubtedly the Union. Land ceased to dominate political debate even in rural Ulster. The Liberals fought the election on support for the Union and for further land reform, but, following the Ashbourne Act,[85] there was little difference between the Liberals' position and the Conservatives on either of these questions. The Liberals had failed to meet the challenge of an expanding electorate. The Ulster Reform Club 'failed to provide the central organisation for the Liberals that had been envisaged'.[86] Local party organisations were not prepared to carry out the necessary amount of registration work, preferring to leave it to a few individuals who were swamped by the vastly increased size of the electorate. The *Witness* commented in the aftermath of the election: 'with the exception of four or five county divisions in Ulster the Liberals gave themselves no trouble about the registry and suffered matters to tide on without any guidance or judgement [and] to go by default'.[87] The party was too closely tied to tenant-right associations and failed to appeal to agricultural labourers, arguing that nothing could be done to address their grievances until the farmers' problems were resolved.

The Liberals also suffered because their opponents conspired together to oust them from political representation in Ulster. Because of the Liberal government's policy of coercion, Parnell urged northern Catholics to support the Conservatives in contests where there was no Home Rule candidate unless local Liberals submitted to his demands.[88] For

---

[84] H. Patterson, *Class Conflict and Sectarianism: The Protestant Working Class and the Belfast Labour Movement 1868–1920*, Belfast, 1980, p. 15.

[85] The Ashbourne Act was a measure of land purchase introduced to Ireland by the Conservative administration in the summer of 1885.

[86] Walker, *Ulster Politics*, p. 192.

[87] *Witness*, 18 December 1885.

[88] See *Weekly Northern Whig*, 28 November 1885.

example, in the County Down contests he indicated that if 'the three Whig candidates there would pledge themselves to oppose coercion on all occasions ... it might be best for our friends to vote with them'.[89] The decision of Catholics to abstain or support Conservatives was crucial in as many as six divisions. A local Nationalist newspaper attempted to explain why Catholics had now deserted the Liberals; the defeat of a Liberal candidate in Mid Antrim would not have occurred 'but for the treachery of the Whigs of West Belfast and Derry city'.[90] Parnell's demands that the Liberals oppose coercion and support Nationalists rather than Conservatives in certain constituencies were impossible for the Unionist-minded Liberals to countenance. The well-organised Nationalist Party took advantage of the increased proportion of Catholic electors to maximise their number of MPs. They also showed good tactical awareness by targeting resources at seats they could win. The support of rural Catholic labourers and small and large farmers allowed the Nationalists to virtually monopolise political representation in south and west Ulster.

The 1885 election produced for the first time a clear Nationalist–Unionist politics linked to a Protestant–Catholic division. There was a high degree of religious polarisation in terms of how votes were cast. Excluding those who voted Conservative for purely tactical reasons, nearly all Catholics supported Home Rule candidates while most Protestants supported the Conservatives and in lesser numbers the Liberals.[91] In an atmosphere of heightened sectarian tension cross-denominational voting effectively disappeared. Such a phenomenon only existed so long as Catholics needed the support of Presbyterians to oust Conservatives who were hostile to land reform. McGimpsey comments: 'once this interdependence was disturbed by changes in relative electoral strength the dissolution of the alliance was inevitable'.[92] A parliamentary report of 1885 had indicated that after the franchise reforms half the seats of Ulster had a Catholic majority and the Nationalists duly won a narrow majority of seats in Ulster.[93]

The period between 1870 and 1885 saw the effective undermining of the political power of the landowning class in Ulster. While 'landlords

---

[89] *Ibid.*

[90] *Belfast Morning News*, 4 December 1885.

[91] See P. Collins (ed.), *Nationalism and Unionism: Conflict in Ireland 1885–1921*, Belfast, 1994, p. 7.

[92] C. D. McGimpsey, 'To Raise the Banner in the Remote North: Politics in County Monaghan 1868–1883', Edinburgh University, unpublished Ph.D. thesis, 1982, p. 499.

[93] Nationalists won seventeen out of thirty-three seats in Ulster, and every seat in the rest of Ireland except the university seats at Trinity College. See B. M. Walker, *Parliamentary Election Results in Ireland, 1801–1922*, Dublin, 1978, pp. 130–36.

still retained prominent positions ... in local affairs generally ... the extent of their dominance had been irrevocably questioned by the farmers, Catholic and Protestant, who had developed a new political and social consciousness of their own ... thanks to the agrarian issue'.[94] During its period of success, 'rural liberalism created an alliance between large Protestant tenant farmers, Protestant ... professionals and the Catholic rural middle class'.[95] However, these groups gave the Liberals only transitory support. The professional classes had a tendency to pick their politics according to what patronage was on offer,[96] while the political 'invasion' of Ulster by the Nationalists transformed the aspirations of rural Catholics. The Liberals failed to cope effectively with the challenge of populist Catholic nationalism, and the emergence of Home Rule as the dominant issue in Ulster politics allowed the Conservatives to appear once again as the defenders of the Protestant cause in Ireland. Liberal rhetoric about land reform did not appeal to the newly enfranchised elements in the electorate. By contrast, the Conservatives, in a process of internal democratisation, had successfully integrated large numbers of Protestant labourers into their party and their support was crucial in what proved to be a watershed election.

VIII

At the 1885 election the Conservatives emerged as the clear leaders of unionism in Ulster, winning sixteen seats, including those of two Independents who were later incorporated into the party. Calls had been made for the Conservatives and Liberals to unite their forces against the Nationalist threat, and in the aftermath of Gladstone's conversion to Home Rule such calls proved irresistible. Ulster liberalism, disillusioned by the 'apostasy' of Gladstone, was to disappear as an independent political force for a generation, as former Liberals allied themselves with the Conservatives in the fight against Home Rule.[97] The agrarian tension which the Liberals successfully harnessed to transform the Ulster political landscape between 1870 and 1885 did not disappear altogether for the 'Ulster Protestant, with his tendency to follow his own line come what may, was an individual not easy to gather into, or keep within, a broad united political front'.[98] Evidence of this was the continuing tension which existed between Liberal Unionists and Conservatives in Ulster,

[94] Clark and Donnelly, *Irish Peasants*, p. 252.
[95] Gibbon, *Origins of Ulster Unionism*, p. 108.
[96] *Ibid.*, p. 117.
[97] The Ulster Liberal Party disappeared from the political landscape until 1906 when it was revived following the British Liberals' return to power in that year.
[98] Boyce, *Nineteenth Century Ireland*, p. 201.

and the radical demands made by dissatisfied tenant groups during the long periods of Unionist government after 1886.

The Liberal Party in Ulster believed that by bringing together rural Catholics and Protestants to campaign for common economic rights the deep divisions in Irish society could be healed and Ireland could be reconciled to the Union. It was on this premiss that their political appeal to rural tenants was based. However, this failed to take into account the possibility that Protestant and Catholic tenants had very different ideas about the ultimate aims of the land reform movement. Protestants regarded land reform solely in terms of their own economic interests and were often 'unwilling to engage in any politics which did not appear to promise a direct advance of their immediate interest'.[99] For Catholics, land was a highly symbolic battleground. They regarded the land movement not merely in terms of an economic problem to be resolved but also as a political crusade to dismantle the political system which had developed out of the landowning class, a system which had excluded them from political power. For Nationalists the removal of political power from religious and landowning elites in the 1860s and 1870s was a preparation for native self-rule. The Liberals were powerless when faced with Catholic demands for Home Rule. Most local Liberal leaders were businessmen for whom unhindered access to British markets was central to their economic prosperity. It was inconceivable that they could support such a dramatic change of policy as Gladstone announced at the end of 1885.

The Liberals were now effectively unable to appeal to rural Catholic tenants, who had been the mainstay of their support. On the other hand, they remained attached to the old tenant-right rhetoric to the extent that they were unable to produce an alternative programme which could appeal to the newly enfranchised agricultural labourers. Yet, as Nigel Scotland has shown,[100] gaining the farmworkers' support was the only way forward for the Liberal Party in the counties. But in Ulster, the future of the Union with Britain now dominated the political debate within the Protestant community. As pressure grew for a united campaign against Nationalist encroachment, the Liberals were forced into a political alliance with their former enemies. The dramatic decline in political fortunes experienced by the Ulster Liberals in the early 1880s can be attributed to the extension of Nationalists politics into the Catholic community of Ulster and the reaction this provoked within the northern Protestant community.

[99] Gibbon, *Origins of Ulster Unionism*, p. 117.
[100] See chapter 6, above.

11 Nationalising the ideal: Labour and nationalism in Ireland, 1909–1923

Claire Fitzpatrick

We have, therefore, in Ireland, three revolutionary movements – political, industrial and agrarian – actuated by one immediate common purpose – the establishment of Irish independence, although differing in their ultimate aims. Such divergences would probably manifest themselves in an independent Ireland in a disruption of society. But for the moment and from the standpoint of national and imperial safety, these revolutionary movements must be regarded as one.[1]

Such was the conclusion drawn by an anonymous commentator in a pamphlet entitled *Ireland and International Revolution*, in 1921. The writer pointed out that Irish radicalism was coordinated through three groups: Sinn Féin, Revolutionary Labour, centred on the Irish Trades Union Congress (ITUC) and a 'sporadic agrarian movement'. For the casual observer of the Irish scene, the confusion within the nature of Irish radicalism was great. In many cases the sporadic agrarian movement was coordinated by the labour movement and at other times by the republican movement, but often times it clashed with both. This chapter is concerned with conflict within Irish radicalism, which centred on the relations between Sinn Féin, which had come to steer the nationalist movement, and the Irish labour movement. It focuses on the struggle of Irish Labour to deal with the over-riding nationalist movement, whose radicalism was fast giving way to rise of a conservative nature.

I

The development of the labour movement in the south of Ireland had been a long, slow process. Irish trade unions were predominantly skilled and were dominated by the great British unions. Impoverished labourers had little influence. The leadership was one of 'uncompromising hardhatted respectability'. The ITUC, established in 1894, was the embodiment of this rather respectable and socially conservative 'labour aristocracy'. It has been referred to as the Irish version of 'Lib–Lab'

---

[1] National Library of Ireland pamphlet, *Ireland and International Revolution*, 1921, pp. 7–8.

reformism, and unskilled representation was limited.[2] The organisation of unskilled workers had been tried but was unsuccessful. The spread of British-based unions was the main concern until the foundation of the Irish Transport and General Workers Union (ITGWU) in 1909, when the serious work of organising Irish trade unions began.

By contrast, in the north-east of Ireland, labour politics had been developing at a rapid speed and along other lines. By the turn of the century, Belfast was the dominant centre of trade unionism and labour politics.[3] The trades councils were politically active both at municipal and parliamentary level. Indeed the Belfast United Trades Council, which later became the Belfast and District Trades Union Council, was presenting itself as a viable alternative to the political parties and the basis had been 'laid for future independent working class activity in the city and a break with the idea that workers must be dependent on Tory or Liberal representatives to speak their interests'.[4]

Furthermore, Ireland had a young socialist tradition which was primarily in line with the Marxist social democratic position. At that time, most intellectual and theoretical discussion was articulated within the confines of the wider international socialist movement, then the Second International. Locally, however, politics remained restricted to practical trade union concerns.[5] The arrival of James Connolly in 1895 to form the Irish Socialist Republican Party (ISRP) saw the development of a specifically Irish Marxist doctrine. For Connolly linked socialism with the national question. In a sense the main dilemma of the Irish labour movement can be found in Connolly's claim that 'the cause of Labour is the cause of Ireland, the cause of Ireland is the cause of labour'. He argued that the fight for socialism was a fight for national self-determination. On this point he was at odds with most of the British and continental socialists, and indeed Connolly's main complaint with the Second International, to which the ISRP was affiliated in 1900, concerned the national question. Connolly believed a certain 'false internationalism',

---

[2] C. McCarthy, *Trade Unions In Ireland*, Dublin, 1972, p. 5.

[3] For the history of labour politics in Belfast see: A. Morgan, *Labour and Partition: The Formation of the Belfast Working Class*, London, 1991; H. Patterson, 'Industrial Labour and the Labour Movement, 1820–1914', in L. Kennedy and P. Olleranshaw (ed.), *An Economic History of Ulster, 1820–1939*, Manchester, 1985, and H. Patterson, *Class Conflict and Sectarianism*, Belfast, 1980.

[4] *Belfast and District Trades Union Council, 1881–1951: A Short History*, 70th Anniversary Souvenir, Belfast, 1951, p. 4.

[5] For history of the early labour movement in Ireland, see: J. W. Boyle, *The Irish Labor Movement in the Nineteenth Century*, Washington, D. C., 1989; F. A. D'Arcy and K. Hanningan (eds.), *Workers in Union*, Dublin, 1989, and E. O'Connor, *A Labour History of Ireland, 1860–1960*, Dublin, 1992, which also contains bibliographical details for the earlier period.

which engendered as identification with England, permeated the social-
ists' vision and accounted for the failure of the growth of socialism in
Ireland. It was on this point that Connolly would take the Second
International to task at the Congress in 1902.[6]

Otherwise the ISRP developed a programme loosely based on that of
the Social Democratic Federation (SDF) in Britain.[7] It is fair to say that
Connolly had no primary interest in trade unionism, when he arrived
in Ireland: his concern was the promotion of socialist ideology and
independence, and the programme of the ISRP made no mention of
trade unionism or its demands. Instead, it advocated the establishment
of an Irish socialist republic 'and the consequent conversion of the means
of production, distribution and exchange into the common property of
society, to be held and controlled by a democratic state in the interests of
the entire community'.[8] The very limited appeal of this programme is
confirmed by the fact that the ISRP was disbanded in 1903 and Connolly
went to the United States where he became involved with Daniel De
Leon and was exposed to the intricate workings and ideas of industrial
unionism and syndicalism.

The divide between Connolly and 'Belfast socialism' could not have
been deeper, and brought to light the contentious issue which thwarted
any attempt to create a unified labour movement – nationalism versus
internationalism. The Belfast movement was more attuned to the British
labour movement both politically, with a branch of the Independent
Labour Party (ILP) being established in 1893, and industrially, with a
predominance of British-based unions. As William McMullen, recalled,
'we were nurtured on the British brand of socialist propaganda and all the
literature we read, as well as our speakers, were imported from Great
Britain'.[9] He believed that Belfast socialists saw themselves 'as being part
of a vast international socialist movement' and nationalism was not
regarded as an integral part of socialism: 'Our school of thought had no
nationalist tradition, and was not conscious of, and even if it had been
would have been contemptuous, of a social movement in any other part
of this country.'[10] Moreover, the policy of republicanism presented problems to socialists such as McMullen, who contended that 'it was difficult

---

[6] See A. Morgan, *James Connolly: A Political Biography*, Manchester, 1989, pp. 41–2 and
for background to the whole debate see J. Joll, *The Second International, 1889–1914*,
London, 1974, p. 76.
[7] The programme of the ISRP is reproduced in J. Connolly, *Socialism and Nationalism*, (ed.
D. Ryan), Dublin, 1948, p. 184.
[8] *Ibid.*, pp. 184–5.
[9] W. McMullen, cited in introduction to J. Connolly, *The Workers' Republic*, (ed. D. Ryan),
Dublin, 1951, p. 1.
[10] *Ibid.*, p. 2.

enough to break with Unionist family tradition and embrace socialism, but much more difficult to swallow the hook, line and sinker of Irish republicanism as well'.[11]

Despite the 1907 upsurge in trade union militancy – culminating in the dock strike[12] – the working class in Belfast remained influenced by strong Conservative and Orange affiliations,[13] with its previous history of intra-Protestant conflict within a national context in which labour organisations and conflict were Belfast matters.[14] Orangeism was an integral part of the Protestant workers' way of life, and the working class was an integral part of Orangeism. Indeed, the working class was ruled by a form of Protestant ascendancy, and the values which were nurtured cut across class lines.

Despite his acquaintance with north-east Ulster, Connolly remained convinced that conditions were conducive to the establishment and subsequent active role of a socialist party. With this goal in mind, he planned to inject the Irish labour movement with the politics of industrial unionism he had developed during his time in the USA. While working for the establishment of a strong union and indeed the development of one big union for Ireland and Britain, Connolly aimed at establishing a separate political party. Apparently he did not think that these aims were contradictory. With this goal in mind he established the Socialist Party of Ireland (SPI), with its explicit aim of common ownership of the means of production and distribution of wealth. Its strategy was based on the 'political organisation at the ballot box, to secure the election of representatives of Socialist principles to all the elective governing Public Bodies of this country', and the gradual transference of the political power of the state 'into the hands of those who will use it to further and extend the principle of common or public ownership'.[15] It would give the working class direction but the unions would remain the essential industrial and financial base. In this way, syndicalism and nationalism were deemed compatible, as Connolly argued that whilst the economies of Britain and Ireland would be linked, the political systems would be completely separate.

Given his rather unrealistic interpretation of the aspirations of the labour movement in the north, it is not surprising that Connolly soon

[11] *Ibid.*, p. 4.
[12] See J. Gray, *City in Revolt: James Larkin and the Belfast Dock Strike of 1907*, Belfast, 1985, and E. Larkin, *James Larkin: Irish Labour Leader*, Manchester, 1965.
[13] The following section relies heavily on the work of Patterson, *Class Conflict and Sectarianism* and P. Gibbon, *The Origins of Ulster Unionism*, Manchester, 1975.
[14] Patterson, *Class Conflict and Sectarianism*, p. 143.
[15] The programme of the Socialist Party of Ireland is reproduced in Connolly, *Socialism and Nationalism*, p. 191.

clashed with the leading exponent of socialism in Belfast. At one ITUC conference held in Galway in 1910 a motion calling for the establishment of an Irish Labour Party was defeated when William Walker moved an amendment which held that the only way to secure independent labour representation was to affiliate with the British Labour Party.[16] Walker, one time president of the ITUC, and a Protestant who saw his religion as being synonymous with socialism, was against Independent Catholic political representation and Home Rule. He insisted on the internationalist aspect of the ILP and emphasised that 'my place of birth was accidental, but my duty to my class is worldwide, hence MY INTERNATIONALISM!'[17] Walker's argument reinforced his reformist approach and reaffirmed the goal of working for socialism in the British labourist sense:

The ILP have enabled the Irish in Belfast to unite. James Connolly (Catholic) can – thanks to the spade work of the ILP – come to Belfast and speak to audiences mainly Protestant, and be patiently heard, and it is curious that our Comrade never came to Belfast until he was confident that the ILP had won a tolerant hearing for all classes; and if this can be accomplished in Belfast, what is to prevent the other parts of Ireland from using the same organisation to accomplish all those reforms which – whether we YELL for Socialism or WORK for it – are claimant for adoption.[18]

Eventually an independent Labour Party of Ireland was founded in Clonmel in 1912 but the tensions remained unresolved, and indeed grew deeper after Larkin's defeat in the Dublin lock-out of 1913. During that strike, Connolly was summoned to Dublin to assist James Larkin, the former Liverpool trade unionist and veteran of the 1907 Belfast dock strike, who had established the ITGWU. Together, Connolly and Larkin endeavoured to secure assistance from the British labour movement by way of sympathetic strikes. Yet the British movement failed to respond satisfactorily, partly because it harboured much scepticism concerning the motives of Larkin; soon the British Trades Union Congress discontinued financial support to Dublin. As Ruth Dudley Edwards writes, 'there was a general sense in the British labour movement that it had all gone on too long, that Larkin was uncontrollable and that forces were being unleashed that they could neither contain nor approve'.[19]

[16] *Ibid.*, p. 19.
[17] Walker in *ibid.*, p. 8.
[18] *Ibid.*, pp. 26–27.
[19] Dudley Edwards, *James Connolly*, Dublin, 1981, p. 110.

II

Bitterly disappointed not only by the defeat of the workers in Dublin but also by the poor response of British workers in coming to their aid, Connolly tried to analyse the strike from the position he had developed in America. In *Forward* in 1914, he argued that the 'labour aristocracy' had isolated Dublin, and that sectionalism had killed the strike. He criticised the British for failing to support either the Irish or the concept of the sympathetic strike. Yet he did not lose faith in the central idea of industrial unionism but qualified it by arguing that it could only succeed if there was solidarity, and he advocated an extensive amalgamation process.[20]

The failure of the industrial action in Dublin highlighted the uneven and strained relationship the Irish labour movement had with British labour. This already tenuous relationship was dealt another blow when the British Labour Party (BLP) decided to support the claims of the Irish Nationalist Party, thus antagonising the republican socialists. This decision reopened the debate. Connolly now saw the Irish national struggle against British domination in terms of Lenin's theory of imperialism as the ultimate stage of capitalism.[21] From August 1914 the war and the BLP's decision to support the government completed the break.[22]

For Connolly, however, the war meant more. It appeared to him 'as the most fearful crime of the centuries'. 'In it', he argued 'the working class are to be sacrificed that a small clique of rulers and armament makers may sate their lust for power and their greed for wealth'. He wrote:

We shall continue, in season and out of the season, to teach that the 'farflung battle line' of England is weakest at the point of factual advantage, that a defeat of England in India, Egypt, the Balkans or Flanders would not be so dangerous to the British Empire as any conflict of armed forces in Ireland, that the time for Ireland's battle is NOW, the place for Ireland's battle is HERE.[23]

Written just four months before the Rising, this gives a good indication of the way Connolly was thinking, particularly in deciding what role he would assume. He was a great believer in small nationalist revolutions, trusting that they would end the war and win emancipation for the

---

[20] Connolly, *Selected Political Writings*, Dublin, 1973 pp. 170–1. For another angle, see Morgan, *James Connolly*, in which he argues that Connolly never saw the Dublin lock-out as a proletarian revolutionary offensive or a major tackling of the national question. Rather, the defeat of the Dublin lock-out contributed to the growth in national chauvinist recriminations and it became difficult to sustain a belief in proletarian action, p. 23.

[21] See Ransom, *Connolly's Marxism*, London, 1986 p. 77.

[22] Connolly, *Socialism and Nationalism*, p. 152.

[23] *Ibid.*, pp. 220–1.

working class. By 1915 he was well on the way to playing out his interpretation of history.

Connolly had already helped to form the Citizens' Army, a unit
designed to protect workers from attacks by police and employers' guards
during the 1913 lock-out and inspired by Carson's build-up of the Ulster
Volunteer Force. Connolly took over the command of the Citizens's
Army in 1915 and set to work streamlining and disciplining it, probably
with his original design in mind that it would be the embryo of an armed
revolutionary body. He proposed to make that force the 'best equipped
mentally in Ireland'.[24] On its strategic importance, Connolly had written
that it gave the Irish workers 'arms in their own hands' and would enable
them to 'steer their own course, to carve their own future'.[25] According
to Connolly this would mean a 'complete overhauling and remodelling of
all the training and instruction hitherto given to those corps' and would
involve teaching the corps how to act and fight against an enemy
equipped with superior weapons.[26]

So on Easter Monday 1916 Connolly led the Citizens' Army, 'out for
not only political liberty, but for economic liberty as well', and joined an
eclectic band of rebels united by the desire for an independent Irish
Republic. For Connolly it was an attempt to fuse the two pillars of his
political life, nationalism and socialism.[27] The 1916 Rising brought
labour into direct contact with the struggle for national independence
and catapulted Ireland into a revolutionary situation. Indeed Lenin
commented that the tragedy of the Irish situation was that the workers
had risen too early.[28] Labour had been drawn into the struggle by
Connolly's involvement and for the initial period following 1916 the
movement had to come to terms with the significance of this action.

The relevance of Connolly's socialism to Ireland's political, social and
economic situation formed an integral part of the discussion within the
labour movement. It could either accept the alliance of nationalism and
socialism forged by Connolly, or opt for a policy of moderation and revert
back to its socio-economic aims. The ITUC conference in 1916 was

[24] Connolly, *Socialism and Nationalism*, p. 169.
[25] Connolly, *Selected Writings*.
[26] Connolly, *Socialism and Nationalism*, p. 169.
[27] In their article, '1916–a Workingman's Revolution', *Social Studies*, (1973), pp. 377–98,
S. V. Larson and O. Snoddy claim that the 1916 revolution was one which appeared to
be a perfect picture of a socialist revolution in the way Lenin and Marx envisaged it. They
argue that it was very much in line with what has been dominant tradition in Irish revolutionary politics with regards to participation. Their analysis shows the Rising to have
been primarily the work of workers in alliance with small farmers. Their evidence on the
influence of the works of Connolly on the minds of the participants is not very conclu-
sive.
[28] Lenin, *On Ireland*, n.d.

indicative of things to come and called for the organisation of one big union for each industry. It stressed moderation, based on the argument that the movement was not in a position to rule the political state and that such a position would only be commanded once a strong industrial base was created.[29] This moderate stance marked a divergence from the general fervour of the time and a particular section of the movement was reluctant to distance itself from the nationalist struggle. Two years later, in August 1918, the ITUC Conference held in Waterford pledged solidarity with the international working-class movement. The tone of the speeches was full of emotion and carried away with the fervour of the extraordinary times.[30] Cathal O'Shannon declared Irish Labour's adherence 'to the Russian formula of peace for the peoples on the basis of genuine democracy, the real self-determination of all subject peoples' and renewed 'its welcome and congratulations to its Russian comrades who for twelve months have exercised that political, social and economic freedom towards which Irish workers in common with their fellows in other lands still strive and aspire'.[31] Congress called for affirmation of support for self-determination and also paid special tribute to Connolly, who had been executed by the British in the aftermath of the Easter Rising, setting the future path for Irish Labour within the shadow of his legacy.

However, in the drafting of the Labour Party's constitution of 1918, the problems inherent in the movement became clear. The constitution called for a socialist, collectivist reconstruction of society and stated the aims of (1) complete (public) possession of all national, physical sources of wealth; (2) the collective ownership and control of the produce of the workers' labour; and (3) the democratic management and control of all industries and services by the nation, subject to the authority of the national government.[32]

William O'Brien and Tom Johnson assumed the leadership of the labour moment after the death of Connolly.[33] Johnson was aware of the

---

[29] D. R. O'Connor-Lysaght, 'The Rake's Progress of a Syndicalist: The Political Career of William O'Brien, Irish Labour Leader', *Saothar*, 9 (1983), p. 16.

[30] ITUC/LP, *Annual Report*, 1918.

[31] *Ibid.*, pp. 118–20.

[32] *Ibid.*

[33] Johnson was born in Liverpool in 1872 and always referred to himself as 'Liverpool English'. After reading works by Blatchford, Owen and Morris, he became convinced that socialism was the only political system to combat the social degradation of his home city. He became active in particular socialist groups, joining a branch of the Fabian Society and then the Liverpool branch of the ILP. A clerk by trade, Johnson worked for a veterinary medical supplies firm and in 1903 moved to Belfast to cover the northern part of Ireland for the firm. He joined the Belfast Trades Council in 1904 and became involved in the educational work of the Belfast Cooperative Society which aimed to ensure that the children of working-class parents had adequate access to education. It

acute need for peasant support. He appeared to have a clearer understanding of the importance of the land question than Connolly. In 1916
he had advocated a 'plots for the workers campaign', which called for the
provision of plots for cultivation by landless people,[34] and as early as 1914
he had written:

Landholders must be made to realise that they hold their land in trust for the
community. If it is not made the best use of, the community must assume possession and use it to the fullest advantage. Private profit, in farming as in industry,
must not be allowed to interfere with the national well-being.[35]

Thus when asked to elaborate on the definition of 'nation' during the
drafting of the constitution, Johnson said that the 'working class in the
proletarian sense' was only half of the nation and that there was another
half which was largely of the 'peasant propertied class'.[36] Johnson had
objected to the insertion of the phrase 'common ownership of means of
production', referring, instead, to 'national control' as the urban working
class did not constitute the entire Irish nation and the agricultural sector
had to be taken into account.[37]

The debates on what should constitute membership subscription to
the Labour movement are also revealing, with particular reference to
individual membership and the relationship between middle-class socialists and the working class. P. Coates of the ITGWU said he did not want
to keep the middle class out of the Labour Party as they could help the
working class achieve their objectives.[38] Yet the policy of not allowing
socialist groups to affiliate to the party, which had been adopted in 1914,
was maintained. It appears that the party wanted to continue to have a
purely working class, trade unionist base with no influence from what
were deemed to be organisations 'of a propagandist nature'.[39]
Significantly it was the delegate of the Belfast Trades Council, D. R.
Campbell, who opposed the affiliation of individual members, on the
ground that 'they might not be sound on the industrial question'.[40]

---

was in 1911 that Johnson attended the ITUC where the question of the establishment of
a separate Irish Labour Party dominated proceedings. While Johnson supported the idea,
he was adamant that the party should federate as closely as possible with the British
party. This was an expression of his own identification with the British movement as well
as a regard for the working-class Unionists of north-east Ireland. See J. Gaughan, *Thomas
Johnson*, Dublin, 1980.

[34] Cited in Gaughan, *Thomas Johnson*, p. 78.
[35] *Ibid.*, p. 73.
[36] ITUC/LP, *Annual Report*, 1918, p. 136.
[37] *Ibid.*, p. 136.
[38] *Ibid.*, p. 140.
[39] *Ibid.*, p. 146.
[40] *Ibid.*, pp. 142–3.

III

Sinn Féin had emerged as the dominant force in Irish politics after the 1916 Rising. Disillusionment with conventional politics had enticed nationalists to look for something that would accentuate Ireland's identity, individuality and ethno-centricity. The failure of subsequent Home Rule bills had contributed to the move towards a notion of self-reliance. And yet the type of regime that was to evolve under the leadership of Sinn Féin was not one envisaged by Connolly and hardly the one he had fought for in 1916. His death had left Labour in a predicament, for while the Irish labour movement had stood aloof from the Rising, it became tied to it by Connolly's involvement. His part in the Rising and subsequent execution bequeathed to the labour movement a contentious nationalist legacy which would undermine its effort to maintain class unity, and retain its appeal to the Protestant workers in Ulster. It also caused problems when the labour movement channelled emerging agrarian discontent into direct political action. Then it seemed that the national revolution was turning full circle and what in the 1880s had been a vital impetus for the national movement, in 1917 became a threat to its aims.

In a statement by De Valera can be found the crux of nationalist-dominated politics at the time:

This is not the time for this, for this reason, that the only banner under which our freedom can be won at the present time is the Republican banner ... This is not the time for discussion on the best forms of government ... This is the time to get freedom. Then we can settle by the most democratic means what particular form of government we may have.[41]

The subsequent abstention of the Labour Party from the 1918 election has been imputed to be the pivotal factor determining Labour's fate in the development of Irish politics. It reflected the widespread concern that the workers should not 'split' the national vote. However, it also reflected the demands of the 'non-political' trade union component of the party which focused on building up the industrial side of the movement. Yet, at first the party had considered contesting the election in order:

to provide an opportunity for the workers to prove their adhesion to the principle and policy of the Labour Party, to strengthen the position of Irish Labour in its relations with the international Labour movement, and to prepare the way for a full representation of Labour in any Irish parliament.[42]

---

[41] Cited in M. Moynihan (ed.), *Speeches and Statements by Eamon De Valera, 1917–70*, Dublin, 1980, p. 8.
[42] Cited in B. Farrell, *The Founding of the First Dáil*, Dublin, 1971, p. 33.

However, even this modest strategy angered the republicans and caused considerable dissension within the labour movement, as many believed it would harm the struggle for independence if Labour was to compete against Sinn Féin. For example, the Kilkenny Trades Council and Land League disapproved of running candidates and regarded it as a 'disservice to the country'.[43]

When the question was debated at a special congress in 1918, Campbell of Belfast criticised abstentionism as detrimental to the effort to build up a united labour movement as it would give the nationalists dominance in the south whilst in the north, 'the Conservative' crowd would be given a 'walk-over'.[44] Tom McPartlin said that he realised that many delegates were 'steeped to the neck in some political movements' but that if they had Sinn Féin becoming the dominant power they would have to fight them as they had to fight the rotten and corrupt party in 1914, for 'they would be another political mouthpiece of the capitalist class in this country'.[45] In a letter to McPartlin, P. T. Daly wrote that the decision to abstain from the election practically signalled the adoption of the Sinn Féin policy.[46]

With the increasing popularity of Sinn Féin, the *Freeman's Journal* despaired that:

every other interest in Ireland is now being subordinated to the Republican dream. Yesterday the Bolshevik leaders who, by a narrow majority, seized the control of the Irish Labour Party, resolved to sacrifice the interests of labour on the altar of this impossible policy. The workers of Ireland are to be asked to throw away their votes, and subscribe to Mr De Valera's doctrine that Labour must wait until the Irish Republic is established before attention can be given to its particular needs. While the rest of Europe is engaged upon the work of reconstruction, Irish labour is to be invited to go on fighting the British Empire.[47]

While it has been argued that the new Labour leadership failed to take the initiative to fuse nationalism with socialism by working with Sinn Féin,[48]

[43] *Ibid.*, p. 34.
[44] ITUC/LP, *Annual Report*, 1919, p. 113.
[45] *Ibid.*, p. 105.
[46] University College Dublin Archives (UCDA), McPartlin Papers, letter dated 28 September 1918.
[47] *Freeman's Journal*, 2 November 1918.
[48] Farrell argues that Labour failed to recognise the frailty of Sinn Féin and that its urgent need for a clear run could be used as a political weapon by Labour. He argues that the majority of labour leaders did not see the need to synthesise socialism and nationalism. See Farrell, *Founding of the First Dáil*, p. 44. O'Connor-Lysaght argues that if Labour had allied with Sinn Féin keeping intact its socialist aspirations as long as it upheld the principle of the 'virtual establishment' of the Irish Republic and maintained a policy of abstention from Westminster, this would have handicapped the strategy of the ITUC/LP whose policy was to build up an 'industrial republic', as opposed to participation in the national struggle. See D. R. O'Connor-Lysaght, 'A Saorstát is Born', in S. Hutton and P. Stewart, (eds.), *Ireland's Histories*, London, 1991, p. 43.

the situation was not so clear cut. As Frank Robbins, a member of the Citizens' Army who fought in the Rising in 1916, recalled:

Workers by and large were not attuned to the potential for organised labour involvement in politics. Hence although Madame Markiewicz, after the 1918 election, became the first Minister for Labour, the bulk of trade unionists thought of their trade unionism and their nationalism separately and did not share in Connolly's attempts to unite the two.[49]

Again another contemporary noted:

If the goal and ideology of Sinn Féin and Socialist Republicanism were identical, there would obviously be no need for separate labels and division of action: there would not have been the remotest probability of Irish Labour contesting the recent elections against Sinn Féin, because they would have worked on a common platform. It is clear then that there is a difference.[50]

Underlying all of this was the fact that Sinn Féin took for granted that Labour would assist in fighting the nationalist cause. Labour contributed to the development of this mentality with its general strike against conscription in 1918. The threat of conscription was a rallying point and representatives of Labour, Sinn Féin and the parliamentary party met at the Mansion House to issue the call that they 'deny the right of the British Government or any external authority' to impose compulsory military service on Ireland 'against the clearly expressed will of the Irish people', and declared that the 'attempt to enforce it will be an unwarrantable aggression, which will call upon all Irishmen to resist by the most effective means at their disposal'.[51] The Catholic church also supported the offensive against conscription. It has been argued that the success of the strike against conscription gave Labour political recognition in the eyes of the nation, proving that it could command power when it took the lead, and that the anti-conscription campaign shifted the entire nationalist community to the left.[52] However it seems more likely that Labour's action was treated by the nationalists as mere political expediency and if Labour operated centre stage it did so only because it suited the nationalists to allow it. Many contemporary accounts play down the role of Labour and interpret the conscription crisis as being the most potent impetus to the Sinn Féin movement.[53] As Darrell Figgis recalled:

For everyone – including those who loved us little, but who loved conscription less – looked to the militant party to rescue them, and from every part of the

[49] F. Robbins, *Under The Starry Plough*, Dublin, 1977, pp. 222–3.
[50] S. Sigerson, *Sinn Féin and Socialism*, Dublin, 1919.
[51] Cited in H. M. Henry, *The Evolution of Sinn Féin*, Dublin, 1920, p. 260.
[52] E. O'Connor, *A Labour History of Waterford*, Cork, 1990, p. 142.
[53] S. Desmond, *The Drama of Sinn Féin*, London, 1923, *passim*.

country news came of new members joining Sinn Féin *cummain* [branches] in large numbers.[54]

There was a belief that Labour should join forces with Sinn Féin as the anti-conscription campaign had illustrated the potential of this alliance. Aodh de Blacam writing in the *Republic* noted that Sinn Féin and Labour were attacking the same enemy from different sides and argued that 'the closer the relations between the two bodies, the more will the might of Ireland be intensified, the people held together, national organisation consolidated and made effective'.[55] It appears, then, that Labour's action only lent it credibility in the eyes of the nationalists, and thus not only led Sinn Féin to expect future support for its cause but also alienated Protestant workers in the north from the wider labour movement. Commenting on the strike against conscription, the *Belfast Newsletter* observed:

Protestant trade unionists are strongly opposed to this [the strike], but being in a minority they have been unable to make their protests effective, and the Roman Catholics have had their way. One Protestant trade unionist remarked bitterly to me today, 'this is going to split Irish trades unionism on sectarian lines. It's all very well making a protest; but when you impart the religious and political element into it, it's goodbye to unity'.[56]

The decision to abstain from the elections in 1918, therefore, can be understood in this light. P. S. O'Hegarty recalled that Sinn Féin 'were given the mailed fist. The German Plot, Partition, Conscription – everything combined to throw more and more elements in the country over to Sinn Féin. The Labour Party gave it a free hand; and finally its bitterest opponent, the Irish Hierarchy came over to it'.[57] Piaras Beaslai noted that the majority of people had no reasoned political theories on the subject, and were always most interested in the removal of those grievances or disabilities which weighed heavily on them, and that the vote of the general election of 1918 was essentially an anti-Irish Party parliamentary vote.[58]

IV

The results of the election left Ireland in the hands of a socially conservative party with no constructive policies other than the attainment of self-determination. A comprehensive socio-economic programme did not

[54] D. Figgis, *Recollections of the Irish War*, London, 1921–2, p. 192.
[55] *Republic*, 5 July 1919.
[56] *Belfast Newsletter*, 23 April 1918.
[57] P. S. O'Hegarty, *The Victory of Sinn Féin*, Dublin, 1924, p. 29.
[58] P. Beaslai, *Michael Collins and the Making of Modern Ireland*, Dublin, 1926, p. 227.

feature in the party's platform. Of the Sinn Féin clubs, one chronicler of the times observed that 'social questions such as housing, land division, public health, were seldom discussed and generally the subjects for debate were of the "England's difficulty, Ireland's opportunity" variety'.[59] Eventually the republicans called on Labour to draw up a social programme. This move was motivated not so much by social radicalism, as by lack of alternatives. The social thinking of Sinn Féin was then still dominated by its founder, Arthur Griffith, who by 1918 had ceased to be an asset to the party. A strongly protectionist, socially conservative liberal, influenced by the ideas of Friedrich List, Griffith was distrusted not only by the socialists, but also – because of his support for the concept of dual monarchy and contempt for the republican ideal – by the separatist nationalists who had come to dominate Sinn Féin.

Since the republicans seemed unable to produce any credible alternative, the task of drawing up the new government's policy was given to Johnson. Entitled the *Democratic Programme* (1919) it enshrined the political, economic and social goals of Labour, and according to Johnson, contained 'the basis of agreement between the forward thinking members of the contending parties'.[60] However, his proposals were severely edited and tempered before the programme was eventually adopted by Sinn Féin. As Piaras Beaslai recalled:

It is doubtful whether the majority of the members would have voted for it without amendment had there been any immediate prospect of putting it into force ... Many would have objected to the communistic flavour of the declaration.[61]

Even the tempered version of the *Democratic Programme* was not taken too seriously by Sinn Féin. Its attitude was representative of the purely formal concessions that mainstream republicanism was prepared to make to 'keep labour in the ambit of a political strategy under republican control'.[62] The social policy of Griffith and the military policy of Cathal Brugha were the two facets of Sinn Féin at that time: the concept of a democratic revolution had no place in their political thought. Certainly, Michael Collins did not approve of it, as it obscured the main objective of ridding Ireland of Britain.[63] As Peadar O'Donnell writes, the republican movement was one of 'pure ideals' and 'in the grip of this philosophy, the Republican struggle could present itself as a democratic

[59] C. S. Andrews, *Dublin Made Me*, Dublin, 1979, p. 100.
[60] National Library of Ireland, ms. 17, 139, Thomas Johnson Papers.
[61] Beaslai, *Michael Collins*, p. 259.
[62] H. Patterson, *The Politics of Illusion; Republicanism and Socialism in Modern Ireland*, London, 1989, p. 16.
[63] D. C. Boyce, *Nationalism in Ireland*, Dublin, 1990, p. 327.

movement of a mass revolt without any danger to the haves and the have-nots'.[64] Moreover it seems that at this critical point the 'Revolutionary Dáil' was concerned – first and foremost – with maintaining the morale of a united national movement, and this meant not interfering with existing social policies.[65] While incorporated into legislation, the *Democratic Programme* amounted to little; in the south nationalism was the guiding principle to which all else was subordinated, and De Valera's leadership consolidated this position.

Thus the advent of an Irish parliament, in many ways a revolutionary event, did not signal the beginning of a more radical time for Irish politics. Alice Stopford Green, an active participant in the women's national movement, lucidly observed:

the Irish are a conservative people faithful to law and justice. The whole scheme was in the wildest sense democratic ... there was nothing revolutionary in the Dáil except that it transferred from the English to the Irish the control of the daily life and the destinies of the people of this island.[66]

V

De Valera's 'this-it-not-the-time' attitude handicapped the labour movement in Ireland during the critical years of the Irish national revolution. As the ITUC/LP turned to concentrate on building its organisation and coordinating the workers' agitation, the nationalists protested that Labour's actions were harming the revolution. This was clearly the case when disturbances broke out in the countryside.

Industrial and agrarian direct action was a prominent feature of the years following the Rising until the consolidation of the Free State and the northern state. 1919 had begun with a strike in Belfast as part of the movement to shorten the 54-hour week worked by the shipbuilding and engineering workers which had developed in particular parts of the United Kingdom, beginning on the Clyde in Glasgow. As a result of a ballot taken, 47 hours had been adopted provisionally in most of the shipbuilding and engineering firms and Belfast also adopted a similar modification. However, the decision by the British engineers on 23 January 1919 to agree to 47 hours for six months was unacceptable to the north-eastern workers. From the beginning, the 44-hour strike diverged from

---

[64] P. O'Donnell, *There Will Be Another Day*, Dublin, 1963, p. 12.
[65] Farrell notes that the *Democratic Programme* represented a tactical device designed to secure political support for the new Irish legislative body within the International Socialist movement. See, B. Farrell, 'The First Dáil and After', in *The Irish Parliamentary Tradition*, Dublin, 1973, p. 210.
[66] J. R. Green, *The Government of Ireland*, London, 1921.

the English and Scottish situation. To begin with, the Belfast shipyards were outside the Engineering and National Employers' Federation. There was no organisational harmony among the engineering unions. Eight union branches affiliated to the Belfast District Committee of the Federation of Engineering and Shipbuilding Trades (FEST) were still not affiliated to the Belfast Trades Council and the ITUC/LP.[67]

When the strike began in Belfast in January 1919 the initial reaction of the local press was to emphasise the inherently conservative nature of the working class and to dismiss the idea that revolutionary socialism had any influence on its attitudes. Thus the *Northern Whig* claimed:

If there is any talk about industrial Bolshevism or such things it will be an absurdity, because as far as Belfast is concerned, Bolshevism does not exist. Those who know the average Belfast working man would laugh at the idea of his having anything to do with such a thing.[68]

The *Freeman's Journal* noted: 'the local men in charge of the strike are practically all Unionists; the overwhelming majority of the workers are Covenanters and Orangemen'.[69] *Irish Opinion (Voice of Labour)* noted that 'the workers of Belfast are not revolutionary. We know that well for we have tried and failed, to make them so. They are not the playthings of "Clyde Revolutionaries" ... But they know when they are robbed'.[70] To counter this view, the General Strike Committee (GSC) established the *Belfast Strike Report*, which ran for the duration of the industrial action. The *Newsletter*, which condemned the leadership of the GSC claiming it was influenced by doctrines of Bolshevism and Sinn Féin, denounced the industrial action as syndicalism 'pure and simple'.

The action taken by the Belfast workers had repercussions across the channel and soon various unions were pledging support for the action. On 30 January 1919 the GSC met and received a deputation from Manchester, which had been sent to Belfast to link up the shorter-hours movement on both sides of the channel, and arranged for a delegate from Belfast to visit Manchester. The London District of the ASE decided to join the 44-hour movement and soon the sympathetic strike action was in full force. The *Newsletter* commented that the effort to force out of employment men who had no connection with shipbuilding and engineering had for its aim 'the paralysing of the daily life of the community, and that, we assert, is contrary to trades unionism and democratic principles'.[71]

---

[67] D. R. O'Connor-Lysaght, 'Class Struggle During The War Of Independence and Civil War, 1916–1924', University College Dublin unpublished M.A. thesis, 1981, p. 46.
[68] *Northern Whig*, 25 January 1919.
[69] *Freeman's Journal*, 27 January 1919.
[70] *Irish Opinion (Voice of Labour)*, 8 February 1919.
[71] *Ibid.*

Set in the context of revolutionary upheaval in Europe, the action in Belfast differs considerably. Although it followed the action in Clydeside and maintained a verbal adherence to working-class solidarity, the strike in Belfast differed in content and significance. It was constrained by the confines of the hostile political atmosphere. This was due to the relationship between trade unionism and Unionism. Many Protestant trade unionists were firmly entrenched in their Unionist traditions and many had the conviction that their action was another expression of their Unionism. The *Freeman's Journal* noted: 'it is not paradoxical to say that a majority of the workers regarded the strike as a demonstration which would prove to a sceptical world that Ulster Convenanters were the true exponents of democratic ideas in Ireland'.[72] It was also observed that 'the average Carsonite artisan, strange as it may appear, holds as an article of faith, that extreme Unionism can be harmonised with advanced Labour views'.[73] The *Journal* took this further and pointed to the relationship between industrial and political autonomy:

It is delightfully ironical that at a time when the mass of Belfast workers are backing Sir Edward Carson in his demand for the complete assimilation of Ulster and England, they should be in open revolt against what they call 'English dictation' in their industrial affairs. Nine-tenths of the strikers would argue that only England can rule Ireland, but when it comes to an affair which touches them as individuals they are prepared to fight to the death for the right of Belfast to rule itself.[74]

The Belfast workers were concerned to stress their autonomy and draw a demarcation line between themselves and the movement in the south; they were entrenched in the interest politics of Belfast.[75] The shipbuilders and engineers were the bastions of Unionist trade unionism and fervent in their determination to protect that bastion. That determination had found expression in the formation in 1918 of the Ulster Unionist Labour Association. In 1916 a month after the Rising, the *Belfast Newsletter* highlighted the influence of Larkinism which preached 'anarchical socialism', and noted that 'no more poisonous growth in the body politic of a country could be imagined than this combination of Syndicalism and Revolution'.[76] Unionists were fearful that this growth of labour solidarity

---

[72] *Freeman's Journal*, 3 February 1919.
[73] *Ibid.*
[74] *Ibid.*
[75] O'Connor writes that the dispute reflected contemporary radicalism without changing the isolated and conservative character of local trade unionism. He argues that any attempt to alter the strictly economist basis of action would have transgressed parameters set by craft exclusiveness. E. O'Connor, *Syndicalism In Ireland*, Cork, 1988, pp. 173–4.
[76] *Belfast Newsletter*, 4 May 1916.

would be seized upon by the nationalists and used to derive support from the Protestant working class. Combined with this was an increasing disappointment with the British Labour Party for its adoption of Home Rule, which many Unionists regarded as a signal of the party's disregard for the welfare and interests of the Northern Irish working class.[77] The action of January/February 1919 added to the Unionists' insecurity and heightened their fears of the rapid growth of Sinn Féin and socialism. Unionists claimed it was the 'hand of Sinn Féin at work' and they moved quickly to mobilise the Protestant working class into their spheres of influence. R. D. Bates, the secretary of the Ulster Unionist Council, wrote to Sir James Craig, expressing these concerns:

What one wants to try and get the workers to see is that really no-one is against them, except themselves; that the Question is not a local one, but a national one. The leaders are practically Sinn Féiners, who have taken advantage of some of the rank and file, and as time goes on their action is being found out ... as regards the strikers you may take it less than one quarter are out and out socialists and extremists.[78]

The 44-hours strike in Belfast had been considered a significant victory by the ITUC/LP. Although the demarcation line between north and south had been clearly set, with the south's offers of assistance largely ignored, the action had done something to revitalise the trade union movement. The ITUC experienced a growth in membership from 100,000 in 1916 to 225,000 in 1920 and on top of this there were 30,000 north-eastern workers not affiliated to Congress. Much of the growth in trade unionism occurred amongst the farm workers,[79] due to inflation caused by the war, an increase in the demand for labour and the introduction of tillage which had produced a labour shortage in agriculture.[80]

Land disturbances became a common feature of labour agitation with the steady growth of the unionisation of farm workers. In Limerick, in April 1919, a general strike over the imposition of military special permits for access to the city led to the establishment of what was dubbed the 'Limerick Soviet'. Workers claimed 'the republican capitalist, the shopkeeper nationalist, the "landed" unionist should all co-operate with hitherto despised wage slaves – that the sacrifice made by the wage earner should in some degree be participated in by those who had waxed fat on the toil and sweat of their fellows'.[81]

[77] *Ibid.*, 6 October 1919.
[78] P. Buckland, *Irish Unionism, 1885–1922: A Documentary History of Unionism*, Dublin, 1972, pp. 431–2.
[79] Fitzpatrick argues that this epitomised the twin trends of expansion of agriculture and general trades unionism of the United Kingdom. See D. Fitzpatrick, 'Strikes In Ireland, 1914–23', *Saothar* 6 (1988), p. 31.
[80] *Ibid.*, p. 23.
[81] *Watchword of Labour*, 15 May 1920.

The workers took over the city, commanding control over propaganda, finance, food and vigilance.[82] The action taken at Limerick was not, however, based on pure working-class dissent, as the national struggle had an acute influence on the events.[83] The *Irish Times* declared that the action could no longer be dissociated from the propaganda of the Irish republicans:

> The bulk of Irish Labour, both urban and rural, is restless today, but it is shrewd and intelligent. It will begin soon to recognise the economic limits of the concessions which our staple industries can make to its demands. The Limerick strike and the National Executive's hopes are possible just now, because political excitement runs high, because extremist organisations terrorise public opinion, and because the Irish people, in their insular isolation, have not learned, like the English, the lesson of recent events in Russia and Germany.[84]

It declared the agitation a 'challenge to British Government in Ireland, against which some Irishmen have worked themselves to such a pitch ... so mad that they would prefer a bloodstained and bankrupt Bolshevism to an Ireland safe and progressive under British rule'.[85] It feared that an effort was being made to extend the strike to the rest of Ireland. Furthermore, and here it touched on a critical point concerning the nature of the general state of the labour movements in Ireland, it argued that the strike could not be universal because the 'sturdy and highly organised Labour of north-east Ulster will have nothing to say to it'.[86]

During the course of the strike, the workers appealed to the national executive of the ITUC/LP to call a national strike in support, but after some deliberation the executive decided against taking such action. This decision was criticised by some at the ITUC/LP Congress in Drogheda later that year but, as one shrewd delegate observed succinctly, the national executive could not have taken any other action. He claimed a general strike had to be backed up by guns and that it meant a 'revolution and that unless they were prepared for a revolution there was no point calling a general strike'. Unless the workers were prepared to 'hoist the Red Flag from one end of the country to the other' there was no point condemning the actions of the executive.[87] He observed that the workers were not 'class conscious enough, not educated enough and not ready for

---

[82] J. Kemmy argues that the rise of Sinn Féin to political power had been another potent influence on working-class consciousness. He suggests that the action in Limerick was an assertion of both political expressions of nationalism and socialism. See, J. Kemmy, 'The Limerick Soviet', *Saothar*, 2 (1975), p. 47.

[83] *Ibid.*, p. 46.

[84] *Irish Times*, 23 April 1919.

[85] *Ibid.*

[86] *Ibid.*

[87] ITUC/LP, *Annual Report*, 1919, p. 80.

a general strike', but that when they were, they 'would not need leaders to act'.[88] The *Irish Times* was unsurprisingly blunt in its condemnation of the action:

The truth is that Syndicalism and Bolshevism, with their common motto, 'What is yours is mine, and what is mine is my own', never will make any headway in this country. In our farming classes the sense of property is as sacred and as strong as in the French. Our middle classes are hard working individuals.[89]

The Catholic church spoke out against the action. The Bishop of Ross had commented that there were few countries in the world in which the ownership of property was so widely diffused as in Ireland, and therefore in which the proportion of proletariat to owners was so small.[90] That there was no takeover of private property during the strike is significant for, as Cahill writes, the strikers were aware that it was necessary to preserve a semblance of unity across economic classes so as not to alienate actual or potential middle-class Sinn Féin support.[91] This situation contrasts with the action taken by agricultural labourers when they embarked on an intense period of land seizures during the 1920s.

Later, when farm workers joined forces with creamery operatives, collective seizures were made of creameries in various parts of the country. According to one Labour member, the origins of the agrarian conflict could be traced back to the Land Acts which, he claimed, had erected a class bar between the extensive landowner and the landless farm worker; this was seen as a further instance of the historical lesson of class struggle.[92] Tom Johnson claimed the seizures raised the 'most important question that could be raised in the labour movement or in social economy. It is a challenge – let us made no mistake about it – to the right of property'.[93]

Although it has been argued that Labour should have taken advantage of this situation and tried to develop a social revolution, it appears the Labour leadership was in no way interested in such a thought. Further insight into the political nature of the leadership which shows its overtly moderate nature is offered in the manifesto issued by the Labour Party at Easter 1921. The tone and ideological content of the *Democratic Programme* provided the philosophical framework for the document

[88] *Ibid.*, p. 80. In his account of the action taken in Limerick, Cahill claims that the Soviet was 'basically an emotional and spontaneous protest on essentially nationalist and humanitarian grounds, rather than anything based on socialist or even trade union aims'. L. Cahill, *Forgotten Revolution, The Story Of the Limerick Soviet*, Dublin, 1991, p. 148.
[89] *Irish Times*, 23 April 1919.
[90] National Library of Ireland, 'Ireland and International Revolution', Dublin, n.d.
[91] Cahill, *Forgotten Revolution*, p. 144.
[92] ITUC/LP, *Annual Report*, 1923, p. 49.
[93] ITUC/LP, *Annual Report*, 1921, p. 92.

which was entitled *The Country In Danger*. Claiming it was entitled to speak for the 'organised wage worker', it continued the theme that the synthesis of socialism and nationalism was the key to emancipation:

If in Ireland during the period of storm and stress, when men are united as ever before in a desire to serve their motherland there can be diffused through the mind of the nation this thought; that mutual labour and personal service for the common good is the only basis upon which a just and stable society can be built: then when our political freedom had been won, the way will have been cleared for a peaceful settlement.[94]

The manifesto argued that it was time to give practical effect to the claim enshrined in the *Democratic Programme* that every citizen should have an adequate share of the produce of the nation's labour. It also set out a series of proposals calling for an improvement in the standard of living, a policy of protection and a planned economy involving an extensive 'buy Irish' campaign. On the issue of land, the manifesto argued that 'land is held in trust for the nation; it must be made the most of in maintaining the largest possible number of persons' and advocated that those land-holders holding more than they can cultivate must pay for hired labour or resign parts to those willing to work it.[95] The manifesto said: 'we accept the view that agriculture is, and must remain, the foundation of Ireland's true prosperity'.[96] The manifesto was part of a long tradition which advocated extending property ownership, carrying the thread from Wolfe Tone to Connolly, and arguing that many of the ideas and policies of the programme had been:

advocated for many years with admirable persistence and eloquence by men whose voices today are involuntarily suppressed. Whatever is new or unfamiliar in our programme is necessary in order to protect the interests of 'that large and respectable class of the community – the men of no property'.[97]

Though the document outraged farmers and was virtually ignored by employers, it contained little more than watered-down socialism. No-where in the document was there talk of the public ownership of industry. Johnson, after all, had unsuccessfully opposed the inclusion of that clause in the 1918 Constitution.

The reaction from the farmers, who paradoxically were fundamental players in the national revolution, gave an indication of the prevalent mood and the obstacles facing the Labour Party. The Farmers' Union was formed and aimed to suppress strikes and to act against 'Labour,

---

[94] 'The Country In Danger' reproduced in ITUC/LP, *Annual Report*, 1921.
[95] *Ibid.*
[96] *Ibid.*
[97] *Ibid.*

Socialism and Bolshevism'. In 1923 it published a pamphlet which outlined Labour's policy and cited a speech made at the ITUC/LP Conference which spoke of the breaking of ranches into small holdings and linked this with 'communism' – the abolition of private ownership. Whilst admiration for Labour in parliament was expressed, the trade union movement was attacked for 'strangling Irish farming'.[98]

The antagonistic relationship between Labour and the farmers revealed marked differences in ideology. The *Irish Times* forecast a battle between socialism and anti-socialism and noted:

Sinn Féin as a body, is anti-socialist. The Sinn Féin farmers are as little in love with Labour's claim to control food prices as are the Unionist farmers of North-East Ulster. The agrarian agitation in the West – wholly a Labour movement – is viewed with intense alarm by the shopkeeping proprietors of grazing land.[99]

The agrarian disturbances brought Labour into direct conflict with the nationalist movement. It is clear that as the affinity grew between agricultural labourers and the trade union movement an atmosphere of class war was generated to a certain extent. In the Dáil, Constance Markiewicz spoke of the urgent need to do something so as to ensure the class struggle did not divert attention from the more pressing nationalist struggle.[100] In a file on agrarian outrages, the Minister of Agriculture reported that he had reason to believe that acute agrarian disorder would very shortly manifest itself in the form of a widespread and intensive campaign of incendiarism, and that suitable steps were being taken to cope with this type of irregularism.[101] Darrel Figgis recalled in his memoirs:

If Sinn Féin once slipped into agrarian revolution its national claim for independence would have been lost, its hope for the Peace Conference undone, and its larger plans for the political creation of an independent state through the formation of a constituent Assembly scattered past recovery.[102]

This commitment to nationalism and land exposed the essential problems facing Labour in trying to achieve political success in nationalist Ireland.

VI

The dilemma of political versus industrial action dominated the debate on the future of Labour, and this was accentuated with the advent of

---

[98] NLI, Ms. 19,021, Irish Farmer's Union.
[99] *Irish Times*, 3 March 1923.
[100] *Dáil Eireann Papers*. See also NAD File C.1/90 'Agrarian Outrages'.
[101] NAD File, C.1/90.
[102] Figgis, *Recollections of the Irish War*, p. 185.

partition which split the country and was a considerable blow to the hope of a united labour movement. The industrial action in Belfast in 1919 had already illustrated the difficulty in the way of a strong united labour movement. It had served to underline the main differences in the northern and southern attitudes. The 'carnival of reaction', which Connolly had predicted would follow partition, did result in widening the gulf between the movements. The establishment of the Northern Ireland Labour Party in 1924 strengthened this. Southern Labour was faced, once again, with the question of competing in national politics. On the one hand, there were those who argued that Labour had to abandon politics in order to maintain its independence and not be swamped by the nationalist parties; on the other hand, this argument was countered by those who maintained that in order to advance the cause of Labour the party should make use of the means at its disposal, and, as parliament was such a central function in the government of the country, Labour should be a part of it.

As the new state evolved, it became clear that Labour remained the only voice offering any constructive socio-economic policies. Writing in the *Republic*, a journal edited by Sinn Féiner Darryl Figgis, Eoin McNeill stressed the importance of Labour's position in society and in the national struggle. He argued that 'the only militant leaders' in Ireland who were 'seen endeavouring to think and plan on economic lines for the benefit of those who trust them' were the Labour leaders.[103] McNeill touched on the important point of the economic factor in the national question. He wrote that there were abundant indications that the 'process of our exploitation' was being 'hardened into a centralised policy, and that Irish savings and the unprecedented revenue extracted from us was being used to bring Labour and resources under control of "absentee capitalists"'.[104] He emphasised the importance of Labour's responsibility in the development of the country's future:

it is to Labour we look in the future of Ireland. Its power is increasing each day. That is to say, the nation – or that part of the nation from which the national strength has always derived, and will always derive – is thinking economically as well as politically.[105]

Labour polled very well in the municipal elections of January 1920 taking a quarter of the vote, with 116 trade unionists elected besides labour candidates. The *Irish Times* noted that the advance of Labour meant that Sinn Féin had 'no particle of right to be the sole voice of

[103] *Republic*, 5 July 1919.
[104] *Ibid.*
[105] *Ibid.*

Nationalist Ireland' with Labour sharing control of the largest share of municipal government in Ireland.[106] Later that year, *Watchword of Labour* claimed that the elections had shown that over great areas of Ireland the working-class electors had 'given their votes to a political party, which as a party has no remedy for social distress' and that 'the need of the moment is a clear and independent political action, free from all entanglement with the fears and hesitations of the non-working-class property-owning elements'.[107] Indeed it noted that the danger lay 'in accepting the leadership of non-working-class elements, which will be bound by class interests to restricted courses of action, alike in respect of the workers' needs and the national struggle for freedom'.[108]

The Dáil remained a closed arena for Labour as long as the latter retained its abstentionist policy. Labour issued a statement on its refusal to participate in the parliamentary elections under the Partition of Ireland Act 1920, which, it claimed, did not have the 'valid sanction' of the Irish people:

The Labour Party will take no part in the elections beyond calling up all workers, North and South, to demonstrate their loyalty to Ireland and Freedom by voting only for those candidates who stand for the ownership and government of Ireland by the people of Ireland, or in the words of the Labour party constitution for the abolition of all powers and privileges social and political, based upon property and ancestry, or not granted or confirmed by the freely expressed will of the Irish people.[109]

The issue of parliamentary participation continued to cause dissension. Fears were expressed that entry into the parliamentary fight would split the labour movement in Ireland.[110] Such concern was exacerbated by the realisation that the forthcoming election was not an ordinary election to be conducted in ordinary conditions. The debate on the Anglo-Irish Treaty had consumed all of the Dáil's energy and polarised the country. Sinn Féin was split into two camps. Acceptance of the Treaty by one of these camps had unleashed civil war. Labour took an unequivocal stand in the civil war. It was felt by certain members in the labour movement that Labour could not help but be forced into a situation where it would have to take sides on the issue, and this would split the movement as it had split the country. These fears were expressed by T. Kennedy of the ITGWU, who argued at the Special Congress that it was all right talking about the workers' republic, but when they went before the

[106] *Irish Times*, 19 January 1920.
[107] *Watchword Of Labour*, 24 July 1920.
[108] *Ibid.*
[109] National Library of Ireland, Ms. 17,132, Thomas Johnson Papers.
[110] Special Congress on the Election Policy, in the ITUC/LP *Annual Report*, 1922, p. 70.

working-class electors, the question they would have to decide was whether they were for peace or war.[111] In Tipperary workers met and passed a resolution calling on Labour's candidate, Mr Morrissey, to stand down 'in the interests of national unity'.[112] On the other hand, the *Workers' Republic* declared that:

The fight as between the Republic and the Free State is an integral part of the class war in Ireland and the treachery of the Labour party leaders in not linking the workers and the peasants of Ireland up on the side of the Republic will cost those self same workers and peasants dear in the end.[113]

Within the labour movement itself, a firm link had developed between the far left and a group of republicans who were more open to the socialist teachings of Connolly, as expressed by such figures as Liam Mellowes and Peadar O'Donnell. The growth of such a relationship is significant for a number of reasons. First, it was potentially embarrassing for a labour movement which had adopted a fairly moderate position. Secondly, it posed questions on the nature of the republican position, as it became obvious that the moderate nature of Sinn Féin was tightening its grip on the movement as a whole. Indeed, the republican movement was developing into a middle-class, socially conservative body. It was precisely because of the growing moderation of Sinn Féin that particular republicans formed close links with Labour. This situation was further complicated by the increasing relationship between Sinn Féin and the Labour leadership, which many socialists perceived as a suffocating extension of the bourgeois–nationalist hegemony over the working class, while others saw it as inevitable given the fact that 'so many workers are Republican both in feeling and in principle and so many Republicans are workers in class and sympathy'.[114] The Treaty issue discredited labour in the eyes of the republicans, especially the left-wing republicans who still adhered to some vague interpretation of Connolly's thesis.[115] Some called for the republicans to 'adopt a working class policy',[116] and Peader O'Donnell suggested that:

There is a revolutionary position now. The whole weight of the Labour movement added to the armed Republicans means the knitting of all the forces in the country needed to consolidate and shape the Republic. The Labour Party at present champions Imperialism. The dominating influence is Thomas Johnson. The duty of the Irish Citizen Army is plain. Tom Johnson must be deported. Deport him.[117]

---

[111] *Ibid.*, p. 70.
[112] *Freeman's Journal*, 13 June 1922.
[113] *Workers' Republic*, 9 September 1922.
[114] *Watchword of Labour*, 10 January 1920.
[115] University College Dublin Archives, P/7/B/Mulcahy Papers.
[116] *Workers Republic*, 28 January 1922.
[117] *Ibid.*, 26 August 1922.

However, such calls for socialist republicanism only served to highlight the fragmentation of both socialism and republicanism. Thus, Todd Andrews, a civil servant in the Free State government and active member of the republican movement, dismissed the influence of Connolly on the thinking and motivation of the IRA. He recalled being first introduced to the theory of socialism in an Irish context while travelling with O'Donnell in Donegal:

I felt nothing less than bewilderment at his references to the 'uprising of the masses' or the 'gathering together (with appropriate gestures) of the workers, small farmers and peasants' or the 'expropriation of the landlords and the taking over of the means of production'.[118]

He wrote that the class war of which O'Donnell talked would have been

unknown – even as a phrase – to almost everyone in the movement. In our estimation there were only two classes. There were the British and their dependants and hangers-on ... and the Irish. There was no Marxian slide rule appropriate to Irish social conditions. The difference between a publican living over his shop and a publican living in a detached house in the suburbs was one of the main class distinctions in Ireland, a difference to provoke any kind of war.[119]

On the other hand, the militarism of the republican movement proved to be the main bone of contention for the labour movement. At the 1922 Congress, calls were made for Labour to refuse to take part in the military activities of the IRA and to refrain from civil war:

It is not a war of the masses against the classes. It is not a war that will serve any working class interest. It is not a war that will make the lot of the worker easier ... Starve to death rather than shed your blood in this civil war.[120]

G. Lynch of the Dundalk Trades Council declared:

You failed in the peace efforts, with the result that we are still in the midst of civil war ... we are representing workers, as workers, and though we want to take a neutral standpoint, we are faced continually with the fact that owing to the war activities these people we are representing are being brought down to the starvation level ... It is all right talking about politics, but we are here in the interests of the workers of Ireland as a whole, and we will not shirk our responsibility.[121]

At the same time the IRA complained that many workers were 'actively co-operating with Free State forces', while organised labour had 'up to the present, freely co-operated in assisting the "Free State" and the British Government in their attempts to exterminate the Republican

---

[118] Andrews, *Dublin Made Me*, p. 200.
[119] *Ibid.*
[120] ITUC/LP, *Annual Report*, 1922, p. 106.
[121] *Ibid.*, p. 139.
[122] Irish Republican Army document dated 5 August 1922 cited in the ITUC/LP, *Annual Report*, 1922.

forces'.[122] And M. Harle at the 1922 Congress claimed that 'the majority operating on either side of the combatants are workers'.[123]

While the ITUC/LP was seen as 'Free Stater',[124] there is some evidence to suggest that the ITGWU benefited from the advance of republicanism.[125] It has been argued that 'nowhere was Labour policy more enigmatic, more futile in its waste of opportunity, or more cynically deceptive, than in its response to Republicanism'.[126] However, the republicans' attitude to Labour could be assessed very much in the same terms – no real effort was made by the republicans to exploit certain situations such as the postal workers' strike of 1922.

VII

The fragmentation of working-class politics was further increased by the attitude of the Catholic church.[127] As a body, the church was highly suspicious of the labour movement and the influence of socialism on the individual members of trade unions. During the intense years of 1911 and 1914, as Larkin was busy organising workers and preaching socialism, the church was vitriolic in its attack on the labour movement. As Rumpf and Hepburn have shown, the 'long-term antipathy of the bulk of the Irish population to even milder forms of socialism ... was the product of church influence in the years down to 1914'.[128]

It was the attack on the sacred ideal of private property, so central to catholicism, which was the most feared aspect of the labour movement. The fate of the original *Democratic Programme* owed much to the attitude of the church in the clauses concerning property. Such a definite denial of private property as advocated by Johnson's draft of the *Democratic programme* challenged the very foundations of the church. Though left-wing Catholic intellectuals – such as Frs Peter Coffey and William Moran of Maynooth – tried to reconcile traditional church teaching with socialism, their views 'lost out to a Catholic church which adopted Pius X's condemnations of social modernism'.[129]

---

[123] ITUC/LP, *Annual Report*, 1922, p. 143.
[124] *Workers' Republic*, 16 December 1922.
[125] P. Starrett, 'The Irish Transport and General Workers Union in its Industrial and Political Context', University of Ulster, Coleraine, unpublished Ph.D. thesis, 1989, p. 367.
[126] O'Connor, *Syndicalism In Ireland*, p. 186.
[127] For background to the church and its role in Irish history and society see: D. Keogh, *The Church, Vatican and Irish Politics, 1919–45*, Cambridge, 1986; J. Whyte, *Church and State In Modern Ireland*, Dublin, 1980.
[128] E. Rumpf and A. Hepburn, *Nationalism and Socialism in Twentieth-Century Ireland*, Liverpool, 1977, p. 16.
[129] B. Murphy, *Patrick Pearse and the Lost Republican Ideal*, Dublin, 1991, p. 109.

That the church saw the upholding and protection of property as the way to safeguard the status quo in society is clear in the attitude taken to the industrial unrest and the threats to property made during the civil war.[130] In May 1920 the Bishop of Ross, at a meeting of the Council of Agriculture warned that 'by a Republic, many Irishmen mean a Workers' Republic and they define the workers as the proletariat and propose to take over all sources of production in the country, to run the Government'. He called such a position a 'denial of democracy' for it meant 'government by a class'. He claimed that 'in Ireland there is little room for a social revolution'. Ross even appealed to Unionists in the north, suggesting that partition would weaken the hold of property ownership and 'the hope of excluding revolutionary ideas' would diminish:

The great conservative force in Ireland is the multitude of peasant owners and their families and friends. If the Ulster Unionists retire behind the boundary of the six counties, there will not be that preponderant proportion of the owning classes over the proletariat that exists in unpartitioned Ireland.[131]

As unrest widened, a pastoral letter was delivered during Lent in 1922, by the Archbishop of Dublin, who spoke of the dangers of 'pagan doctrines' which threatened the notion of property:

This Paganism is an ever-present danger, and it is simply the expression of man's fallen nature and the forgetfulness of God. It manifests itself in many ways … in a disregard for the rights of others shown, on the one hand, by a capitalism which looks on the worker as a chattel to hire, rather than a man with a right to a living wage and frugal comfort, and, on the other, by a proletariate [sic] which disregards the natural right of men to hold private property … Justice will demand that the worker receive an honest wage for his daily toil to enable him to live in decent comfort … Justice will also demand that the natural right of men to hold private property be respected.[132]

During the civil war, Cardinal Logue issued a pastoral letter which condemned the destruction of 'life and property' which, he wrote, was part of a 'campaign of plunder, raiding banks and private houses, seizing the lands and property of others, burning mansions and country houses, destroying demesnes and slaying cattle'.[133]

---

[130] Brown writes that 'Irish Catholicism increasingly became a badge of national identity at a time when the church also felt able to propound doctrines that enshrined the rights of private property. In a nation where nationalist aspiration was so often rooted in the farmer's rigorous attachment to his land, all this helped to ensure the Church's continued role in Irish life even though at difficult moments during the Land War and the War of Independence ecclesiastics felt obliged to oppose the tactics employed by political activists'. See T. Brown, *Ireland: A Social and Cultural History, 1922–1985*, London, 1981, p. 29.

[131] *Irish News*, 1 May 1920.

[132] Archbishop of Dublin's Church Archives, pastoral letter dated 24 February 1922.

[133] *Ibid.*, 22 October 1922.

On another level, the church appears in some instances to have questioned the merits of the labour leadership to guide the workers, the overwhelming majority of whom were Catholics. Revd John Flanagan of the Pro Cathedral, Dublin, in a speech at the Catholic Truth Society's conference, urged workers to make sure that trade union officials were practising and instructed Catholics, and made note that Johnson was the only Protestant. *Voice of Labour* responded by saying the Irish labour movement was not a sectarian movement and that it was not the duty of labour leaders to instruct the rank and file of organised labour in catholicity.[134] Nevertheless this attack on socialist ideas and condemnation of the sporadic agrarian and industrial action was damaging to Labour, as the church had a great influence over the bulk of the trade union membership as well as on Irish society in general.

VIII

By 1923 the national revolution in Ireland had run its course and the conservative state which came into being enshrined its own nationalist mythology and fought off any threats to its position. Nationalism remained the dominant ideology. But it was a conservative nationalism and all radical aspects of the separatist movement were kept under control so as not to disturb the new state. As Sinn Féiner P. S. O'Hegarty wrote in 1923:

The Irish nationalist tradition has always been national rather than proletarian, and it takes quite a quantity of inoculation for the jargon of which the modern world is so enamoured to take root here.[135]

The action of the labour movement was kept in check by the nationalists and cramped by the problem of trying to maintain a united Irish labour movement, which was hopelessly insoluble especially once the country was partitioned in 1920. The workers split over and over again, as the civil war and the Catholic church introduced new variables. On the other hand, the radicalism of the nationalist movement must be called into question, for apart from its goal of national independence, there was no real revolution, and no claims to radically change Irish society. As for the labour movement, it was in a binding predicament. To turn its back on the national revolution completely and espouse internationalism would have alienated a large section of its trade union support. For Labour, there was no clear path forward – for that path had been blurred from the moment when the 'cause of Labour' had been equated with the 'cause of Ireland'. In 1923, both causes were found wanting.

[134] *Voice of Labour*, 20 October 1923.
[135] P. S. O'Hegarty, *The Victory of Sinn Féin*, Dublin, 1924.

12   Land, people and nation: historicist voices in the Highland land campaign, *c.* 1850–1883

John Shaw

I

Conventional wisdom has tended to presume that the political movement for land reform in the Highlands of Scotland grew organically and unproblematically out of the crofting community itself,[1] and that the victories of the Crofters' Party in the elections in 1885 and 1886 moved by some ineluctable process from the spontaneous outbursts of anger characteristic of the 'land war' of the first half of the 1880s.[2] In the best of such accounts outside influences are never neglected and a subtle and variegated picture of the land reform campaign has been presented.[3] The concern here will be to examine the complex historical construction of the crofting community behind the political movement arguing the crofters' case. This means focusing upon the relationship between the images of culture, language and community projected by the land reform movement. At the heart of this lay the question of land and the rich and culturally specific meanings it took on in relation to what was thought of as the ancient nation of the Celts.

Liberalism was engaged by the land question over a much wider area and longer period than the Highlands of the 1880s.[4] It is the extent to which land and community (and ultimately nation) became cognates that distinguishes the problems which the Liberals experienced over crofters'

---

[1] See I. M. M. Macphail, 'The Napier Commission', *Transactions of the Gaelic Society of Inverness* (henceforth *TGSI*), 48 (1972–4), pp. 435–72; 'Prelude to the Crofters' War, 1870–80', *TGSI*, 49 (1974–76), pp. 159–88; 'Gunboats to the Hebrides', *TGSI*, 53 (1982–4), pp. 531–67; D. H. Crowley, 'The "Crofters' Party", 1885–92', *Scottish Historical Review*, 35 (1956), pp. 110–20; J. G. Kellas, 'The Crofters' War', *History Today*, 12 (1962), pp. 281–8.

[2] The Crofters' Party put up six candidates in the election of 1886 and won, see J. Vincent and M. Stenton (eds.), *McCalmont's Parliamentary Poll Book of all Elections 1832–1918*, London, 1971, Part II, pp. 5, 30, 118–19, 205, 236, 253–4.

[3] For instance James Hunter, *The Making of the Crofting Community*, Edinburgh, 1976.

[4] Eugenio F. Biagini, *Liberty, Retrenchment and Reform: Popular Liberalism in the Age of Gladstone, 1860–1880*, Cambridge, 1992, pp. 56–9, 62, 139, 186–91 (where land reform is discussed as an exception to the rule of *laissez-faire*), 303–4; Jonathan Parry, *The Rise and Fall of Liberal Government in England*, London, 1993, pp. 4–5, 17, 210, 243–5, 262; cf. chapter 10 above, pp. 253–75.

rights in the Highlands and, more famously, in Ireland.[5] One context was the cultural particularity of much of the crofting region, which was not only not English, but not simply Scottish – it was Celtic. This distinctiveness was preserved in the Gaelic language, oral tradition, the use of Gaelic in religious observance and so forth.[6] The dramatic tension of the land crisis of the 1880s was coloured by the immediacy of such traditions. Distinctions between an *echt* culture of the people and the images of the culture presented in the political campaign are now notoriously difficult to make. As Charles Withers suggests, the paucity of sources 'makes it difficult to understand the cultural production *of* the Gaels as opposed to the cultural productions *imposed* on them'.[7] In relation to contemporary political argument about land reform and the status of the crofting community, such traditions were recast within a historicist interpretation which attempted to present anew the virtues of peasant proprietorship.[8]

This historicist interpretation was of long provenance but gained momentum from the mid-nineteenth century and placed the land question and the revival of things Celtic in a symbiotic relationship. Peasant institutions were recast by Gaelic enthusiasts determined to resurrect the historical status of the culture and political institutions which lay behind the community. It was land that gave a corporeality to visions of culture and community and that also provided the connective tissue between a range of often vague historical and cultural assertions and the material suffering and struggles of the crofters. It connected a *volk* concept of the 'Highland people' with the people that lived in the Highlands. The historicist reconstruction of the status of the peasant and Celtic revivalism fused land and community and this fusion structured and filled out political argument. In this process a pre-existing vision of the

---

[5] See, for instance, N. D. Palmer, *The Irish Land League Crisis*, New Haven, 1940; J. E. Pomfret, *The Struggle for Land in Ireland, 1800–1923*, Princeton, 1930; Samuel Clark, *Social Origins of the Irish Land War*, Princeton, 1979; Sally Warwick-Haller, *William O'Brien and the Irish Land War*, Dublin, 1990. On Scotland and Ireland comparatively see James Hunter, 'The Gaelic Connection: the Highlands, Ireland and Nationalism, 1873–1922', *Scottish Historical Review*, 54 (1975), pp. 179–204. On land as an issue in popular politics elsewhere, see P. Jones-Evans, 'Evan Pan Jones – Land Reformer', *Welsh Historical Review*, 4 (1968), pp. 143–59; J. P. D. Dunbabin, 'The "Revolt of the Field": The Agricultural Labourers' Movement in the 1870s', *Past and Present*, 26 (1963), pp. 68–97; Reg Groves, *Sharpen the Sickle*, London, 1981, pp. 39–111; Nigel Scotland, *Methodism and the Revolt of the Field: A Study of the Methodist Contribution to Agricultural Trade Unionism in East Anglia 1872–96*, Gloucester, 1981; Alun Howkins, *Poor Labouring Men: Rural Radicalism in Norfolk, 1872–1923*, London, 1985.

[6] Charles W. J. Withers, *Gaelic Scotland: The Transformation of a Culture Region*, London, 1988, p. 328 and *passim*.

[7] *Ibid.*, p. 327.

[8] Clive Dewey, 'Celtic Agrarian Legislation and the Celtic Revival: Historicist Implications of Gladstone's Irish and Scottish Land Acts 1870–1886', *Past and Present*, 64 (1974), pp. 30–70.

Highlands was rearticulated, supplemented and offered back to the people who, in the wake of the 1884 Reform Act, were a newly potent force.[9]

II

Incidents between the 1850s and the 1880s which prefigured the land war can now be set in the context of wider patterns of resistance to the Highland clearances than once would have been recognised.[10] Such incidents illustrate the way in which direct action by crofters was interpreted by sympathisers trying to give wider political articulation to their case. On the island of Bernera in 1874 persistent interference with previously accepted grazing practices led to resistance by crofters and to consequent evictions. The ensuing conflict resulted in legal action over an assault upon a sheriff officer and an affray in Stornaway which led to four arrests. These men were acquitted and the eviction notices on the Bernera crofters were allowed to lapse.[11] The political interpretation of this incident was fitted into a wider conspectus. Immediately after the trials an anonymous pamphlet with the revealing title *Report of the Trial of the So-called Bernera Rioters* was produced in Edinburgh, claiming to give an account of the proceedings.[12] Moreover, in their defence, an unknown person retained an Inverness lawyer, Charles Innes, the Conservative agent for Inverness-shire – not an obvious person to defend the crofters' interest. Matheson, the Bernera landlord, was the Liberal MP for Ross-shire from 1847 until 1868, when he was succeeded by his nephew.[13] The possibility that the Conservative Innes might have been willing to use the incident to embarrass the Liberal Matheson cannot be overlooked. Not only is party affiliation a factor in interpreting the political uptake of land disputes but what we know of these incidents themselves has been refracted through this prism.

Later the same year, in Swainbost, a similar situation pertained. Crofters had grazing rights on Swainbost links which, and the language is

---

[9] On constructions of the Highlands as a geographical and cultural entity, see Peter Womack, *Improvement and Romance: Constructing the Myth of the Highlands*, London, 1989; Charles W. J. Withers, 'The Historical Creation of the Scottish Highlands', in Ian Donnachie and Christopher Whatley (eds.), *The Manufacture of Scottish History*, Edinburgh, 1992, pp. 143–56.

[10] E. Richards, 'How Tame were the Highlanders during the Clearances?', *Scottish Studies*, 17 (1973), pp. 35–50; 'Patterns of Highland Discontent, 1790–1860', in R. Quinault and J. Stevenson (eds.), *Popular Protest and Public Order*, London, 1974, pp. 75–114.

[11] *The Highlander*, 25 April 1874; on the Bernera incident, see MacPhail, 'Prelude to the Crofters' War', and on conditions on Bernera, J. S. Blackie, *The Scottish Highlander and the Land Laws*, London, 1885.

[12] Anon., *Report of the Trial of the So-called Bernera Rioters*, Edinburgh, 1874.

[13] *The Highlander*, 25 April 1874.

significant, had been held 'since time immemorial' until 1872. Then the Mains of Swainbost had been let to a Mr Sutherland who was given sole rights to most of this grazing. Rather than offend the chamberlain, the crofters rented it from Sutherland from 1872 until 1874 but anticipated a reduction in their rent to the landlord which was not forthcoming. They told the factor that they were not paying Sutherland until they had seen the proprietor. He agreed to amend the situation but did nothing and the crofters marched to see the proprietor in Stornaway. In response the factor intercepted them and agreed to reinstate their original right.[14]

Patterns of conservative resistance, and of struggles to retain or recover putative traditional and moral rights, are common strands in radical argument.[15] This is the case in the description of the events at Bernera and Swainbost advanced in the reforming journal, *The Highlander*, but it was developed beyond the defence of customary right. *The Highlander* was established by the radical John Murdoch a year before these incidents and from its inception it addressed the Highland land question in ways that assumed a continuity between the land and a putative nation. It did so in a period when there was little more than sporadic bursts of popular anger from which to build a reforming movement.

Murdoch's credo is apparent from his earliest utterances in the new journal:

We this day place in the hands of the Highlanders a journal which they can call their own. This we do with the distinct view of stimulating them to develop their own industrial resources and encouraging them to assert their nationality and maintain that position in the country to which their numbers, their traditions and their character entitle them.[16]

In this way the economic base of the Highland region was linked to assumptions about nationality. The preservation of the race, of the 'particular type of humanity to which they belong' was seen as imperative.[17] Aspects of nationhood went much further than this because 'there are sentiments and tendencies of thought; there are fragments of an ancient polity – traditions of the older time – hanging about us'.[18] Sentiment was a key factor in the development of the reconstruction of the Highlands as a political community. 'Contemning [*sic*] the senti-

---

[14] *The Highlander*, 12 December 1874.

[15] For a discussion of this, see E. P. Thompson. 'The Moral Economy of the English Crowd in the Eighteenth Century' and 'The Moral Economy Reviewed', in *Customs in Common*, London, 1991, pp. 185–258, 259–351.

[16] *The Highlander*, 16 May 1873.

[17] *Ibid.*

[18] *Ibid.* Murdoch had previously argued that the idea that the Highlands had recently been delivered from feudalism was bogus and that in fact the feudal system was built upon the ruins of the clan system; John Murdoch, 'The Clan System', *TGSI*, I (1871–2), pp. 31–43.

ments of our people was very nearly akin to despising themselves, and that very naturally led to the very general practice of undervaluing even the material wealth around us.'[19] A link was thus forged between the sentiments from which nationhood was seen as being constructed and the material resources. It is a short step from there to raging about the abuse of the land and its occupants: 'There are our rivers, our lochs, our moors. Are they for no better purposes than sport while our people are half idle in their bothies and the nation wants food from the land?'[20] For Murdoch the problem of Highland land was a dimension of a wider crisis of national self-confidence. Given that he did not believe that the sentiments of nationhood he wished to see were a political force in the mid-1870s, the assertion of nationhood amounts to an attempt to define the Highlands and Islands as a political community. This was given further resolution by setting it against the other side of the land controversy – the landlord.

> So without any straining after effect, and without anything to distrust as to our own or our contributors' statements, we may say that there is within the limits of *The Highlander* itself a positive demonstration that our country, from one end to the other, is labouring under the malign influence of a vicious land system.[21]

The earlier assertion was of frustrated nationhood and the radical project being raised upon it was to define the crofting community as a vital dimension of nationality and also as the victim of the present tenurial system. These categories were conflated in a way that allowed the community to be asserted as the necessary political raw material from which a movement could be built. This was developed to a point where *The Highlander* itself was seen as a 'positive demonstration' of the nation it attempted to highlight.

By mid-1874 it was being argued that 'even the humble crofters can make themselves heard sometimes, although they are proverbial for their quietness. Indeed the idea was beginning to be entertained that the whole Highland peasantry have been too quiet and submissive'.[22] The linkages forged between the land, the people and the nation meant that direct action by the people could be seen as an expression of the nation. Aligning themselves with such resistance the contributors to *The Highlander* extended this lifestyle to historically encompass a national past. It became the legitimating idiom of an infant movement concerned with the land issue in an area increasingly seen as being bathed in a Celtic twilight.

[19] *The Highlander*, 16 May 1873.
[20] *Ibid.*
[21] *Ibid.*, 12 July 1873.
[22] *Ibid.*, 25 April 1874.

III

The new sensibility was not only rooted in the Highlands and Islands. Highland exiles were largely responsible for creating an elaborate support system for the bounded and putatively beseiged language and culture.[23] In the cities of the south during the 1860s and 1870s Highland enthusiasms were expressed in formal associations. In Glasgow a Sutherland Association was founded in 1860, a Skye Association in 1865, a Tiree Association in 1870 and a Lewis Association in 1876. There was also a Mull and Iona Association, a Ross-shire Association, an Islay Association, an Appin Society, a Coll Society and an Ardnamurchan, Morvern and Sunart Association. Similar societies prospered in Edinburgh and the London Gaelic Society was described as the 'old and patriotic parent of all our Celtic Societies'.[24] The most significant of the new Gaelic societies, the Gaelic Society of Inverness, was founded in 1871 and was followed by others in Glasgow, Greenock, Aberdeen and Dundee.[25] During the 1870s they promoted the teaching of Gaelic, many campaigning for a chair in Gaelic at Edinburgh University. Whilst in their earlier days many of them deferred to the notable landowners of their localities, they played a vital role in asserting a positive series of images of the particular nature of the Highlands which was developed prior to the 1880s. Their activities were reported in publications like the *Celtic Magazine*, started in 1876, which also carried articles on Gaelic and comparative philology; the need for a Gaelic professorship; the literature, song and language of the Highlands and histories of the clearances and depopulation.[26]

Important anterior frameworks were thus established to articulate grievances and give them a coherent context which was intelligible to sympathisers. Support was recruited from those with no personal connection with the Highlands but politically aligned with the crofters' case and possessing a sentimental view of Highland life. Mathilde Blind, in her narrative poem *The Heather on Fire*, presented just such a picture and also raged against the injustice of the clearances.[27] She was the step-daughter of the German exile, Karl Blind, himself a noted folklorist who

[23] For a general history of the Gaelic language and culture in this period, see Withers, *Gaelic Scotland*, especially pp. 327–401.

[24] *Celtic Magazine*, 3 (1878), p. 173. The London Society had long made a cause of defending the language and enjoyed its centenary, *ibid.*, 2 (1877), pp. 353–66.

[25] *TGSI*, 1 (1871–2).

[26] This included a continuing discussion of the status of Macpherson and the Ossian legend, *TGSI*, 1 (1871–2), p. 3. See also 'The Ossianic Controversy, between Dr Hately Waddell and Hector Maclean, Islay', *Celtic Magazine*, 1 (1876), pp. 343–55, 372–8; 2 (1877), pp. 116–19.

[27] Mathilde Blind, *Poetical Works*, London, 1900, pp. 89–153. This poem is dedicated to Captain Cameron of the steamer *Lochiel* for resigning rather than carry the police expedition to suppress the Skye crofters in 1884, p. 89.

studied the comparative folklore of Shetland and Germany.[28] It all provided orientation, helped to complete an overarching historical picture into which the events at Bernera, Swainbost and later the 'crofters' war' could be fitted. This was especially valuable at Westminster where it could help MPs sympathetic to the crofters' cause to approach other potential sympathisers – a stock piece in the armoury of land-reforming Liberal MPs like Charles Fraser-Mackintosh, member for Inverness-shire, who went on to represent the Crofters' Party.

IV

A negative view of Scottish Gaels and their historical culture had grown out of Scottish Enlightenment concerns with Gaelic antiquity. Colin Kidd has recently suggested that an enlightened 'conjectural sociology undermined the values associated with Gaeldom' and according to a stadial theory of social progress Scottish Gaels were seen as having stagnated in a primitive condition.[29] Prior to the Fenian rising of 1865–6 there was broad agreement that Scotland, like Ireland, was overpopulated through irresponsible procreation and bad agriculture which demanded free trade, especially in land.[30] By the 1860s, however, rising enthusiasm for Celtic culture and language in both Ireland and Scotland fed into a growing lyric historicism in England.[31] Overstating this would risk caricature, but there is little doubt that the intellectual climate was less hospitable to doctrinaire political economy than it had been during the 1850s.[32] The questioning of political economy came from various directions. Jevons' marginal utility theory threatened a central plank – the labour theory of value – and, by the late 1860s, John Stuart Mill had repudiated the wages fund theory. The influence of Comte and the inductivist approach was a source of further questioning, particularly through his influence on Mill and Frederic Harrison. An economic historicism devel-

---

[28] Karl Blind, 'New Finds in Shetlandic and Welsh Folk-lore' *The Gentleman's Magazine*, 252 (1882), pp. 353–71; 'A Grimm's Tale in a Shetland Folklore Version', *Archaeological Review*, 1 (1888), pp. 346–52.

[29] Colin Kidd, 'Gaelic Antiquity and National Identity in Enlightenment Ireland and Scotland', *English Historical Review*, 109 (1994), pp. 1197–1214.

[30] For instance, John Stuart Mill wrote that 'the best system of landed property was that in which land is most completely the subject of commerce'; J. S. Mill, *Political Economy* in *Collected Works*, ed. E. E. C. Priestley, London, 1965, vol. I, p. 839. Mill's views on land in the Celtic areas were later cited with approval by land reformers, see *The Highlander*, 26 July, 2 August 1873; 25 May 1875.

[31] Dewey, 'Celtic Agrarian Legislation and the Celtic Revival'.

[32] G. Kitson Clark, *Churchmen and the Condition of England, 1832–1885*, London, 1973, pp. 190–313; Stefan Collini, Donald Winch and John Burrow, *That Noble Science of Politics: A Study in Nineteenth-century Intellectual History*, Cambridge, 1983, pp. 249–75.

oped in Ireland through Cliffe Leslie and J. K. Ingram and in England from Rogers, Cunningham and Toynbee.[33]

Such disputes were also reflected in historical jurisprudence which was influenced by German thought. Names which have been associated with this turn include Maine, Pollock, Vinogradoff, Bryce, Maitland, Hancock and Ritchie.[34] It is arguable that the historicist reaction moved from here to political economy and Sir Henry Maine in particular influenced economic thought.[35] The historicist vision, and that part of it which focused upon the Celtic communities, was part of a wider uptake of German scholarship in mid-Victorian educated society.[36]

Aspects of this historicism acted as a pre-condition for a sociology that accorded a new value to the communitarian, to custom and the collective.[37] In one mode it questioned the predominance of contractarian and individualist thought. Significant in this was the realisation that custom was not necessarily inflexible but could evolve, as Maine had argued, with the society in which it operated. Moreover, the cohesiveness of a society was rooted in the relationship between custom and belief. The historical journey undergone by developed societies was one from the dominance of status to the dominance of contract.[38] This suggested that the tenets of political economy were historically relative, the child of a particular historical moment. The premature imposition of the laws of commercial society to societies properly dominated by status, custom and the communitarian could only lead to devastating social dislocation. Given this, the re-evaluation of peasant proprietorship could be envisaged.[39] A formerly despised group could be seen as possessing ancient virtues like loyalty, industriousness and thrift. The Celtic periphery could now appear on centre stage.

In the case of Ireland these developments raised up more dangerous

---

[33] Dewey, 'Celtic Agrarian Legislation and the Celtic Revival', pp. 35–6.

[34] *Ibid.*

[35] J. W. Burrow, *Evolution and Society: A Study in Victorian Social Theory*, Cambridge, 1966; G. A. Feaver, *From Status to Contract*, London, 1969; R. C. J. Cocks, *Sir Henry Maine: A Study in Victorian Jurisprudence*, Cambridge, 1988; Sir Henry Maine, *Ancient Law*, London, 1861; *Village Communities East and West*, London, 1871; *Early History of Institutions*, London, 1875; *Early Laws and Customs*, London, 1878.

[36] A. W. Coats, 'The Historicist Reaction in English Political Economy', *Economica*, 21 (1954), pp. 143–53; T. W. Hutchinson, *A Review of Economic Doctrines 1870–1939*, Oxford, 1953, pp. 28ff.; J. W. Burrow, *Evolution and Society*, pp. xv, 136, 235; J. W. Burrow, *A Liberal Descent: Victorian Historians and the National Past*, Cambridge, 1981, pp. 97–228.

[37] C. J. Dewey, 'Images of the Indian Village Community: A Study in Anglo-Indian Thought', *Modern Asian Studies*, 6 (1972), pp. 291–328; 'The Education of a Ruling Caste: The India Civil Service in the Era of Competitive Examination', *English Historical Review*, 88 (1973), pp. 262–85.

[38] Maine, *Ancient Law*, pp. 170, 311–12.

[39] C. J. Dewey, 'The Rehabilitation of Peasant Proprietorship in Nineteenth-century Economic Thought', *Modern Asian Studies*, 6 (1972), pp. 291–328.

possibilities. Outrages on the land, the Fenian rising and then the various forces feeding into the nationalist movement in the 1870s, reinforced this and coloured responses to Celtic revivalism.[40] In Scotland such constraints upon the development of a sentimental view of the Highlands were less severe. Highland Jacobites had long been an object of nostalgia and Queen Victoria's promotion of a Highland identity coupled to a view of the Highlanders as passive victims of the clearances had solidified into received opinion.[41] Defeat following the '45 and pacification by force alongside the harnessing of the Highland martial tradition to the service of the crown led to a reputation for quietism. It was this and the resultant cultural disorganisation and loss of self-esteem that informed Murdoch's complaints.[42] All this played a part in enabling the transformation of the image of the inefficient sluggard into a survival of the tragic and shattered clan system.

V

The consideration of the national past and the relative status within this of Gaels and Picts had long troubled Scottish historical scholarship during its golden age between 1750 and 1820. George Chalmers had, between 1807 and 1824, begun to make up for the paucity of written evidence on the Dark Ages through the study of place names, language and archaeology.[43] He laid the basis for a balanced view of the ancient Celts at a time when Macpherson's *Ossian* 'had divided the world into idolators and detractors'.[44] This contrasted sharply with John Pinkerton, who had earlier approached the Dark Ages with a more erratic understanding of etymology and was ferociously anti-Celt.[45]

The writing of William Forbes Skene, son of the close friend of Sir Walter Scott, James Skene of Rubislaw, represents one early connection between this historical scholarship and the developing historicism. Highland born, he studied philology in Germany in 1827 and had become an

---

[40] The land agitation in the mid-1880s happened against the backdrop of the Phoenix Park killings, the bomb in the Home Office (that exploded) and the bomb in the offices of *The Times* (that did not). The same edition of *The Times* that reported these two bombs also reported the trial of crofter agitators from Glendale (Skye) in Edinburgh. See *The Times*, 16 March 1883.

[41] Eric Richards, 'How Tame were the Highlanders During the Clearances?' questions the actual extent of their timidity but the prevailing *image* was doubtless one of passivity.

[42] T. M. Devine, *Clanship to Crofters' War: The Social Transformation of the Scottish Highlands*, Manchester, 1994, pp. 209–10.

[43] George Chalmers, *Caledonia*, 3 vols., London, 1807–24. Vol. III deals with the Dark Ages.

[44] James Anderson, 'William Forbes Skene: Celtic Scotland v. Caledonia', *Scottish Historical Review*, 46 (1967), p. 141.

[45] John Pinkerton, *Enquiry into the History of Scotland, etc*, 2 vols., London, 1789.

enthusiastic Germanophile who learned both Gaelic and Welsh and eventually, in 1881, became Historiographer Royal for Scotland.[46] His earlier work differentiated clan histories but his *magnum opus, Celtic Scotland,* presented a more complete history, arguing that in ancient Scotland the tribe was the historic unit of social organisation, and emphasised the blood ties cementing chief and kinsmen.[47] Here the clan had two special features. First, there was originally no concept of private property – ownership grew out of communal property. Secondly, the primary social unit was not the family but the community.[48] Skene believed that this ancient system had been shattered, partly as a result of the economic differentiation of personal from communal wealth deriving from differences in ability, but also from the effects of the centripetal force of Scottish Lowland government.[49]

It should be noted, however, that Skene administered the hated 'destitution test' for relief during the famine, which was seen by many as an imposition of heartless political economy.[50] He was deeply involved in relief work during the famine in the 1840s, becoming secretary of the Edinburgh section of the Central Board of Relief.[51] Aware of the disapprobrium that 'the test' brought, he ascribed the animosity to ignorance of the longer-term restructuring that the 'test' would bring.[52] His veneration of Highland history and tradition must be set against this contempt for the ways of contemporary Highlanders.[53] Skene was not of a piece with those who created a historicist connection between Highland history and the present state of the Highlands. In spite of this he was a proponent of an important understanding of early Scottish history which helped to inform this historicism. The introduction of the first volume of the *Transactions of the Gaelic Society of Inverness* commended Skene for editing *The Dean of Lismore's Book.*[54] He helped furnish historical valida-

---

[46] Anderson, 'William Forbes Skene', p. 142; T. M. Devine, *The Great Highland Famine: Hunger, Emigration and the Scottish Highlands in the Nineteenth Century,* Edinburgh, 1988, p. 128.

[47] W. F. Skene, *The Highlanders of Scotland,* 2 vols., London, 1837; *Celtic Scotland: A History of Ancient Alban,* 3 vols., Edinburgh, 1876–80.

[48] Skene, vol I, p. 138. This finds an echo from Murdoch, who stressed the role of filial feeling that bound the community together, that the reciprocity of the system meant that the chief could not be despotic, and that the law of Tanistry, by which the most able son could become heir, was once general to the system, suggesting that primogeniture, the defining characteristic of the Anglo-Saxon system, was not natural, Murdoch, 'The Clan System', pp. 31–43.

[49] Skene, *The Highlanders of Scotland,* vol. I, pp. 139, 335.

[50] T. M. Devine, *The Great Highland Famine,* p. 135.

[51] *Ibid.,* pp. 91, 124.

[52] Skene to Sir Charles Trevelyan, 21 February 1848, Scottish Record Office HD7/47, quoted in *ibid.,* p. 136.

[53] *Ibid.,* p. 128.

[54] *TGSI,* I (1871–2), p. 3.

tion for what became a constitutive element in the wider claims made in the crofters' name and was notable for asserting that the orthography of certain early manuscripts suggested the linguistic and cultural independence of the central and northern Highlands and questioning the view that Ireland was the parental home of the Gael.[55] His later writing emerged into a political environment charged by activity in a direct if inchoate way in Bernera and Swainbost and, in an organised form, through the Gaelic societies and their publications. Skene's emphasis on philology helped fuel the concern for Gaelic. His stress on the history of legal structures meant that the reforming eye could easily be drawn from there to the question of land tenures.[56]

John Stuart Blackie was the most prominent Celtic enthusiast actually connected to the land reform campaign. Like Skene, he had studied in Germany between 1829 and 1830 – history under Heeren in Göttingen and theology under Schleiermacher in Berlin. He also followed lectures by Boeckh, Neander and Raumer.[57] As professor of Latin at Aberdeen University and then of Greek at Edinburgh he championed university reform and was one of the best known Scots of his day.[58] His nephew, the editor of his published notes, described him as 'German in training, Greek in spirit, and cosmopolitan in sympathy'.[59] This classical training and German education coloured his views of the history of the Highlands, its language and the nature of the community. Blackie was a Liberal with evangelical principles but had a temperamental sympathy for the old Moderate party in the Church of Scotland.[60] He prided himself on not being a slavish party man and supported reform in 1832. In mid-life he flirted with the Conservatives but opposed reform in 1867 and felt a highly qualified warmth for reform again in the 1880s.[61] His political heterodoxy, coupled with his importance in the land campaign and Celtic movement, should caution against assuming that the construction of the Highland community being advanced was merely a

[55] W. F. Skene, 'Introduction' to Sir James McGregor, *The Dean of Lismore's Book*, ed. Thomas McLaughlin, Edinburgh, 1862.

[56] For an example of the jurist line, see Cosmo Innes, *Lectures on Scottish Legal Antiquities*, Edinburgh, 1872.

[57] J. S. Blackie, *Notes of a Life by John Stuart Blackie*, ed. A. Stodart-Walker, Edinburgh, 1910, pp. 37–66. The notes were largely compiled between 1869 and 1872.

[58] J. G. Duncan, *The Life of Prof. John Stuart Blackie ... by Various Eminent Writers*, Glasgow, 1895; H. A. Kennedy, *Professor Blackie: His Sayings and Doings*, London, 1895; Anna M. Stodart, *John Stuart Blackie: A Biography*, Edinburgh, 1895.

[59] A. Stodart-Walker, 'Preface' to Blackie, *Notes of a Life*, p. vi.

[60] Blackie, *Notes of a Life*, pp. 22–5. He thought that he detected a sympathetic resonance of such views in the sermons of his hero, Schleiermacher, *ibid.*, p. 23.

[61] *Ibid.*, pp. 208–61 esp. 209–31; J. S. Blackie, *Democracy: A Debate between Prof. Blackie and E. Jones*, Manchester, 1885. This was Ernest Jones the former Chartist and the debate took place in 1867.

radical political device to beguile the Highlanders by creating an ennobled vision of their history to garner their support. The cultural production of this communitarian vision was politically complex, drawing on
credible scholarship, and itself containing diverse motives which were
articulated within the campaign for land reform. Legal history and a new
understanding of the significance of the Highland past, reinforced by a
restitution of status and the collective, provided the life spark of a
community's past that was re-presented to that community. Blackie
moved freely between the linked elements of the associational life of land
reform and Celtic revivalism.

A non-Highlander, Blackie first became aware the problem of Highland
depopulation and distress in 1856 whilst staying at Braemar.[62] His reaction
was horror and typically his initial analysis of the problem drew upon his
training as a classicist. He interpreted relations in the Highlands through
the optic of the struggle over land between 'the plebeian and patrician party
in classical Rome'.[63] This drew upon Pliny's contention that the great
estates were the ruin of Italy.[64] Pliny remained a touchstone for his interpretation of the agrarian problem into the land reform movement of the
1880s. The analogue was the Gracchi, seen as the patriotic group who,
resisting the greed of the senators for more land ('the besetting sin of every
aristocracy'), achieved their aim of a commission on land, 'such as the
friends of the crofters in the Highlands now propose for the repeopling of
the old depopulated homes of the clans'.[65] This also connected with his
anti-democratic sentiments, since the regrettable democratisation of the
old constitution had resulted from the same senatorial greed.[66]

Skene studied philology in Germany, Latin and Greek were Blackie's
main professional interests and language further tied together classical and
German influences. Of particular significance was the role of the origin
and development of language in the determination of a politics of culture
and community.[67] The influence of the Scottish historical school during
the eighteenth century upon Herder and German *Aufklärung* scholarship
has attracted comment.[68] Herderian perspectives on culture, language
and *volk* were highly mediated by the 1820s and 1830s and it would be the

---

[62] Blackie, *Notes of a Life*, p. 190.
[63] *Ibid.*
[64] *Ibid.*; John Stuart Blackie, *What does History Teach us?* London, 1886, p. 43; *Braemar Ballads*, Edinburgh, 1856.
[65] Blackie, *What does History Teach us?* p. 43.
[66] *Ibid.*
[67] Such thought about language and political association had deep roots in the *Aufklärung*, e.g. J. G. Herder, *Essays on the Origin of Language: Prize Essay given to the Royal Academy of Sciences, 1770*, Berlin, 1772; F. M. Barnard, *Herder's Social and Political Thought: From Enlightenment to Nationalism*, Oxford, 1965, pp. 54–87.
[68] Roy Pascal, 'Herder and the Scottish Historical School', *Publications of the English Goethe Society, 1939–39*, new series, 14 (Cambridge, 1939), pp. 23–42.

subject of another essay to map such influences on Skene, Blackie and others. Nonetheless, the similarity of their general concerns are clear and find further common ground in the stress placed upon the importance of education (*bildung*) in the formation of national character. For Blackie, as for Herder, it was the guarantor of tradition and of progress – it was a restraining discipline but it also conjured up potentialities.[69] Blackie led the campaign for the establishment of a chair in Gaelic at Edinburgh University. This was seen as an aspect of the redevelopment of the culture that would help to facilitate the reconstruction of the community. Highlanders, like the Poles and the Irish, had been overwhelmed but not assimilated; the land had been denuded and devastated but 'the Highlanders though humiliated and degraded, are not extinguished'.[70] Blackie advised the Gaelic societies, even in the attempt to establish a new professorship, to 'go to the people, and you will find them ready to support you, that is, if you have the right inspiration'.[71] Recourse to the people was necessary for support but also for moral arbitration.

To Blackie, 'folk-literature', which 'consists of popular songs', was a great corpus of literature.[72]

> I value these Scottish songs, I have got from these Scottish songs more than I have got from Homer, Aristotle, or Plato; or from all of them put together. The Scottish songs are full of the wisdom – the wisdom of life, sagacity, humour, pathos; full of everything that makes a man a man; full of everything which constitutes poetry.[73]

Song played a significant part in the formation of national character: 'You are essentially a lyrical people; I have heard a common woman express herself in the language of poetry.'[74] Furthermore, 'it has been said that "poetry makes rich the blood of the world"; and I say that "poetry makes rich the blood of the people"'.[75] Folk-songs are now regarded by historians as troublesome sources[76] but an acceptance of the historical validity of such material was central to the construction of the cultural

---

[69] This was also a view imbibed by Mill via Coleridge, J. S. Mill, *On Bentham and Coleridge*, ed. F. R. Leavis, London, 1950, p. 131; Barnard, *Herder's Social and Political Thought*, pp. 167–8.

[70] J. S. Blackie, *Gaelic Societies, Highland Depopulation and Land Law Reform* (inaugural address to the Gaelic Society, Perth, 7 October 1880), Edinburgh, 1880, p. 3.

[71] J. S. Blackie, 'Address to the Annual Assembly of the Gaelic Society of Inverness, 1876', *TGSI*, 5 (1875–6), pp. 13–14. Blackie was elected 'chief' of the society that year.

[72] In the manner of, if not directly influenced by, Herder. See, for instance, J. G. Herder, *On the Effects of Poetry on the Customs and Morals of Nations in Ancient and Modern Times*, 1778; Robert T. Clark Jnr., *Herder: His Life and Thought*, Berkeley, 1969, pp. 251–81.

[73] Blackie, 'Address to the Gaelic Society of Inverness, 1876', pp. 14–15.

[74] *Ibid.*

[75] *Ibid.*

[76] For discussions of this in relation to Highland history, see Eric Richards, *A History of the Highland Clearances*, 2 vols., London, 1982, 1985, vol. II, pp. 288–92.

identity in question here. It was seen as a historically determinate force but one that continued into the present. Songs lamenting and complaining of eviction and migration predated the land war of the 1880s. The Skye poet Mairi Mhor (Mary Macpherson) celebrated in verse the victory of the Bernera crofters in 1874 and urged action on land reform.[77] Alongside her protest she advanced a 'moving evocation of the self-sufficient communities of Skye in the days before the potato famine and mass migration' and she carried this message into the ceilidhs of Celtic enthusiasts and Land Leaguers.[78] She was also a supporter of Fraser-Mackintosh and accompanied him on election tours during 1882.[79] Poetry and songs of protest provided one of the more energetic modes of the land reformers and one that, through its connections with the cultural tradition and language, seemed itself to be evidence of continuity with the older world.

The character of the people was formulated in a language of 'blood' and 'fire' and set in the context of the retrieval of ancient institutions, community and literature. Blackie too identified them as a group ennobled and victimised.

We Scotch, English-speaking or Gaelic-speaking, are Gaels. Our very names prove that we are. And I say that it is a disgrace and a shame to us, inheriting that blood – the Combination of Celtic fire with the stubborness and sagacity of the Saxon – to say that this Gaelic language has existed only to be kicked out of this world.[80]

Defending the language created a conduit between the campaigner and the student of philology.[81] In this respect Blackie represented a sophisticated shift away from earlier Scottish ventures in comparative philology which asserted rigorous connections where he saw only affinities.[82] A special status was accorded to Gaelic because it was said to be a very close 'modification' of 'the Aryan dialects of Greece and Rome'.[83] The language was fixed in its location within a complex with land and people

---

[77] D. E. Meek, 'Gaelic Poets of the Land Agitation', *TGSI*, 49 (1977), pp. 50–1.

[78] D. E. Meek, 'The Role of Song in the Highland Land Agitation', *Scottish Gaelic Studies* 16 (1990), pp. 7, 11.

[79] *Ibid.*, p. 7.

[80] Blackie, 'Address to the Gaelic Society of Inverness, 1876', p. 14.

[81] See, for instance, William Morrison, 'Notes on the Affinity between German and Gaelic', *TGSI*, 5 (1875–6), pp. 64–71.

[82] He cites Revd T. Macpherson, *Philological Systems Delineated*, Edinburgh, 1859 and *Maclean on the Celtic Language*, London, 1840. He also credits Grimm and Heyne (*sic*) with redeeming the subject. J. S. Blackie, *The Gaelic Language: Its Classical Affinities and Distinctive Character*, Edinburgh, 1864, pp. 6–8. T. O'Neill Russell optimistically claimed that their verb structure represented the only substantial difference between Irish and Scots Gaelic; 'The Gaelic Language; Scotch and Irish Dialects', which ran in *The Highlander* throughout 1874.

[83] Blackie, *The Gaelic Language*, p. 1.

by suggesting an elective affinity between language and landscape. First, the Celtic modifications of the Aryan dialects were described, by means of a version of the pathetic fallacy, as relating to and phonetically echoing 'the granite bluffs of Bretagne, the green hills of Erin, the slaty precipices of Wales, and the heather-tufted glens of North Briton'.[84] Secondly, Gaelic suffered compared with English which was the rising and dominant language but also compared with other Celtic languages. Blame for this lay at home and abroad – in 'a lack of kindly concern for, and patriotic sympathy with the Celtic people as a peculiar race', and also an 'unworthy misprision' on the part of Highlanders.[85]

Saving the soul of the people could be brought about through education and the best vehicle for this was Gaelic. Claims were made for Gaelic over Latin, Greek and English.[86] The promotion of Gaelic teaching in schools was a subject of recurrent debate in the articles and correspondence of *The Highlander*.[87] Blackie's analysis identified the people as the repository of the language and said of teaching Gaelic:

Such a question could never have been raised except in an anomalous state of society, where the upper classes generally speak one language and the lower classes another. Under such circumstances, the upper classes are apt to imagine that they confer a boon on the lower, by presenting them with their more aristocratic organ of utterance, whilst the lower classes are apt to look on their mother tongue as an impediment rather than a help in the way of that rise in the world, which is the true heaven of every Scot.[88]

The crofting community was implicitly narrowed to the old realms of Gaeldom and the linguistic and cultural nation of the Gaels to the lower classes, that is the crofters and cotters, and was set against an intrusive Anglophone elite.

At the annual assembly of the Gaelic Society of Inverness in 1876, at which Blackie made a great impact with a speech demanding the salvation of the soul of the Highlands, Fraser-Mackintosh made his final address as 'chief' of the society. He remembered the cultural aims of the

---

[84] *Ibid.* Topography was discussed in relation to the derivations of Gaelic placenames. Alexander Mackenzie, 'Local Topography', *TGSI*, 1 (1971–2), pp. 23–31.

[85] Blackie, *The Gaelic Language*, pp. 4–5.

[86] *Ibid.*, p. 2. This was also a theme in an important speech made by Brougham in 1860, *Inaugural Address of Chancellor Brougham at Edinburgh University*, Edinburgh, 1860. English was described by Blackie as lacking the purity of the Celtic languages, *Celtic Magazine*, 2 (1877), p. 153.

[87] See also H. C. Gillies, 'Reasons why Gaelic should be Taught in Highland Schools', *TGSI*, 6 (1876–7), pp. 23–6; *Free Press*, 27 November 1876. By 1886 Secretary of State for Scotland Trevelyan could promise that 'the department gives every encouragement to the appointment of Gaelic teachers', suggesting that at least the principle had been recognised by the Liberal government, *Hansard*, vol. CCCII (1886), pp. 1762–3.

[88] J. S. Blackie, Letter, 'Gaelic in Highland Schools', *The Highlander*, 21 February 1874.

society but pointed to how the old problems of strict entails and impoverished proprietors, coupled with poor communications, price fluctuations and farm enlargements, had impoverished the people. The resulting famine had been used as justification for depopulation. He advocated redefining the role of the society to marry its original aims to new imperatives.

It would be right to establish, here in the capital of the Highlands, a society from which should emanate a desire for the collection of much that is interesting from a glorious past, *and for the furthering and fostering of efforts for the amelioration of the present*.[89]

The formal recruitment of the Inverness Society was a paramount moment in the unifying of the purposes of cultural enthusiasts and land reformers reached through the redefinition of the problem as a much vaster struggle to save the soul of the nation.

In December 1877 they debated the way the land laws had been historically misrepresented.[90] The previous year a paper given to the society by Colin Chisholm, a past president of the London Gaelic Society,[91] discussed 'misapplied capital and the cultivators of the land in the Highlands' and their consequences during the clearances.[92] Many of the better-known activists of the campaign, like Murdoch, Alex Mackenzie, Fraser-Mackintosh and so forth, were associated with the Inverness Society. A federation of Celtic societies was established in 1878 and was soon active in publicising crofters' issues.[93] It was substantially through the connections of such activists and this associational experience that the Highland land campaign grew. This associational experience amounted to more than its formal connections. It promoted a historicist understanding of what constituted the Highlands in its reformulation of land, language and people and the crofters were given a political meaning as a community in advance of the agitation of the 1880s.

---

[89] Charles Fraser-Mackintosh, 'Address to the Gaelic Society of Inverness, 1876', *TGSI*, 5 (1875–6), pp. 2–3. The original objects of the society stated the aims of preserving the language, promoting the literature and culture of the Gael and to 'vindicate the rights and character of the people', *ibid.*, p. v. Land reform is not singled out as an aspect of these rights at this stage.

[90] John Mackay, 'Errors regarding the *Elections* of Chiefs and the Land Laws', *TGSI*, 7 (1877–8), pp. 212–20.

[91] *Celtic Magazine*, 2 (1877), p. 153.

[92] Colin Chisholm, 'The Clearance of the Highland Glens', *TGSI*, 6 (1876–7), pp. 174–88; *Celtic Magazine*, 3 (1878), pp. 378–88.

[93] This federation was proposed by Charles Fraser-Mackintosh, 'Supplement', *Celtic Magazine*, 3 (1878), inter. pp. 320–1.

VI

Under pressure from the explosion of unrest, which started in Skye during the winter of 1880–1 and then spread beyond, and also from the land reform movement, a part of which was organised within the Liberal Party through MPs like Fraser-Mackintosh, Gladstone and Harcourt agreed to grant a royal commission on crofting on 28 February 1883.[94] It was chaired by Lord Napier and took evidence in sixty-one places throughout the region.[95] The Napier Commission deliberated against a background not just of unrest in the crofting townships but of renewed vigour from the land reform associations. These included a Skye Vigilance Committee established in Glasgow in 1881 by John Gunn Mackenzie and Angus Sutherland.[96] The London Highland Land Law Reform Association (HLLRA) was effective from June 1882 with the enthusiastic Donald Murray as its first secretary. The HLLRA appointed John Macpherson, a hero of the Glendale troubles in Skye, as a lecturer. This no doubt aided recruitment and by June 1882 it claimed to have 5,000 crofters among its members.[97] In Sutherland, the Sutherlandshire Association was largely inspired by Glasgow-based Angus Sutherland whose famous speech in Helmsdale was a moment in its growth.[98] In 1884 the Edinburgh HLLRA merged with the Free Church-dominated Highland Association which further helped its development.[99]

The land war, with its attendant arrests, imprisonments and the creation of genuinely local martyrs, not only focused attention upon the Highlands but also helped to connect the crofters more effectively to the broader movement. The concerted popular action that Murdoch had hoped for as early as 1874 seemed to be coming to fruition – the nation was at last speaking for itself. Connections of personnel like John Macpherson seemed to consolidate the homogeneity of the idea of the nation articulated by the Gaelic enthusiasts and land reformers and the crofting population. The two were even more firmly bonded together

---

[94] For a general account see Hunter, *Making of the Crofting Community*, pp. 130–206; on press reactions to the Skye rebellions, *The Highlander*, 23 March 1881; *Scotsman*, 17 April 1882; on the lionising of those prosecuted, A. Mackenzie, *The Isle of Skye, 1882–1883*, Inverness, 1883, pp. 37–8; on parliamentary arguments over a commission, *Hansard*, ser. 3, vol. CCLXVII (1882), p. 1032; vol CLXIX (1882), p. 227; vol. CCLXXIV (1882), pp. 227–8; vol. CCLXXVI (1883), p. 853.

[95] *Royal Commission of Inquiry on the Condition of Cotters and Crofters in the Highlands of Scotland, 1883–4*, 5 vols. (henceforth *Napier Commission*), *Parliamentary Papers 1884*, vols. XXXII–XXXVI.

[96] James Cameron, *The Old and the New Hebrides: From the Days of the Great Clearances to the Pentland Act of 1912*, Kirkaldy, 1912, p. 44.

[97] *Oban Times*, 3 May, 28 June 1884; *The Times*, 14 June 1884.

[98] D. W. Kemp, *The Sutherland Democracy*, Edinburgh, 1890, pp. 37–9.

[99] *Ross-shire Journal*, 27 June 1884.

through the experience of the Napier Commission, as reformers such as Murdoch, the Reverend Murdo MacAskill of Greenock, Alick Morrison of the Lewis branch of the HLLRA, John Macdonald of the Ardna-murchan, Sunart and Morvern Association of Glasgow, and several Free Church ministers helped to prepare witnesses and evidence.[100]

The fear that overrepresentation of landlords on the commission would lead to a biased report proved largely unfounded, although the resultant report pleased few.[101] The reasons for the displeasure on the part of land reformers are revealing. Security of tenure had always been a chief aim of the reform campaign and the report did not offer this.[102] A range of improvements were suggested in local communications, fish-eries, education and the administration of justice, which were welcomed but seen as not going far enough. The most novel proposal involved establishing communal townships of crofts on estates over the Highland region.[103] This was a cause of alarm amongst proprietors and factors and both MacKenzie of Gairloch and Conservative MP and improving land-lord, Cameron of Lochiel, appended memoranda to the report recording their disagreement.[104]

It might be expected that the land reformers would welcome a scheme to create a communal system of townships, especially since the available quantity of land was acknowledged as requiring special attention: 'The occupiers of an existing township should have the right to claim from the proprietor an enlargement of the existing township, in regard to arable land and common pasture.'[105] Where overcrowding was an issue and deemed to be the landlords' fault, land was to be gradually recovered for

[100] *Napier Commission, Evidence*, vol. I, p. 290; vol. IV, pp. 3070, 3138; *Report*, vol I, pp. 2–3; Philip Gaskell, *Morvern Transformed: A Highland Parish in the Nineteenth Century*, Cambridge, 1968, pp. 94–6.

[101] The commissioners included several prominent landowners including Napier, who owned a Lowland estate; Cameron of Lochiel, a model Highland landlord and Conservative MP; and Sir Kenneth MacKenzie, a Liberal landlord and Lord Lieutenant of Ross and Cromarty from 1881. The reform movement was represented by Fraser-Mackintosh, Liberal MP for Inverness Burghs from 1874 to 1885 who was sympathetic to the crofting interest, but from 1886 he was a Unionist representing the county seat and was defeated by another crofters' candidate, Dr MacGregor, in 1892; in addition Sheriff Alexander MacDonald, a native of Skye and a Gaelic literary enthusiast who made pithy comments about landlords (see Magnus MacLean, *Literature of the Highlands* London, 1903, pp. 170–2). On the composition of the commission see *Napier Commission: Warrant Appointing Commissioners and Secretaries*, vol. I, pp. v–vii.

[102] Security of tenure was offered only to those with a rent of over £6, a figure which would have excluded most crofters. In his objection Fraser-Mackintosh suggested a figure of £4. *Napier Commission: Memorandum by Mr Fraser-Mackintosh of Drummond, MP*, vol. I, p. 137.

[103] *Napier Commission: Report*, vol. I, pp. I–III.

[104] *Napier Commission: Memorandum by Sir Kenneth Mackenzie, Bart.*, vol. I, pp. 113–18; *Memorandum by Donald Cameron of Lochiel MP*, vol. I, pp. 119–36.

[105] *Napier Commission: Report*, vol. I, p. 26.

the crofting township under investigation by a sheriff substitute. In saying this, the commissioners envisaged it having the force of law.[106]

The problem with this remedy bears directly upon the historicist analysis which underpinned so much of the land reform case and the issue was not just the generosity of the settlement but its relevance in relation to the historical depiction of the crofting community already developed by the land reforming movement. The Napier Commission posited a solution based upon a vision of the crofting community as historically an unproblematic peasant community, organised in townships, operating under patriarchal authority. Such an interpretation simply had no relevance in many areas. A historian of Shetland, which had no Celtic background to reformulate, has pointed out that 'there was no folk memory at all of any such Golden Age' and this remedy would have been irrelevant if not completely disastrous.[107] In this respect Orkney and Shetland are the most significant areas not to fit the reformers', or Napier's, paradigm of the crofting community. There was a certain amount of unrest in Orkney[108] but very little in Shetland and both have been thought of as relatively inactive.[109] The Nordic background of the northern isles denied them the Celtic roots so important in the land reformers' construction of the crofting community. This is an aspect of the way in which the crofting region was politically defined and in this definition the language and culture of the Gael was a more significant factor than the prevailing tenurial system alone.

Land reformers in the Gaelic-speaking areas offered a vision of the history of the community which validated a much greater claim to autonomy than the patriarchal image represented by the Napier Commission. The reforming vision was historicist but was tailored to altogether more immediate imperatives. It gave a venerable meaning to the history of community but also addressed itself to current political needs, underpinning claims for fair rents and security of tenure. The continuity of land and people may have been present in Napier's conception of the crofting township but was addressed to a people that had already politically defined themselves in ways that promised so much more.

[106] *Ibid.*, p. 92.
[107] Brian Smith, 'Shetland and the Crofters Act', in Laurence Graham (ed.), *Shetland Crofters: A Hundred Years of Island Crofting*, Lerwick, 1987, p. 5.
[108] W. P. L. Thomson, *The Little General and the Rousay Crofters: Crisis and Conflict on an Orkney Crofting Estate*, Edinburgh, 1981.
[109] Brian Smith, 'Shetland and the Crofters Act', p. 6; in 'Shetland Archives and Sources of Shetland History', *History Workshop Journal*, 4 (1977), p. 212, he also suggests that the system of debt-bondage and truck in Shetland made rebellion much less likely there. On the background to this system, see Jonathan W. G. Wills, 'The Zetland Method', in Barbara E. Crawford (ed.), *Essays in Shetland History*, Lerwick, 1984, pp. 161–78.

VII

Dissatisfaction with the outcome of the Napier Commission boosted the land agitation in general. Whilst the particular recommendations may not have pleased many, the implicit acknowledgement of the need for change did. The unrest in the crofting townships that had been in abeyance during the commission's deliberations revived and the reform movement was now in a position to claim that it was giving political expression to the dilemma of the entire region. The possibility of electoral reform gave this a new urgency and optimism. By 1884 the tide was moving with the HLLRA which grew throughout that year and beyond. By August, Gladstone had promised legislation on crofting.[110] A bill was discussed but not acted upon prior to the fall of Gladstone's administration in 1885. The most striking feature of the campaign was the organisational development of the land reform movement. At their conference in Dingwall in September 1884 the movement formulated a programme which included security of tenure, compensation for improvements made to crofts, and a land court, which had been included in the Irish Land Act of 1881, but rejected by Napier.[111] The HLLRA announced that they would only support candidates at the next election who publicly approved the 'Dingwall programme' and also pledged their support for a land bill to this effect. Electoral reform in 1884 dramatically increased the electorate in the crofting regions, increasing the size of some seats by hundreds of per cent. The prospect and reality of these new political conditions heightened the propaganda effort. The HLLRA stated its aims thus:

The object of the HLLRA is to effect by unity of purpose and action such changes in the land laws as will promote the welfare of the people ... The cause has many friends ... but the success of the movement must depend upon the unity and determination of the Highland people ... Unity is might, and with might on their side the people will soon succeed in obtaining their rights.[112]

'The people' in this reckoning represented a culturally rooted political identity developed over a long period in a complex with land, language and culture.

---

[110] *The Times*, 1 September 1884. Gladstone had his own historicist interpretation of the position of the crofters, see W. E. Gladstone to Sir William Harcourt, 19 January 1885, in *The Gladstone Diaries*, ed. H. C. G. Matthew, Oxford, 1990, vol. XI, *July 1883–December, 1886*, pp. 277–9. Gladstone's diaries also suggest that he read very widely in the writings of Blackie between the late 1850s and the mid-1880s.

[111] *Napier Commission, Report*, vol. I, pp. 50–1.

[112] Scottish Record Office, GD 1/36/1 (2), HLLRA tract, *Shoulder to Shoulder*.

13 The Welsh radical tradition and the ideal of a democratic popular culture

Richard Lewis

I

Most accounts of Welsh radicalism in the late Victorian and Edwardian eras tend to stress the extent to which it was still wedded, albeit with declining fervour, to the shibboleths of popular liberalism: land reform, disestablishment and temperance. It was a political tradition that was unwilling, or unable, to address the changing problems and politics of urban and industrial south Wales, a political environment increasingly marked by class conflict and a widening chasm between the interests of capital and labour. Labour was seen by most Welsh Liberals as something to be either confronted or contained, not embraced as part of a fundamental re-evaluation of the values and objectives of radical politics.[1] Lib–Labism is portrayed as offering a prolix 'progressivism' which hardly made up in the sheer volume of its wordy good intentions what it lacked in substance, namely policies to tackle the social ills of urban and industrial Wales.[2] Into this intellectual vacuum intruded various brands of ethical and 'scientific' (i.e. Marxian) socialism. In an amazingly short period of time the enemies of the people ceased to be the landlords, the Anglican clergy and the brewers. They were replaced by the coalowners and their hired lackeys, the managers, collectively defined as the 'bosses'.

It was a conceptual rupture so profound that within less than fifteen years the lay-preacher leadership of the South Wales Miners' Federation (SWMF), the great embodiment of Welsh working-class social, economic and political independence, had been replaced by card-carrying

---

[1] The best account of the relationship between south Wales liberalism and Labour is to be found in K. O. Morgan, 'The New Liberalism and the Challenge of Labour: The Welsh Experience, 1885–1929', *Welsh History Review*, 6, 3 (June 1973). See also his comments in Morgan, *Rebirth of a Nation, Wales 1880–1980*. Oxford and Cardiff, 1981, pp. 134–55. In addition, see D. Tanner, *Political Change and the Labour Party, 1900–18*, Cambridge, 1990, pp. 207–8.

[2] For a withering indictment of the linguistic limitations of south Wales Lib–Lab 'progressivism', see Peter Stead, 'The Language of Edwardian Politics', in D. B. Smith (ed.), *A People and a Proletarian: Essays in the History of Wales*, London, 1980.

communists.[3] Even more important was the creation of an independent political labour movement which articulated its objectives by means of a socialist vocabulary and an anti-capitalist rhetoric. By the late 1920s most of industrial south Wales and certainly the coalfield was as uniformly Labour as it had been Liberal only just over a decade earlier. Whilst some writers are very willing to acknowledge underlying elements of continuity within the working-class politics of industrial Wales,[4] the failures of popular liberalism, the old home of Welsh radicalism, to respond to the 'rise of Labour' is seen to trigger a decisive break with the values and aspirations of a radicalism forged in an essentially rural context. Elements of continuity are, however, seen in essentially personal terms; translation rather than displacement of leaders. A good and typical example is the general secretary of the Cardiff, Barry and Penarth coaltrimmers' union, Samuel Fisher, Baptist and teetotaller, who in 1920 described his politics as 'Liberal now Labour'.[5]

A further dimension has recently been added to this interpretation by a critical re-evaluation which has called into question the underlying liberal intentions of much of the intellectual basis of late nineteenth-century Welsh rural radicalism. Owen M. Edwards, usually portrayed as the rather saintly author of much that established and celebrated the peasant and craft values which were seen to be the essence of the Welsh rural democratic ideal, is the subject of his re-assessment. His rejection of the materialist values of modern urban and industrial society, and his manifest loathing of bourgeois capitalist society, are this main claims to being seen as a radical. His desire to disseminate the sturdy, self-reliant skills and values of the rural working population through universal education is his main claim to being seen as a democrat. Yet, as a recent study has shown, Edwards really belongs to an essentially reactionary tradition in European, and especially German and French thought, which idealised a rural society of harmony and order. He despised the commercial middle class, especially the English middle class, as uncultured philistines; but he feared the proletariat of any nationality. His solution was a return to the land, the creation of a society of small holders and independent craftsmen, well educated, deeply religious and governed by wise rulers. Despite his lauding of the peasantry, Edwards also expressed a high regard for the virtues of true aristocracy. There is within these ideas

---

[3] The case for a decisive break in the continuity of leadership is made most starkly and most eloquently in G. A. Williams, *The Welsh in their History*, London, 1982, pp. 185–6.

[4] See Peter Stead, 'Working Class Leadership in South Wales, 1900–1920', *Welsh History Review*, 6, 3 (June 1973) pp. 329–53. Even G. A. Williams is forced to admit that the changes were often as much by 'translation' as by 'displacement'; Williams, *The Welsh in their History*, p. 186.

[5] See Fisher's entry in *Who's Who in Wales*, Cardiff, 1920.

a strong whiff of the anti-democratic, anti-individualism and anti-liberalism of the European extreme right.[6]

If for some the only solution to the ills of Welsh society lay in rolling back the waves of industrialisation, urbanisation and Anglicisation, others took a more measured view of the perceived problems and the solution, even if they also shared many of Edward's rural ideals. In the rapidly expanding economy of south Wales in the Edwardian era, there existed a loosely knit coterie of social radicals whose anxieties about the dangers emerging in the industrial and urban communities of the region caused them to seek solutions very different from the 'back to the land' ideas of Edwards or the state socialism of the ILP. They sought, instead, to channel and control the waves of social and economic change; to inculcate the perceived culture and values of the Welsh peasantry and rural artisans among the urban proletariat. They sought to elevate the low tastes of the masses, with their apparently inexhaustible appetite for passive and commercialised entertainment and spectator sports; to foster a sense of citizenship and equip the workers with an ability to select wise and responsible leaders; and to rekindle their spiritual instincts, and get them to appreciate the inspirations and consolations of religion, through a religion conscious of its social as well as its soul-saving purposes. In short, they sought to foster in urban and industrial areas of the Principality the ideal of a democratic popular culture which it was believed existed, or had existed, in rural Wales. From this would develop the ultimate objective – a harmonious community, spiritually, politically and socially at peace with itself. The objectives were clear but the means of achieving them were less so. Instead of denouncing or challenging the agencies and institutions of the Welsh proletariat, the advocates of this ideal of popular culture sought instead to engage with them; to see in them traits which could be cultivated and leaders who could be cajoled into support for the ideal. It is this group of social radicals, usually academics and public servants, operating in an ill-defined 'progressive' twilight zone encompassing the most radical wing of popular liberalism, organised labour and ethical socialism, which provided the most consistent attempt to invest the Welsh radical tradition with a new sense of purpose in the Edwardian era.[7]

[6] E. Sherrington, 'O. M. Edwards, Culture and the Industrial Classes', *Llafur*, 6, (1992), pp. 28–41.

[7] The existence of this group/coterie has long been acknowledged by Welsh historians, but its long-term significance has been ignored or discounted, or has been too focused around the personality of Thomas Jones. See, for example, Peter Stead, *Coleg Harlech, the First Fifty Years*, Cardiff, 1977, pp. 16–17. A more critical view can be found in D. B. Smith, 'The Rebuilding of the SWMF, 1927–1939', University of Wales unpublished Ph.D. thesis, 1976, pp. 444–8. See also 'Wales through the Looking Glass', in D. B. Smith, *A People and a Proletariat*.

II

Of the main personalities associated with this movement, only one is well known outside Wales. Thomas Jones, whose role as a participant in, and a chronicler of, the high politics of the Lloyd George/Baldwin era has given him a reputation and a status beyond the confines of his native country,[8] was also the promoter of an ideal of a popular democratic Welsh culture. It was an ideal which differed in some key respects from that of Owen M. Edwards, but which also derived much of its intellectual force from similar sources and influences. Unlike Edwards, however, Thomas Jones was the product of industrial and proletarian Wales. He sympathised with organised labour and flirted with socialism, at least of the Fabian variety. Whilst he was often repelled by the beer-sodden leisure pursuits of many coalminers, he was also inspired by their capacity to tackle the problems which confronted them through the various agencies of collective self-help.[9] He did not despise the Cooperative Societies, the working mens' clubs or the trade unions. These he saw as signs of hope, which, together with a more worldly and socially concerned form of nonconformity, he hoped would rescue south Wales society from conflict and chaos.

Both Jones and Edwards had been heavily influenced by the late nineteenth-century revival in interest in the idealist philosophers of both the Hegelian and the ancient Hellenic varieties, and in particular by the ideas of the Scottish neo-idealists, whose chief advocate was Edward Caird. Both Jones and Edwards had studied at Glasgow University and were influenced by Caird. When Caird left Glasgow for Oxford, his post was taken by his Welsh-born disciple Henry Jones, who soon rose to eminence himself as a proponent of neo-idealist thought. Henry Jones was to provide the social radicals of south Wales with a philosophical underpinning for their ambitions, though his ideas were often received in an attenuated and partially understood form. It was during a well-publicised visit to his homeland in late 1907 that Henry Jones expressed alarm at the spread of class war and materialist socialist ideas amongst key sections of the working classes of industrial south Wales.[10] It triggered amongst many Welsh liberal intellectuals a new concern to develop a strategy which would reharness the energies of organised labour for

---

[8] There is now a very full account of the life and influence of this extraordinary man: E. L. Ellis, *T. J.: A Life of Dr Thomas Jones, CH*, Cardiff, 1992.

[9] See, for example, Thomas Jones's comments in *Welsh Broth*, London, 1950, pp. 27–39.

[10] *South Wales Daily News*, 12 December 1907. The social and political reflections of this much neglected figure, and the mechanisms by which his ideas were popularised in south Wales, can be found in D. Boucher and A. Vincent, *A Radical Hegelian: The Political and Social Philosophy of Henry Jones*, Cardiff, 1993, pp. 95–133.

Welsh radicalism. Whilst the collection of Welsh academics and administrators who clustered together to try to forge a new idealist progressive alliance with organised labour rejected state socialism, they were willing to accept many of the criticisms of unbridled free-market capitalism which had helped the Independent Labour Party to make rapid headway amongst many of the younger labour activists in south Wales in the Edwardian era. They were certainly not averse to using the state as an agency to control the free market and bring about a more just society. Seizing on those facets of idealist thinking which saw the state in a positive light, they began to stress how it could be used as an agency which could promote the moral as well as the material well-being of the people. The criticism of free-market capitalism was frequently combined with an attack on what they saw as the world-rejecting mentality of Welsh (and Scottish) Calvinism. Thomas Jones summed up this outlook: 'Selfishness was not to be overcome by postponing its gratification to the next world but by social service in this. The State was a moral institution and civic duty a spiritual function.'[11] Thus public service was on a par with a religious vocation. As a recent study has shown, these ideas were in the vanguard of British social thought in the early twentieth century.[12]

Within a burgeoning academic, bureaucratic and legal elite in south Wales, these idealist concepts proved to be powerful in promoting the search for a new radical consensus. The targets of this strategy were the labour activists, identified as the key opinion-formers among the working classes. Social service and education, especially adult education, would allow the leading lights among the idealist coterie to gain access to this formative element. Not exclusively Welsh, one very prominent figure was the Scottish neo-idealist professor of philosophy at Cardiff, J. S. Mackenzie. As the chairman of the Welsh district of the Workers' Educational Association (WEA), Mackenzie declared his purpose was to promote a democracy governed by the principle of the rule of the many 'under the guidance of the wise'.[13] The author of an influential text, published in 1890, which presented the idealist case for social reform, Mackenzie's influence was to extend well into the third and fourth decades of the century, especially among those active in settlement and relief work in the depressed areas of inter-war south Wales. He was particularly influential

---

[11] T. Jones, 'Biographical Sketch' in W. Smart, Second Thoughts of an Economist, London, 1924 p. xxii. This mentality is also reflected in the comments of Jones and his wife on the birth of their daughter in 1909. Thomas wrote of how he hoped she would be 'as good a citizen as her mother', and his wife wrote of how she regarded child-rearing as the 'highest duty we owe the state'. Quoted in Ellis, T.J., p. 117.

[12] José Harris, 'Political Thought and the Welfare State 1870–1940: An Intellectual Framework for British Social Policy', Past and Present, 135 (1992), pp. 116–41.

[13] Glamorgan Gazette, 1 November 1911.

with those entering the nonconformist ministry, though he was always anxious to stress the need for a secular morality to underpin social reform.[14]

Another key non-Welsh figure amongst this circle of social radical activity was Ronald Burrows, the rather patrician professor of Greek at Cardiff in the 1900s. The first warden of the university settlement in one of the city's most impoverished districts, although he often called himself a 'Christian socialist', he was in essence a Tory democrat.[15] His aristocratic instincts caused him to hanker after the reinforcement of 'that spirit of obligation, which in the past has been so distinctive of our national life, [and] is still a great tradition in our upper classes'. He sought to extend this spirit to the whole of the 'employing class'. It was its absence which he saw as creating the 'bitter Nihilist spirit' of the revolutionary left, as cruel and relentless in its turn as that of the Industrialism which it seeks to destroy. Education and social work, through agencies such as the university settlement movement, were the ways to translate into modern life the 'friendly personal relations between individuals that did at least something in our villages to sweeten life and blunt the edge of political differences'.[16] However, he shared with Tom Jones and Mackenzie a sympathy with organised labour and the Cooperative movement. Both movements possessed the potential to breed a sense of responsibility amongst the working classes which, if matched by equally responsible behaviour by employers, and judicious social reform by government, could remove the dangers of class conflict. Whilst working at Glasgow University under Gilbert Murray, Burrows had become very active in the social and political life of the city. In Glasgow in the 1890s he came to the conclusion that the activities of unscrupulous employers were the main cause of social discontent amongst the masses, and the main spur to the spread of extremist political thought amongst them. Working closely with the Glasgow Trades Council, he led a major campaign against 'sweating' for which he was awarded a silver-topped walking cane by the council. This was an achievement about which he proudly boasted in the WEA classes of south Wales, to prove that the educated upper classes were really on the side of the workers.[17] He also shared with Thomas Jones (who knew Burrows whilst in Glasgow, and was heavily influenced by him) and Mackenzie an enthusiasm for adult education as a means of

[14] J. S. Mackenzie, *Introduction to Social Reform*, London, 1890. See the comments of the Revd M. Watcyn Williams in M. Mackenzie (ed.), *J. S. Mackenzie*, London, 1936, pp. 89–90.

[15] G. Glasgow, *Ronald Burrows: A Memoir*, London, 1934, pp. 87–8.

[16] R. Burrows, 'Evolution or Revolution', in *Welsh Outlook*, January, 1914, pp. 27–8.

[17] See his comments to the Barry branch of the Workers Educational Association in May 1907, *Barry Dock News*, 17 May 1907.

educating the intelligent activist elements within the ranks of labour into an awareness of their responsibilities.[18] In fact Burrows tended to regard the more sober political outlook of the skilled working class – the artisan – as something to be fostered and transmitted to the children of the unskilled poor. He once described this as the main purpose of the university settlement movement.[19]

III

It was the labour problem which was the main impetus for the south Wales social radical clique. Despite the fact that at least some of their number, such as Tom Jones, were strong supporters of female enfranchisement, they displayed little interest in the question of women's suffrage. There was only one female among them who made any significant contribution – Elizabeth Phillips Hughes, who described herself as a 'radical democrat', the former head of Cambridge Teacher Training College for Women, who retired to her home town of Barry, in south Wales, in 1899 and devoted her life to the promotion of social and political reform.[20] Although she was a strong supporter of votes for women, she was highly critical of the actions of the suffragettes, and was as concerned as her male colleagues with how the organised working class could be induced to follow the paths of reform rather than revolution.[21] Also, her interest in improving educational provision for women was as much concerned with developing and enhancing the skills of women in their role as homemakers and mothers as it was with providing them with the knowledge necessary for the exercise of the political responsibilities which she anticipated them acquiring.[22] As with all those active in the social radical network in south Wales, she believed strongly in the power of education to provide, in a phrase she used frequently, a 'solid knowledge' of the issues and problems confronting society.

Concern with the way that the organised working-class movement was apparently susceptible to the appeal of doctrines of class conflict and revolutionary change grew in the years up to 1914. This led to a greater urgency in the desire of this select group to form an alternative radical

---

[18] Thomas Jones states that he and Burrows founded the Glasgow University branch of the Fabian Society. Jones, 'Biographical Sketch', pp. 27–8.

[19] See the letter from Burrows in *South Wales Daily News*, 5 March 1908.

[20] For E. P. Hughes, see the entry in the *Dictionary of Welsh Biography* and also in *Who's Who in Wales*, Cardiff, 1920. Her career as an advocate of female education in Wales is illuminated further in W. Gareth Evans, *Education and Female Emancipation: the Welsh Experience, 1847–1914*, Cardiff, 1990, *passim*.

[21] She did organise a number of public petitions in favour of votes for women in Barry. See *Barry Dock News*, 21 January 1907, 7 June 1907 and 7 December 1907.

[22] See *The Highway*, 2, 17 (February, 1910), pp. 75–6.

agenda to the one being offered by the far left. Radical but not revolutionary, it was willing to accommodate the growing anti-capitalist sentiment of the activist elements within the labour movement. In 1914 this loose coalition of middle-class radicals found a mouthpiece in the form of the monthly journal *Welsh Outlook*.[23] This magazine tried to overlay questions of social reform and the resolution of industrial conflicts with a strong sense of Welsh national sentiment. Blood was thicker than class,[24] but this did not mean that issues of social justice could be ignored in the pursuit of some form of Welsh national harmony. This was a rather soft, sentimental, type of nationalism which displayed little or no interest in political autonomy for Wales, nor was it much exercised about the fate of the Welsh language. They tended to seek a distinctive and recognised role for Wales within the empire. Believing that the empire would survive if it recognised diversity, they sought 'home rule' in areas such as educational and religious policy, which they believed were of crucial importance to the Welsh people. Elizabeth Hughes, in particular, liked to emphasise the different requirements of the English and the Welsh in matters of educational policy in terms of racial differences, in a phraseology which jars today. In 1884 she declared that differences of race, far from being regretted, should be 'deepened and perpetuated'. This, she argued, would strengthen and not weaken the empire. She remained fearful that the imposition of a purely English pattern of education on the Welsh would destroy these 'racial' differences.[25] Writing in 1917 she reiterated her views with less restraint and wilder generalisation: 'We *are* a different race. We are much more susceptible to our human environment than the more sturdy Englishman, and because of our greater adaptability we unconsciously, not infrequently, mislead those who are not of our race and hide the many fundamental differences which undoubtedly exist.'[26] Welshness was an attitude of mind, reinforced by education, religion and the fostering of a myth of racial distinctiveness, and certainly not something to be institutionalised by political separation from the British empire.

[23] For the background and wider significance of this journal, see Gwyn Jenkins, 'The *Welsh Outlook*, 1914–33', *National Library of Wales Journal*, 34 (Winter 1986) pp. 463–92. See also Ellis, *T.J.*, *passim*.

[24] This phrase was actually used by Burrows in the *Welsh Outlook* article mentioned above. This article was particularly significant because the editor of the journal, none other than Thomas Jones, stated that the views expressed 'crystallised' the ideas of the magazine.

[25] E. P. Hughes, 'The Higher Education of Girls in Wales with Practical Suggestions for the Best Means of Promoting It', National Eisteddfod Prize Essay, Liverpool, 1884. Quoted in Evans, *Education and Female Emancipation*, p. 137.

[26] Proposed statement on the Education Bill to be submitted to the president of the Board of Education by the WEA Welsh District, 6 October 1917. WEA District Records, Cardiff.

IV

Also, although there was a strong anti-militarist strand within Welsh radical tradition, none of the leading figures within the south Wales social radical coterie opposed the First World War. On the contrary, most of them were strong supporters of the war effort, but they were all anxious to use the war as an opportunity for radical reform. Unsympathetic, or even downright hostile to critics of the war, they drove the anti-war activist, John Thomas, out of his job as district secretary of the WEA.[27] However, they seemed to revel in the expansion of state power which the vigorous prosecution of the conflict required, because they saw that the resources could be redirected to more constructive uses when peace came. To them 'reconstruction' did not mean a return to the conditions of 1914, but an opportunity to use state power to build a new society. In endorsing the Welsh WEA's plans for educational reform, the *Welsh Outlook* made this position clear:

no plea of the costliness of the scheme must stand in the way. A country which is rightly prepared to spend six million pounds a day on warfare must be prepared to spend vastly more than it has ever done before on the making of men and women capable of building the new world which must emerge if our victory is to be anything more than a meaningless bubble in the stream of time.[28]

The war made issues of social reform more stark, and the survival not just of Wales but of Britain and its empire depended on the willingness of the workers to provide the means to defeat the Germans. However, the apparent willingness, in the summer of 1915, of Welsh coalminers to stop work in pursuit of an industrial relations grievance shocked the members of the social radical circle and as the industrial relations climate in the coalfield worsened they became even more disturbed. It was then that the ideal of a democratic popular culture was offered as a means of resolving the festering conflicts of industrial Wales in general, and the coalfields in particular.

Daniel Lleufer Thomas, was an undergraduate contemporary of Owen M. Edwards at Oxford in the 1880s, and one of a group of Welsh-speaking students who used their time at the university to foster a Welsh cultural and intellectual revival.[29] He was regarded at the time, and he

---

[27] E. P. Hughes took a particularly hard line with those hostile to the war effort. Interview by the author with Dr John Thomas, Manchester, April 1972.

[28] *Welsh Outlook*, January 1917. R. H. Tawney was a close friend of Thomas Jones and through him with the south Wales social radical circle. They were also allies in an attempt to force Lloyd George to adopt a much more radical reform programme. T. Jones, *Whitehall Diaries* (ed. K. Middlemass), London, 1969; see entries for 28 September 1916 and 16 December 1916. See also Ellis, *T.J.*, pp. 195–6, and J. M. Winter, *Socialism and the Challenge of War*, London, 1974, p. 169.

[29] K. O. Morgan, *Rebirth of a Nation*, p. 100. See also *Dictionary of Welsh Biography*.

certainly regarded himself as a radical progressive,[30] but as the stipendiary magistrate for Pontypridd and the Rhondda who sentenced the rioters in the Tonypandy disturbances of 1910 he was denounced by many on the left. He wrote and spoke in generally sympathetic terms abut the trade union movement and he was an active supporter of the Cooperative movement. A believer in co-partnership, he hoped that at some point the workers of south Wales would be able to take a direct stake in their enterprises and that the wages system would give way to cooperative enterprises or employee share-ownership schemes which would remove the root causes of class conflict and antagonism between capital and labour.[31]

It was, however, in the area of religion that Thomas felt the biggest obstacle to social reform in Wales existed. It is too often forgotten just how wedded the Welsh radical tradition was to the political agenda set by militant dissent. As a close ally of Thomas, the Revd Gwilym Davies once commented that Thomas thought that the main problem of Wales was not so much social as theological: its Calvinistic obsession with saving souls for the next life. It was an 'other-worldliness' in which religion 'came to be considered as a matter of man's soul and "life hereafter," with little if any relation to the conditions of his physical existence. In practice it meant that a man could, on his way home from a fervent prayer meeting, walk through a bad slum and feel nothing of its horror. He was immune.'[32] As a number of writers have shown, Welsh nonconformity put up a staunch resistance to the spread of socialist ideas, and socialists were regularly denounced as infidels and atheists. There were notable exceptions to this: some ministers, such as R. Silyn Roberts, another member of the south Wales social radical clique, embraced socialism and sought to reconcile it with their religious beliefs, but they were unusual.[33] Even prominent nonconformists anxious to promote a 'progressive' alliance between Labour and popular liberalism seemed unable to accept the need for a worldly dimension to their message of salvation. To those, such as R. J. Campbell, who argued that salvation of the soul could be made easier by social reform, the Lib–Lab MP, William Brace, in 1907, made the uncompromising statement that 'social reform was only

---

[30] Many Home Office officials regarded him as being far too lenient and understanding with the rioters. See Jane Organ, *Conflict and Order: The Police and Labour Disputes in England and Wales, 1900–1939*, Oxford, 1987, pp. 161, 196.

[31] D. Lleufer Thomas, *Labour Unions in Wales – Their Early Struggle for Existence*, London, 1901, pp. 25–6.

[32] G. Davies, *Welsh School of Social Service, 1911–25*. Cardiff, 1925, p. 4.

[33] See Christopher Turner, 'Conflicts of Faith? Religion and Labour in Wales, 1890–1914', in D. R. Hopkin and G. S. Kealey (eds.), *Class, Community and the Labour Movement: Wales and Canada, 1850–1930*, Cardiff, 1989, pp. 67–86.

possible with the redemptive spirit of Jesus Christ'.[34] The saving of souls must precede the saving of men's bodies. The main organ of south Wales progressivism, the *South Wales Daily News*, was equally forthright in 1908 in an attack on J. S. Mackenzie when he suggested that it might be appropriate for children to be given moral instruction detached from the teaching of the scriptures. In an editorial it declared that 'lack of a biblical basis is inimical to moral growth'.[35] It was such attitudes which drove many young people out of the chapels and into purely secular activities within the trade union movement. Thomas realised that the drift of the young labour activists away from the chapels was in no small measure a rebellion against the soul-obsessed spirituality of the preaching. What he feared was that, within one generation, it would be displaced in the minds of the majority of those active in the labour movement by a soulless materialism. It was a trend which Thomas feared and sought to reverse.

Thomas struggled, with limited success, to encourage the Welsh nonconformist churches to take on board a social dimension to their ministry. In 1908 he supported the visit to south Wales of R. J. Campbell and the propagation of the social gospel of his 'New Theology'.[36] Of greater long-term significance was the establishment in 1911 of the Welsh School of Social Service. An inter-denominational organisation, this derived most of its driving force from those in the nonconformist churches who accepted the need for a message of social amelioration as well as personal salvation in the teaching of the chapels, and it was designed to create networks of like-minded people, from all walks of Welsh life. The material as well as the spiritual well-being of the people was to be their concern. Operating on the basis of 'collegiality' and 'corporate thinking', this body was to be a key agency in promoting social radical values among Welsh opinion-formers, and it was also the means by which the older Welsh rural radical traditions and the idealist principles of the social radicals were required to address the horrendous social and economic problems of inter-war south Wales. Within its deliberations there were constant references to how the 'democratic' values of the Welsh 'peasant' culture, 'traditions guarded by the simple folk of the countryside', could be brought to the benighted masses of industrial and urban Wales.[37]

Another 'network' which brought Thomas in contact with organised labour was the Workers' Educational Association, the Welsh district of which, from the summer of 1915, he chaired. It was in this capacity that

[34] *Barry Dock News*, 15 February 1907.
[35] *South Wales Daily News*, 30 September 1908.
[36] *Llais Llafur*, 20 November 1909.
[37] Welsh School of Social Service, *Memoranda for a Conference on Education in Wales, 1881–1931*, Carmarthen, 1931, pp. 11–12.

Thomas gave an address at the National Eisteddfod in Bangor in August 1915, with memories of the coal strike still fresh in his audience's memory. Although essentially an argument for extending university extra-mural education, the speech was also one of the clearest statements of the nature of the Welsh ideal of a democratic popular culture. He saw in the traditions of the rural areas – the innumerable local eisteddfods and literary circles, the adult classes of the Sunday schools and the bardic traditions – a living democratic culture.[38] It was a tradition which promoted harmony and understanding as it was open to all, irrespective of social background or rank. It was a culture that had been rudely disrupted by industrialisation, commercialisation and the 'intrusion of a large non-Welsh element'. The result was that there was a danger of the ideals of nationality and religion being repudiated 'in some of the industrial districts in favour of an illusory ideal of a cosmopolitan, and perhaps to some extent materialistic brotherhood'. His solution was for the University of Wales, through an expanded programme of extra-moral work, to seek the 'reconciliation of individualism and socialism – opposite, yet complimentary standpoints'.[39] Public service and civic duty were to be means by which the educated amongst all social classes would guide the Welsh people back to their cultural roots, from which would grow a harmonious social order. However, for Lleufer Thomas, there were two pressures which would militate against this harmony. The attitude of employers was one major factor, the growing chasm between them and their employees made more pronounced, Thomas noted in March 1917, by the advent of the motor car, causing managers to live, geographically, apart from the workers. The other factor was their failure to see the necessity for a humane and humanising education for both employers and employed.[40] Thomas was equally concerned with the spread of Marxian ideas amongst the labour activists of industrial south Wales, a fear made more urgent by the explosion of adult classes in 1916–17 held under the aegis of the Labour College movement. His solution was not to attack these classes, but to offer the workers an attractive alternative by a massive extension of the provision of orthodox liberal adult education. His fear was that employer hostility to any form of workers' education, combined with post-war fiscal retrenchment, would scupper such a response.[41]

[38] D. Lleufer Thomas, 'University Tutorial Classes for Working People', *Transactions of the Honourable Society of Cymmrodorion* (1916), pp. 69–135.
[39] *Ibid.*, pp. 94–5.
[40] Thomas's views and fears in this field are well brought out in his evidence, as chairman of the Welsh WEA, to the royal commission on university education in Wales, chaired by Viscount Haldane, in 1917. *Royal Commission on University Education in Wales*, vol. III, Minutes of Evidence (Cmnd. 8993), 1918. Minutes for 23 March 1917, pp. 66–76.
[41] *Ibid.*

It was an issue to which Lleufer Thomas was to return as chairman of the Industrial Unrest Commission for Wales. Concerned as much with the ideological as with the social and economic basis to the wartime unrest, its recommendations, published in 1917, reflected the semi-corporatist inclinations of the south Wales social radical group to which Lleufer Thomas belonged.[42] The power of organised labour would be both recognised and contained by the institutionalisation of relations between capital and labour. The power of capital would be circum-scribed by having all employers compelled to belong to associations which would send representatives to national and district councils for all major industries. Discipline would be in the hands of the respective employer and employee associations and unions.[43] The state would guide and control industries through more *dirigiste* policies, but would also be responsible for the education of employers and employed into a deeper understanding of each other's problems and needs. Whilst the Unrest Commission was seen by Marxian critics as a device for preserving a crumbling and discredited capitalist system, the tone of the proposals actually reflected the growing anti-capitalist sentiments of the organised working class in south Wales. The 'Labour' representative on the com-mission, Vernon Hartshorn, although by 1917 increasingly seen as the acceptable face of socialist labourism, was still a severe critic of the nature of private ownership of the means of production, distribution and exchange. The secretary to the commission, Edgar Chappell, an ethical socialist, and fellow member of the social radical circle around Thomas Jones, used the commission to expose the iniquitous nature of coalowner control over the mining industry.[44] The hostility of the coalowners to the commission's proposals was significantly more virulent than anything that came from the socialist left in south Wales.

V

The Industrial Unrest Commission probably marked the high point of the political influence of the south Wales social radicals, and of the neo-idealism which underpinned their ideas. Thereafter the polarisation of

---

[42] *Commission on Enquiry into Industrial Unrest: Division No. 7. (Wales and Monmouthshire)* (Cmnd. 8668), National Library of Wales.

[43] For the thinking behind the unrest report, see Edgar Chappell, 'The Struggle for Industrial Control', *Welsh Outlook*, November 1917, pp. 391–4.

[44] Chappell took over the editorship of the *Welsh Outlook* from Tom Jones, but his anti-capitalist views were too strong for the Liberal radical coalowner and MP David Davies who financed the magazine. On one occasion Davies suppressed one of Chappell's edito-rials which contained a vitriolic attack on the south Wales coalowners. This incident is examined in Trevor L. Williams, 'Thomas Jones and the "Welsh Outlook"', *Anglo-Welsh Review*, 64 (1979), pp. 38–46.

electoral politics, and the bitter industrial conflicts of the 1920s, made the ideas of this grouping look peculiarly out of place. It is, therefore, easy to dismiss them as an intellectual dead end. In south Wales both organised labour and organised capital rejected the corporatism inherent in the Industrial Unrest Commission's proposals. The nonconformist churches, which had proved very unwilling to take on board a social dimension to their mission in the Edwardian era, still clung tenaciously to their commitment to a message of individual salvation, and, in any event, declined as a social and political force in the inter-war years. The gentle cultural nationalism of the south Wales social radicals was soon to be replaced by a less accommodating form with the foundation, in the mid-1920s, of Plaid Cymru.[45]

Yet it would be wrong to see this flowering of social radicalism as in some ways a political and intellectual cul-de-sac. The downplaying of the individualist facets of traditional liberal thought, and the lauding of the state and direct state action as an agency of social improvement, were ideas which were easily absorbed and carried forward by middle-class converts to the Labour Party. The almost religious quality that was given to the ideal of public service, whether through politics and administration or by voluntary agencies, was something that was also accepted by Labour, which quickly became the dominant political force in the region.

The mechanisms for transmitting these ideas were disrupted by the demise of Lib–Labism, but there was, of course, a good deal of continuity in terms of personnel who, while operating in the new context of independent political action and socialist rhetoric, still functioned with ideas acquired in an earlier era. More directly, the workers' education movement (despite being riven by a deep ideological dispute), through the WEA and the university extra-mural departments, provided direct access to large numbers of working-class political activists. By the 1930s the WEA and the university extra-mural departments were educating a significant slice of the 'secondary leadership' of organised labour in industrial Wales: the branch secretaries, ward councillors and lodge committee men[46] – the people who made the movement actually work. It even provided a new route to the minds of the working class for the significant minority of Welsh nonconformist ministers who were influenced by the neo-idealists. They found in adult education, and the voluntary social service response to unemployment in the inter-war years, a new sense of

[45] The *Welsh Outlook* was hostile to the new form of nationalism; see its editorial July 1926.
[46] For details of the growing influence of the WEA in south Wales in the 1930s, see R. Lewis, *Leaders and Teachers: Adult Education and the Challenge of Labour in South Wales, 1906–1940*, Cardiff, 1993, pp. 191–233.

mission in the benighted working-class communities of the coalfield.[47] Above all, the social radicals' emphasis on community, over individual and class, was something which was absorbed by, and to a large extent diluted the full impact of Marxist influence on, the leaders of thought and action within the Welsh labour movement.

This stress on community was particularly strong with regard to the voluntary social service response to the heavy structural unemployment of the inter-war years. The social service movement in south Wales was in fact dominated by members of the old Edwardian south Wales social radical clique.[48] Thomas Jones and Percy Watkins, another prominent figure in the old social radical coterie, saw in the appalling plight of the coalfield in the late 1920s and early 1930s new opportunities to restore the mission of Henry Jones, J. S. Mackenzie, Ronald Burrows and Lleufer Thomas to establish an ideal of popular culture in the numerous unemployed clubs and settlements of the valley towns. Percy Watkins saw the unemployment problem as a barrier to the emergence of an educated democracy in Wales, but he also saw the social service response to unemployment as a challenge to convert the 'new leisure' into an opportunity to foster the old Welsh ideal of a democratic popular culture.[49] The idealisation of rural virtues remained, but now there was again the constant assertion that adult education would not succeed in fostering a new popular democratic culture if it was confined to the 'intellectual aristocrats of the countryside'.[50] Within the Welsh social service movement, and its strong adult education dimension, there were features which had a resonance for many working-class activists in industrial south Wales. There was a rejection of the kind of mechanistic materialism which had kept many working-class activists away from the Communist Party, but it was always combined with a sustained ques-

---

[47] By the early 1930s nonconformist ministers were the largest single occupational group among WEA tutors in south Wales; Welsh Department of the Board of Education, *Education in Wales, Memorandum No. 5, Report on Adult Education*, London, 1937, tables 12, 40.

[48] Both Jones and (Sir) Percy Watkins, after a period in Whitehall as very senior civil servants, returned to Wales to assist in the coordination of the semi-voluntary social service response to unemployment. Watkins became secretary of the Welsh department of the National Council of Social Service, which dispensed funds to the various clubs and settlements in the coalfield. Jones was secretary of the Pilgrim Trust charity. Both of these were very influential positions in the blighted communities of south Wales.

[49] Watkins wrote and spoke very extensively on these themes. See, for example, 'Adult Education and the New Leisure in Wales', in *Wales and the New Leisure*, Llandyssul, 1935, pp. 45–51, and also *Adult Education among the Unemployed of South Wales*, London, 1935. The echoes of the ideas of the earlier period were still very loud. For Watkins' earlier career, see his autobiography, *A Welshman Remembers*, Cardiff, 1944.

[50] Percy Watkins, 'Adult Education and Welsh Tradition', *Cambria*, 2 (Summer, 1930), pp. 3–7.

tioning of the moral basis of the economic system which produced the grotesque social order that obtained in industrial south Wales in the 1930s.[51] Above all there was the incessant stress on the idea that education of the mass of the people was essential for democracy to work. In 1935 Thomas Jones acknowledged that the social service and adult education movement, far from reconciling the unemployed to their fate, could actually foster discontent and that rational discontent was a thoroughly desirable phenomenon. 'It was', said Jones, 'the essence of democracy that they should have intelligent citizens and the maximum number of effective individuals in their midst'.[52] The whole movement, which touched the lives of many more ordinary men and women than any political party,[53] cannot simply be dismissed as an ameliorative diversion from the growth of a socialist political consciousness amongst the Welsh working class. Rather it has to be seen as an integral part of the process which ultimately generated a demand for state action in the areas of welfare reform and expanded public provision for health and education.

Those who argue that the Welsh radical tradition failed to come to terms with the new politics of industrial and urban Wales, and thus lost out to a rising socialist labourism, need to qualify their argument by taking account of the role and influence of a new social radicalism in Edwardian south Wales, which was carried over into the new political order in the region. It formed a bridge between the old Liberal radicalism and the new socialist labourism. As the south Wales social radicals always sought, wherever possible, to go with the grain of both popular and governing elite sentiment, their ideas were perhaps, ultimately, far more significant in their impact than those, such as Marxist theories, that usually ran against it.

[51] See the comments of the Revd G. M. L. I. Davies, 'Fundamentals', in *Wales and the New Leisure*, pp. 61–3.

[52] *Montgomeryshire Express*, 5 January 1935.

[53] In 1934 there were over 180 social service schemes for the unemployed in south Wales. One scheme in the Rhondda had thirty separate clubs catering for over 6,000 unemployed men and 650 unemployed women. J. Davies, 'Time to Spare in Wales', in *Wales and the New Leisure*, pp. 7–9.

Part IV

Consciousness and society: the 'peculiarities of the British'?

14 Platonism, positivism and progressivism: aspects of British sociological thought in the early twentieth century

Jose Harris

I

For the past thirty years social and intellectual historians have puzzled over the question of why there was no sociological theory in Britain: of why it was that, in the late nineteenth and early twentieth centuries, when sociology was being established as a major theoretical enterprise and academic discipline in many other western countries, in Britain alone sociological theory remained weak, peripheral and largely unacknowledged both by the universities and by the wider intelligentsia. Why, so it has often been asked, were there no great British analysts of society and social action, comparable in range and method to such theorists as Weber, Durkheim, Mosca, Pareto and the authors associated with the 'Chicago school': theorists who fundamentally challenged and changed the way in which people interested in social questions thought about social cohesion, social conflict, social stratification and social transformation? That Britain *had* once had a 'grand theorist' in the person of Herbert Spencer is not denied: but though Spencer lived till 1903, his work after the 1860s is widely dismissed as moribund and wholly out of tune with the intellectual revolution of the late nineteenth century.[1] Similarly, it is not denied that there *was* a 'sociological movement' in late-Victorian, Edwardian and inter-war Britain, nor that, rather surprisingly, Britain was the first country in the world to have a nationally based 'Sociological Society' (founded by Patrick Geddes and Victor Branford in 1904).[2] But this movement is usually portrayed as an insignificant and largely amateur affair, tainted with post-Gladstonian faddism, and excessively concerned with questions of moral improvement, civic

---

This chapter is a revised version of 'The Spell of Plato in English Social Thought', a paper given as the Sir John Neale Lecture in English history at University College London, December 1992.

[1] Talcott Parsons, *The Structure of Social Action*, Glencoe, Ill., 1937 (1949 edn) ch 2.

[2] R. J. Halliday. 'The Sociological Movement, the Sociological Society and the Genesis of Academic Sociology in Britain', *Sociological Review*, n.s., 16 (1968), pp. 377–98.

consciousness and social reform. Despite the ambitious meta-theories of Patrick Geddes, it nurtured no great analytical minds capable of developing sociological theory as a new form of systematic critical philosophy, a new world view.

In this chapter I am going to consider this question from several different angles. First, I shall review the specific arguments put forward by historians of the social sciences about the 'failure' of British sociology and the reasons given for that failure. Secondly, I shall consider whether social analysis in Britain was in fact so half-baked, peripheral and lacking in intellectual content as many of its critics claim; and I shall suggest that a great deal of innovative theorising about modern societies was in fact occurring in many different contexts – not necessarily under the label of academic sociology. Thirdly, I shall suggest that – quite regardless of its intrinsic intellectual merits or demerits – the 'sociological movement' in early twentieth-century Britain was of major significance as a social and cultural phenomenon, and of underrated importance in the history of 'progressive' politics and of wider social thought.

II

Firstly, then, the debate on why there was no serious sociological theory in Britain. This debate has been a familiar commonplace of *sociological* writing since the 1920s and 1930s, when the deficiencies of British theory were first pointed out by Talcott Parsons and other members of the powerful Chicago school; but it first entered into mainstream *historical* discourse with two important works that appeared in 1958. In that year a Stanford intellectual historian, H. Stuart Hughes, published a justly famous book on the modernist reconstruction of European thought which still remains perhaps the most widely read and influential overview of trends in European intellectual history in the early twentieth century. In Hughes' study British social theorists were conspicuous by their absence; and Britain generally appeared fleetingly throughout the book in one guise only – namely, as the tranquil backwater of cautious empiricism to which a variety of dynamic and innovative European theorists fled when their own societies became too unpleasant and dangerous to hold them (often in the process losing or compromising their 'purity' as theorists).[3] Also in 1958, the distinguished Cambridge historian, Noel Annan,

---

[3] H. Stuart Hughes, *Consciousness and Society: The Reorientation of European Social Thought 1890–1930*, 1958, (first English edn 1959, repr. 1974), pp. 13, 53, 71. The only British thinker of the period whom Hughes acknowledged as a major innovator was Bertrand Russell (pp. 397–8), who specifically rejected the possibility of 'sociology' or any other kind of theory of society.

delivered a Hobhouse Memorial Lecture on the theme of 'The Curious Strength of Positivism in English Political Thought'. This lecture – dedicated to the memory of Leonard Hobhouse, the first person to hold a chair of sociology in a British university – specifically addressed itself to the question of why it was that only in Britain had the traditional discipline of political philosophy *not* been displaced and superseded in the nineteenth and twentieth centuries by the newer discipline of theoretical sociology.

In Britain alone among post-Victorian nations, Annan argued, social debate had remained fixed in the familiar and well-worn channels of liberal *political* thought: English theorists continued *ad nauseam* to pose traditional and unanswerable questions about 'state, society, will, rights, consent, obligation' – whereas in other industrial cultures social thought had shifted decisively away from the study of individuals and their rights to the study of social groups and their roles and functions: from analysis of society in terms of choice and rational will to analysis of society in terms of large impersonal forces. This peculiarly British failure to embrace the new sociology Annan ascribed to a variety of factors (not all of them self-evidently compatible with each other). At a structural level he blamed the integration and stability of British social and political life and the relative absence of profound structural crises in the form of blood-feuds, invasion, racial domination and scarcity – all of which, Annan implied, had forced intellectuals in other societies to eschew vacuous optimism and to analyse social order in terms of 'needs' and 'functions' rather than 'progress' and 'morality'. And at an intellectual level the failure was due to certain chronic deficiencies in the outlook of Britain's intellectual elite: to an inability to liberate themselves from moralism and reformism; to an obstinate belief in gradualist social evolution; and above all to a peculiarly British concentration upon the pivotal role of the autonomous rational individual – a focus that Annan identified as the inner core of 'positivism' at the heart of British social and political theory. The consequence of these attitudes, so Annan claimed, had been a general impoverishment of intellectual life throughout the first half of the twentieth century, and an almost total failure among British social theorists to understand the structure of society, the nature of social conflict or the 'totality' of social facts.[4]

Annan's analysis raises a number of problems that I can mention only briefly here. Perhaps the most trivial, though possibly the most confusing, of those problems is his equation of 'positivism' with an emphasis upon rational will and reductionist individualism – even though many philoso-

---

[4] Noel Annan, 'The Curious Strength of Positivism in English Political Thought', *L. T. Hobhouse Memorial Lecture*, 28, London, 1959, esp. pp. 8–10, 15–18.

phers and social scientists might use the term 'positivism' in precisely the opposite sense, to indicate the view that society is *not* a heap of separate, choosing, purposive individuals, but a structured organism governed by predetermined and predictable natural laws.[5] A more fundamental problem than this mere idiosyncracy of language is that much of Annan's argument was fundamentally circular: it redescribed the phenomenon it sought to explain, by ascribing British cultural resistance to sociology to the prior fact that British culture was inherently anti-sociological. This may or may not have been true; but, *if* it is true, it tells us nothing beyond what the argument had assumed already.

Nevertheless, Annan's central theme was taken up and developed by many subsequent historians, some of whom attempted to account for it in more genuinely historical terms. A major essay on *The Origins of British Sociology* by Philip Abrams was published in 1968 as a preface to a collection of extracts from nineteenth- and twentieth-century British sociological writings. Abrams was much less patronising than Annan had been about the past deficiencies of British social thought, and very willing to acknowledge the many serious attempts made by Victorian and Edwardian theorists to describe, comprehend and explain the working of society. Unlike Annan, Abrams identified a long sequence of British institutions, coteries and individual theorists who had undertaken systematic analysis of both their own and other societies. He pointed to the widespread growth of Victorian national and provincial social science associations; to the intellectual vitality of Victorian and Edwardian social anthropology; to the attempt to provide a national forum for sociology through the medium of the Sociological Society; and to a long list of speculative social theorists from J. S. Mill and Herbert Spencer through to L. T. Hobhouse and Bruno Malinowski who had tried to develop systematic theories both about the nature of society in general and about the logical processes of social-scientific method.[6]

Even so, Abrams came to the conclusion that the history of sociological thought in Britain had been one of ultimate failure. Like Noel Annan he laid much of the blame upon a deeply ingrained cultural inheritance of rationalism and atomism embodied in the 'master paradigm of Adam Smith'.[7] Abrams' specific complaint was that although the quality of specific social enquiries in Britain had often been high, there had been a prolonged and damaging divorce between two quite different sociological

---

[5] On the ambiguities of 'positivism' see Jennifer Platt, 'The Sociological Construction of "Positivism" and its Significance in British Sociology, 1950–80', in P. Abrams, J. Finch, R. Dean and P. Rock (eds.), *Practice and Progress: British Sociology 1950–1980*, London, 1981, pp. 73–5.

[6] Philip Abrams, *The Origins of British Sociology: 1834–1914*, Chicago, 1968, pp. 3–153.

[7] Abrams, *The Origins of British Sociology*, pp. 8–9.

traditions – between a speculative, analytical tradition derived from evolutionary theory and philosophy, and a statistical, descriptive, fact-finding tradition largely subservient to government, social work and practical social reform. This divorce Abrams portrayed as fatally embodied in, and reinforced by, the organisation of social studies in British universities, and above all in Britain's foremost social science institution, the London School of Economics. At the LSE from 1912 onwards social enquiry had been formally divided between a theoretically oriented Department of Sociology, and a practical and applied Department of Social Science and Administration – a division that Abrams implied was to have disastrous consequences for the growth of sociology in Britain over the next half century.[8] A further source of intellectual weakness Abrams saw as lying in the very character and structure of British society in the early twentieth century and in its open, expanding, liberal, reformist elite – an elite that continually absorbed social critics and analysts into practical public administration, and diverted them from the more rigorous, creative and subversive practice of analytical sociology.[9] The result, in Abrams' view, was that the most distinguished works of British sociology tended to be limited, concrete and empirical studies like those of William Beveridge on unemployment or Arthur Bowley on living standards: they were not macroscopic theoretical investigations of the social fundaments of class, status and power.

Arguments of this kind have echoed throughout historical writing on the social sciences and sociology over the past twenty years, though with some interesting variations in what historians have seen as the crucial factors in British sociology's intellectual failings. A study by Geoffrey Hawthorne in 1978 laid much of the blame upon the malign influence of the long shadow of Herbert Spencer. Reaction against Spencer's deductive methodology and obsessive belief in timeless and universal social laws drove many would-be sociologists into unreflective pragmatism and reformism; while those who continued the quest for a grand theory of society could not escape from the suffocating blanket of Spencer's progressive evolutionary positivism.[10] This view was strongly criticised, however, by Stefan Collini in an important article in the *European Journal of Sociology*. He suggested, on the contrary, that it was the predominance of post-Hegelian *idealist* thought in early twentieth-century Britain that had undermined earlier belief in an autonomous 'natural science of society', and had led to a revival of interest in the purposes of the state

---

[8] Abrams, *The Origins of British Sociology*, pp. 107–13.
[9] Abrams, *The Origins of British Sociology*, pp. 148–9.
[10] Geoffrey Hawthorne, *Enlightenment and Despair. A History of Sociology*, Cambridge, 1976, pp. 90–111.

and other questions of traditional *political* philosophy.[11] Collini was followed by Reba Soffer writing on 'Why do Disciplines Fail?' in the *English Historical Review* of 1982. Soffer ascribed the deficiency of British sociology to its failure to 'take seriously evidence of social irrationality', and its 'myopic faith in social evolution', which had 'prevented sociologists from [recognising] systematically the realities of social dysfunction and disorder'.[12] Moreover, sociologists had failed in Britain, not through their reformism but through the lack of it, since 'all that they offered was a view of society which uncritically endorsed existing social tendencies'.[13] Lawrence Goldman, on the other hand, in a series of articles published in the early 1980s, suggested that since way back in the mid-Victorian era critical sociological theory in Britain had been thwarted by too close a connection with reformist public administration – and by too close an attachment to liberal presuppositions about peaceful and piecemeal social change and the normality of progress.[14]

All these interpretations differ in their precise details, but all appear to agree that Britain was in some sense singular in failing to adopt sociological theory as a predominant cultural paradigm in the nineteenth and early twentieth centuries. Before we explore this point further, however, it may be useful to identify some of the questions that arise from both the similarities and the differences between these various viewpoints. The most obvious of these questions concerns the actual nature and character of Britain's 'failed' sociological tradition. Was it the case, as Annan suggested, that British sociology failed because social theorists in Britain could rarely see beyond the narrow confines of the atomised rational individual? *Or* was it the case, as Collini suggested, that the problem was quite the opposite one – that social theory was monopolised by anti-empirical post-Hegelian idealism and could not bring itself to focus upon scientific analysis of individual action? Was British sociology unduly 'moralistic' or, on the contrary, was it flawed by excessive faith in the model of moral neutrality and detachment, supposedly characteristic of political economy and natural science? Was it the case, as Abrams suggested, that the hallmark of British sociology was a cautious and

[11] Stefan Collini, 'Sociology and Idealism in Britain 1880–1920', *Archives Européennes de Sociologie*, 1 (1978), pp. 3–50.

[12] Reba Soffer, 'Why do Disciplines Fail? The Strange Case of British Sociology', *English Historical Review*, 97 (October 1982), pp. 787–802.

[13] Soffer, 'Why do Disciplines Fail?' p. 781.

[14] Lawrence Goldman, 'The Social Science Association, 1857–1886: A Context for mid-Victorian Liberalism', *English Historical Review*, 101 (January 1986), pp. 95–134. Unlike most contributors to this debate, Goldman warned against the pitfalls of setting up unhistorical standards of what constitutes good sociology (Lawrence Goldman, 'The Origins of British "Social Science": Political Economy, Natural Science and Statistics, 1830–1835', *Historical Journal*, 26, 3 (1983), pp. 587–616).

limited empiricism: or was Professor Soffer right in claiming that empiricism was always subordinate to grand and vacuous theories of social evolution? Were British sociologists seduced away from creative thought by an excess of zeal for reform, or was their problem the opposite one, that they fatalistically acquiesced in 'existing social tendencies'?

I shall come back to these questions shortly, when I turn to considering what British sociological theorists actually thought. However, this central problem of correctly identifying the British sociological tradition by no means exhausts the problems that arise from this debate. A majority of the writers whom I have cited concur in blaming the strongly 'reformist' character of British sociology for the subject's conceptual weakness and imply that, if only British sociologists had been systematically excluded and estranged from government, their discipline might correspondingly have flourished.[15] Such a point may well have some force: yet a moment's reflection about the situation in other countries must instantly dispel the claim that the embrace of reformist government was somehow peculiar to Britain. On the contrary, almost the exact converse is true. Durkheimian sociology in France grew up in the very bosom of the French state, and was vigorously sponsored by French ministers of education as a form of semi-official civic ideology for the Third Republic.[16] In imperial Germany, social theorists like Max Weber, Ferdinand Tönnies and George Simmel were closely involved with reformist bodies like the Verein für Sozialpolitik and were financed and patronised by a wide range of government-sponsored academic foundations working under the umbrella of the Kaiser Wilhelm Institute (though it should be noted that there were – surprisingly – no formal university chairs in sociology in Germany until 1927).[17] In an American context both the funding and the fruits of academic sociological research were 'closely tied to public social policy from the 1890s onwards' and sociology was viewed as 'an indispensable study for intelligent, responsible citizenship'.[18]

---

[15] See especially, Abrams, *The Origins of British Sociology*, pp. 34, 39–40, 47–9, 106.

[16] George Weisz, 'The Republican Ideology and the Social Sciences', in Philippe Besnard (ed.), *The Sociological Domain. The Durkheimians and the Founding of French Sociology*, 1983, pp. 115–16. Steven Lukes, *Emile Durkheim. His Life and Work: A Historical and Critical Study*, Cambridge, 1973, pp. 372–8.

[17] Dieter Kruger, 'Max Weber and the Younger Generation in the Verein für Sozialpolitik', in Wolfgang J. Mommsen and Jurgen Osterhammel, *Max Weber and his Contemporaries*, 1987, London, pp. 71–87; Bernard vom Brocke, 'Die Kaiser-Wilhelm-Gesellschaft im Kaiserreich', in Rudolph Vierhaus and Bernhard vom Brocke, *Forschung in Spanningsfeld von Politik und Gesellschaft, Geschichte und Struktur der Kaiser Wilhelm/Max Planck-Geschichte und Struktur der Kaiser Wilhelm/Max Planck-Gesellschaft*, Stuttgart, 1990, pp. 110–12.

[18] Reba Soffer, 'Why do Disciplines Fail?', pp. 776–9, 790–1.

A similar point may be made about the question of 'moralism'. Durkheim and his followers in France laid a great deal of emphasis on treating moral values as neutral 'social facts'. Yet the French 'solidarist' movement (which had close affinities with 'ethical' sociologists in Britain) drew much of its moral inspiration from Durkheim; and the political and pressure-group activities of the Durkheimian school reveal that they were deeply committed to injecting a new critical 'scientific' morality into the various tiers of French state education.[19] In Germany Max Weber defended the conception of a sociology or social science that was value-free; yet a great deal of Weber's writing consisted not of detached clinical analysis of social institutions but of the defence of the values and public morality of a state-centred nationalist liberalism.[20] Whatever else may be claimed about the relative deficiencies of British sociology in this period, it cannot therefore be the case that those deficiencies may be simply attributed to the unique attachment of British social theorists to moralism, improvement and progressive liberal partisanship.

III

I want now to turn to a brief examination of what British social thinkers actually thought and wrote about society and social relationships in the late nineteenth and early twentieth centuries. I have purposely used the rather limp term 'social thinkers' rather than 'sociologists', because it seems arguable that at least part of the confusion which surrounds the subject is a terminological one, and that a great deal of serious social analysis *was* going on in Britain at this time, not under the institutional label of sociology, but under other academic umbrellas – in the form of political economy, classics, history, philosophy, theology, biology, anthropology, ethics, and social and political science. As A. D. Coats, Alon Khadish and other historians of political economy have shown, there was an implicitly sociological dimension to much late-Victorian and Edwardian writing on economic thought, even though economics and sociology were often consciously ranged against each other as antagonistic academic disciplines;[21] and it was not until the 1920s and 1930s

[19] Roger Geiger, 'Durkheimian Sociology under Attack; The Controversy over Sociology in the Ecoles Normales Primaires', in Besnard, *The Sociological Domain*, pp. 120–31. On the institutional connections between solidarism and British sociology, see Gustav Spiller, 'Discussions: The Moral Education Congress', *Sociological Review*, 2, 1 (1909), pp. 69–73.

[20] W. J. Mommsen, *The Age of Bureaucracy. Perspectives on the Political Sociology of Max Weber*, Oxford, 1974.

[21] A. W. Coats, 'Sociological Aspects of British Economic Thought (ca. 1880–1930)', *Journal of Political Economy*, 75, (1967), pp. 706–29; Alon Khadish, *The Oxford Economists in the Late Nineteenth Century*, Oxford, 1982, pp. 123–5, 127–52.

that algebra and analytical positivism effectively purged sociology from academic economics. Likewise much Edwardian and post-Edwardian *political* thought largely turned its back upon the atomistic utilitarianism of past years, and explicitly engaged with the more 'sociological' categories of 'community', collective 'mentalities', social 'organisms' and 'pluralism' (often in the process explicitly rejecting the traditional political philosopher's focus upon the uniqueness and social transcendence of the 'sovereign' state).[22]

A sociological dimension was even more marked in many other academic disciplines. The study of classics in early twentieth-century Britain was enormously invigorated by the rise of a young generation of classical scholars – Alfred Zimmern, Gilbert Murray, Francis Cornford, Jane Harrison – who drew upon 'sociological' ideas to illuminate ancient history.[23] Leading philosophical journals like *Mind* and the *Proceedings of the Aristotelian Society* frequently carried articles on sociological themes, reviewed sociological works, and even on occasion sponsored conferences and symposia on theoretical aspects of social questions.[24] Learned publications like the *Journal of the Royal Statistical Society* and reports of Section F of the British Association were full of articles on the social dimensions of demography, anthropometry and vital statistics very similar to those which appeared in *L'Année Sociologique* and the *American Journal of Sociology*. Between 1908 and 1914 the Cambridge historian John Neville Figgis published a long series of analytical and speculative lectures and articles on the relationship between capitalism, religion, morality, social structure and political power that might well have been described as sociology – if Figgis had not also happened to be a theologian and an Anglican priest.[25] Even Professor Soffer, who is generally critical of the conservative bent of British academic life in this period, nevertheless concedes that psychology and political science were 'revolu-

---

[22] A. D. Lindsay, 'Political Theory', in F. S. Marvin (ed.), *Recent Developments in European Thought*, London, (1919), pp. 164–80; Ernest Barker, *Political Thought in England 1848–1914*, London, 1915 (2nd edn 1928).

[23] Jane Ellen Harrison, *Themis. A Study of the Social origins of Greek Religion*, with a chapter by F. M. Cornford on 'The Origin of the Olympic Games' Cambridge, 1912 (revised edn 1927); Gilbert Murray, *The Rise of the Greek Epic*, 1907; Alfred Zimmern, *The Greek Commonwealth. Politics and Economics in Fifth-Century Athens*, Oxford, 1911; Murray's work was hailed in the *Sociological Review*, Oxford, 2, (April 1908), p. 193, as a major breakthrough for the 'truly sociological and synthetic method'. Zimmern was an active member of the Sociological Society and a regular contributor to sociological journals.

[24] B. Bosanquet, 'The Relation of Sociology to Philosophy', *Mind*, n.s., 6, 21 (1897), pp. 1–8; Sydney Ball, 'Current Sociology', *Mind*, n.s., 10, 38 (1901), pp. 146–71; 'Symposium: The Ethical Principles of Social Reconstruction', *Proceedings of the Aristotelian Society* [*PAS*], n.s., 17 (1916–17), pp. 256–99; H. W. Hetherington, 'The Conception of a Unitary Social Order', *PAS*, n.s., 17 (1917–18), pp. 286–316.

[25] J. N. Figgis, *Religion and English Society*, London, 1910; *Civilization at the Cross Roads*, London, 1912; *Churches in the Modern State*, London, 1913.

tionary disciplines' in British universities in the early twentieth century:[26] yet much of what went on in those disciplines – such as, for example, the study of crowd behaviour or group irrationality – would in France or North America have passed for sociology.

This point can be demonstrated most clearly by looking more closely at the activities known to the Edwardians as 'social philosophy' and 'social science'. When complaining about the absence of academic 'sociology', most of the critics whom I have cited largely ignore the fact that ten new departments of 'social science' were set up in provincial and Scottish universities between 1900 and 1925. Where mentioned at all, these new departments are portrayed as primarily concerned with descriptive fact-finding and with vocational training in social work – both activities, so it is argued, simply exemplifying the weak, non-theoretical and reformist character of British sociology.[27] Yet the introduction of social science in universities like Birmingham, Leeds, Nottingham, Glasgow and Edinburgh was a direct offshoot not just of Edwardian social work but of Edwardian philosophical idealism – and of the social, educational and civic reform movements of which idealism was an integral part.[28] The earliest promoters of these social science departments were not social workers or statisticians but classical or neo-Hegelian idealist philosophers – men like Sir Henry Jones and Hector Hetherington at Glasgow, J. H. Muirhead at Birmingham, and Edward Urwick at the London School of Economics. The core of research and teaching carried out in the early days of these departments was not into social work nor into applied statistics; it was into what was called 'social philosophy', a term that had an ancestry in British intellectual history going back to J. S. Mill, and whose major exponent in Edwardian England was the idealist philosopher Bernard Bosanquet. By 'social philosophy' Bosanquet and his colleagues meant a very wide-ranging theoretical perspective that attempted (as the works of Mill had done) to integrate the traditional study of ethics and political philosophy with the newer disciplines of economics, anthropology, psychology and sociology.[29] Such an approach may have been so wildly overambitious and comprehensive as to be doomed from the start to failure; but it bore little relation to the narrowly descriptive and atheoretical studies parodied by some of the above-cited histories of British sociology.

[26] Reba Soffer, *Ethics and Society in England. The Revolution in the Social Sciences 1870–1914*, Berkeley, Ca., 1978.

[27] Abrams, *The Origins of British Sociology*, pp. 106, 110–11.

[28] Andrew Vincent and Raymond Plant, *Philosophy, Politics and Citizenship: The Life and Thought of the British Idealists*, Oxford, 1984, esp. pp. 132–49.

[29] Sandra den Otter, 'The Search for a "Social Philosophy": the Idealists of Late Victorian and Edwardian Britain', Oxford University D. Phil. thesis, 1990.

The hallmarks of this approach to the study of society may be found very clearly in the early work of sociologists and social scientists at the London School of Economics. Archival evidence suggests that, contrary to the account given by Philip Abrams, in the early days of the LSE there had been close cooperation between the teaching and research programmes of the Department of Sociology and the Department of Social Science. Sociological theory was taught in both departments by Edward Westermarck and Leonard Hobhouse, and both departments laid great emphasis upon the empirical observation of society as well as on social theory.[30] It is true that the Social Science Department between 1912 and 1920 produced a series of largely descriptive studies which set out to measure the practical impact of the 'new' Liberal social reform legislation of 1906–14, but this was precisely the kind of sociological monitoring of public policy that was currently being undertaken by social scientists in Wilhelmine Germany (and to a lesser extent in Durkheimian France).[31] Moreover, the intellectual core of the Social Science Department's work, and one that deeply penetrated all these practical surveys, was the study of 'social philosophy', as exemplified in the teaching and writing of the department's senior professor, Edward Urwick.

The key theme of Urwick's teaching was the application of classical philosophy to analysis of the social structure and social problems of the present day. He and his disciples used works such as Aristotle's *Politics* and Plato's *Republic* and *The Laws* as texts for the study of contemporary social relations, ethical consciousness and state power.[32] Similar themes were explored in the writings of many other social philosophers of the Edwardian and post-Edwardian generations: in Bernard Bosanquet's *The Philosophical Theory of the State* (1899), in Hetherington and Muirhead's *Social Purpose* (1918), in Muirhead's *The Influence of Plato in Anglo-Saxon Philosophy* (1931), and, at a more popular level, in the writings of H. G. Wells, who claimed that 'Plato, not Comte, is the true type of a sociologist'. [33] Plato was continually cited as the forerunner of modern 'organicism' and his use of 'myth' was invoked to explain the transcendent,

[30] Jose Harris, 'The Webbs, the COS and the Ratan Tata Foundation', in Martin Bulmer, Jane Lewis and David Piachaud, *The Goals of Social Policy*, London, 1989, p. 49.

[31] The *Schriften des Vereins für Socialpolitik*, Leipzig, regularly featured articles on the impact of public policy on such questions as agricultural wages, housing and living standards. Durkheim's *L'Année Sociologique*, cinquième section, carried articles on policy issues, and regularly reviewed work on applied sociology being carried out in England, Germany and the United States.

[32] E. J. Urwick, *The Message of Plato. A Reinterpretation of the Republic*, London, 1920; *The Social Good*, London, 1927.

[33] E. J. Urwick, 'Sociology and Social Progress', *Sociological Review*, 3, 2 (April 1910), pp. 137–49; H. G. Wells, 'The So-called Science of Sociology', *Sociological Papers*, 3 (1906), pp. 357–69.

non-utilitarian elements in human association, while his practical proposals for social organisation were often cited by reformers as though they were 'designed to be put into operation in modern England ... as if they were debating a bill before the House of Commons'.[34] Nor was the classical frame of reference confined to works of political philosophy. On the contrary, studies of ancient history were continually mined to provide an analytical framework for such themes as community, racial efficiency, the role of women and the organisation of family life; and the political and social structures of Edwardian Britain were continually viewed through the lens of subversion of civic virtue by plutocratic corruption, as patterned in the downfall of Athens or the transition from republican to imperial Rome.[35] Throughout the period from the 1890s down to the Second World War the inheritance of Greece and Rome provided social theorists and social scientists with a constant battery of conceptual tools and historical examples with which to explain and engage with the changing social institutions of the modern world.[36]

The persistence and omnipresence of this classical frame of reference may perhaps be seen as confirmation of the claim that, in marked contrast to other western cultures, Britain singularly failed to generate a school of modern theoretical sociology during the half century before the Second World War and remained stuck in the outworn grooves of polit-ical philosophy. Whether a classical framework was necessarily a proof of 'anti-modernism', however, seems very much open to question. The use made of classical writings by Edwardian social philosophers suggests that, far from subscribing to an old-fashioned ontological individualism, they turned to the ancient philosophers, and particularly to the works of Plato, precisely because they found there a theory of 'community' and of collective social action that was lacking in the established mainstream of English political thought.[37] This was certainly in striking contrast to the

---

[34] R. Nettleship, *Lectures on Plato's Republic*, London, 1897 (second edn 1901), pp. 134–5, 303; Urwick, *The Message of Plato*, *passim*; G. C. Field, 'Plato's Political Thought and its Value for Today', *Philosophy*, 16, 65 (July 1941), pp. 227–41.

[35] C. Dawson, 'Progress and Decay in Ancient and Modern Civilizations', *Sociological Review*, 16 (1924), pp. 1–10.

[36] For the role of Greece and Rome in the wider culture of the period, see Frank Turner, *The Greek Heritage in Victorian Britain*, New Haven, 1981), pp. 74–6, 244–63, 358–68, 414, 446; and Frank Turner, 'British Politics and the Demise of the Roman Republic: 1700–1939', *Historical Journal*, 29, 3 (1986), pp. 557–99.

[37] A very striking example was R. M. MacIver's *Community: A Sociological Study. Being an Attempt to Set out the Nature and Fundamental Laws of Social Life*, London, 1917, pp. 51–2, 81–2, 92–3, 223, 282–4, 389. MacIver's book was published when he had become a professor of sociology at Toronto, but it was written in the philosophy department at Glasgow – a fact which illustrates the very high degree of overlap between the two disci-plines during the Edwardian era. MacIver recorded that he had set out with, but found himself compelled to abandon, the traditional utilitarian assumption that 'community' and 'society' did not exist.

great onslaught upon classical studies that was being launched by positivist sociologists in Third Republican France.[38] But the constant and
easy movement from the contemporary industrial world to that of fourth-
century Athens was just as much a hallmark of the German tradition of
social thought as of the British; and it was also commonplace in much
North American sociological writing until at least the 1920s.[39] Indeed the
idioms in which Max Weber worked – a mixture of classicism, neo-
Hegelianism, historicism and utilitarianism – almost exactly replicated
the framework of much British social science and social philosophy of this
period; and it remains an abiding mystery why Weber's work was so little
known in Britain until much later in the twentieth century.[40]

IV

Late-Victorian and Edwardian sociological thought was therefore
nothing like so minimal in scope nor so marginal in character as many of
its critics have claimed. Sociological ways of thinking penetrated into a
wide range of academic disciplines; and many studies that in France or
North America would have been classed as sociology were carried out
under the aegis of some other intellectual umbrella. Moreover, far from
being confined to university-based elites, the mixture of modern sociology and classical political thought supplied an idiom for the understanding of modern societies that was in widespread use in more popular
and vernacular contexts throughout the first three decades of the twentieth century. The 'social service' movement, the 'social survey' movement, the 'guild of help' movement, the women's suffrage movement, the
town-planning movement, the adult education movement and many
aspects of 'new liberalism' at the grassroots, were all animated by an
understanding of modern society that was visibly indebted to the thinking
of fourth-century Athens:[41] thinking that was mediated and made intelli-

---

[38] Bernard Bosanquet, 'A Question of Method', *Charity Organisation Review*, n.s., 30,
(June–Dec. 1911), pp. 287–302.

[39] See, for example, the entry on Plato by Leon Brunschwigg in *The Encyclopaedia of the
Social Sciences*, vol. XII, New York, 1934, pp. 158–60; and numerous articles in the
International Journal of Ethics, published from 1893 to 1918 in Philadelphia, and thereafter
in Chicago.

[40] A mystery that cannot be explained simply with reference to a cultural gap between
British and German traditions; Weber's countryman, Ferdinand Tönnies, was widely
cited and indeed published extensively in both British and North American philosophical and sociological journals.

[41] This point could be demonstrated much more fully than I have space for here, and is
worth a more detailed study in its own right. See, for example, 'Commentary: The Basis
of Politics', *The Ploughshare. The Quaker Organ of Social Revolution*, 4, 1 (Feb. 1909), pp.
3–7; 'Model Towns and Communities: Plato's *Republic*', *Garden City*, n.s., 1, 1 (1901),
pp. 16–18; Sybella Gurney, 'Civic Reconstruction and the Garden City Movement',

gible by the immense popularity of cheap translations of the classics.[42] In many voluntary and communitarian organisations such a vision of society did not rival but complemented and harmonised with the kind of evolutionary sociology constructed by thinkers such as Hobhouse, Westermarck and Geddes. Indeed, such an idiom – incorporating elements of both idealism and scientific 'naturalism'[43] – appears to have been uncannily attuned to many sectors of that widely ramifying, public-spirited, voluntaristic culture that prevailed in Britain between the third and fourth Reform Acts – a culture that was distinctively different from both the 'atomism' of the earlier Victorian period and the interventionist state bureaucracy of the mid-twentieth century.[44] Overall, there seems to me very little evidence to support the view that late nineteenth- and early twentieth-century British intellectuals – either in universities or in more populist spheres – were inherently reluctant to analyse human behaviour in terms of 'society' or collective social groups. There is I think a great deal of evidence to support the opposite view: namely, that a vast range of intellectual, academic and more practical activities – ranging from economics, philosophy and history, through to ethics, biology, social work and civic reform – acquired a strongly 'sociological' dimension.

The fact remains, however, that no single major school of sociological theory emerged in Britain during this period, and many intellectuals and students of society remained nervous or diffident about the term 'sociology'.[45] Major British analysts of society in the early twentieth century owed their primary allegiance to disciplines other than sociology; and, even among theorists with a strongly sociological bent, 'sociology' was not often viewed as a proper focus for the organisation of an academic degree course of a university department.[46] The reasons for this outlook varied in different contexts and among different thinkers, but only rarely

Sociological Review, 3, 1 (1910), pp. 35–43; J. Strong, 'A Clearing House of Civilisation', *Progress*, 1 (106), p. 3; 'Quality or Quantity', report of an Oxford Summer School, *Social Service Review*, 11 (1930), pp. 159–60; A. D. K. Owen, 'The Social Survey of a City', *ibid.*, pp. 186–91.

[42] Turner, *Greek Heritage*, pp. 431–46.

[43] Sydney Ball, 'Current Sociology', p. 171.

[44] There seems little ground for accepting Geoffrey Hawthorne's claim (*Enlightenment an Despair*, p. 111) that the enterprise of constructing an ethical-cum-evolutionary sociology was dead by 1914, due to 'a complete lack of interest in the attempt'. On the contrary, the evidence of reformist periodicals suggests that, from the 1890s through to the 1930s, it was of obsessive interest throughout the middle and lower echelons of civil society.

[45] *Positivist Review*, 139 (January 1904), pp. 165–7.

[46] At the London School of Economics, for example, the study of sociology was established as, and remains to this day, a component subject of the synoptic degree known as the B.Sc.(Econ.). Even Victor Branford, who was most active among the sociological community in trying to promote university chairs in sociology, was even more keen on promoting an injection of sociology into other disciplines.

can it be ascribed to mere cultural conservatism or intransigent attachment to an abstract 'individualism'. A relevant factor in some circles was that the term 'sociology' was still closely associated with the 'positivism' taught by disciples of Auguste Comte – a system of thought which many British theorists from J. S. Mill onwards had viewed as vitiated by reductionism, scientism and false determinism. In Urwick's words, the Comtean vision of a 'general sociology' was inherently doomed to failure, because the totality of data about human society was 'necessarily unknown and unknowable'; and the fact that several leading members of the Sociological Society had close links with the English variety of 'Comtism' may well have been a liability in many quarters.[47] There were, however, other and perhaps more important reasons for the non-emergence of sociology as a distinct and separate field of knowledge. One such reason was the persistence of the widespread belief among many British intellectuals that 'society' was not in itself an autonomous sphere of existence, but that it was partnered by and premissed upon the prior existence of politics and law.[48] Such a view did not preclude the possibility of 'sociology', but it slanted its character in a certain direction. Another view, strongly held by Patrick Geddes and his followers, was that sociology – and indeed all forms of social enquiry – was a 'civic' rather than an 'academic' pursuit: though fostered by scientists and philosophers, 'the work was to be done locally by volunteers (not by trained workers from universities) and to be publicised in the local town hall'.[49] A rather different position (though certainly one shared by the Geddes school) was the continuing powerful attachment of many thinkers in Britain to the view that the study of human behaviour was an unbroken seamless web: that history, social science, philosophy and anthropology were all interrelated with each other, and that sociology was not so much an autonomous discipline as a slant of mind that held them all together. In the words of Ernest Barker, president of the Sociological Society in the mid-1930s, 'There is no need to quarrel about names and the boundaries of studies, if sociology produces good fruits'.[50]

[47] A case, perhaps, for seeing 'positivism' as an adverse influence on British sociology: but the 'positivism' of the English disciples of Comte (exemplified in such organs as the *Positivist Review*, the *Reformer* and the *Humanitarian*) seems very remote from the tradition of positivistic individualism identified by Noel Annan. On English suspicion of the term 'sociology', see Urwick, 'Sociology and Social Progress', pp. 137–8.

[48] Powerful examples of this kind of argument may be found in H. C. Dowdall, 'What is a Society?', *Proceedings of the Aristotelian Society*, n.s., 25, (1924–5), pp. 19–40; R. G. Collingwood, 'Political Action', *PAS*, 29 (1928–9), pp. 155–76; and J. MacMurray, 'The Conception of Society', *PAS*, 31 (1930–1), pp. 127–42.

[49] Martin Bulmer, *Essays on the History of British Sociological Research*, Cambridge, 1985, pp. 10–11.

[50] Barker, *Political Thought in England*, p. 160.

These views were very apparent in the deliberations of the Sociological Society from its foundation. The society was very strongly committed to the promotion of what it called the 'sociological habit of mind' among both its members and the wider public. But for most of its members this meant infiltrating existing disciplines rather than promoting sociology as a discrete and exclusive subject in its own right: in other words, sociology was to be pursued, not as a specialist discipline, but as an intellectual outlook and set of assumptions which were to guide and integrate other areas of knowledge. This was apparent in the fact that the vast majority of members and contributors to the Sociological Society were and continued to be not professional sociologists but historians, philosophers, classicists, economists, biologists and anthropologists, with a sprinkling of practical politicians, administrators and social workers – most of them apparently quite content to pursue sociology within the context of these other disciplines and spheres.

A further explanation for the relative weakness of British sociology lies rather outside the scope and timespan of this paper and applies not merely to sociology but to all aspects of the social sciences in Britain (and possibly indeed to the natural sciences as well).[51] This stems from the fact that the development of the social sciences in the early twentieth century was so closely tied up with a framework of philosophical idealism, and with an 'organic' model of society that to a certain extent united and supplied a common language for both the 'idealist' and the 'evolutionary–positivist' traditions. This framework remained strong in many areas of the social sciences until the inter-war years: and down to the 1930s both Plato and Hegel were used as points of reference in British sociological writing at least as commonly as Comte and Durkheim. This vantage point, which attempted to embrace both the study of subjective 'consciousness' and 'natural laws of society', offered the latent potential for a highly sophisticated variety of sociological theory which might have transcended the limitations of both styles of thought.[52] But both idealism and sociological naturalism were being sapped in Cambridge by G. E. Moore and Bertrand Russell from the 1900s; and at the time of the founding of the Sociological Society in 1904 Russell himself had publicly questioned the logical validity of 'sociological' inquiry.[53] Idealism remained strong in the provincial and Scottish universities until well into

---

[51] On the latter point, see Roy Porter, 'Sir Charles Snow and the Two Cultures', paper given to the Wellcome Institute for the History of Medicine, Oxford University, November, 1994.

[52] See the discussion in Peter Winch, *The Idea of a Social Science and its Relation to Philosophy*, London, 1958, esp. ch. 2.

[53] *Sociological Papers*, 1, 1 (1904), 244. See also B. Russell, 'On the Notion of Cause', *Proceedings of the Aristotelian Society*, n.s., 13, (1912–13), pp. 1ff.

the 1920s; and, as I have shown, idealist philosophers in those universities were also vigorous promoters and practitioners of the new social sciences. In the 1930s, however, philosophical idealism throughout Britain went into precipitate decline in the face of the onslaught of linguistic positivism. This collapse brought intellectual crisis, not merely for old-fashioned philosophers but for many of the newer social sciences as well – in fact for all those areas of social enquiry in which idealism had provided a powerful normative theory and methodological base. The new positivism of the 1930s – a positivism which begins to look far *more* like the type of positivism denounced in the 1950s by Noel Annan – made discourse about social groups and the normative frameworks that held them together increasingly difficult and barren. The result was that throughout the social sciences there was a retreat into studies that were either largely mathematical and analytical – as in the case of economics – or into studies that had little or no problematic philosophical basis, such as the measurement of poverty, population, unemployment and nutrition. One of the main casualties of this crisis was grand speculative sociology with its deep roots in organic and idealist moral and political philosophy.[54] It is from these developments of the 1930s that one should date the characteristics that historians have ascribed to British sociology since its nineteenth-century origins – namely, its lack of interest in a general theory of 'society', its concentration on quantitative and descriptive studies, and its estrangement from the kind of large-scale structural, functional and normative questions posed by sociologists in other societies and cultures.

One final and more speculative factor that is difficult to document precisely but that resonates through many of the sources of the period, is that the very nature of British society made it perhaps inherently less amenable than other comparable societies to large-scale 'sociological' analysis – at least in so far as that term was universally understood in the late nineteenth and early twentieth centuries. In all the countries including Britain where 'sociology' was emerging as a new disciplinary perspective around the turn of the century, discourse about social relations was rooted in the notion of society as an 'organism' (a term that was sometimes used in a purely biological sense, but more often to imply some kind of moral or spiritual or 'subjective' as well as merely physical identity). Such a notion was fraught with difficulties in any context; but it was peculiarly problematic for a society such as Britain, with its highly voluntarist and pluralist *internal* social structure, and its uniquely

---

[54] For a contemporary discussion of this crisis see the dispute between Karl Mannheim and Morris Ginsberg on 'The Role of Sociology as a Discipline in Universities', Mannheim Papers, University of Keele, Box II, file (e), early 1940s.

cosmopolitan and imperial *external* ties.[55] Any realistic account of British society in this period, whether it was based on idealist 'consciousness' or material structures and functions, had to take account both of the intense localism and variety of British institutions and culture and, simultaneously, of British political and economic encirclement of the globe. Any equation of the activities of the 'social organism' with what went on inside the political boundaries of the United Kingdom was therefore doomed to fail. By contrast, the more self-contained, state-centred and *dirigiste* regimes of France, Germany and other continental nations may have lent themselves more readily to grand social theories of an 'organic' kind. Such a possibility, with all its obvious pitfalls, deserves much more precise and detailed exploration than I have space for here. But, if even in part true, it would help to explain in historical and contextual terms the apparent 'failure' of theoretical sociology in Britain, the relative 'success' of more limited and localised British studies, and the eventual collapse, not just in Britain but elsewhere, of the 'organic' model of sociology in the face of the changing structural realities of the modern world.

[55] On the difficulties of applying the 'organic' model to cosmopolitan and individualised societies, see Ferdinand Tönnies, 'Present Problems of Social Structure', *American Journal of Sociology*, 10 (1904–5), pp. 569–88.

Index